MARCHING WITH SHERMAN

Conflicting Worlds: New Dimensions of the American Civil War
T. MICHAEL PARRISH, *Series Editor*

MARCHING
— WITH —
SHERMAN

Through Georgia and the Carolinas
with the 154th New York

Mark H. Dunkelman

Louisiana State University Press)(Baton Rouge

Published with the assistance of the V. Ray Cardozier Fund
Published by Louisiana State University Press
Copyright © 2012 by Mark H. Dunkelman

DESIGNER: Mandy McDonald Scallan
TYPEFACE: Minion Pro

ISBN 978-0-8071-4378-0

Book Club Edition

For my aunt,
Floris Dunkelman Sarver

Contents

Maps and Illustrations

ILLUSTRATIONS *(following page 132)*

General William Tecumseh Sherman

Corporal John Langhans

Lieutenant Colonel Lewis D. Warner

Army wagons in Atlanta

Georgia state capitol, Milledgeville

Destruction of the Ogeechee River railroad bridge

Fountain in Forsyth Place, Savannah

Sherman reviewing troops in Savannah

Winnsboro, South Carolina

Chesterfield, South Carolina

United States Arsenal in Fayetteville

Corporal Job B. Dawley

MARCHING WITH SHERMAN

History and Memory

My introduction to Civil War history came in stories my father heard from his grandfather—stories of General William Tecumseh Sherman's March to the Sea. Harold Dunkelman and his sister, Floris, were raised on a western New York farm by their parents and their mother's father, John Langhans, a veteran of the 154th New York Volunteer Infantry. In 1929, when my father was sixteen and my aunt was nine, John Langhans died. His Civil War stories survived in their memories.

More than two decades later, during my boyhood in suburban Buffalo in the 1950s, Dad related the tales to me. They transported me to my great-grandfather's side. I could picture him tramping down a red dirt Georgia road in a long line of blue-clad soldiers, taking pigs and chickens over the protests of white plantation and farm owners and marveling at the mobs of black people flocking to Sherman's army and freedom.

According to my father, one newly freed slave insisted he wanted to accompany our ancestor back to Cattaraugus County to work on the family farm. With no need for a hired hand, John tried to dissuade the man. The freedman persevered, however, and followed my great-grandfather north after his muster out until John finally managed to elude him.[1]

Dad could not remember the black companion's name. I wondered if somewhere a black boy of my age heard tales from his father of an ancestor's flight to freedom in the company of a young New York soldier. Could the same story's strands spin out over time in different places, among different people? As much as our family legend hinted at John Langhans's wartime experiences, it left plenty unsaid.

My father and aunt also inherited relics of their grandfather's Civil War service. Aunt Floris preserved six letters he sent home from the front. Here, in his own words, my great-grandfather told me about drilling in Atlanta and watching ships load with cotton on Savannah's wharves. And his letters chronicled a campaign overlooked in our family stories—Sherman's march through the Carolinas, which has generally been neglected by history in favor of the March to the Sea. Yet it was in a letter from North Carolina that John described roads lined with crowds of jubilant blacks, affirming one theme of our family stories. His letters ended with proud reflections on the momentous events he had experienced. They reinforced my concept of Sherman's marches as a great adventure and a striking crusade for freedom.[2]

During the Civil War centennial I began to study the conflict. During those years, newspapers and television were flooded with images of southern blacks conducting sit-ins, boycotts, and marches and whites responding with a furious backlash of arrests, brutality, and murder—sometimes carried out under Confederate flags. A century after my great-grandfather helped to liberate slaves during Sherman's marches, their descendants were still struggling for equality. I could not articulate them at the time, but I grasped connections between Sherman's marches and the 1960s' marches on Washington and from Selma to Montgomery.

A 1957 reprint of Sherman's memoirs and a worn copy of Lloyd Lewis's 1932 Sherman biography taught me that our family legend had ignored a key feature of the two marches: the devastation wrought by Sherman's men. In his wartime letters and postwar stories, John Langhans had neglected to mention what Sherman termed "a hard species of warfare." The general estimated his army caused $100 million worth of damage to Georgia alone, $80 million of it "simple waste and destruction." Clearly our family tales depicting Sherman's marches as a rambunctious picnic excursion and joyous liberation mission were greatly simplified and purified. What harsh scenes had my great-grandfather omitted from his accounts?[3]

Lewis called Sherman a "fighting prophet" and presented the marches as an Old Testament epic in which a stern visionary of relentless war led a pilgrimage of destruction, visiting woes upon Georgia and the Carolinas like the plagues of Egypt, his host plundering and devouring all in its fifty-mile-wide path like a great swarm of locusts, leaving in its wake pillars of fire and smoke. Ruin and lamentation were the lot of the white population overrun by Sherman's horde, while tens of thousands of blacks fled slavery in an immense exodus to freedom, praising God and the general and his men for their deliverance.[4]

Biblical analogies to Sherman's marches date from the war itself. Shortly before Savannah fell, the commander of the 154th New York's division, Brigadier General John White Geary, wrote, "The state of Georgia is about as badly destroyed as some of the tribes of the land of Canaan were by the Israelitish army, according to Biblical record." Thomas Maguire, owner of a Georgia plantation ravaged by Geary's troops, remarked that the scene reminded him of the sacking and burning of Jerusalem by the Babylonians, albeit on a smaller scale. Clearly my great-grandfather had taken part in episodes more terrible than those in our family legend.[5]

Among Dad's trove of our ancestor's Civil War relics was a small box containing three cotton bolls. According to family legend, John Langhans had picked them during the March to the Sea. We considered the cotton a remarkable relic of our ancestor's service but paid little attention to the pretty box, its lid adorned with an image of a woman holding a fan. As best my father and aunt could remember, the cotton bolls had always been stored in it; our ancestor had brought them home together from the war. Some thirty years after I first saw the box, an expert at the Metropolitan Museum of Art informed me that it appeared to be of American origin and dated from the mid-nineteenth century—so our family legend was plausible.[6]

If the box was indeed a souvenir of the march, it begged some questions. Where did John Langhans obtain it? Did he take it from a table in a Georgia parlor or from a dresser in a Carolina bedroom? Who lost this feminine curio to a Yankee souvenir hunter? Was she the wife or daughter of one of the protesting plantation owners of our family legend? Did she herself protest the loss?

I started to ponder those questions in a Buffalo movie theater in 1961, as the re-released *Gone with the Wind* introduced me to a southern view of Sherman's march that counterpointed my triumphal northern one. Sherman's army remained an offstage menace in the film until an unforgettable scene at Tara, where Scarlett O'Hara confronted and killed a solitary Yankee—a leering, loathsome villain who represented each and every one of Sherman's soldiers, I realized, including my great-grandfather. Turning to Margaret Mitchell's Pulitzer Prize–winning novel, I found a scene omitted from the movie in which Sherman's men pillage Tara and set it afire, causing Scarlett to battle the blaze and save the house. Here were images of the March to

the Sea starkly at odds with those of my family legend. I did not realize
it at the time, but I had absorbed a reciting of southern myth that has
never been surpassed in force or influence.[7]

Mitchell's book and the movie it inspired are prime artifacts of the
Lost Cause—a powerful, nostalgic myth that twists history by extolling
the lifestyle of the Old South, lauding the alleged harmony between
masters and slaves, vindicating and defending the Confederacy's legiti-
macy and righteousness, and glorifying the Redemption that toppled
Reconstruction, when black political power was subdued and white
supremacy was firmly reestablished. In praising the heroism, gallantry,
and sacrifice of Confederate soldiers and civilians, it ignores factors
that helped to doom the would-be nation: battlefield blunders, rampant desertion, widespread dissent, and tens of thousands of southern
men—white and black—who fought for the enemy. In exaggerating
the extent of Yankee wartime destruction and inaccurately blaming it
for southern postwar impoverishment, it denies other factors including the economic, social, and political consequences of emancipation.
Rising from the prostrate South like a spirit, the Lost Cause myth was
a direct manifestation of Confederate wartime nationalism and in-
vigorated the postwar southern interpretation of the conflict. Handed
down through the generations in oral and written histories, in monuments and relics, and in movies like *Gone with the Wind,* it continues
to inspire adherents today. To certain white southern families with
deep roots in Dixie, the Confederate past is a palpable presence, and
the Lost Cause myth is its purest expression of pride.[8]

I began to wonder about those protesting white southerners encountered by my great-grandfather and the 154th New York. Theirs
were voices—like the voice of my ancestor's black companion—that I
longed to hear. Eventually I went to seek them.

In July 1978, my wife, Annette, and I reached Atlanta halfway through
a summer road trip. By that time my youthful interests had coalesced,
and I had been working for several years on a history of my great-
grandfather's regiment. I had visited all of the 154th New York's battlefields but had yet to follow its route on Sherman's marches. Now my
opportunity had arrived. Before we left Atlanta, however, I planned a
special day. It would start with my first-ever Civil War relic hunt and
end with a concert downtown.

A well-known Atlanta relic collector had agreed to be my guide.

Annette and I met Bill at his house, and he drove us through unfamiliar city streets to a dead end. He parked the car, slipped on his metal detector's headset, and handed me a spade, and we entered a patch of woods. As we clawed our way through the underbrush in the heat and humidity, we soon were dripping sweat. But Bill had brought us to the right place—a little-known battlefield of the Atlanta campaign. He got plenty of detector hits, and I dug bullets and shell fragments left and right. Then Bill asked us, "Y'all start itchin' yet?" We did not pay him much mind. He had already asked if we could "smell them snakes" and informed us that we Yankees were out of our element in the Georgia woods, where only a redneck could safely prowl. So we took him as an affable joker and ignored his question. When we were satisfied with our booty, Bill drove us back to his house and we parted.

That night Annette and I went to see a great lineup of country music stars play at the Omni auditorium. About halfway through the show, we finally understood Bill's question. We started itching. By the next morning our arms and legs were thickly dotted with ugly red welts. Something had attacked us in the woods, but what we did not know.[9]

Plans had been made, however, so we headed east out of Atlanta along the 154th New York's route to the sea. Now and then I stopped the car and hopped out to take a photo. But our agonizing sores were a constant distraction. That evening we arrived in Savannah and stopped at the first drugstore we saw, seeking diagnosis and relief. The woman behind the counter looked us over and said, "Why, y'all must be Yankees. You got chiggers!"

John Langhans had marched into Savannah as a victor, but Dixie had defeated his descendant. The druggist's suggested remedy—covering the bites with clear nail polish—offered scant relief. The itchy sores kept us in misery. I wrote off the trip as a fiasco, a journey that would have to be remade someday under better conditions. Rather than following the 154th New York's route through the Carolinas, we morosely meandered on our way home.

Two years later I concocted a grandiose second attempt at the trip, one that I hoped would result in a book to follow my by then forthcoming regimental history. I proposed to the National Geographic Society "to retrace on foot, following the same timetable," the 154th New York's route on the March to the Sea, pondering "the reaction of residents along the route today as well as the historical realities of the march." I had convinced two photographer friends, Christopher L. Ford and Robert S. Sherman, to join me on the trek. In addition to their camera skills, I knew Chris and Bob would be ideal companions. Chris's Confederate ancestry would appeal to certain southerners we met along the way, I figured, and it just seemed right to have a Sherman along.[10]

Two weeks after I mailed my inquiry to the society's Washington offices, a senior editor drafted a reply rejecting the proposal. When I think now about how much trouble Chris Ford, Bob Sherman, and I could have stumbled into wandering afoot through Georgia in the early 1980s, I realize the rejection was a blessing in disguise. The time for me to make the trip had yet to come, but the idea behind it was firmly lodged. I wanted to follow the 154th New York's route through Georgia and the Carolinas, to relate the wartime events and their memory more than a century later and to seek connections between the two.[11]

Today, fifty years after I first read Sherman's memoirs, eight feet of my office shelf space are lined with books on the general and his campaigns. Within this voluminous literature, surprisingly few books are concerned solely with the marches. Their authors have generally stressed the military perspective rather than the civilian and the March to the Sea over the Carolinas campaign. The three most recent books—two of them short overviews—briefly touched on a subject germane to this study: southern memory of the marches.[12]

Other books fall into the category of combined campaign studies, analyzing Sherman's marches together with the simultaneous campaign in Tennessee, or the Atlanta campaign, or the campaigns of Confederate general Thomas J. "Stonewall" Jackson. Another group compares the marches to warfare of other eras, including Vietnam, ancient Greece, World War II, and the age of terrorism after September 11, 2001.[13]

Lloyd Lewis's biography appeared a few years after one by the British military historian and theorist B. H. Liddell Hart. Decades passed before another Sherman biography was published in 1971. The twentieth century closed with a spate of biographies, by five historians. Sherman has also been the subject of dual biographies pairing the general with his comrade Ulysses S. Grant and with his opponent Joseph E. Johnston. Biographical portraits of Sherman range from prophetic mastermind to tormented barbarian, reflecting the competing myths of North and South.[14]

Sherman's letters have been published in three edited compilations. Two older volumes include correspondence from the pre- and postwar years; a recent collection offers a wide selection of wartime letters. Sherman is generally acknowledged as one of the better writers to emerge from the war, and his copious and verbose letters provide a wealth of thoughts, occasionally rash and intemperate, on his famous marches.[15]

Sherman and his marches appeared sporadically, often as an unseen presence, in postwar fiction through the turn of the century. The overwhelming impact of Margaret Mitchell's opus largely dampened the ardor of novelists for Sherman's marches until another century turned. In the most significant recent work, E. L. Doctorow memorably characterized Sherman's army as both an ominous, distant, humming brown cloud and a grotesque creature writhing over the roads of Georgia, consuming all in its path.[16]

A comprehensive portrait of Sherman's men emerged in Joseph T. Glatthaar's *The March to the Sea and Beyond,* which utilized hundreds of soldiers' letters and diaries to explore their attitudes concerning the Union cause, foraging and destruction, and white and black southerners. Glatthaar's book has special significance for me—it includes several quotes from my great-grandfather's letters, one serving as the final chapter's epigraph, and reproduces a wartime portrait of John Langhans as representative of Sherman's soldiers. My ancestor would doubtless be proud of his presence in the book.[17]

This book forms a unique hybrid by intertwining four other types of literature on Sherman's marches: regimental histories, accounts of southerners in Sherman's path, studies of myths and legends of the marches, and reports by postwar travelers in Sherman's wake. Regimental histories, published in profusion in the postwar era, typically included an itinerary of the marches based on official records from federal and state archives and soldiers' diaries and letters, enlivened occasionally by human-interest anecdotes and musings about the campaigns' significance. Together with other modern works in the genre, the regimental history I was researching during my chigger-plagued trip used similar materials to attain similar results.[18]

Marching with Sherman expands the chronicle by utilizing many additional sources. The 154th New York was severely depleted in numbers by the time of the marches, but enough diaries and letters survive to detail the regiment's experiences and the soldiers' reactions to them.

About ten diaries shape the core of this book, with their daily itineraries and commentary pinpointing the regiment's routes and roles in both campaigns. A consistently reliable diarist was the regimental commander, Major (later Lieutenant Colonel) Lewis D. Warner, whose lengthy, observant, well-informed entries were the basis of his official campaign reports. To reflect my reliance on these sources, my narrative of the marches adheres to the diary format.

Because Sherman's army was incommunicado during the two campaigns, the soldiers had opportunities to send mail only during pauses at Savannah and in North Carolina. Writing to their families and friends, they composed broad overviews reflecting each writer's particular slant on his experiences. Their letters provide analysis of the campaigns lacking in their diaries.

In their writings, the soldiers generally ignored punctuation and uppercase and misspelled words to varying degrees. For smoother reading, I have corrected those mistakes when quoting from these writings, leaving the passages otherwise unchanged.

A handful of regimental veterans recorded memories of the marches in postwar reminiscences. In published memoirs, Charles W. McKay provided a regimental history with few personal anecdotes, while Marcellus W. Darling only related memorable personal experiences. Former officer Alfred W. Benson took yet another approach in an 1874 speech, composing a general overview that ignored regimental history and the personal anecdote but summarized the campaigns' major features in the colorful prose of a skilled writer. His vivid account tended to romanticize, but he also dealt frankly with some unsavory aspects of the marches. In general, however, Benson evoked memories that fit neatly into northern myths.[19]

The papers of Edwin D. Northrup—an outsider who wrote a history of the 154th New York but failed to publish it—include notes he made while regimental veterans reminisced. Memories of Sherman's marches were relatively few compared with those of earlier campaigns. However, Northrup interviewed several veterans who recalled the incidents that led to a dozen casualties near Snow Hill, North Carolina, thus lifting a veil of mystery from that episode.[20]

Underpinned by the wealth of soldiers' diaries and letters, this book's account of the 154th New York's marches through Georgia and the Carolinas provides a broader range of voices and opinions—and offers a deeper examination of the campaigns—than those generally recorded in the regimental histories of a century ago. With the regimental perspective as its foundation, this study adds a second viewpoint—that of southerners who lived along the 154th's route—and proceeds to examine both as they are altered by time and memory.

The March to the Sea and the Carolinas campaign were warfare against civilians on a massive scale, but the victorious soldiers of the 154th New York seldom wrote about their encounters with vanquished white southerners. In his letters home, John Langhans made only one general reference to "the people of the South" and related a single anecdote of a boy he encountered.[21]

Likewise, in the sizable literature on Sherman's marches, historians have generally neglected the interaction between Sherman's men and southern civilians. A scant three books have been devoted to depicting the campaigns as perceived by southerners. Two of them date from the Civil War centennial. John M. Gibson's 1961 account relied too often on northern sources to succeed fully as a study from the southern perspective. In 1964, Katherine M. Jones published a compilation of writings by women who encountered Sherman's army, including some who resided in the path of the 154th New York. In the most recent and only analytical study, Jacqueline Glass Campbell examined a host of issues in the conflict between Sherman's men and Carolinian women. The works of Jones and Campbell emphasize that Sherman's war was directed largely against women and children.[22]

For this book I sought wartime writings by Georgians and Carolinians who resided along the 154th New York's path to provide a southern view of the campaigns. I also sought southern counterparts to the veterans' reminiscences to reveal early shapes of memories of the marches. Finally, as I contemplated a trip along the regiment's route, I sought descendants of the Civil War inhabitants with family legends and relics similar to my own. Could I find a Georgian or Carolinian equivalent of my cotton bolls?

"History isn't just what happens in the past," Laurel Thatcher Ulrich emphasized. *"It is what later generations make of it."* In a study of southern historical memory, David Goldfield wrote that history and memory are not distinct. "They evolve from each other, and their interaction produces the flexibility that enables traditions to survive through centuries of change." As the Civil War generation bequeathed memories

to its descendants, Sherman's marches entered the realm of myths and legends. Only in recent years have scholars begun to investigate those flourishing legacies.[23]

In *Sherman's March in Myth and Memory,* Edward Caudill and Paul Ashdown described competing northern and southern memories of the March to the Sea. The authors chose to concentrate on the Georgia march as the foundation of the Sherman myths, overshadowing the important but underappreciated Carolinas campaign. Their neglect of the latter march is regrettable, but their findings in general characterize memories of both campaigns.[24]

In the postwar years, Caudill and Ashdown asserted, white southerners remembered Sherman as an agent of destruction and humiliation and his march as the deathblow to the Old South's splendor. They never forgave his villainy in exterminating their antebellum culture. Sherman was their antihero, a barbaric terrorist who had shattered Old South myths of superior southern warriors and contented slaves. Although Sherman was in fact a peacetime friend of the South who offered generous surrender terms to his Confederate adversary, southerners despised him as a menacing madman and the cruel despoiler of a civilized and cultured Eden. The North, in contrast, lauded Sherman as a brilliant eccentric, a humane tactical genius, and a modern, innovative hero who waged war much like the efficient manager of a well-run factory. His march symbolized the superiority of northern industrial progress over the South's backward, aristocratic culture and represented the absoluteness of southern defeat.[25]

Sherman's marches became "a staple of the American pageant," observed Civil War scholar Mark Grimsley, "seared into the memory of everyone who experienced them and millions who only heard of them." Memory gave birth to myth. "As the years went by," Grimsley continued (in words I connected with), "Union veterans told their children about the raids and white southerners in the path of the war told theirs. Grandmothers put pen to paper and reminisced for future generations about the coming of the Yankees. Everyone struggled to answer the same question: What did it mean?"[26]

Lost Cause adherents agreed on an answer. The marches were "indiscriminate and all-annihilating," an immoral form of warfare. Grimsley noted that this myth went hand in hand with theories that the South was beaten by sheer force rather than military art (or internal discord), that it engaged in a "chivalrous struggle" whereas the North fought a "brutal, destructive war," and that the complete collapse of its economy was due to Yankee raiding rather than the failure of the Confederate financial system and the loss of billions of dollars of wealth in slaves. Faith in the myth has never waned, Grimsley observed. Sherman's damn Yankees remain etched in southern memory as the personification of evil: "thieves, murderers, rapists, arsonists, trespassers," the perpetrators of a "Dixiecaust" that resulted in utter devastation. But the historical record belies those claims. Sherman ordered his men to mete a "directed severity" to the population in its path, discriminating between hostile, aristocratic slaveholders and the generally more neutral or friendly lower classes. The soldiers were politically astute enough to understand the distinction and usually behaved accordingly. They also were restrained by their strong moral values, their empathy with the civilians they encountered, and official policy, reinforced by orders from their commanders. Grimsley considered Sherman's marches to be a model of enlightened restraint compared with the much more brutal raiding expeditions of the Hundred Years' War or the modern total warfare of World War II (of which Sherman's campaigns are often said to be precursors). But when Grimsley advanced the concept of directed severity in an Atlanta newspaper during the 140th anniversary of the March to the Sea, he received hate mail from irate southerners. The scorched-earth myth is firmly embedded in southern memory.[27]

Nurtured by this mythology, legends of Sherman's marches have spread like kudzu in the South. For fourteen years, University of Georgia folklorist Elissa R. Henken collected, analyzed, and categorized such legends from throughout the state. Aware that Sherman was considered a fiend incarnate whose army razed not only Georgia and the Carolinas but much of the South as well, Henken was surprised to find that legends detailing destruction were paradoxically outnumbered by "stories about the places that Sherman did *not* destroy." The tales revealed several motifs. Towns were reportedly spared because Sherman had a girlfriend living there during his antebellum stay in the South, or because of a Masonic tie between the general and a resident (despite the fact that Sherman was not a Mason), or because he found the place simply too beautiful to destroy. Many of the legends thrive in towns that Sherman never passed through. Henken considers them expressions of Lost Cause pride in which the ogre Sherman is tamed by the influence of southern civilization, most often by genteel but tough and wily women.[28]

In addition to preservation legends regarding towns, Henken

recorded family legends about the saving of a single house or property. These tales also generally feature women, determined and fierce "steel magnolias" who outwit, tame, or defeat Sherman and his men through cunning, defiance, or violence. Candid Southerners have acknowledged the unreliability of these legends. The inhabitants of Screven County, Georgia (through which the 154th New York passed), believed so strongly that the Yankees ransacked and burned every house, historian Dixon Hollingsworth wrote, "that each family seemed to be compelled in later years to devise some explanation as to why its home was spared." But Sherman's men did not wantonly burn houses, Hollingsworth observed, and usually left enough provisions on a farm to support a family for a few days. "In fact they marched by hundreds of Screven County homes without even infringing on the privacy of the families."[29]

In a 1952 book on Georgia's antebellum homes, Margaret Mitchell's good friend Medora Field Perkerson related several preservation legends. In one, General Sherman encountered children playing in the garden of a handsome old house. Mistaking the place for a girls' boarding school, he ordered that it be spared destruction. "Since its antebellum neighbors also remain," Perkerson commented, "one is forced to conclude this is indeed legend." She found such tales to be harmless, "a pretty bit of sentiment and a rare-enough local compliment for the general."[30]

The Reverend J. A. W. Thomas of Marlboro District, South Carolina (through which the 154th New York marched), wrote three decades after Sherman passed that many sad stories of "hidden spoons and trinkets, buried demijohns, and incised feather-beds" could be told. "But these legends rightly belong to those who were the participants in those fearful times, and through them to their descendants. So, as a fair historian, we will not trespass on family matters." Roughly a century later, historian Marion Little Durden of Jefferson County, Georgia (also traversed by the 154th), described family legends of Sherman's marches as undocumented but "dear to the hearts of all Southerners." As dear, no doubt, as my family legends have been to me. Unlike Reverend Thomas, I wanted to hear those southern tales, to see the hidden trinket.[31]

My two unsuccessful attempts only whetted my desire to follow the 154th New York's path through Georgia and the Carolinas. My plan was hardly original. In tracing the regiment's footsteps, I would shadow previous followers of Sherman's route. Shortly after the Civil War ended, northern journalists traveled the path of the marches to report on conditions in the defeated South. In the following decades, others occasionally made the trip. Most recently, a number of writers and other commentators have rambled through Georgia and the Carolinas to collect memories of the marches.[32]

For his 1984 book comparing Sherman's marches to the war in Vietnam, James Reston Jr. made the trip and recorded the opinions of people he met along the way. The Alabamian adventurer Jerry Ellis followed the March to the Sea on foot for a 1995 book that is more given over to ruminations on the modern South and his love life than the historical legacy. In a similar vein, North Carolinian filmmaker Ross McElwee set off to follow the march in his 1986 documentary but meandered into a series of encounters with southern women that distracted him from the Sherman quest. Ten years later, thirteen Christian intercessors followed Sherman's route on foot through the three states in "Operation Restoration," seeking to relieve through prayer "some of the deep and persistent wounds affecting Southerners even today." A collateral Sherman descendant from Maine followed his ancestor's route through Georgia on a bicycle in 2004 and reported his findings in his hometown newspaper and a Web site. In his 1998 best seller *Confederates in the Attic,* Tony Horwitz visited Atlanta and briefly headed east, but abandoned his pursuit of the March to the Sea for other destinations.[33]

More than half a century after I first heard stories of my great-grandfather marching with Sherman, and decades after my two failed attempts to follow his regiment's path, the time came for me to try the trip again. The account of my journey that closes this book follows a long literary tradition in measuring memories of the two marches.

For more than a year and a half during 2005 and 2006 I planned the trip. Consulting official Civil War military maps, I plotted the 154th New York's route in state atlases and on county highway maps. Correspondence linked me with people to visit at archives, libraries, and historical societies. I made arrangements to speak in seven towns along the way, expecting excellent opportunities to gather present-day memories of the marches. The military maps identified property owners on the roads the regiment followed. I had the good fortune to contact certain of their descendants, some of them still inhabiting the ancestral homesteads.

I left my home in Providence, Rhode Island, on a January morning in 2007 and three days later was in Atlanta. My intention to walk the route had vanished with my youth. Over the next six weeks I drove about 3,500 miles along the regiment's 850-mile path through the three states. My days alternated between peaceful jaunts along country back roads, hours spent in archives and libraries, and conversations with folks along the way. A couple of river crossings were inaccessible, but otherwise I traced the 154th's march thoroughly, visiting virtually every city, town, village, and hamlet that the regiment did. At my seven lectures I engaged in dialogues with attendees during lengthy question-and-answer sessions. In memorable moments, I met with descendants in homes that the soldiers had seen, and I listened to family tales of wartime episodes. I kept long days and chronicled them in an illustrated journal. When I left Raleigh for home, I had two boxes full of accounts by southerners who had encountered the Yankees along the 154th New York's route, both wartime writings and postwar reminiscences. I also had collected numerous modern-day memories and legends.

Most of the people the soldiers confronted during the marches were women and children. Many of the white men were away serving in the Confederate army, and those that remained—the elderly and infirm, those exempt from service—tended to flee Sherman's advance, herding male slaves and livestock to hiding places, leaving the women and children, white and black, to fend for themselves. Although I found wartime writings by white members of both sexes, much of the material I gathered consisted of women's postwar memoirs. Many of them were young girls or teenagers during the war, daughters of the class particularly targeted by Sherman and his men—slaveholders. They were patriotic Confederates who expected a victory to ensure the continuance of their privileged lifestyle. They joined their mothers or struck out on their own to do war work, volunteering in soldiers' aid societies and hospitals. They labored and sacrificed and accepted their new responsibilities dutifully. They found the traditional rituals of courtship and marriage disrupted by the war. Some were forced to separate from their families by becoming refugees. They had hated the Yankees before Sherman arrived; in his wake they hated them all the more. They viewed northerners as a separate people, lacking decency and common values.[34]

    These girls grew up to play a prominent role in promoting the postwar mythology of the Lost Cause. Southern white women were by tradition record keepers, and those of the war generation naturally took up the pen to record their memories. Fierce fighters in a cultural battle, the Confederate daughters wrote reminiscences that indoctrinated following generations in the myth. Their memoirs emphasized their war work, their self-sacrifice, and their loyalty to the cause. The writing was cathartic, helping to reconcile them to the bitterness of defeat and the loss of a future they had dreamed to inherit.[35]

During Reconstruction, these women generally neglected history as a medium for telling their war stories. By the late nineteenth century, a combination of factors had emerged to encourage them to write their reminiscences. Much to their dismay, a pro-northern interpretation of the war had gained general acceptance nationwide. In their eyes, the reconciliation theme that had become popular in the North needed an antidote. The success of *Century* magazine's popular "Battles and Leaders" articles prompted them to write and peddle their reminiscences. In the 1880s and 1890s, they began in earnest to publish their diaries and memoirs. During that era clubs and associations proliferated as popular social outlets for middle-class women. One such organization formed in 1894 proved to be the greatest disseminator of white southern women's war reminiscences.[36]

No group more ardently espoused the Lost Cause than the United Daughters of the Confederacy (UDC). The organization grew rapidly in the decade after its formation, increasing its membership tenfold. While it appears UDC members were predominately middle class, the leadership was drawn from socially elite descendants of the planter class, and the group portrayed itself as elite. The UDC's objectives were social, philanthropic, educational, memorial, and historical. Members advocated a divinely mandated "true" history that idealized plantation culture, defended slavery, and vindicated the Confederacy. To counter the malign influence of biased northern histories, the UDC supported the creation of state historical archives, gathered reminiscences from Confederate veterans and women, wrote historical articles for newspapers and magazines, and established national and state history committees to channel their efforts.[37]

The UDC was dedicated to recording the story of every white southern woman in the war. Indeed, the organization charged its members to write accounts of the war, rejecting the objective methods of professional historians in favor of their claimed divine sanction. The

UDC did not distinguish between fact-based history and stories that offered moral judgments. Over and over, in public pronouncements and private correspondence, UDC officers stressed their sacred imperative. The sentimental and romantic results of this godly ordained view of history held great appeal to white southerners.[38]

The UDC suggested certain works as models for would-be writers, steering clear of books by northern historians. The national historical committee instructed state divisions and local chapters on the proper principles, presentation, and organization of historical papers, including guidelines for formats down to paper size. It never dictated the content of the members' accounts, but it did suggest appropriate subjects, including women's reminiscences. The collection and publication of memoirs extended through the twentieth century and continues today. In the process, the UDC archives grew to include many second- or thirdhand stories of long-lost ancestors. As a consequence of the group's influence, thousands of narratives were written in similar ways, telling similar stories. Each was infused with the organization's concept of "true" history, while collectively they presented a single narrative devoid of interpretative variety. The women of the UDC understood that this powerful narrative voice could silence competing accounts.[39]

Early on, the UDC tales were an important element in turning the southern interpretation of the war into a national one, but their influence has waned in recent decades. Katherine Jones utilized some of them in her anthology, whence they found their way into certain popular histories of the marches. But scholarly historians have refrained from using them (and similar reminiscences found in county, church, and family histories) as source material.[40]

I have chosen to include UDC accounts for what they are—highly partisan memories presented according to the strict stipulations of dedicated apologists for the Confederate cause. It is no surprise that they were filled with vituperative language that spread Sherman hatred throughout the South. A UDC memoirist from Chesterfield, South Carolina—a town the 154th New York passed through with fateful results—described Sherman's men as a horrid, filthy, insolent, miserable horde of locusts who swarmed, devoured, desecrated, destroyed, pillaged, burned, ruined, frightened, perpetuated indignities upon, and violated the sanctity of homes and all that was prized and cherished. But the modern southern myth outdoes the scathing UDC accounts

in exaggerating the marches' harshness. At their core, contrary perhaps to expectations, the UDC stories largely support the thesis of
directed severity. In general, they paint a picture of Sherman's marches
much like that sketched by the wartime sources. But they also contain
material not found in the wartime writings—elements of a legendary
nature.[41]

Reading the UDC and other reminiscent accounts, I noticed
similarities to the modern-day legends collected by Elissa Henken.
The old stories shared certain motifs with the new, of steel magnolias
or Masonic ties preserving properties against Yankee misdeeds. At
least one of Henken's stories—of a Sandersville woman and her cry-
ing baby—links directly to the old reminiscence literature. Henken
assessed the tale as a legend illustrating the powerful civilizing effect of
southern womanhood, unaware that it was a close retelling of the story
of Mrs. L. F. J. (told herein in Chapter 5), which was first published in a
South Carolina newspaper, then reprinted an 1885 collection of South
Carolinian reminiscence literature, and finally included in Katherine
Jones's 1964 book. Henken's source for this particular legend was passing along a local story with long roots.[42]

I discovered numerous stories in the reminiscence literature that fit
folklorist Jan Harold Brunvand's definition of modern-day urban legends: odd, whimsical tales told as if factual and often set in a particular
place; tales that seem believable and seem to apply to a particular situation but crop up repeatedly in varying versions, spread orally or in
print. Urban legends are typically attributed to a friend of a friend;
the handed-down southern postwar reminiscences often came from a
long-dead ancestor (separated from the teller by a generation or two)
or the friend of one. Legend tellers, Brunvand notes, "are simply passing on what they assume is a bit of truth." And so it appears to have
been with the southerners who related tales of sitting women, dropped
corn, escaped cows, single kind Yankees, dramatic piano interludes,
and other themes revealed herein. These legends have no parallels in
wartime writings, but they form a bridge to today's apocryphal Sherman tales.[43]

The stories of the thousands of African Americans who encountered
Sherman's men have largely gone untold. Unlike white southern-
ers, the largely illiterate blacks left virtually no written records.
The lack of reliable source material from such significant actors in

the drama of the marches is highly regrettable. Their voices can be heard, however, in the accounts of about three dozen former slaves from counties traversed by the 154th New York. They were among twenty-three hundred ex-slaves interviewed from 1936 to 1938 by employees of the Federal Writer's Project of the Works Progress Administration (WPA). Like much of the white reminiscence literature, these black accounts offer vintage memories. A few of the former slaves were centenarians whose recollections reached back three antebellum decades, but most had been young children during the war. Their stories, like those of their white counterparts, were no doubt shaped (or misshaped) by memory's quirks. Some responses to their usually white interlocutors were perhaps calculated. Their accounts can be described as impressionistic, but they are the only pictures we have from the African American perspective. Those three dozen aged black southerners recited testimony that has to stand for thousands of their silent brethren. Their words, suspect perhaps in their accuracy, are nonetheless valuable for their rarity.

Interviewers transcribed the ex-slaves' stories in the Uncle Remus style of Joel Chandler Harris. Such imaginatively spelled attempts at rendering dialects seem inappropriate in a twenty-first-century study. Consequently I chose to spell the WPA quotes correctly. This measure increases clarity (as with the corrected soldiers' spelling) and perhaps bestows on those long-gone people a measure of dignity denied them in life by their contemporaries.[44]

In the end, I found accounts by southerners along the entire length of the 154th New York's route through Georgia and the Carolinas, ranging from reliable wartime writings to embellished postwar reminiscences to an odd batch of legends to handed-down family tales much like my own—the long-ago inspiration for this book. *Marching with Sherman* follows a single Union regiment through Georgia and the Carolinas, introduces some of the southerners in its path, and considers evolving memories of those events along that specific route. When the story begins in the late summer of 1864, the soldiers of the 154th Regiment are resting by a river outside Atlanta, unaware that they are about to march over a landscape of history and into a fog of legend.

Atlanta Is Ours at Last

THE good news arrived at noontime on Friday, September 2, 1864, when an order reached the camp of the 154th New York Volunteer Infantry at Paces Ferry on the Chatta-hoochee River: Pack up and prepare to march to Atlanta. During the night the Confederate army had abandoned the city. After four months of marching and fighting over the rugged terrain of northern Georgia, a grueling and bloody campaign—the toughest the regiment had endured in two years of service—was coming to an end, capped with success.[1]

The soldiers quickly struck tents, packed gear, formed behind an artillery battery as brigade rear guard, and wound their way toward Atlanta. They stopped for an hour at Peachtree Creek, the site of their last battle, where entrenchments, shattered trees, and graves scarred the landscape. At dusk they passed through the abandoned Confeder-ate earthworks encircling the city. Then, with flags flying and drums beating, they marched through the streets of Atlanta and sang along as a band at the head of the division blared a familiar tune, "Battle Cry of Freedom." A few delighted Unionist residents waved handkerchiefs in response. Camp was pitched on a common a few blocks south of City Hall.[2]

Late that night a few stragglers caught up. Some did not reach camp; three comrades of Company I spent the night in an arsenal. The men found plenty of tobacco in the city, and each grabbed two or three plugs. Other than that, Atlanta's pickings were slim. The stores were mostly emptied, cleaned out by the Confederates.[3]

Heavy showers fell the next morning as the regiment marched south beyond the city's fairgrounds to an abandoned Confederate fort. The storms continued all day, and the men huddled in their tents. Nearby, the charred carriages of two large siege guns smoldered in the rain. Dawn brought clearing weather. As church bells rang, the

regiment moved camp about a half mile west, to a grove on the Mc-
Donough Road. A nearby brick house was occupied as brigade headquarters.[4]

Settling in, the men wrote home of the "glorious news of taken
Atlanta," as Quartermaster Sergeant Newton A. "Dell" Chaffee put it.
The 154th New York was part of the 2nd Brigade, 2nd Division, 20th
Corps, in the army commanded by Major General William Tecumseh
Sherman. Identifying the units by their badges, the soldiers proudly
referred to their "White Star Division" and "Star Corps." Thus Private
Emory Sweetland of Company B exulted, "Hurrah! Atlanta is ours at
last. The glorious old Star Corps had the honor of taking the city at
last, and my division was the first (by about fifteen minutes) to raise
the flag in this, the commercial capital of the Confederacy." Sergeant
Marcellus W. Darling of Company K wrote that he was prospering
in the famous Gate City of the South, adding, "The White Stars have
done some fighting since the fourth of May last." Sergeant Addison L.
Scutt of Company C summarized the Atlanta campaign as "one of a
great many exposures and some hairbreadth escapes" and admitted, "I
have seen all the fighting I care about."[5]

A string of battles had decimated the 154th. "We have only got
about 100 guns in our regiment now," noted Corporal Milon J. Griswold of Company F; the regiment had embarked on the campaign with
roughly 240 present. Now the ten companies averaged only fourteen
soldiers each present for duty. But the cruel cost had purchased a great
victory. "Now the old flag floats in triumph over Atlanta," Griswold
boasted, "where but a short time ago floated the ensign of treason and
rebellion against a glorious Union. But that rebel ensign can never
more wave in triumph where our gallant leader (Major General W. T.
Sherman) and his army go."[6]

"Sherman has demoralized the Johnnies very bad," declared First
Lieutenant and Quartermaster Edgar Shannon. "I think this is the
worst blow they have had in a long time." The magnitude of Atlanta's
loss to the Confederacy was incalculable. The city was a railroad hub
and home to railroad support and service industries. Its factories and
warehouses produced and stored everything needed to arm, equip,
clothe, and feed rebel armies. It housed administrative headquarters
for enemy quartermaster, commissary, and medical departments.
Among the cities of the Confederate States of America, Atlanta was
second in importance only to Richmond. The war had stagnated into a

bloody draw during the summer of 1864. Atlanta's capture lifted northerners' spirits dramatically—and boosted Abraham Lincoln's chances
of reelection in the November presidential contest. No wonder that
a veteran of Company C, Charles W. McKay, boasted in his postwar
memoir of "a glorious campaign ending in complete victory."[7]

September 1864 marked the second anniversary of the 154th New
York's muster into the service of the United States. At its organization, the regiment numbered 948 officers and enlisted men. Eight
of its companies were recruited in Cattaraugus County and two in
neighboring Chautauqua County. Two days before the 154th entered
Atlanta, the bimonthly muster rolls listed 148 officers and men present for duty (about 100 of whom, as Milon Griswold estimated, were
musket-toting enlisted men). Disease, disabilities, discharges, and
desertions had taken a fair share of the other 800 soldiers, but most of
them were casualties of combat at Chancellorsville, Gettysburg, Chattanooga, and the fights of the Atlanta campaign: Dug Gap on Rocky
Face Ridge; Resaca; New Hope Church; Pine Knob; near Kennesaw
Mountain; and Peachtree Creek.[8]

Additional manpower to bolster the regiment was found at home.
Fifty-six men volunteered in western New York in the late summer
and early fall of 1864 to serve in the 154th for one year. They rendezvoused at Dunkirk, were examined and mustered in, and boarded
railroad cars for the long journey to Georgia. The skeletal band of
hardened veterans awaited the new men with some resentment. The
recruits had received a bounty of $300 from Cattaraugus County, and
the veterans were indignant to learn that a property tax had raised
the bounty money. Emory Sweetland regretted that his fellow citizens
would pay "Negroes, jailbirds, and everything and anything to fill up
the war-worn and battle-stained ranks of that noble old regiment, the
154th New York, and save their own precious hides."[9]

General Sherman likewise denigrated the volunteers being sent
to replenish his army as "niggers," "bought recruits," and "refuse."
Historian Bell Irvin Wiley similarly termed late-war recruits "sorry
specimens of humanity" but admitted, "A substantial portion of them
became creditable soldiers." More recently, William Marvel has argued
that many late-war recruits provided "raw material just as good as the
soldiers of 1861," showing grit by volunteering during bloody 1864.
Post-1862 volunteers composed one-fifth of Sherman's army, but most

of them had been hardened by participation in the Atlanta campaign. Only several hundred green troops were to join the army at Atlanta, including those bound for the 154th New York.[10]

Most of them reached the regiment on October 29, 1864. If the veterans expressed any bitterness to the recruits, it went unrecorded by both groups. On the contrary, recruit Private Levi D. Bryant of Company G wrote that the veterans were "pleased to see us." It seems that hard feelings vanished (or were repressed) when the veterans welcomed the recruits to the regiment. After all, the newcomers were friends, neighbors, and kinfolk from back home—which preserved the 154th's sense of community—and regardless of their large bounties, they were volunteers, not despised draftees or substitutes.[11]

Seven recruits who were ill were taken to hospitals and did not make it to the regiment. Forty-eight men were assigned to different companies as privates. The other new man, the Reverend William W. Norton, joined the field and staff officers as regimental chaplain. With the additions, the regiment's strength grew to 205 on the October 31, 1864, muster roll, with each company averaging about a score of men. The recruits formed about a quarter of the total.[12]

That the regiment was understrength was reflected in its officer corps. Colonel Patrick Henry Jones was detached to command the 2nd Brigade. When Lieutenant Colonel Dan B. Allen was discharged for disability and left Atlanta for home, Major Lewis D. Warner took command of the regiment. Adjutant William Clark, Quartermaster Edgar Shannon, Surgeon Henry Van Aernam, and Chaplain Norton completed the field and staff. Only four captains commanded companies: Alfred W. Benson (Company D), James M. Gallagher (E), Byron A. Johnston (F), and Commodore Perry Vedder (H). First Lieutenants Homer A. "Dell" Ames, Stephen Welch, John F. Wellman, and George C. "Guy" Waterman led companies A, C, G, and I, respectively. The other two companies were commanded by first sergeants: William H. Casten (B) and George J. Mason (K).[13]

Without exception, the soldiers were familiar with the higher chain of command. Major Lewis Warner had commanded the regiment for much of the Atlanta campaign and would lead it for the rest of the war. He was respected as hardy, brave, unassuming, patriotic, capable, and always on hand for duty. Colonel Patrick Jones had long led the 154th New York until he assumed command of the 2nd Brigade (which also included the 33rd New Jersey, 119th New York, 134th New York, 73rd Pennsylvania, and 109th Pennsylvania) by seniority during the Atlanta campaign. Jones was courageous, charismatic, self-assured, ambitious, well connected politically, and idolized by the men. When Jones was absent, Colonel George W. Mindil of the 33rd New Jersey took brigade command. A fine soldier, Mindil was nonetheless disliked by members of the 154th, who preferred their own Colonel Jones. They considered Mindil to be a mean-tempered, severe disciplinarian and denigrated him because he was Jewish.[14]

Commanding the 2nd Division was Brigadier General John White Geary, a Pennsylvanian and Mexican War veteran who organized a regiment at the outbreak of the Civil War and led a brigade for about a year before taking command of the division he would head (slightly altered on the April 1864 formation of the 20th Corps) until the end of the war. Geary was as much a politician as a soldier, a shameless self-promoter who exaggerated his abilities to newspaper correspondents and inflated his achievements in grandiloquent, overlong after-action reports. The men of his White Star Division feared him as a hot-tempered, harsh disciplinarian.[15]

The single recent change in command was at the corps level. After Major General Joseph Hooker was bypassed for a promotion in July 1864, his request to be relieved as 20th Corps commander had been readily accepted by Sherman. Hooker's replacement was Major General Henry W. Slocum, a New Yorker and West Point graduate who had risen from regiment to brigade to division to corps command. Private Charles W. Abell of Company E met Slocum at his Atlanta headquarters and thought him jovial and good natured. In the coming campaign, Slocum would head a larger command, and Brigadier General Alpheus S. Williams, commander of the 1st Division, would lead the corps. A Connecticut native and Michigan resident, Williams was another Mexican War veteran. Appointed a brigadier general early in the Civil War, he had commanded his division for two years by the time it entered Atlanta. Geary resented him as a rival, but the men of the corps revered "Pap" Williams.[16]

Commanding the army was Major General William Tecumseh Sherman, a native Ohioan, graduate of West Point, veteran of years of service in the South and in California, and superintendent of a Louisiana military college at the outbreak of the Civil War. As a brigadier general in Kentucky, he had suffered a nervous breakdown. In supporting Ulysses S. Grant's thrust into Tennessee in the spring of 1862, he earned Grant's appreciation and friendship. Their partnership was sealed at the battle of Shiloh. Sherman was promoted to major general and became Grant's most trusted subordinate. After the triumphs at Vicksburg and Chattanooga, when Grant accepted overall command of the Union armies in March 1864, Sherman succeeded him as commander in the western theater and validated Grant's trust with the successful Atlanta campaign. A bundle of nervous energy, voracious intellect, and rapid-fire chatter, the tall, lanky, carelessly dressed Sherman had a wrinkled face, close-cropped sandy beard, and red hair that bristled like a rooster's comb. The uncertainty he had felt early in the war was behind him—his confidence as an independent commander had grown during the recent campaign. With the capture of Atlanta he had earned a reputation as one of the Union's foremost generals. Now he contemplated a campaign unprecedented in conception and scope. He was sure of the confidence of his soldiers, who hailed him familiarly as "Uncle Billy."[17]

After the hardships and hazards of the campaign, the soldiers welcomed the return to routine camp life during the occupation of Atlanta. Sherman issued an order congratulating the army on its accomplishments; it was now to rest, draw new clothing, and be paid. Everyone knew that the hiatus would be limited and another campaign would ensue. As Dell Chaffee put it, "General Sherman believes in keeping to work." In the meantime, the men laid out company streets, dismantled a barn for its lumber, and constructed huts roofed with their tents. But several days of work came to naught. A week after setting up the McDonough Road camp they moved to a nearby pine grove and rebuilt their huts there. When the recruits arrived and constructed their own shanties, Private John Langhans of Company H likened his new home to "a hen roost or a temporary pigpen" but deemed it better than a cloth tent.[18]

While the enlisted men made do with huts, the officers found more homelike shelter. Captain Alfred Benson and First Lieutenant Alexander Bird of Company F moved into the large brick house occupied as brigade headquarters. Quartermaster Edgar Shannon, Quartermaster Sergeant Dell Chaffee, and Acting Commissary Sergeant Marcellus Darling inhabited the abandoned house of a wealthy secessionist, sleeping in a four-poster bed, storing their clothes in an armoire, and enjoying a library of scavenged newspapers and novels. Even Major Warner, usually content to live like the enlisted men, succumbed to temptation and occupied a deserted house.[19]

The soldiers kept busy standing picket, drilling, policing camp, working on fortifications, guarding cattle, cleaning their muskets for inspections, and holding dress parades. Private James W. Clements of Company E found the routine to be unnatural, "for I cannot hear the bullets whistle around me now as they did this summer." When the recruits arrived, Lieutenant Alex Bird was assigned to drill them in three hourly sessions each day. Major Warner wrote his official report of the Atlanta campaign and labored over the regimental muster rolls and other paperwork. On Sunday, October 30, Chaplain Norton preached to the regiment for the first time. Officers and enlisted men brushed up their uniforms and equipage before reviews of the brigade by General Geary and of the division by generals Slocum and Sherman.[20]

"I have a great deal better times than I expected so far," John Langhans wrote after his first week in camp; he was tough, healthy, and "growing fat every day." By and large, the soldiers were well fed during their stay in Atlanta, enjoying soft bread, fresh meat, mixed vegetables, beans, and coffee and sugar. When circumstances forced them to settle for fewer rations, they got by on hardtack, bacon, beef, rice, and pea soup. "I *always* had *enough* to eat," wrote Charles Abell, "and that was good too."[21]

After the rigors of the Atlanta campaign the veterans' uniforms and gear were ragged; consequently they drew new clothing and equipage. To First Lieutenant Horace Smith of Company H, the issues—which included an extra pair of shoes for each man—portended "a big move somewhere." The soldiers adorned their new uniforms with the white star badge of the 2nd Division, 20th Corps. The evening Major Warner issued them nearly every man had them on at dress parade.[22]

About two weeks after arriving in Atlanta, Marcellus Darling noted, "They owe us eight months pay now." Many of the men were broke, among them Charles Abell, who admitted, "I live on other men's pockets." The long-awaited day arrived on October 12, when the regiment marched to brigade headquarters and was paid. Most of the men allotted much of their pay to their families, retaining only small sums for themselves. Private Jesse D. Campbell of Company D was typical. Of the $214.64 he received, he left a check for $190 with the paymaster to be sent home to his parents.[23]

After two years at the front, popular pastimes like singing, card games, and sports had become too mundane for general comment; the soldiers rarely mentioned amusements in their letters and diaries. Alfred Benson sat through a miserable minstrel show at an Atlanta theater; Private George Eugene Graves of Company D called it the flattest performance he ever saw. Private William D. Harper of Company F spent spare hours reading his pocket testament, mending his clothes, and napping. Alexander Bird bought a guitar. Corporal Job B. Dawley of Company K had his portrait taken by an unknown photographer and sent it home.[24]

"Our company is small," Sergeant Milton D. Scott of Company F informed his brother, "only ten present and two of them is sick." Many of the soldiers had a touch of scurvy, but it did not keep them from duty. In general, their health was good. The veterans were acclimated to Georgia's weather, hardened to living in the field, and used to army rations, but the recruits experienced a difficult adjustment. "Most of the new men have the *diarrhea*," Chaplain Norton observed. About half of the recruits were hospitalized. Some recovered in time for the coming campaign, but seven of the forty-nine remaining recruits— and ten veterans—were sent to northern hospitals, part of an army-wide purge of unfit soldiers. The recruits were introduced to another tormenting aspect of army life: lice. "I find some on me," Levi Bryant noted, "in spite of all I can do."[25]

One member of the 154th New York, Private Reuben R. Eggleston of Company C, died during the stay in Atlanta, expiring at the division hospital of chronic dysentery on the night of September 29. He was buried the next day in a cemetery containing two acres of Confederate graves and a smaller section for the Federal dead. Geary's 2nd Division had its own plot in a corner of the graveyard, with a marble monument and a sod lawn, surrounded by a white picket fence taken from a city yard. In the postwar years, Eggleston and the cemetery's other Union dead were reinterred in the Marietta National Cemetery.[26]

The 1864 political campaign stirred excitement in camp. In the presidential contest the Democratic candidate, former Union army commander George B. McClellan, stood on a peace platform, while the Republican incumbent, Abraham Lincoln, advocated a steadfast prosecution of the war. The New York State gubernatorial contest pitted Republican Reuben E. Fenton—the congressman representing Cattaraugus and Chautauqua counties—against the Democratic incumbent, Horatio Seymour, whom the soldiers widely considered to be a Copperhead (as war opponents were termed). Running on the Republican ticket to replace Fenton in Congress was the 154th's own Surgeon Henry Van Aernam, who was opposed by Democrat Jonas K. Button, a wealthy farmer from Van Aernam's hometown of Franklinville.[27]

News of the Democrats' convention and McClellan's nomination reached the 154th two days after marching into Atlanta. "Their supporters in the army," Emory Sweetland predicted, "will be about as scarce as angels' visits or Uncle Sam's greenbacks." "The army is for Lincoln almost unanimous," wrote Dell Chaffee, "and this is one of Uncle Abe's regiments." Naturally, Fenton and Van Aernam also drew the men's support. Before Election Day fell on Tuesday, November 8, New York State soldiers cast their ballot by power of attorney. Among the 150 veterans, Major Warner guessed, not more than 5 or 6 voted for McClellan. The recruits, Levi Bryant declared, were unanimous "for Old Abe." A decided majority of the rest of Sherman's army also favored Lincoln. The president would be reelected by a substantial margin, Warner predicted, but when the soldiers finally left Atlanta in mid-November, they were still uncertain whether Lincoln had been returned to office.[28]

Fenton and Van Aernam both won their races. Van Aernam was discharged from the service on November 5 and left Atlanta the next day aboard a hospital train. "It was a sad day to our boys when he left," noted Horace Smith. Van Aernam took his seat in Congress in December 1865; he would go on to serve three subsequent terms.[29]

Before Atlanta fell, the war-weary citizens of the North appeared ready to desert the Union cause, and Abraham Lincoln predicted his own electoral defeat. But Sherman's triumph, together with other timely victories, renewed sagging hopes and bolstered drooping spirits like an elixir, revitalizing the North and swinging political support back to Lincoln and the Republicans. By helping to capture and then occupying the Gate City, the 154th New York had performed one of its most significant achievements of the war.[30]

$$\left[\ 2\ \right]$$

The Gate City

WITHIN days after Atlanta fell, the enemy cut the railroad between Chattanooga and Nashville. That logistical lifeline connected Sherman to supply depots in the two Tennessee cities and points north. If it remained cut, his army could not survive. Communications were quickly restored, but General John Bell Hood, after resting his defeated Confederate army, moved in early October to strike the railroad in northern Georgia. In response, Sherman marched the bulk of his army after Hood, leaving the 20th Corps to hold Atlanta. Fearful of an attack and unable to man the lengthy outer lines, the corps worked day and night for a week to erect an inner circle of fortifications around the city. Once the situation clarified, the men relaxed, trusting their commander to handle the enemy. "Old Billy Sherman is a-going to fix them," wrote Charles Abell, "if they don't play out."[1]

With Hood's disruption of the supply line, the troops were reduced to half rations, and feed for the horses, mules, and cattle grew short. Consequently thousands of troops and hundreds of wagons were sent from fifteen to thirty miles into the countryside to gather fodder. The 154th New York had briefly gleaned foodstuffs from Virginia farms in 1862, but now the regiment foraged systematically for the first time in two expeditions. The first, from October 16 to 19, carried the men twenty miles southeast to Flat Rock Shoals on the South River. The second, from October 26 to 29, took them east through Decatur to the vicinity of Stone Mountain. The tramps revealed they were a bit out of shape, but together with ample corn for the animals, they brought in large supplies of sweet potatoes, flour, and hams for themselves. Between the two expeditions, the regiment rode a train of flatcars southeast to East Point, at the junction of two railroads, where it guarded pioneers who were tearing up the track; the rails would be used to repair the broken railroad north of Atlanta.[2]

The foraging and railroad-wrecking excursions proved to be re-hearsals for the coming campaign. Sherman noted that his men took to foraging "like ducks to water. They like pigs, sheep, chickens, calves, and sweet potatoes better than rations. We won't starve in Georgia." Indeed, the soldiers saw they could live luxuriously on Georgia's bounty. After one expedition, Emory Sweetland enjoyed a breakfast of sausage, beefsteak, bread, tomatoes, pickles, and coffee. Beyond the plenty, the men found a certain satisfaction in plundering Georgian farms. As Horace Smith put it, "We had a gay time harvesting corn for those old Reb farmers."[3]

Alfred Benson thought Atlanta was "a fine town," an opinion shared by his regimental comrades, who admired its splendid houses and yards and architectural gems including a female seminary, a medical col-lege, a courthouse and town hall, and churches. James Clements paid Atlanta the ultimate compliment, from a Yankee perspective: he said it looked like a northern town. As pleasant as the men found it, how-ever, Atlanta was battered. The evacuating Confederates had burned trainloads of ammunition, exploded magazines, spiked cannons, and dumped shells and powder in mud holes. During the siege, Union cannon had fired thousands of rounds into the city, which several of the men described as badly torn to pieces by shells. Commercial and residential structures alike showed damage, and some were nearly demolished. Private Mervin P. Barber of Company E attended service at a church that had been struck by a shell. Many Atlantans had dug bombproof shelters in their yards, reinforced with heavy timbers and cotton bales. Marcellus Darling expressed qualified sympathy for the subterranean shelter seekers. "It is hard I know, but such is war and so it is. We have all got to stand it."[4]

Dell Chaffee reported that nearly two hundred women and chil-dren had been killed in Atlanta during the bombardment. This was inaccurate; that amount probably encompassed all the civilian casual-ties, including the wounded. A southern newspaper correspondent reported almost five hundred deaths, but an Atlanta diarist recorded about twenty fatalities. Historians who have closely studied the avail-able evidence consider the diarist's figure to be most accurate, and the reporter's number to be highly inflated Confederate propaganda.[5]

Henry Van Aernam estimated that Atlanta had about 4,000 inhab-itants when the city fell. The population, which stood at 9,554 in 1860, had swelled to some 20,000 or more by 1864, only to dwindle during the siege as refugees sought safer environs. Van Aernam detected distinct types among those who remained. There were wealthy, virulent secessionists, who hypocritically took an oath of allegiance to the United States and clamored for safeguards to protect their property. Then there were renegade northerners, who expected sympathy and protection on account of their birthplace but had aided the rebellion and were now praying for McClellan's election. Among this group the soldiers spotted some familiar faces.[6]

Brothers and native New Englanders Joseph and Isaac Winship owned the Winship Machine Company. Their brother-in-law, former Cattaraugus County resident John Boutelle, worked at their iron foundry and machine shop, which was said to be worth half a million dollars. Although many of Atlanta's northern-born residents were Unionists, Van Aernam pegged the Winships and Boutelles as staunch Confederates. From the start of the war, their company's production had been given over to shot, shell, and cannons. Architect John Boutelle Jr. had helped to construct Atlanta's defenses, his wife and daughters had nursed ailing southern soldiers in hospitals, and two of his sisters were married to rebel soldiers. As president of the Atlanta Hospital Association, Isaac Winship's wife, Martha, met trainloads of sick and wounded Confederate soldiers, cared for them in hospitals and her home, buried them when they died, and marked their graves.[7]

Isaac and Martha Winship fled Atlanta when Hood's army evacuated the city, so the soldiers of the 154th New York encountered the families of Joseph Winship and the elder and younger John Boutelle. Although Henry Van Aernam doubted their loyalty, Hannah Winship Boutelle claimed many years later that she and her husband were Unionists and she and her daughters had nourished and nursed wounded Union soldiers. Whatever their loyalties, the Boutelles were laid low by Atlanta's fall. "The war has blasted and desolated everything here," Van Aernam noted, "and they are pretty poor now." Projectiles had repeatedly struck their house and shell fragments had wounded two of them. Van Aernam had no sympathy for the family. In his opinion, slavery and greed had demoralized them and made them rebels— treachery would prove to be as bitter to them as it had been to Judas.[8]

Having survived prison in Virginia following their capture at Gettysburg, many members of the 154th New York were incarcerated at the prisoner-of-war camp at Andersonville, Georgia. But their comrades in Atlanta knew little about the place until August 1864, when Private Sidney Moore of Company D returned to the regiment after escaping from the camp and told the men about overcrowding and death among the scorbutic and debilitated prisoners.[9]

The large brick house that served as 2nd Brigade headquarters belonged to a Confederate officer serving at Andersonville. James Ormond, a former Floridian, owned three elegant stores downtown. He later reflected that he was a well-off, contented man when the war began, the owner of some fifty slaves. The first years of the conflict did little to diminish his happiness or prosperity. But when Sherman's army approached Atlanta, Ormond was caught in the war's web. Although too old to be conscripted, he nonetheless enrolled in the 2nd Georgia Reserves as a second lieutenant and was sent with his regiment to guard prisoners at Andersonville. He was soon appointed the post's adjutant.[10]

After Atlanta fell, Ormond received a furlough and returned to the city to find his property occupied by the Yankees and various officers quartered in his house. In a memoir, Ormond reported that his wife, Elizabeth, and three children were generally well treated by the enemy. He recalled 2nd Brigade commander Colonel George Mindil as a gentleman who was courteous to the family and did all in his power—not always successfully—to prevent thievery and vandalism by his men. When a soldier stole the Ormond silverware, Mindil had him arrested and the property restored. However, an officer stole Ormond's son's pony.[11]

In a postwar reminiscence, Henry Van Aernam related his encounter with the family. Elizabeth Ormond's children were sick with typhoid fever, and Van Aernam received permission from General Geary to doctor them. He also provided Mrs. Ormond with food; in gratitude, she cooked his meals. In their recollections, Van Aernam did not mention James Ormond's visit to Atlanta, and Ormond did not mention Van Aernam's care of his family. Their stories ran parallel but never intersected.[12]

Andersonville was on the minds of many members of the regiment who had family or friends among the prisoners. When a citizen who was going south through the Union lines offered to deliver mail to the prison, the men took advantage of his kindness and wrote to their captive friends. Whether the man fulfilled his pledge was never discovered.[13]

For a while, members of the regiment had ample opportunities to consort with Atlanta's citizens. Edgar Shannon made many acquaintances among the inhabitants, with mixed impressions, finding some to be intelligent but others foolish for refusing to work despite being half starved. The men inevitably turned their eyes toward the females. Shannon informed his girlfriend that "there are some handsome young ladies here," but they were ardent rebels. He enjoyed talking with them and eliciting their opinions of the Yanks. Alfred Benson admired pretty women during a tour of the city and enjoyed a visit to a family of fine girls. James Clements, on the other hand, found little to admire in the local women. "They're most all built like a ten-foot slab," he wrote, "a little round on the belly and rather dark complexion, but I think the cause of that is chewing tobacco and snuff."[14]

In the postwar years, veterans recalled playful encounters with Atlanta women. Private Zeno Besecker of Company I remembered astonishing a group who sought a light for their pipes by wrapping a pinch of powder in a wad of paper around the tip of his bayonet, topping it with a percussion cap, and hitting it. When the paper burst into flames, the women exclaimed, "That is a Yankee trick!" Private Clark E. "Salty" Oyer of Company G recalled allowing a woman to pass through his advanced picket post, knowing she would be stopped at the main picket line and prohibited from proceeding. When he returned to the main line and found the detained woman seething, he jovially arranged for her to obtain a pass.[15]

The nighttime sight of the White Star Division's camp enchanted one young Atlanta woman. From her window, Mary Rawson Ray had a fine view of the house General Geary occupied as his headquarters, surrounded in all directions by the tents of his men. The brightly illuminated house and the campfires dotting the surrounding hills reminded her, she wrote in her diary, of Aladdin's dazzling home in the tales of the Arabian nights. That night Ray was "carried to dreamland by the music of the bugle." Her fantasy was soon to be rudely interrupted.[16]

Less than a week after his troops entered Atlanta, General Sherman ordered the expulsion of the inhabitants. He was resolved to make the city strictly a military post, with no interference from civilians. He gave them a choice: Go north or go south. A bitter correspondence regarding the order's justification ensued between Sherman, Atlanta's mayor, and General Hood, inspiring several pithy pronouncements by the Yankee general, the most famous: "War is cruelty, and you cannot refine it." The order stood.[17]

Members of the 154th New York commented on several aspects of the expulsion order. Milon Griswold noted the residents' sorrow. But Marcellus Darling endorsed the logistical necessity; the army needed all the supplies that could be delivered to the city. Horace Smith noted that the citizens were sent away as quickly as possible. Those who chose to go south were sent through the lines under a flag of truce to a railroad stop called Rough and Ready, while the rest were shipped by rail north of the Ohio River.[18]

Some thirty members of the regiment were assigned to guard duty during the expulsion. By the end of September, about 1,650 people—with their furniture and household goods—had been hauled in railroad cars, wagons, and ambulances to Rough and Ready, where they were turned over to the Confederate army. An equivalent number boarded trains in the city's battered depot to go north. When it was over, the only civilians left in Atlanta were about fifty white families—mostly Unionists who passed a closely scrutinized application process in order to stay—and an unknown number of blacks, most of whom simply refused to leave; many of them would depart Atlanta when Sherman's army left the city.[19]

Quartermaster Edgar Shannon took charge of seventy wagons to transport women and children south. He entered every house along two main streets and rounded up fifteen families, including quite a number of young women. The caravan took eight hours to make the ten-mile trip to Rough and Ready, where it arrived at midnight to find the Confederates waiting. After transferring the people and their belongings to the Confederates' wagons, Shannon visited with the enemy for a couple of hours. Then he climbed under a wagon to sleep, "dreaming of Johnnie Reb dressed in gray and the fair ones going the other way."[20]

On the morning of September 12 Mary Rawson Ray rushed to the home of relatives, who were scheduled to leave that day. At their gate she found soldiers loading baggage into two huge army wagons. Then her relatives emerged from the house, bid her a sad good-bye, climbed aboard two ambulances, and slowly departed. Returning home, Ray witnessed similar scenes. She finished her walk thoroughly dejected.[21]

Mary A. H. Gay, a die-hard Confederate spinster from Decatur, joined the evacuees heading south. In a postwar memoir she bemoaned the confusion and disquiet of Atlanta yielding to the alien enemy, portraying the Yankees as brutes bent on utterly impoverishing and humiliating the citizens, their vile curses, boisterous laughter, and vulgar jokes echoing in the deserted streets. At Rough and Ready the civilians—mostly female, Gay recalled, from aged grandmothers to babes in arms—were deposited on the cold ground as drizzle saturated their clothing. One evacuee later stated they were herded like cattle into some woods, where hundreds formed a mournful chorus and sang a sentimental song of home.[22]

Accounts of the evacuation published years after the war by the United Daughters of the Confederacy (UDC) conformed to that organization's potent Lost Cause propaganda. Most UDC accounts were of postwar origin, but the occasional wartime writing saw print, such as a September 1864 letter by Mary Ann Mecaslin, submitted for publication by a descendant. Mecaslin and her husband were uncertain whether to go north to his family in Baltimore or south to her folks in Augusta, Georgia. Mecaslin anguished over the dilemma, but in the end she and her husband went north. More typical was the postwar, secondhand UDC story of Neppie Jones, a loyal Confederate who naturally decided to go south. She packed a box with valuables and keepsakes and hired a man to convey it to the depot. When she left her house, Yankees swarmed through it and took what they wanted. (The account typically characterized the enemy as crude foreigners, "uncouth Hessians and Irishmen in blue.") At the depot, Yankees stole her box, stripping Jones of everything "except memories and love."[23]

Elizabeth Ormond and her three children went north. James Ormond applied to a Union quartermaster for his family's transportation before he returned to his duties at Andersonville. The Ormonds packed as many household goods as they could into a freight car before Elizabeth and the children clambered aboard. They left Atlanta in better condition than most others. Elizabeth Ormond had prospered selling provisions to the Yankees, and her profits were sewed up in her clothes.[24]

Stationer and bookseller Samuel P. Richards also chose to go north. When the Yankees entered Atlanta, Richards noted in his diary, they did not disturb private homes. Consequently he was shocked when he went downtown and found soldiers and a crowd of locals, white and black, looting his store. Nevertheless, he was able to save much of his stock and stow it in his house, where it remained unmolested. The Yankees "generally behaved pretty well," he wrote. Richards was granted the use of an entire boxcar to haul north his books and other effects.[25]

When the Yankees marched into Atlanta, ten-year-old Carrie Berry wrote in her diary, "We were afraid they were going to treat us badly." Her fears soon dissipated; she found the enemy to be orderly and well behaved. "I think I shall like the Yankees very well," she wrote. When her father arranged for the family to remain in Atlanta, Berry sadly parted with expelled relatives and witnessed the city's ruin, but she voiced no bitterness toward the enemy. She described the family's Yankee guard as "a very good friend to us." Long after Sherman's men left Atlanta, the city filled with returnees, who ostracized the Berrys and others who had remained during the occupation as collaborationists.[26]

The Yankees caused racial upheaval, Samuel Richards noted in his diary, by assuring African Americans of their freedom. The blacks consequently became impudent and indifferent to the wants of their former masters. In the UDC story of Neppie Jones, "servants"—as slaves were euphemistically called—were "faithful and sympathetic" until Atlanta fell. But when the Yankees arrived, "they deserted their household tasks, seated themselves in rocking chairs on the front porch and gaily called to passing soldiers." That egregious misconduct disgusted Yankee officers staying at the Jones home, one of whom declared that he had not left his home "to fight for their kind." In this tale, white northerners and southerners were united by racism.[27]

In his later years, the African American William Ward recalled that when the Yankees arrived in Atlanta he wondered whether Sherman would keep him enslaved. But young, able-bodied black men were welcomed to work for the Yankee army. Finally convinced of his freedom, Ward joined the ammunition train and remained with it until the end of the war. Along the way, he spread the news of liberation to thousands of his people.[28]

The expulsion of its residents further transformed Atlanta. Joshua Hill, the mayor of Madison, Georgia, visited Atlanta in late October and found "one prolonged scene of desolation." Gone was the hubbub of thousands of civilians, replaced by the clockwork of military routine. "The silence that reigns," Hill wrote, "is only broken by the sound of moving masses of men, trains of wagons, squadrons of cavalry and occasionally a railway train." As Sherman had promised, Atlanta had become a military post.[29]

Soon after the 154th New York entered Atlanta, the soldiers began to speculate about the future. Some hoped they would remain to garrison the city. Others foresaw Sherman moving northeast to a climactic battle. Still others surrendered to uncertainty. "How long we shall remain here I know not," Jesse Campbell wrote. "It may be two days or it may be all winter. The latter, I hope."[30]

Meanwhile, Sherman was making plans that would settle the issue.

When word of Atlanta's fall reached Lieutenant General Grant, the Union army commander asked his trusted subordinate what was to be done next. In response, Sherman proposed on September 20 to march across Georgia with sixty thousand men, living off the countryside. Hood's army remained a threat, but Sherman believed that troops in Tennessee under Major General George H. Thomas could contend with it. Sherman repeatedly pushed his proposal. "I can make this march," he wired Grant a famous promise on October 9, "and make Georgia howl!" On November 1, Grant suggested by telegraph that Sherman "entirely ruin" Hood before undertaking his march. Sherman replied the next day that Thomas had enough troops to confront Hood. Grant immediately wired his permission for the march.[31]

Sherman's army remained ignorant of his plans. By the end of October, members of the 154th New York sensed a move was imminent, although the specifics remained unknown. In subsequent days, several unfit men were sent away to hospitals, surplus muskets were turned in, and the regiment's spare baggage and papers were packed up and shipped to Nashville in the care of Sergeant Norman H. Gray of Company A, who consequently missed the coming campaign.[32]

As November opened, all sorts of rumors circulated regarding the army's destination. As Horace Smith observed, however, "No one but Sherman knows [for] certain." From their posts at the division hospital, Surgeon Van Aernam and Emory Sweetland (doing duty as a steward) offered the most accurate predictions. Van Aernam stated the army would march to "Savannah or some other point on the ocean or gulf." Sweetland wrote that the "great raid" would carry four army corps to Charleston or Savannah, without significant opposition. The men realized they would be incommunicado during the campaign and warned their families of the consequences. Chaplain Norton informed his daughter that, even if the march was successful, it would be a long time before he could write home again. Sweetland cautioned his wife, "You will probably hear hard stories through rebel sources about our being all cut to pieces or captured but you must not believe them."[33]

The handful of newspaper reporters accompanying the army would likewise be unable to file reports until communications with the North were reestablished. Ironically, the journalist whose accounts eventually reached the largest audience did not make the march. The *New York Herald*'s David P. Conyngham had covered the Atlanta campaign, but he left the city to cover the Tennessee campaign. He subsequently returned to Sherman's army at Savannah and accompanied it through the Carolinas. When the war ended, he published his compiled reports as a popular book. His March to the Sea account—falsely presented as his own—was based on the dispatches of a fellow *Herald* reporter who made the march.[34]

The 154th New York received marching orders on the afternoon of November 5. After an hour's delay, the men finally left camp at 3 p.m. They marched a couple of miles east of the McDonough Road, passed the outer line of fortifications, pitched camp in a thicket, and settled in for the night. The next day, a Sunday, Chaplain Norton conducted a service. Two hours later the regiment packed up and returned to its old camp. The next day new orders arrived: Be ready to march at a moment's notice. For several days following, the regiment's arms were stacked on the color line, and the men slept with their cartridge boxes and cap pouches strapped on. While waiting, they speculated about Atlanta's fate. Emory Sweetland offered the most accurate prediction: "We shall probably destroy what is left of Atlanta when we leave it."[35]

The future came into closer focus on November 8 and 9, when General Sherman issued orders dividing his army into the Right Wing, composed of the 15th and 17th Corps, under the command of Major General Oliver Otis Howard, and the Left Wing, consisting of the 14th and 20th Corps, commanded by Major General Slocum. A division of cavalry under Brigadier General Hugh Judson Kilpatrick would receive special orders from Sherman. The orders also stipulated procedures to be followed in the upcoming campaign regarding transportation, foraging, destruction of resources, and relations with the black population. His army of approximately sixty-two thousand men had a "special purpose," Sherman declared, but it remained a mystery to the rank and file. It was sufficient for the men to know that it involved a departure from their present base, the general stated, "and a long and difficult march to a new one."[36]

Emory Sweetland noted a significant factor in the upcoming campaign: "Sherman goes with us." The soldiers expressed unbridled confidence in their commander. "I will risk W. T. Sherman with the best general the Rebs have," Sweetland declared. The army knew nothing but victory with Sherman at its head, Milon Griswold wrote. In the upcoming march, "If General Sherman undertakes to go there, he will go, in spite of the whole Confederacy." The general basked in his army's adulation. The men would follow him anywhere, Sherman boasted, however hazardous. "They think I know every road and by-path in Georgia," he noted. Indeed, Sherman had traversed the state as a young officer; he was familiar with the territory his army was about to cross and had studied it deeply in preparation for the march. He reciprocated his men's confidence. "The army," he declared, "is in magnificent heart."[37]

Mid-November brought the destruction of Atlanta. Initially, three 20th Corps regiments drew up plans to destroy buildings using explosives and fire. Sherman intervened and ordered his chief engineer to demolish with battering rams and other heavy equipment, using fire only to consume the wreckage. As it happened, however, explosives and fire were used to destroy structures—and vagabond Union soldiers started enough fires to cause widespread additional damage.[38]

Daytime of November 11 passed quietly. After dark Major Warner and his fellow diarists penned laconic entries as flames broke out in Atlanta. "In evening fires in town," Warner wrote. "Hot times," wrote Sergeant Joshua R. Pettit of Company A; he reported soldiers had set some thirty buildings afire. The men were called to arms at 11 p.m., and after watching the blazes for a while, they stacked arms on the color line and slept with their straps on.[39]

In the burning, battered, and largely abandoned city, there was no sleep for young Carrie Berry. "We were frightened almost to death last night," she wrote the next day. "Some mean soldiers set several houses on fire in different parts of the town. I could not go to sleep for fear that they would set our house on fire. We all dread the next few days to come for they said that they would set the last house on fire if they had to leave this place." Only when the Berrys were assigned a guard did their concerns ease a bit.[40]

Over the next several days, while Yankee arsonists torched houses in Atlanta, the engineer troops kept busy. The railroad tracks running north were destroyed on November 12. On Sunday, November 13, fires burned day and night along all the railroads around Atlanta. The 154th New York was inspected that morning and heard a sermon from Chaplain Norton in the afternoon. The demolition of the city intensified. Government buildings and depots were set afire or blown up with powder. Among the first structures to fall were the iron foundry and shops of the Winship Machine Company. On November 14, the regiment received orders to march the following morning. Before turning in for the night, the men packed up and watched large fires consume Atlanta.[41]

The city was reduced to "a perfect mass of ruins," wrote an area woman. Weeks after the Yankees departed, a Confederate officer arrived in Atlanta for an inspection. The railroad depots and car shed, machine shops, foundries, rolling mills, arsenals, laboratories, and armories had been battered to pieces and burned. About four hundred houses survived; some four thousand had gone up in flames. Five churches survived; four did not. The medical college was saved, but the female seminary was torn down and other schools were destroyed. Two-thirds of the city's shade trees had vanished. Thousands of animal carcasses littered the streets. Cemetery headstones and monuments were smashed, vaults were opened, and coffins robbed of their silver nameplates. The suburbs—including the Ormonds' neighborhood—were reduced to "one vast, naked, ruined, deserted camp." In the Yankees' wake came the scavengers: "bushwhackers, robbers, deserters, and citizens from the surrounding country," all engaged in plundering what little was left.[42]

On the night of November 14, as the sky over Atlanta glowed and swirled with smoke and flames, Major Warner closed his diary entry, "Expect to be off tomorrow." The way was open from the ruined Gate City of the South into the heart of Georgia. The 154th New York was poised to march with Sherman into history.[43]

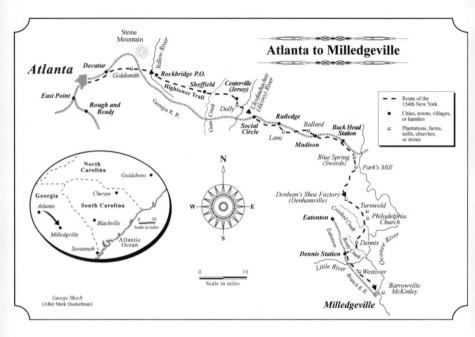

Atlanta to Milledgeville

Atlanta

Stone Mountain

Decatur
Goldsmith

Rockbridge P.O.

Sheffield

Centerville (Jersey)

Hightower Trail

Yellow River

Georgia R. R.

East Point

Rough and Ready

Dally

Gum Creek

Social Circle

Rutledge

Ballard

Buck Head Station

Lane

Madison

Blue Spring (Swords)

Park's Mill

Ulcofauhachee (Alcovy) River

Denham's Shoe Factory (Denhamville)

Turnwold

Crooked Creek

Eatonton

Philadelphia Church

Dennis

Oconee River

Eatonton

Rocky Creek

Dennis Station

Little River

Branch R. R.

Westover

Barrowville
McKinley

Milledgeville

Route of the
154th New York

Cities, towns, villages,
or hamlets

Plantations, farms,
mills, churches,
or stores

North Carolina

Goldsboro

Cheraw

Georgia

Atlanta

South Carolina

Blackville

Milledgeville

Savannah

Atlantic Ocean

0   50
Scale in miles

N
W   E
S

0   10
Scale in miles

George Skoch
(After Mark Dunkelman)

To Denham's Shoe Factory

*T*uesday, November 15, 1864. Marching orders arrived before daylight. At 7:00 a.m. the soldiers of the 154th New York moved out of their Atlanta camp carrying thirty days' rations in their knapsacks and sixty rounds of ammunition in their cartridge boxes. The regiment led the 2nd Brigade eastward on the Decatur Road beyond the fortifications, where a halt was made while the wagon train was untangled at the rear of the column. The men then entered DeKalb County and passed through Decatur, which they found ablaze and mostly destroyed. After tramping a few more miles, they camped about midnight near the James W. Goldsmith farm, a few miles south of Stone Mountain. The day's march totaled fifteen miles.[1]

Major Warner closed his diary entry this night, "We are now entered upon a campaign which for brilliancy of conception has not been surpassed during the war. May success attend us." A decade later, Alfred Benson stressed the audacity of "the most hazardous undertaking of modern warfare" and dramatized the strategic situation: Sherman's army would either march triumphantly to the sea or "fall back over the long line, defeated, demoralized, routed, it may be destroyed." Other veterans remembered the excitement of embarking on the campaign. It was delightful to enter a new region, Marcellus Darling recalled, where there were plentiful provisions, good roads, and fair weather. Everyone was in good spirits to be marching in hostile country unopposed.[2]

The men cast rearward glances at the doomed Gate City. "The last I see of Atlanta," wrote James Clements, "was the flames and smoke curling around over the tree tops as I march along." Ten years later, Alfred Benson recalled "the overhanging cloud of smoke by day and the almost blood red glow by night, reminding us of the destruction of war, and of the ruin we had wrought."[3]

Flames also spread ruin in Decatur. Exactly a year after the 154th passed through the village, Martha Amanda Quillin remembered watching from her veranda as fires erupted for miles in each direction. A church and an academy burned and blanketed her neighborhood with smoke. As flames roared, Yankee soldiers yelled and swore, and frightened neighbors screamed. Fourteenth Corps regiments passing through the village the following day described it as half ruined and desolate. Quillin attributed the preservation of her home to the presence of some Yankee officers who used her sitting room as their headquarters.[4]

In later years, ex-slave Camilla Jackson stated that her master fled Decatur, taking his slaves with him. When the refugees returned, they found the Yankees had torn down the slave quarters, so the blacks moved into the master's roomy mansion until their cabins were rebuilt. The opposite was more likely to occur: Sherman's men might destroy a "big house," especially if vacant, but spare the slave quarters. (The dwelling of a white slave owner was called "the big house" regardless of its size. Unlike the white-columned mansion of popular imagination, most of them were modestly proportioned.)[5]

Wednesday, November 16, 1864. Divisions, brigades, and regiments routinely took turns marching in the lead. So on this day Geary's 2nd Division headed the 20th Corps, Colonel Patrick Jones's 2nd Brigade led the division, and the 154th New York, having led the brigade the previous day, now took the rear. The men marched at 8:00 a.m. and proceeded east at a quick pace on good roads through gently rolling countryside. In the afternoon they crossed the Yellow River, entered Gwinnett County, and passed Rock Bridge Post Office. (A typical southern post office, one of Sherman's staff officers observed, was merely a planter's homestead.) After a tramp of fifteen miles, they camped at 4:00 p.m. near the Newton County line.[6]

Following Sherman's orders, the army foraged a living from the land. In his memoir, Alfred Benson described the procedure. Every morning fifty men were detailed from each brigade to take the advance and gather provisions. Riding confiscated horses and mules, they returned at night carrying large sacks of provisions, with pigs and chickens dangling from their saddles, all of it confiscated from hapless citizens. The army was now beyond the regions stripped during the October foraging expeditions, and provisions were plentiful. On this day the men enjoyed meals of sweet potatoes and fresh pork.[7]

The New Yorkers delighted in detailing the bounty foraged from Georgia farms. "We had all the sweet potatoes, fresh pork, chickens, ducks, geese, sheep, honey, and all of the molasses we wanted," Gene Graves wrote later in the campaign. "We would go in the fields and pull all the peanuts we could eat, and sugar cane." Major Warner compiled a similar list and concluded, "In fact everything that the country produces is taken and turned to the use of the soldier or his animals. So clean is the work done that I much doubt whether a forlorn hope of caterpillars can winter where our army has foraged."[8]

Foraging was just one of the woes the army visited on farm and plantation owners. On this day, when the regiment passed Thomas Maguire's Rock Bridge plantation, Maguire was hiding in the woods, leaving his family to face the Yankees without him. This proved to be typical behavior by white male residents in the army's path, often prompted by rumors of mistreatment of southern men by Sherman's soldiers. When Maguire returned home the next afternoon, he was glad to find that his family had not been abused, although much of his property was destroyed. He listed the damage in his diary: his cotton gin and screw, stables, barn, carriage, wagon, tack, and fences were burned; his steers, sheep, chickens, geese, corn, and potatoes were gone; machinery was smashed to pieces; cotton bales and straw piles were smoldering; and the yard was littered with dead horses and mules. In the next few days Maguire roamed his grounds, trying to thwart droves of neighbors seeking plunder. Despite the devastation, he retained some optimism. His house survived, he was doctoring one lame horse, and his family was in good spirits. "We are all cheerful," he wrote, "and hopeful that the worst is past and the Yankees gone, I hope forever."[9]

Maguire also reported that he successfully hid some provisions from the enemy. On the approach of Sherman's men, farm and plantation owners routinely concealed livestock, food, cotton, and valuables in gardens, forests, and swamps—and the Yankees became adept hunters of the hidden goods. Postwar stories of these hide-and-seek games are legion. As an aged veteran, Private Charles H. Field of Company B told his grandson of following wagon tracks into a forest to a pile of brush concealing barrels of hams. In a similar tale, former slave Lucy McCullough of Walton County, Georgia (which the 154th New York traversed), remembered male slaves driving heavy wagons over rain-soaked ground to hide cotton in the woods, making it easy for the Yankees to follow the ruts and burn the cotton.[10]

Southerners often buried their foodstuffs and valuable personal effects. But Sherman's men often discovered them by systematically combing properties, probing the ground with their ramrods and bayonets. If they struck something solid, they started digging. Southerners swore that Yankee bayonets were divining rods that could locate silver anywhere. In their hunt for buried loot, the soldiers even opened recently dug graves. Sometimes they turned up booty, other times they exhumed corpses. One cunning Georgian dug a deep hole, placed his silver at the bottom, covered it with a thick layer of dirt, and buried a dead dog above that. Curious Yankees dug up the dog, quit in disgust, and left the treasure undetected.[11]

One reason for Yankee hide-and-seek success was the help of slaves. In one postwar UDC story, a Georgia plantation owner took elaborate steps to hide his foodstuffs and valuables in camouflaged pits and treetop aeries and his animals in pens and coops deep in the swamps. The crafty fellow did not hide everything, however, but left some stuff to be easily found. His strategy worked. A foraging party raided the plantation, took what was readily found, and departed. The family was giving thanks for their deliverance when the Yankees returned, led by one of the plantation's slaves, who proceeded to reveal all the hiding places. While that treacherous slave connived with the enemy, the story went, a group of weeping loyal slaves dissuaded some Yankees from digging up a young man's fresh grave in the family cemetery.[12]

"We dared not trust the servants" to conceal valuables, declared Sarah Ann Tillinghast of Fayetteville, North Carolina. In postwar reminiscences, she and other white women detailed steps they took to prevent black treachery. A Georgia family hid their goods by night while their slaves slept. A South Carolina woman ordered her male slaves to hide a large box of meat and told them, "Now this is for you. If you show it to the Yankees you must look to the Yankees for more."[13]

In their later years, some blacks boasted of carrying out wartime hiding duties diligently. A WPA narrative told of two South Carolina slaves who took a herd of mules into a swamp and guarded them until the Yankees passed, when they returned the animals to their grateful master. In the postwar years, whenever the two black men brought up the rescue of the mules, their former owner would give them a little cash. But when one of the blacks told the mule story for the umpteenth time, the white man exclaimed, "Look here Alf, I done about paid for sixteen mules and there was but fifteen in the drove."[14]

Some white women wrote of concealing valuables upon their persons, trusting the Yankees to behave decently (despite their loathsome reputation), whereby the goods went undetected. A South Carolina woman remembered the transformation of a neighbor from thin to stout. Hearing that the Yankee brutes took everything but the clothing on one's back, she had tied bags of provisions around her waist and covered them with layers of dresses. Another South Carolinian told of women tying stockings and silverware to the hoops of their skirts.[15]

Thursday, November 17, 1864. The 154th marched at 5:00 a.m. as the division's advance guard, deploying pickets in front of the column. For the second straight day—contrary to custom—Geary's division led the 20th Corps, so the regiment was in the extreme advance. There were many rich plantations along the road, a former Indian path known as Hightower Trail. The men marched through the hamlet of Sheffield, crossed Gum Creek, entered Walton County, and continued through Centerville (today called Jersey). Major Warner estimated the day's tramp at about sixteen miles. Halt was made at sundown on the Dally farm, near the Ulcofauhachee (present-day Alcovy) River.[16]

James A. Mobley was young boy on the family farm near Centerville when the Yankees arrived. As an octogenarian, he related a typical hide-and-seek anecdote in a memoir published by the UDC. His uncle's silver was hidden in a trunk beneath a Masonic apron. An officer lifted the trunk's lid and noticed the silver—loot that was allegedly irresistible to any Yankee. But being a Mason, he ordered his men, "Get out, there's nothing there but a few worthless relics."[17]

The Masonic motif is widespread in southern Sherman lore. The loyalty of the brotherhood was strong enough to bridge the gap between enemies, and incidents did indeed bind northern and southern Masons during the marches—but not as often as present-day legends would have it. Preservation tales are rife of homes being spared because of Masonic ties between southerners and Sherman or his soldiers (generally officers). Any such legend involving Sherman is apocryphal—the general was not a Mason. Many of the others are spurious as well.[18]

According to family legend, the Yankees treated the Dally farm with a light touch. Some foodstuffs disappeared, but root vegetables went undisturbed in the garden, and mules went undetected in remote swamps. The house and outbuildings were left intact. The foraging concerned widow Diannah Dally less than the security of her two teenaged daughters. She made sure the girls remained out of sight until the soldiers left. While some southern women awaited the Yankees with valuables hidden on their persons, feeling free from harm, others awaited the enemy in fear, shocked by rumors of misbehavior and rape.[19]

In their war against white southern women, Sherman's soldiers deployed a deeply resented tactic—the invasion of females' bedrooms. As historian Lisa Tendrich Frank observed, before the war such a violation was rare, unacceptable, and unforgivable. Sherman's men made it a common practice. They intentionally ransacked women's bedrooms, rummaged through their lingerie, cavorted in their dresses, and destroyed their letters and journals. Elite women were particular targets and often were more outraged by these assaults than they were by other plundering on their plantations. Women who hid precious possessions in their bedrooms, confident that the Yankees would not disturb those sacrosanct spaces, were sorely disappointed—the opposite usually proved to be the case. Sherman's men felt that elite white women deserved this treatment as retribution for their spirited devotion to the Confederate cause. A violated home also cast aspersions on southern manhood (for failure to provide protection) while demonstrating Yankee power. The women in turn considered the soldiers to be inhuman brutes. Rather than crushing their Confederate allegiance, the disrespectful behavior of Sherman's men strengthened it. The women remained defiant, their resolve and dedication unbowed, their hatred of the Yankees more bitter than ever.[20]

Like other of Sherman's generals, 20th Corps commander Alpheus Williams sought to curb excesses by his troops. On this night he ordered his brigade commanders to prevent straggling and unauthorized gunfire, which had been noticeable during the day. If necessary, they were to deploy flankers to keep their men together. Seeking to conserve ammunition, he added that the slaughter of animals must be done by means other than shooting. Three days later Williams repeated the edicts and prohibited the burning or destruction of any buildings except by his orders.[21]

Far to the north on this day, the soldiers' families and friends opened a local weekly newspaper and found an article headlined "Sherman's March." It predicted the army would rapidly sweep from Atlanta to Charleston, South Carolina, "carrying terror, dismay, and destruction through the Confederacy, and creating a panic from which the rebellion can never recover." The destination was wrong, but the rest of the forecast was prescient. "The next few weeks," the article concluded, "while we wait the news of his arrival upon the coast, will be weeks of intense anxiety and excitement."[22]

Friday, November 18, 1864. The 154th packed up and started at 5:00 a.m. on what became a very warm day. Jones's brigade moved with the Left Wing pontoon train. The caravan crossed the Ulcofauhachee and followed Hightower Trail to the southeast. About 9:00 a.m. the regiment entered Social Circle. The village appeared to be an aristocratic place to Sergeant Andrew D. Blood of Company A, but David Conyngham's sources described it scornfully as a collection of dirty shanties, monkeylike blacks, and "half-naked, snuff-begrimed white women." Social Circle escaped the arson that consumed much of Atlanta and part of Decatur. Perhaps the soldiers were content to burn cotton, fences, and farm machinery, or General Williams's orders were keeping them in line.[23]

One Social Circle store was stocked with sorghum, a substance that figures in many stories of Sherman's marches. Andrew Blood was amused to see his comrades emerge from the store with their tin cups and bare hands full of the sweet, sticky syrup. It was a common sight, Alfred Benson recalled in his memoir, to see groups of soldiers by a roadside filling their canteens with sorghum. In another postwar reminiscence, First Lieutenant John F. Wellman of Company G remembered a pushy sweet-toothed recruit getting a dunking in a plantation sorghum barrel. Benson remembered a comrade whose hair was so often matted with syrup that the men nicknamed him "Sorghum." In postwar UDC stories, the Yankees invariably used sorghum to vandalize. Social Circle's Maggie Garrett, who was four when the Yankees came, decades later told how they unstopped a barrel of sorghum and flooded her home's cellar.[24]

Wherever Sherman's men went, animals were seized or slaughtered, and foodstuffs of all kinds disappeared into the army's capacious maw or were maliciously wasted. With winter near, civilians in the army's trampled wake faced famine. How did they survive? Seventy-eight years after the Yankees visited her family's Social Circle plantation, Fannie Burton described the means in a memoir for her descendants. Burton's father and older brothers were away in the army, leaving her mother in charge of ten children and the slaves. The Yankees stripped the family's corncribs and smokehouse and ransacked their house, but kind and considerate soldiers paid for meals and left a barrel of sorghum. Most important, they suggested the Burtons pick over their campsite, where plenty of partially butchered animals and other useful items had been left behind. Meanwhile, neighbors returned some stray cows, the newly freed blacks agreed to stay and work the plantation, a few bales of cotton were sold to procure necessities, and friends and relatives donated shoats and chickens. That winter the Burtons missed luxuries like coffee and sugar, but they had an abundance of cornbread and dairy products. They never went hungry and "were always very happy." With the help of family and friends, Burton's story emphasized, a determined woman, plucky children, and compliant blacks could endure the hardest of times in good spirits.[25]

Leaving Social Circle behind, the 154th followed the Georgia Railroad (which other of Geary's troops destroyed) into Morgan County to Rutledge Station, where the men stopped for dinner. They were allotted twenty minutes for their meal, in which time one mess captured a pig and butchered, fried, and ate it in time to march. Each messmate was assigned a task—build a fire, haul water, prepare coffee. While they ate, the men watched other 2nd Division troops demolish the depot and water tank and tear up and burn the track. After dinner they marched beside the railroad before pitching camp around sunset near the Jesse Ballard property, about a mile from the town of Madison. They had covered about eighteen miles. "This has been the best day's march we have made," wrote Major Warner, "and through the richest country."[26]

Among the plantations the regiment passed was that of Dawson B. Lane. Unlike most white males in the army's path, Lane stayed on his place to meet the Yankees, together with a few rabidly rebel white women and some aged blacks. In the 1860 census, Lane's personal property was assessed at $20,000, much of the value in slaves. By 1870, his worth had plummeted to $1,500. Sherman's men had an antipathy for well-to-do aristocrats, and their plantations generally suffered the consequences. But the drastic wartime decline in their worth owed more to emancipation than to foragers. The war's destruction was not a significant factor in the postwar South's economic stagnation.[27]

Near Lane's plantation was a small farm rented by Ellen Peck Farrar and her mother. The wife of a Confederate soldier, Farrar had borne twins less than three weeks before the Yankees arrived and was still confined to bed. Nine months later she described the experience in a letter. The family lost its livestock and the contents of its smokehouse but was not left entirely destitute. Some corn survived in a barn, and a large potato hill was untouched. So in August 1865, Farrar had plenty of food to eat or to barter and was "making tolerable." Her twins ate all kinds of vegetables and fruit and were "the healthiest children I ever saw."[28]

Saturday, November 19, 1864. The men marched at 5:00 a.m. and entered Madison, the Morgan County seat, at daybreak. They spent a couple of hours in the town and enjoyed themselves immensely. They judged Madison to be the finest place they had seen in Georgia, beautiful, wealthy, and aristocratic, with tastefully painted houses and fine lawns. It began to rain as they scattered throughout the village. When the bugle called "fall in," they returned with full haversacks and armloads of hams and chickens, indicating Madison was as plentiful as it was prosperous.[29]

Led by excited blacks to places to plunder, the soldiers looted the commercial district. Pillagers flung bales of dry goods, hardware, and harnesses through the windows of well-stocked stores. Locked doors were forced open, and shelves and cellars were emptied of goods. Whatever was not taken was scattered promiscuously about. Alexander Bird returned to the regiment toting bottles of brandy and whiskey.[30]

The Yankees burned Madison's jail, depot, and commissary, Emma High recalled in a UDC memoir, but the village's homes were spared. High remembered that her mother pleaded for protection as the daughter and wife of Masons. In response, an officer assigned a safeguard to the house, and the soldiers treated Mrs. High courteously. One Yankee scamp got his comeuppance from the Highs' loyal black cook when he stole money she had made selling gingerbread to the soldiers. High closed her account with a romantic touch. As the Yankees were about to leave town, she recalled, they stacked arms on the lawn of a neighbor, whose rose garden was bursting with blooms. The soldiers wove garlands of roses to festoon their muskets, all the while singing and joking. Thus adorned, they marched out of Madison in fine spirits.[31]

According to a secondhand UDC account, the home of Mary Talbot Leak likewise benefited from the Masonic tie. Looting was well under way when a large wardrobe in Leak's late husband's bedroom yielded Masonic regalia. With that discovery, a Yankee captain immediately ordered his men to return every valuable they had taken and posted guards to protect the family from further molestation.[32]

General Williams detached the 2nd Division at Madison for a special assignment: to destroy the line of the Georgia Railroad eastward to the Oconee River and to burn the railroad bridge there. While the rest of the 20th Corps marched south toward Eatonton, Geary's men set off on their mission. The 154th halted for dinner at Buckhead Station, where the water tank, stationary engine, and railroad buildings were demolished. Then, while Geary sent a detachment ahead to destroy the Oconee bridge, the regiment continued along the railroad during the afternoon, stopping several times to rip apart the track.[33]

Here was another hallmark of the march. In his memoir, Alfred Benson described how Sherman's men destroyed railroads. The rails were pried from the ties, the ties were piled and set afire, and the rails were put over the pyres until red-hot, whereupon the soldiers grasped them at either end and twisted them into kinks, or bent them into odd shapes (forming the letters "US" was a favorite), or wrapped them around tree trunks, dubbing the results Sherman's neckties, hairpins, corkscrews, doughnuts, or pretzels. At times an entire brigade lined up along a quarter mile or so of track and heaved it over to dismantle and destroy it.[34]

About four smoky miles were made before the 154th halted at Blue Spring (today called Swords). After a brief rest, the men continued to work until dark. In all, Geary's men destroyed about five miles of railroad and great quantities of surplus ties and stringers. Camp was pitched about two miles west of the Oconee River, on the rich plantation of Leonidas A. Jordan, commonly known as Colonel Lee Jordan. Jordan's father, one of Georgia's wealthiest planters, had died in 1856 and left his widow and only child an estate worth more than $800,000 (approximately $20 million in today's dollars), including bank and railroad stocks and plantations in five counties.[35]

William Harper called the evening at Jordan's Blue Spring place a first-rate time. Andrew Blood thought it laughable to see the men chase Jordan's animals and gather his crops; he guessed they killed as many as forty hogs. The officers gave the men a free hand. After butchering Jordan's livestock and plundering his crops, they torched his outbuildings. Geary estimated that 280 bales of cotton and 50,000 bushels of corn went up in flames.[36]

Descendants of Buckhead's Thomas P. Saffold told of a Yankee atrocity at Blue Spring. One of Saffold's many slaves was a little boy who had helped to hide his master's horses and mules. When Geary's men asked the lad the whereabouts of the animals, he claimed ignorance. As a result, the story went, the Yankees hanged him at Blue Spring. Numerous postwar tales were told of Sherman's men hanging southerners to make them reveal hiding places, but typically the alleged victim was an elderly white man who was concealing silver or money, and he lived through the ordeal.[37]

During the day the 154th suffered its first casualty of the campaign when Corporal Leonard L. Hunt of Company B disappeared. Initially it was thought he deserted, and so the company muster roll listed him. But months later, Hunt's comrades learned he had been captured by the enemy while foraging. The Confederates turned him over to Union authorities at South East Ferry, Georgia, on February 27, 1865, and he was discharged seven months later at Elmira, New York.[38]

Sunday, November 20 1864. A wet night was followed by a rainy day. The regiment left Blue Spring at 7:00 a.m. and slogged southward on a muddy road. Three hours later it reached the Oconee River and followed the western bank to the south, past Park's Mill and into Putnam County. When squads of Confederate cavalry took potshots at Geary's men from the opposite shore, the general sent a small detachment across the river to drive them away. The day was bad and the country was rough, but there were many fine plantations along the route, and foraging was productive.[39]

The Park's Mill complex included an inn, a mill, blacksmith and carpenter shops, a store, a saloon, a brickyard, a post office, and a ferry. The lord of this thriving realm, Judge James B. Park Sr., owned real and personal property worth $80,000, including more than sixty slaves. Geary's men burned the mill, destroyed the ferryboats, and took all the livestock and provisions. Judge Park's home survived, and as the years passed, legends emerged to explain the supposed anomaly. Mrs. Park was said to have successfully pleaded with the soldiers to spare the house. Specifics passed on by her son, who was ten in 1864, added a popular motif: his mother had told an officer that her absent husband was a Mason. Consequently guards were stationed, and the family went unmolested. According to another tale, sparks from the burning mill set the house's roof on fire, and a faithful slave beat out the flames with wet blankets to save the dwelling. The fact that a steady rain fell all day casts some doubt on this loyal slave story.[40]

When darkness fell, Geary's division stopped at perhaps the most unusual establishment the 154th New York encountered in the South. James C. Denham owned more than one hundred slaves and fourteen hundred acres. His largely self-sufficient plantation housed blacksmith and carpenter shops, a sawmill and gristmill, a brick kiln, a candle house, a winery, a commissary, and a post office. In all this, it was similar to Judge Park's plantation and the plantations of other wealthy landowners. What made Denham's operation uncommon was a substantial tannery and leather goods factory that employed dozens of German immigrant shoemakers, who lived in a cluster of homes called Denhamville. The white foremen and overseers lived in the Denham home, whose attic housed a textile shop where workers produced clothing for the more than two hundred Denhamville residents.[41]

Here Geary's division found a rich plantation to plunder and a progressive manufactory to destroy. Throughout the war, Denham had produced shoes, boots, saddles, bridles, and harnesses in great quantities for the Confederate army. Geary described the factory as "one of the most extensive establishments of the kind in the South." When a rumor spread that a large number of shoes worn by enemy soldiers came from Denham's factory, the men looked forward to destroying the place.[42]

James Denham and his family were absent. After driving his livestock to a hiding place, Denham and his wife fled on Friday, November 18, to join relatives in another county. On Saturday the Denham slaves were sent away. What happened to the German families is unknown. As Geary's men settled in on Sunday night, the 154th pitched camp in a patch of woods, where the trees offered some protection from the steady rain. A slave who had been left behind was appalled to see the Yankees cut open bales of cotton and spread bunches of it on the ground for bedding.[43]

During this day Geary's skirmishers and foragers captured a large number of mules, cattle, and horses. Joshua Pettit, on duty with the brigade ambulance corps, had brought in thirty-nine horses the previous day. On this Sunday he and Private Thomas N. Bliton of Company D went out hoping to repeat the success. Instead, they got lost. "Was out all night," Pettit wrote in his diary. "Stayed in a nigger shanty."[44]

When Pettit and Bliton left the next morning, the cabin's usual occupants might have accompanied the two Yankees, if they were not already following the army, which was, Sergeant Francis M. Bowen of Company I reported, "getting perfectly black with Negroes and wenches that fall in with the 'Yanks.'" The flocking of African Americans to Sherman's army was "one of the features of the great march never to be forgotten," Alfred Benson wrote a decade later. The crowd came from all directions, through woods and over byways, hauling a motley assortment of possessions: "sacks of cornmeal, jugs of sorghum, old bed quilts, silk umbrellas, pots, pans, kettles, babies, apple butter, old clothes in endless variety and in all the advanced stages of dilapidation, band boxes, gamecocks, feather beds, hams, hoecakes, natural leaf [tobacco]." They had no particular place to go, Benson recalled, other than to follow the army. "They scarcely knew only this—that behind them there was slavery, before them freedom."[45]

Over time, a substantial number of African Americans joined the regiment and attached themselves to officers and enlisted men as cooks and servants or served as teamsters and pioneers. Occasionally they were paid a minimal salary; often they worked without wages. Several cases were documented. "Company I has got two mules and a darky who help to carry our loads," Francis Bowen noted. Corporal George P. Brown of Company A linked up with a freedman in Madison who stayed with him almost to the end of the campaign. Regimental veterans recalled that Corporal Oziah F. Adams and Private James Copeland of Company D had a black cook who was an outstanding wrestler and earned his white handlers hundreds of dollars in bets in matches with black opponents. Alfred Benson's servant accompanied him all the way to Elmira, where the regiment was discharged in June 1865. Some soldiers coerced blacks to serve. After the war a company comrade recalled that Private John S. Belknap of Company G forced a former slave to be his servant, despite the fellow's reluctance to leave his mother.[46]

Members of the 154th New York had encountered black people during their service in Virginia and Tennessee, but never in the numbers they found in Georgia and the Carolinas. The soldiers—for all their racism—marveled at the slaves' thirst for freedom and delighted in helping to break their bonds. In his memoir, Alfred Benson recalled the freed people's jubilee in terms alternately disparaging and admiring. The "ignorant chattels," whose concepts were "undefined, imperfect, and crude," were certain of one fact: "that the day of deliverance had surely come." Somehow they understood that the success of the Union army meant the end of slavery, and so they flocked to Sherman's men. "So it was," Benson concluded, "that while our advance was a line of fire and a very track of desolation, it opened a grand highway to freedom."[47]

In later decades, aged blacks along the regiment's route remembered various reactions to the coming of Sherman's army. Some had eagerly awaited the invaders; others had dreaded their arrival. Della Briscoe recalled that the slaves on her Putnam County plantation were frantic with fear, having heard horrific stories about the Yankees. The blacks on Alec Bostwick's Morgan County plantation mistook the Yankees for a slave patrol and fled to the woods. A mother at another plantation put her children to bed, wrapped herself in a blanket, and told the Yankees that the family was sick with fever. The ruse repelled one group of foragers, but a second was not fooled and looted the cabin. A story handed down by a white family told of an elderly slave named Billy, who came upon his master making preparations for the Yankees' arrival and asked what he was doing. "Getting ready for Billy Tecumseh Sherman," was the reply. No, exclaimed the slave, backing away wide eyed—Billy did not want "to come see" Sherman.[48]

The Yankees took from whites and blacks alike. Some former slaves cursed Sherman's men as bitterly as their white owners did. "The damn Yankees come to our place [and] they done everything that was bad," recalled Aunt Ferebe Rogers of Baldwin County, Georgia. Mary Woodward was ten or eleven when the Yankees came to her Fairfield District, South Carolina, plantation. She was wearing a string of beads, a present from her mistress. A forager took the beads, hung them around his horse's neck, and rode off, leaving Woodward sobbing. More than seventy years later, she still nursed a grudge against "that Yankee scamp." Another former South Carolina slave remembered a grandmother's tale: the Yankees took everything from her but a young chicken that ran into the woods and escaped detection. The pullet's eggs subsequently helped the family get on its feet again. That hen fit a certain type of legendary motif—tales of lone remaining animals surviving the Sherman onslaught.[49]

Clinging to the belief that bonds of affection tied master and slave, southern whites were haunted by the desertion of many of their blacks. UDC memoirs berated the turncoats and celebrated the contented and loyal "servant" of Lost Cause myth. Only the worst blacks followed the Yankees, Confederate diehards proclaimed; the best blacks stayed at home with their owners and were faithful even after emancipation. A prime example was Uncle Isaac, a slave on the Madison plantation of William Henry Newton. Newton's granddaughter later told the tale in a UDC narrative worthy of a novel. When Newton enlisted in the Confederate army, he entrusted the care of his wife and children to old Uncle Isaac. Wherever Kitty Newton went, Uncle Isaac followed close behind, armed with a dirk to protect his mistress. When the Yankees came, Uncle Isaac stood ready to kill the man who touched her. When the war ended, William Newton returned home and found Uncle Isaac still on duty, having helped Mrs. Newton gin several bales of cotton to give the family a new start. "Real Southern families," the storyteller averred, respected loyal and devoted blacks like Uncle Isaac. In truth, however, many blacks remained on the plantation chiefly out of self-interest; they were elderly or did not want to part with their family members. What casts doubt on the Uncle Isaac story is a detail—the Yankees were reportedly members of Sherman's staff, which could not have been the case.[50]

Some Yankees, like some white slave owners, coerced, convinced, or connived with black females to engage in sexual relations. Sena Moore was twelve years old when Sherman's men reached the plantation she lived on near Winnsboro, South Carolina. Decades later she recalled that a Yankee wanted her to go off with him, but she refused. He then persuaded another girl to leave with him. She returned six months later, pregnant with the Yankee's child.[51]

Modern historians have variously interpreted the scanty sources regarding Sherman's men and sexual relations. Joseph Glatthaar found very little evidence in soldiers' writings to suggest much sexual contact between Sherman's men and black women, while Jacqueline Glass Campbell contended that encounters between the two must have been common. Lee Kennett noted occasional references to black mistresses of white officers. All three agreed that rapes of white women were rare, but Campbell observed that evidence regarding assaults on poor white women is lacking.[52]

Federal military law provided women—white and black—with the opportunity to accuse Union soldiers of sexual crimes (and, significantly, of plunder, pillage, and other depredations). Across the entire South, approximately 450 Union soldiers were charged in courts-martial for rape or attempted rape of women of both races and all ages and social classes. Sherman's men, used to invading and plundering the homes of southern women, may have felt entitled to assault their persons as well. For their part, southern women likely knew of their ability to bring charges, although the movement of the army hampered prosecution. In any case, only two of Sherman's men were tried for rape.[53]

According to Emory Sweetland of the 154th New York, the soldiers were sexually active with black women and poor white women alike. A deeply religious man, Sweetland kept his wife abreast of the sinful goings-on in the regiment. When the Georgia march ended, he informed her from Savannah as frankly as he could about his libidinous comrades. "You would be very much shocked," he wrote, "if you knew how much demoralized (in regard to morals) that nine-tenths of the soldiers have become. The lower class (both black and white) in the South seem to be totally ignorant of the meaning of the word 'virtue,' and both officers and men appear to have cast off all the restraints of home and indulge their passions to the fullest extent. Many of the officers keep quadroons for private use." Sweetland promised to reveal additional details when he returned home. In their absence, his candid comments shed some lurid light on a shadowy aspect of the march.[54]

[4]

To Milledgeville

Monday, November 21, 1864. On a rainy morning, Geary's men set fire to James Denham's tannery, shoe factory, cotton gin, and cotton. The only part of the complex to survive was the one-hundred-foot-tall brick smokestack. A Confederate official reported that the loss greatly impaired the operations of the government's clothing depot in Richmond. Denham's house and slave quarters were ransacked but spared. A neighbor who came by to view the scene and to scavenge the abandoned Yankee camps found "a wreck"—"smoking ruins, and private papers scattered all over the plantation!" Another neighbor noted, "Everything in the house was badly used up."[1]

A Denham family legend tells of a neighborhood mother who gave her young son fifty cents to buy a new pair of shoes at Denhamville. On his way to the factory the boy encountered a mounted Yankee, who asked where he was going. When the lad explained, the soldier pointed to a column of smoke and told him, "You're too late." Over the years, tall tales of the factory's demise found their way into print. One asserted that Sherman himself ordered General Slocum and the entire Left Wing to destroy Denhamville. Another contended that Slocum slept in the Denham house for a week while his men methodically demolished the place. But Sherman and Slocum were not on the scene; nor was the entire Left Wing. A third story claimed that despite the Yankees' best efforts, the towering smokestack refused to fall. The smokestack indeed still stands, but whether Geary's men attempted to topple it is uncertain.[2]

Leaving the smoldering factory behind, the 154th New York marched at 7:00 a.m., sloshing along muddy roads. That morning the regiment passed near Turnwold plantation, the property of Joseph Addison Turner, publisher of the *Countryman,* a weekly newspaper produced on the plantation—a unique endeavor in the history of

American journalism. The paper had almost two thousand subscribers throughout the Confederacy and was lauded by southern editors. But for all of his contemporary fame, Turner might have been lost to history had he not hired a teenaged typesetter from nearby Eatonton, the Putnam County seat. At Turnwold, Joel Chandler Harris gained an intimate knowledge of plantation life, absorbed the stories and songs of slaves, plumbed Turner's extensive library, and published his first literary efforts. In his free time, he hunted rabbits and sold the pelts to Denham's shoe factory and to Turner, who, in addition to his other enterprises, manufactured fur hats.[3]

Behind Turnwold's two-story big house sprawled the cabin that housed the newspaper's print shop, a kitchen, a storehouse, a tannery, a distillery, the hat shop, and quarters for hired hands and slaves. Turner, who described slavery as "a just, a humane, and a useful institution," was considered a benevolent master who allowed his twenty-odd chattels to earn some money by growing their own crops.[4]

Rumors, false reports, and the absence of news befuddled southerners in Sherman's path with crippling psychological effects. Most white men chose not to stay on their property and face the enemy. When the Yankees approached Eatonton, a woman reported, "The men like someone crazy were running in all directions to the woods." Only a few remained. Wild, extravagant stories and contradictory reports likewise paralyzed Turner with uncertainty. When he learned on Sunday, November 20, that the Yankees were at Park's Mill, he sent his mules to be hidden in a swamp. He decided to remain at Turnwold "and take things as they might arise."[5]

Geary's main column bypassed Turnwold, but foragers visited the plantation. Turner's buildings and press went undamaged, however, and his paper did not miss an issue. In detailed accounts of interactions between invader and invaded in the *Countryman,* Turner referred to Yankees, Irish, and Germans in lowercase as a sign of disrespect. Yet his despised enemies surprised him with their docility.[6]

On Sunday a handful of foragers stole Turner's gold watch, silver spoons, whiskey, tobacco, fiddle, and a hat or two apiece. Not intimidated, he engaged them in repartee and scolded one man who brandished a revolver. He filled another fellow's canteen with whiskey and toasted his health. He snidely called them gentlemen, offered them seats, and "overwhelmed them with politeness, and hospitality." He asked them to pay for everything they took, "just as though we expected pay."[7]

On this Monday a foraging party of twenty or thirty men arrived at Turnwold. They rounded up mules, horses, a wagon, some saddles, and three of Turner's slaves. Only one of them entered the house and outbuildings, an Irishman whom Turner described as a murderous rogue who looked more like Abe Lincoln or a monkey than a man. The Irishman claimed he was a hatter; Turner offered him a job. The Irishman took a hat; Turner sarcastically asked for payment. When the fellow could not carry all the hams from the smokehouse, Turner gave him a hand. The two joked and laughed as they loaded the hams into Turner's wagon.[8]

As Turner joshed with Yankee foragers, his young printer's devil sat on a roadside fence while Geary's division passed. Years later, Harris described the soldiers as imposing in numbers but not in appearance. As he watched them slosh through ankle-deep mud in a fine mist under leaden skies, "the glamour and romance of war were dispelled." There was nothing gay about the vast procession but the temper of the men, who cracked jokes, sang snatches of songs, and pelted the boy with hundreds of friendly comments. To Harris the panorama seemed to be a wild dream. After all he had read in newspapers of Confederate victories, it seemed impossible that Sherman's army could be plunging through the once peaceful region. When the last of the Yankees passed, he hopped off the fence and returned to Turnwold. Never had he seen the plantation so quiet. The slave quarters were largely deserted; the younger generations had followed the Yankees. He came across an old black woman huddled beside her supine husband in a fence corner. "He dead, suh!" she informed him. "But bless God, he died free!"[9]

At Philadelphia Church, Geary's column took the road heading to Milledgeville, Georgia's capital. An officer posted a note in the sanctuary imploring the soldiers not to deface or destroy anything within its walls. The Yankees obeyed the injunction, Joseph Turner reported, but to his dismay, some local boys scribbled on the walls and in Bibles and hymnbooks.[10]

The 154th New York crossed Crooked Creek and stopped for dinner near a plantation where Colonel Moses White of the 37th Tennessee, commander of the post at Eatonton, was captured. After the short break the sodden march continued. The men covered about twelve miles in all and camped at dark at the Dennis farm and mill on Rooty Creek. That night the weather cleared and frost covered the ground.[11]

Back at Turnwold, Joseph Turner published his regularly scheduled issue of the *Countryman* the next day, and in subsequent weeks he filled it with comical accounts and corny riddles and puns about the Yankee invasion, including a parody in verse, "Old Sherman's Gone": "The southrons he did much abuse / Though sociable and gay / When he was burning Denham's shoes / And scared his folks away." Satirizing the racial upheaval following the Yankee liberation of the slaves, Turner wondered whether he was the subject of Georgia governor Joseph Brown, Jefferson Davis, Abraham Lincoln, or an African king. "Judging from the airs which the colored gentry give themselves, about now," his guess was the last.[12]

A good portion of the area's black population had vanished with the Yankees. Even scarcer were mules and horses. The harshness of the scouring varied, Turner reported, with people living in the path of the main column on direct highways faring better than their neighbors on back roads overrun by foragers. He warned of anarchy in the enemy's wake. It was a splendid time, he averred, for mean people of both races to take revenge against their local adversaries.[13]

Months later, Turner closed his coverage of the invasion with a letter to General Sherman. "Our folks are not as much subdued as you think they are," he declared. Southerners were divided into two classes: patriots who resisted the Yankees until physically overpowered, and those who submitted to save their property but retained their Confederate loyalty. In the end, Turner suggested, the only way to subdue southerners was "to kill 'em—kill 'em all, sir."[14]

Tuesday, November 22, 1864. Snowflakes flew in a cutting wind as the regiment took to the frozen road at 6 a.m. Dennis's mill and cotton went up in flames. Geary's pioneers built a footbridge over Rooty Creek for the infantry to use; the horse-drawn artillery and ambulances forded the stream. From Dennis Station the men followed the Eatonton Branch Railroad to the Little River, which they crossed on a pontoon bridge, and entered Baldwin County. After a dinner break the march continued.[15]

About two miles beyond the river the men came to Westover, another plantation belonging to Colonel Lee Jordan, on whose Blue Spring property the 154th had camped three nights before. The 850-acre spread's big house was one of the most stately homes the regiment encountered in the South. Scattered on the grounds were an office, kitchen, commissary, washhouse, smokehouse, carriage house, harness shed, springhouse, and the slave quarters. A stylish roadside fence opened to an ornate garden with geometric beds cut by paths and set off by low brick walls. Trees shaded ornamental shrubs clustered on emerald expanses of lawn.[16]

Basing his account on a *New York Herald* report, David Conyngham stated that Jordan was surprised by the Yankees' approach (which seems unlikely) and fled (which was quite likely), leaving Westover to its fate. The plantation was plundered of its foodstuffs, but Jordan's overseer, a former New York State resident named Allen, saved the opulent big house by welcoming Geary and his leading officers inside and plying them with the contents of the wine cellar. In appreciation they ringed the mansion with guards. Enlisted men peered wistfully through the windows at the celebration. Allen drank until he passed out and was put to bed by his guests. When he awoke, he found the house unmolested.[17]

So Jordan's magnificent big house reportedly survived the passage of Geary's men. But the following day some foragers were shot by Confederate soldiers at Westover, and on November 24 a detail from the 14th Corps was ordered to clean the place out. They captured several rebels, scattered the rest, entered the house, and wrecked its furniture and decorations. The house itself survived, however, and in the next few months Jordan renovated it and offered it for sale.[18]

According to a postwar UDC tale, Lee Jordan outfoxed the Yankees with a canny hide-and-seek trick. Anticipating the enemy's arrival, he gathered some of his slaves and told them he wanted new gateposts placed by the driveway. He timed their work so the holes were dug but the posts not yet placed when the dinner bell rang. When the blacks went off for their meal, Jordan secretly stashed gold coins in both holes and covered them with dirt. Later, the slaves returned and installed the gateposts atop the treasure. No one ever discovered the cache, and Jordan recovered his gold.[19]

At 5:00 p.m. on this Tuesday, the 154th New York came to a halt on the outskirts of Milledgeville, where Geary's division reunited with the rest of the 20th Corps. Mayor Boswell B. DeGraffenreid had surrendered the city to advance elements of the corps and begged that residents and homes be protected. The soldiers could see refugees hurrying out of town. When darkness fell, the regiment fixed bayonets and marched through the city with flags flying and music playing. Andrew Blood thought he had seen many places handsomer than Milledgeville, but he found some attractive buildings, including the statehouse. Alfred Benson later recalled it as an insignificant country town, with inferior architecture and a generally shabby appearance. The men paraded through the city's east side, crossed the Oconee River, marched less than a mile, camped around 9:00 p.m., and did picket duty throughout a chilly night.[20]

James Clements considered it a privilege to march through Georgia's capital, despite not seeing Governor Joseph Brown or any of the state legislators, who had all fled. Georgia's government had crumbled quickly when the enemy threatened. A motley force of 500 men was assembled to defend the capital, among them cadets from the Georgia Military Institute and about 150 convicts. The legislators issued blustery vows to repel the invaders or die in the attempt. But on November 18 the solons left their papers on their desks, abandoned the statehouse, and purchased transportation to take them out of town. Those unable to make a deal left on foot. Governor Brown and his family departed the next day, and the tiny makeshift military force retreated, leaving the city defenseless.[21]

Postwar reminiscences by Dr. Robert J. Massey, head of a Confederate army hospital, and an Atlanta refugee, Miss A. C. Cooper, recalled the panic on Sherman's approach. Rumors swirled for days as mounted scouts dashed in and out of town, unable to bring certain news. Stories said Sherman's men burned all the houses and killed all the women and children, white and black, in their path. People swore the Yankees had horns on their heads. The city's white population had swelled with refugees in recent weeks, but it plummeted as most of the male residents fled and women wondered where to go. For Sherman was "a huge octopus," Cooper declared, who "stretched out his long arms and gathered everything in, leaving only ruin and desolation behind him." According to Dr. Massey, "everyone left who could."[22]

In her diary, Anna Maria Green, the daughter of the superintendent of the state asylum, denounced the frightened legislators who passed a law levying troops (but exempted themselves) and then paid for a train to hurry them away. Her Confederate allegiance stronger than ever, Green defied the occupying Yankees. Expecting the worst from the enemy, she was surprised when General Slocum received her father kindly and assigned a guard for the asylum.[23]

Another ardent rebel, Rebecca Ann Harris, described the "reign of terror" a week after the Yankees departed Milledgeville. Houses were entered throughout her neighborhood, but she guarded her back door, refusing Yankee requests for food, drink, and sundries. In Harris's opinion, many Milledgeville residents suffered greatly from fear; her mother seemed to age twenty years. But she refused to kowtow to the Yankees. Against the advice of housebound friends, she fearlessly strode through town to demand a guard. "Stand aside and permit a lady to pass," she snarled to loitering Yankees. When an impudent soldier asked if she was a "secesh" (short for secessionist), she proudly replied, "I am a southern woman." When some soldiers asked the spinster if there were any young ladies in her house, she gave them an ugly look.[24]

Throughout Georgia and the Carolinas, a spiteful war of words was waged between spitfires like Rebecca Ann Harris and Sherman's men. Years later, unreconstructed rebel women relished their best ripostes. In her UDC reminiscence, Milledgeville's Mattie Hanna proudly recalled her reply when a Yankee offered her two dollars a week to housekeep for his mother in the North. "Thank you, I was not raised to be a Yankee servant," she sneered. She delighted in being "a damned little rebel." The Yankees left her and other patriotic southern girls with "sickened hearts."[25]

Wednesday, November 23, 1864. For the first day since the march began, the regiment rested. Some of the men did picket duty while others explored Milledgeville. Camp was at Barrowville, the plantation of Colonel William McKinley, who hid in the woods and left his wife and children to face the enemy without him. Guy C. McKinley was six years old at the time. More than six decades later he related hide-and-seek tales involving his father and a pair of slaves. Under William McKinley's supervision, a trustworthy slave buried some silver so cleverly that a Yankee pitched his tent over the spot and slept unwittingly above the treasure. But when McKinley and one-armed Uncle York buried valuables in the blacksmith shop's furnace, the Yankees quickly uncovered the loot, aided by Uncle York's treachery. The traitorous slave also revealed McKinley's hiding place in the woods. While the patriarch underwent those humiliations, General Geary and his staff treated the ladies and children with courtesy. Some attributed the kindness to the presence of a Yankee aunt who had been stranded in Georgia by the war.[26]

More than half of Milledgeville's approximately four thousand residents were black. Alfred Benson remembered that they were "very obsequious" in welcoming the Yankees. Now the large numbers of blacks accompanying the army and flocking to it from the countryside joined those already in the city. The Yankees treated them badly, alleged the *Confederate Union,* one of Milledgeville's two weekly newspapers, robbing them of money, clothing, and anything worth stealing. But the paper later reported that many of the city's blacks departed with the enemy. The editor found it remarkable that they included those least expected to leave and—invariably—those who had been pampered with too many liberties.[27]

Rebecca Ann Harris deplored the upheaval in race relations. The blacks accompanying Sherman's army, she complained, were "more insolent than the Yankees." When her teenaged nephew threatened to blow out the brains of a black man who had pushed him off a sidewalk, she reprimanded the boy, certain he had to behave himself in front of the despised blacks as well as the hated white soldiers.[28]

Boisterous blacks joined a mob of soldiers in the deserted state capitol, an imposing gothic structure set on a twenty-acre square in the center of town. Halls that had echoed days before with bold threats against the Yankee invaders now resounded with the shouts of drunken revelers and greedy trophy hunters. Armfuls of books were tossed out of the state library's windows and trampled in the mud. The treasurer's office was looted of freshly printed state currency. Marcellus Darling carried a bundle of it back to camp and slept "rolling in riches." Alfred Benson recalled winning and losing fortunes of it in card games. Charles McKay took a different souvenir: a two-foot cutlass, one of a stockpile meant for the vanished state troops. He used it until the end of the war to cut tent poles and behead chickens.[29]

Members of the regiment were in the audience when a group of tipsy officers held a mock legislative session in the capitol. They repealed Georgia's secession ordinance, resolved "that Sherman's columns will play the devil with the ordinance and the state itself," and proposed that the state's reconstruction be left in the hands of "Uncle Sam's blue jackets." When one of their fellows scurried into the chamber and bellowed that the Yankees were coming, the revelers imitated the flight of the legislature and scrambled from the room. The next day, at the Baptist church adjacent to the statehouse grounds, some of the same jokers held a mock funeral for the "departed" Governor Brown.[30]

The ransacking of the capitol outraged Milledgeville residents. Rebecca Ann Harris's blood boiled when she viewed the vandalism and contemplated "how grandly those wretches sat in state there." For days the building was knee-deep in papers, and public documents littered the square and nearby streets. The explosion of a nearby powder magazine shattered windows and damaged plaster at the capitol and the churches on the square. The surrounding fences were broken down, and Yankee horses ruined trees on the property by chewing off their bark.[31]

In her later years, former Baldwin County slave Snovey Jackson greatly exaggerated the destruction when she said postoccupation Milledgeville was "just tore up" after the Yankees "burned and destroyed everything" and left "nothing more than a cow pasture." The state arsenal and penitentiary, the railroad depot, and bridges were burned, but the capitol, the governor's mansion, two warehouses, a mill, a foundry, and a factory were spared the torch. And like Social Circle and Madison, Milledgeville escaped the destruction of homes. Two or three houses in the outskirts were burned, the *Confederate Union* reported, but none in the city. Looting was prevalent, however, and the abandoned homes of state officials suffered the most damage. Fences and outbuildings throughout the city were demolished for firewood. Decades later, local lore asserted that the Yankees vandalized St. Stephen's Church, burning its pews, defacing its interior, and pouring molasses into the organ pipes.[32]

Two weeks after the enemy departed Milledgeville, *Confederate Union* editor Seth N. Broughton cataloged Yankee crimes in his first postoccupation issue. Robberies were common, he reported. High-ranking officers overlooked "disgusting scenes of plunder and rapine" and refused requests to protect private property. To detail all the enormities perpetrated by the enemy would fill a volume, "and some of them would be too bad to publish." Sherman's men were in high spirits and considered Georgia vanquished, Broughton observed, but the people's spirit was unconquered.[33]

A week later, however, Broughton tempered his assessment. Most of the Yankee outrages were perpetrated in abandoned homes; occupied homes saw "but few acts of diabolism." Few women or children had been insulted or molested. Many had feared the city would be burned and were relieved when the Yankees assured them otherwise. In a few weeks, Broughton predicted, public offices would again be doing business "as though Sherman had never been in a thousand miles of Milledgeville."[34]

Richard M. Orme, editor of the rival *Southern Recorder,* also conceded that the Yankees had behaved themselves to some extent in Milledgeville. They respected families that stayed indoors while robbing them of everything outside, he wrote, whereas country folk were frequently mistreated and their houses sacked. Yankee vandalism would result in increasing hatred of them throughout the state, Orme declared; property loss had united the people more closely than ever. The postoccupation columns of both Milledgeville newspapers urged farmers to bring food from the countryside to the impoverished city.[35]

Members of the 154th used this idle day to do their part in stripping Milledgeville and vicinity of provisions and brought to camp the usual bounty. Alex Bird and Dell Ames rode about eight miles into the countryside, stole a buggy, and loaded it with food and bunches of cigars. Corporal Nelson H. Fisk returned to camp with a roll of butter in his pocket to flavor Company G's pancakes and sweet potatoes.[36]

Yankee foragers had a great penchant for honey and sometimes suffered when swarms of bees drove them from the gums. But First Sergeant Richard J. McCadden of Company G boasted, "I think we can rob beehives to perfection." One of the recruits, Private Joseph Moyer of Company I, became expert at a special technique. He fearlessly grabbed a hive, hoisted it on his shoulder with its mouth to the rear, and ran. The bees instinctively headed toward their old territory, creating chaos in Moyer's wake but leaving him unscathed with his hive full of honey.[37]

Apart from the authorized foraging parties, untold numbers of freelancers—commonly called bummers—slipped away from the main column to forage on their own. In his memoir, Alfred Benson defined bummers as reckless spirits with a love of adventure and a desire to plunder who primarily gathered food. But truth compelled him to add that vicious bummers pillaged, stole, robbed, and burned, and the ruin they wrought was a sad but common sight. The march's brilliance was dimmed by the foul blot of their unworthy exploits, Benson confessed. Bad men were to be found among soldiers as well as civilians, and it was an oft remarked fact that army life, more than any other experience, revealed the good qualities of worthy men and the ragged edges of rascals. Under such demoralizing influences, Benson lamented, even chaplains succumbed to temptation and looted. (Whether he was referring to regimental chaplain William Norton is uncertain.)[38]

Major Warner deplored the actions of the bummers. "Many acts of wanton vandalism are perpetrated which nothing can justify," he wrote. Families of helpless women and children were completely stripped of food and the utensils necessary to cook and eat, left sitting "in dumb apathy, surveying the ruin," pleading—too often in vain—for some provisions to be spared for the coming winter.[39]

No doubt members of the 154th New York were guilty of pillaging. There is no reason to exempt them from the generalization of Sherman's troops made by David Conyngham: devil-may-care soldiers who "made themselves quite as much at home in the fine house of the planter as in the shanty of the poor white trash or the Negro. They helped themselves, freely and liberally, to everything they wanted, or did not want. It mattered little which." With the exception of Major Warner's comments, the soldiers were silent on the subject in their wartime writings, perhaps hesitant or ashamed to mention the matter to loved ones. Warner did not cite any incidents in his diary or his official campaign report. Colonel Patrick Jones, in his report, claimed that pillaging was uncommon in his brigade. His officers and men "behaved with much consideration and propriety during the march," he wrote, "and but few instances of wanton destruction of property or pillage occurred." Like other officers, however, Jones might have been selectively blind in overlooking misconduct. Aside from Alfred Benson, the regiment's postwar memoirists neglected to discuss pillaging.[40]

Perhaps conscience compelled certain members of the regiment to behave themselves. Decades later, Charles Field told his grandchildren about a flock of turkeys guarded by an elderly man on a Georgia farm. Field recalled he was the only forager who did not have the heart to take a turkey; he paid the old man for one of the birds.[41]

Anticipating the march's second phase, Left Wing commander Slocum and 20th Corps commander Williams issued orders meant to increase their commands' efficiency and discipline. When not destroying railroads, Slocum directed, the soldiers should march fifteen miles per day, guarding their wagon trains carefully, and foraging could be done by authorized parties only. All useless or surplus wagons were to be destroyed. If the enemy burned bridges along the army's route, the troops were instructed to "deal harshly with the inhabitants near by, to show them it is for their interest not to impede our movements. Should the enemy burn corn and forage on our route," Slocum added, "houses, barns, and cotton-gins must also be burned to keep them company." Williams ordered the trains to be kept compactly together and the troops to help move wagons up hills and over bad roads. There was to be no straggling during halts, for attacks by enemy cavalry were probable, and "scattered troops are at the mercy of the enemy."[42]

As they rested outside Milledgeville, members of the 154th New York digested the orders. At regimental headquarters, Major Warner thought the army had reached a milestone. "This seems to be the end of the first stage of our journey," he noted in his diary. "May the second be equally successful."[43]

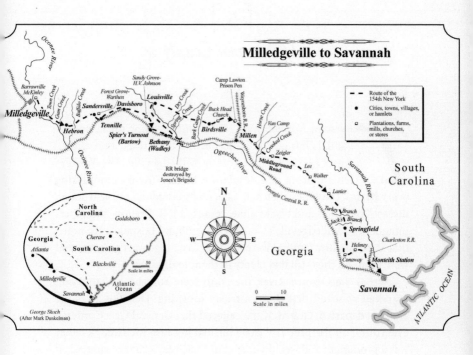

Milledgeville to Savannah

Route of the
154th New York
● Cities, towns, villages,
or hamlets
□ Plantations, farms,
mills, churches,
or stores

Oconee River

Barrowville
McKinley

Milledgeville

Town Creek

Gum Creek

Buffalo Creek

Forest Grove-
Warthen

Sandersville

Hebron

Davisboro

Tennille

Oconee River

Sandy Grove-
H.V. Johnson

Louisville

**Spier's Turnout
(Bartow)**

**Bethany
(Wadley)**

RR bridge
destroyed by
Jones's Brigade

Spring Creek

Dry Creek

Bark Camp Creek

Buck Head
Church

Birdsville

Camp Lawton
Prison Pen

Waynesboro R.R.

Horse Creek

Millen

Van Camp

Crooked Creek

Zeigler

**Middleground
Road**

Lee

Walker

Lanier

Ogeechee River

Georgia Central R. R.

Savannah River

**South
Carolina**

Turkey Branch

Jack's Branch

Springfield

Charleston R.R.

Helmey

Conaway

Monteith Station

Savannah

Georgia

ATLANTIC OCEAN

N

W ● E

S

0   10
Scale in miles

Inset map

North
Carolina

Goldsboro

Georgia

Cheraw

Atlanta

South Carolina

Blackville

Milledgeville

0   50
Scale in miles

Atlantic
Ocean

Savannah

George Skoch
(After Mark Dunkelman)

To Screven County

*T*hursday, November 24, 1864. "This morning the last of the vandals left our city and burned the bridge after them," Anna Maria Green wrote in Milledgeville. The Yankees left suffering and desolation behind them, "embittering every heart." The experience had "effectually cured the reconstruction disease" in whites and blacks alike, reported J. R. Bratton, the superintendent of Milledgeville's Confederate military hospitals. He noted that some wealthy families were reduced to eating sweet potatoes and were thankful they still had plenty of them to dig.[1]

Across the Oconee River, the 154th New York broke camp and marched at seven o'clock on a frosty morning. Decades after the Yankees departed, Guy McKinley alleged that General Geary ordered everything on the property to be burned because McKinley's father was a prominent and wealthy man, but McKinley's Yankee aunt asked another general for a guard, and they prevented any arson. So a merciful Yankee thwarted a malevolent one. All that was left to eat when the soldiers departed, McKinley recalled, was a barrel of split peas. He claimed he ate pea soup for months.[2]

This day's march was slow, as the column had to wait for the wagon train to get out of the way. The route ran through a rough country of pine forests dotted with few clearings. Geary's division had a hard time traversing some swampy terrain and crossing a rickety bridge at Town Creek. After a midafternoon stop for dinner, the men resumed the march. They made no more than twelve miles for the day and camped for the night near the west bank of Gum Creek, where they enjoyed bountiful suppers.[3]

Among the properties stripped this day was a small farm belonging to Harriet Howard, an elderly and childless widow. Seven years later Congress established the Southern Claims Commission to reimburse southern Unionists who had lost property to the Federal forces during the war. To receive recompense, applicants had to prove their loyalty. Of approximately 22,300 claimants throughout the South, only a third were able to meet the standard, among them Howard. She put a value of $1,231.50 on her losses and was granted $881.00 in reimbursement.[4]

General Sherman had accompanied the 14th Corps from Atlanta to Milledgeville. Now he rode with the 20th Corps, passing Geary's division around noon to the men's hearty cheers. At night the general and his staff camped in the midst of the Gum Creek bivouac. Major Henry Hitchcock, Sherman's judge advocate, described the striking scene in his diary. The house Sherman occupied stood in the dense shadows of a pine forest. Campfires lit the skies and sounds filled the air: sentries paced and called, tents hummed with conversation, mules brayed, and cattle lowed. "Our big droves of cattle provoke frequent remarks by natives," Hitchcock noted. "They are larger now than when we left Atlanta."[5]

By this time, Sherman's army had metamorphosed into something more than a body of troops. Behind each brigade, ex-slaves wrangled great herds of packhorses and mules burdened with all sorts of provisions and an infinite variety of items brought in by bummers. By the time the 154th reached Savannah, only two of the mules in its herd had come from Atlanta; the rest had been confiscated along the way. Regimental Wagoner Theodore C. Harns and three other men once captured forty mules in a single sweep.[6]

Friday, November 25, 1864. The march commenced at 6:30 on another frosty morning. Crossing Gum Creek, the men entered Washington County, passed through Hebron, and halted for dinner at noon near Buffalo Creek. For the first time since the march began, they heard sounds of combat as skirmishing broke out in the swamp ahead. The Confederates had destroyed all the bridges across the eight channels of the half-mile-wide creek. General Sherman was annoyed by the delay and threatened to burn a nearby house in retaliation. While their commander fumed, the rank and file relaxed, and the engineers rebuilt the bridges and repaired the roads. After dark the 154th crossed the creek and swamps and camped on a steep hillside.[7]

Foragers visited the Hoyles of Hebron, refugees from Atlanta. Before their arrival, the family inhabited a land of plenty, surrounded by wealthy neighbors and living better than they had since the war began.

Two months after the army passed, Imogene Hoyle lamented, "It is impossible for us to live here, as the Yankees have destroyed everything in the way of provisions."[8]

Saturday, November 26, 1864. The regiment marched at 6:00 a.m. as guard to the brigade train and made six miles on a pleasant morning. Up ahead, the leading 20th Corps units drove away enemy cavalry. When the advance entered the Washington County seat, Sandersville, it was greeted by shots fired from houses and the courthouse. The street fighting angered Sherman, who ordered the burning of the courthouse. The skirmish was over when the 154th arrived at noon. The men ate dinner and spent about two hours in the village. They found Sandersville to be a pretty place, with some impressive buildings. The neat little town was soon pillaged.[9]

Ella Mitchell, age nine when the Yankees arrived, recalled the event decades later. Her stories of pillaging bummers were plausible, but she added a tale that cast doubt on all the others. In it, Sherman ordered all of Sandersville to be razed. A local pastor begged the general to spare the town. Sherman refused to change his mind until the preacher tried a Masonic sign. As a result the town was saved, and another apocryphal story of Sherman as a Mason was added to the legendary canon.[10]

When Sherman arrived, Mrs. L. F. J. was a teenaged widow of a Confederate soldier living with her mother-in-law in Sandersville. Five decades later, she recalled in graphic detail the depredations of "Yankee ruffians," "fierce-looking men" casting "hateful leers from their red eyes" who foraged "with savage delight." But then her reminiscence took a gentler, more legendary turn. She was granted a guard, she related, as the daughter of a Mason. Her baby's cries caught the guard's attention. On learning of the child's hunger, this sympathetic Yankee brought the family some provisions and was rewarded with a home-cooked meal. The single kind Yankee who stands in sharp moral contrast to his brutish comrades appears repeatedly in southern tales. He is a legendary motif, so well known as a type to appear in postwar southern fiction.[11]

According to white women's postwar memoirs, of some five hundred Sandersville residents in 1864, only five adult white males remained to meet the Yankees. When the enemy passed and the men finally returned to town, they dug up hidden guns and patrolled the streets at night, fearing trouble from stragglers and renegade blacks.

Meanwhile, women scavenged what they could from vacated camps. Some were said to have survived on corn left behind where the Yankees had fed their livestock. Such "dropped corn" legends are common in the reminiscence literature, bolstering the myth of Sherman's marches as total devastation.[12]

While the main body of the 20th Corps looted Sandersville, two miles southeast of town bummers descended on Forest Grove plantation, owned by the widow of a slain Confederate colonel. According to family lore, Sarah Wicker Warthen, several daughters, and approximately fifty slaves were at Forest Grove when the Yankees arrived. A captain told Warthen to vacate the house; it was to be burned. She obstinately refused. With that the bummers—mostly Germans, according to the story—stripped the dining room of its silverware, drenched the carpets with syrup, torched the outbuildings and cotton bales, and forced the slaves to depart, leaving small black children clinging to Warthen in tears. Other tales told of items saved. A daughter slipped a single teaspoon into her pocket. The late colonel's sword escaped detection buried in a creek bed. Slaves loaded the family piano aboard a wagon and drove it around back roads until the Yankees departed. When a bummer picked up a glass dome containing artificial flowers and was about to smash it, a Warthen girl begged him to spare it, explaining that she had made it. The soldier acquiesced and carefully set it on the floor.[13]

From Sandersville the 154th marched south some five miles to Tennille (or Station Number 13) on the Georgia Central Railroad, where the 1st Division burned the depot and storehouses. The only occupants to be found were white, black, and mixed-race females; as usual, all the men had fled. The regiment moved east along the railroad for two miles and camped in the woods next to the tracks. Around midnight, the men were aroused by a false alarm and stood under arms for two hours. When an expected attack never materialized, they moved to a new position and went back to sleep. Mervin Barber attributed the panic to cows roaming a nearby field.[14]

Sunday, November 27, 1864. The march began at 7:00 a.m. and followed the line of the railroad. Each brigade was assigned a two-mile segment of track and ordered to destroy it thoroughly. The men covered five miles, halting frequently to tear up track and bridges and burn cotton, and then marched rapidly about ten miles to Davisboro (Station

Number 12), where they collapsed around 10 p.m. without putting up their tents.[15]

Monday, November 28, 1864. Jones's brigade was detached from the division and ordered to accompany the corps headquarters train to Spier's Turnout (Station Number 11, today called Bartow). The 154th started at 10:00 a.m. and led the brigade at a fast pace over eleven miles of fine, level countryside, passing from Washington County into Jefferson County. On reaching its destination at sunset, the regiment was posted for picket duty overnight.[16]

Among the properties the 154th passed this day was Sandy Grove, the large Jefferson County plantation owned by Herschel V. Johnson. The former U.S. senator, state circuit court judge, two-term governor of Georgia, and 1860 Democratic vice presidential candidate was now a Confederate senator. Johnson was known by reputation to the soldiers of the 154th New York, but none of them mentioned his plantation in their diaries or letters, so details of what transpired there are lacking. The outcome, however, was predictable. In 1860, Sandy Grove was worth $123,400, three-quarters of it in slaves. Four years later, when the Yankees approached, the slaves buried Johnson's silver and other valuables in the garden and planted a bed of collards above the stash. Jones's brigade discovered the hiding place, plundered the plantation, and liberated the slaves, and Johnson's wealth vanished. He never recovered from the blow. The Yankees "destroyed nearly everything I possessed" and "reduced me from comfort to poverty," he later wrote. He worked hard to get back on his feet, practicing the strictest economy and sacrificing many comforts, to no avail. He died in 1880 a poor man.[17]

Tuesday, November 29, 1864. Jones's brigade marched at 7:00 a.m. and covered seven miles, passing through Bethany (today called Wadley) and stopping at Bostwick Station (Number 10½) around noon on a very warm day. After dinner, the men spent the rest of the daylight hours destroying four miles of track from the station to the Ogeechee River, where they found a massive railroad bridge. They crossed the river and camped on its east bank. Major Warner observed, "Our course is marked by a line of fire."[18]

"Fires were lit on every hand," Alfred Benson remembered a decade later, "and the flames from burning fences, barns, dwellings, mills, and cotton everywhere lit up the line of march, making our advance a track of fire, leaving a barren waste." Not entirely barren—most inhabited homes escaped the flames, as did other structures. Public buildings were set afire, according to Emory Sweetland, with the exception of churches and schoolhouses. The soldiers burned pine knots in their campfires and were blackened by the soot. Years later, General Sherman stated he knew no more agreeable sensation than "the sight of our camps by night, lit up by the fires of fragrant pine-knots."[19]

A postwar memoir by Mrs. S. E. McCroan of Bethany included a couple of legendary aspects. McCroan's mother's household was relatively unscathed for a familiar reason: the matriarch had donned the patriarch's Masonic regalia, which brought a rescuer to their aid. As bummers ransacked McCroan's house and premises, she noticed a lone Yankee observing the scene as though he was ashamed of his comrades. He accompanied her to General Geary's headquarters and procured a guard, who cleared her house of bummers. McCroan's fear of the enemy had faded on contact, "for in every army, no matter how hostile, there are kind-hearted men ready to defend the weak"—like her single kind Yankee, representative of a legendary motif.[20]

Wednesday, November 30, 1864. Most of the day was spent destroying the Ogeechee River railroad bridge, consisting of three tracks over stout trestles, supported by a huge stone stanchion. An artist for the popular weekly *Frank Leslie's Illustrated Newspaper* sketched soldiers wielding crowbars and sledgehammers to tear up track and topple telegraph poles on one end of the bridge while a smoky fire consumed the other.[21]

"Had a good deal of fun ferrying a family of niggers across the river," Alex Bird noted in his diary. Years later, John Wellman recalled that the blacks appeared on the opposite bank hoping to cross and join the soldiers. The New Yorkers shoved planks across the narrow but deep Ogeechee, and the refugees used the lumber as floats. All crossed without incident except one hefty woman who made a frightened lunge for shore and grabbed Wellman, tumbling both of them into the water. Wellman marched away dripping wet, to the amusement of his comrades. This silly incident stands in stark contrast to the infamous and deadly one that played out nine days later, when the 14th Corps abandoned a crowd of blacks on the shore of Ebenezer Creek, leaving them prey to pursuing Confederates.[22]

Jones's brigade marched up the west bank of the Ogeechee, recrossed the river, entered Louisville, and camped on the outskirts of town, rejoining Geary's division and the rest of the 20th Corps. During the six-hour, fifteen-mile tramp "the roads was quite muddy and the night very dark," noted William Harper; a fog rolled in so dense that men got lost gathering wood for campfires. Consequently the soldiers saw little of Louisville. Perhaps they had a dim view of a pavilion market in the town square where general goods and slaves were sold, or the ruins of the town jail and other buildings, which 14th Corps troops had burned in previous days.[23]

Louisa Bothwell Scott later told her granddaughter typical stories about Yankee vandalism and theft in Louisville. Other of her tales cast the enemy in a better light. She gave them credit for rescuing residents' belongings from burning buildings, although there was much damage despite their efforts. She recalled that General Slocum assigned two trustworthy soldiers as guards for a family, and an officer provided the same clan with food.[24]

This day brought relief from a terrifying ordeal at the nearby plantation of a judge and his family. His wife later described it in a compendium of Confederate women's stories. In addition to the usual accounts of plundering bummers, she told two shocking tales. In one, the Yankees dug up a fresh grave and unearthed a black baby, which they did not bother to rebury. In the second, a black man reported that a trunk full of gold and silver was hidden on the property, and when the judge denied its existence, bummers hanged him repeatedly until he lost consciousness. (Without judging the reliability of this story, it should be noted that numerous unsubstantiated legends recount such hangings.) On this day came a change of fortune—organized elements of the 20th Corps arrived at the plantation. Unlike their rowdy and violent forerunners, these troops were orderly and benevolent. An officer assured the judge's wife of protection, cleared the house of bummers, provided the family with rations, and reported the hanging incident to General Slocum, who unfortunately was unable to do anything about it.[25]

Unlike the hapless judge, most Jefferson County white men were absent when the Yankees arrived, hiding with their livestock deep in the swamps. A handed-down story expressed scorn for these male refugees. After the Yankees left Louisville, it was said, an elderly woman encountered three former fugitives rushing somewhere and asked them if they were going again. Going where, inquired one of the puzzled men. To your swamp hiding spot, the sarcastic lady replied.[26]

A twentieth-century Jefferson County history told of two young children of a Louisville minister who "picked up stray grains of corn and parched them for food"—another instance of the dropped corn legend.[27]

Thursday, December 1, 1864. The 154th marched at 8:00 a.m. as guard to the Left Wing headquarters train and pontoons. The course crossed level, sandy countryside cut by numerous swamp-bordered streams. Major Warner observed that the enemy could use the terrain well to impede the army's progress, but the men met no opposition and kept a steady pace all day, crossing Dry, Spring, and Bark Camp creeks and passing from Jefferson County into Burke County. After covering about eighteen miles, they camped at dusk on the east bank of Bark Camp Creek. Twentieth Corps commander Alpheus Williams once again issued orders prohibiting unauthorized gunfire by foragers.[28]

Gunshots erupted when foragers and Confederate cavalry collided. In their later years, veterans recalled narrow escapes. Privates Joseph Putnam of Company H and Ebenezer C. Sherman of Company D told of eluding squads of enemy horsemen. Theodore Harns remembered he and Private Thomas D. Spiking Jr. of Company F were chased from a farmhouse and fled through the woods to a large plantation, where they found a sleeping Confederate. Shaken awake, he guided the Yankees to a neighboring place, where they captured two more rebels. Harns and Spiking reached camp that night accompanied by three prisoners, a score of horses and mules, and an unknown number of newly freed slaves. Marcellus Darling described how he and a partner hid under a farmhouse bed while rebel cavalrymen searched the premises. The home's occupants—a young woman and her mother—denied there were Yankees present. They saved his life, Darling asserted, "for it was death for foraging in those days." Aware that his tale portended a romance of reconciliation, he added, "As stories go I should have married that little southern girl, but I didn't." After several such close calls Darling resolved to be more careful, but he nevertheless continued to take risks.[29]

A couple of miles from the 154th's campsite stood the Bark Camp Baptist Church. Several days after the Yankees passed, an entry was made in the church's minutes book: "This was the regular day for Conference but owing to General William T. Sherman's Yankee raid, there was no meeting. We of Bark Camp do hereby place on record our solemn protest; also our thorough contempt for the vandals who desecrated our church."[30]

Friday, December 2, 1864. The fog that hovered when the march began at 6:00 a.m. cleared off and left bright, warm weather and dry roads. The day's tramp took the men through the old settlement of Birdsville and across Buck Head Creek. They camped for the night near the eastern bank, at Buck Head Baptist Church. Sergeant Harrison Coe and William Harper of Company F got lost in a swamp while foraging and had to wade through a mile of water to reach the regiment.[31]

"Passed some of the finest plantations we have yet met with," recorded Major Warner. That of Dr. William B. Jones at Birdsville was "a very wealthy place," noted Alex Bird; General Geary described it as "one of the finest in this part of Georgia." Sitting in a grove of old live oaks, an imposing mansion reflected Jones's exquisite taste and the lucrative production of thousands of acres of cotton fields. The plantation was often called Birdsville after the small cluster of buildings—an inn, apothecary, store, and post office—across the road from the big house. By the time of the war, Jones had converted some of the hamlet's buildings into slave quarters.[32]

The Yankees' visit naturally became the subject of Jones lore. A Georgia historical marker for Birdsville, erected in the 1950s or 1960s, gave the state's imprimatur to a family legend: "This mansion was spared Sherman's torch by the heroic resistance of its mistress." According to this classic steel magnolia preservation tale, an order was given to fire the house. From a bed in her second-story room, the ailing Sidney Ann Elizabeth Jones saw smoke rising outside the window. The Yankees figured the fire would force her to flee, but she refused to budge. The chastened enemy put out the fire and the big house was saved. Details added a ghastly touch to this tale. A few days before the Yankees arrived, Sidney Jones gave birth to twins—hence her confinement to bed. The babies died after birth and were buried behind the big house in the family cemetery. Making their usual search for valuables, the Yankees dug up the fresh graves and uncovered the tiny corpses.[33]

Near the 154th's campsite, the Buck Head Baptist Church lost its pews, books, and carpets, the Reverend Washington L. Kilpatrick reported. At the end of the month he listed his personal losses: livestock, poultry, grain, fodder, foodstuffs, flatware, cotton, gin house, carriage and harnesses, shoes and clothing, razors and combs, and nine slaves, all but one of whom escaped and returned. Most area blacks, however, had departed with the army and remained absent. A number of frightened white neighbors had fled, and their abandoned houses were destroyed. Women had suffered no indignities while their men were in hiding. Despite his losses, Kilpatrick hoped to make do by close economy. The Yankees had left behind some broken-down horses, poultry, and untouched potato banks. He and his neighbors had been stripped of their possessions, but—remarkably—not of their morale. "People are generally in good spirits and laugh over their losses," he wrote, "—have not seen more than two long faces."[34]

Saturday, December 3, 1864. On a warm day the 154th did not get started until noon, when the 2nd Division moved out at the rear of the 20th Corps as guard to the wagon train. It was slow going through what General Geary described as "a long and almost impassable swamp." An afternoon rainstorm added to the misery, and Geary and his officers and men labored hard to move the wagons through the mire. The 154th crossed the Waynesboro Railroad about three miles north of Millen and stopped for dinner as darkness fell. After making a total of ten tough miles, the regiment camped at about 10:00 p.m. near the Van Camp farm. Under unknown circumstances, Thomas Spiking was captured in Sylvania, the Screven County seat, roughly twenty-five miles to the east. Spiking had escaped previous close calls, but this time he was sent to a prisoner-of-war camp in Florence, South Carolina.[35]

About five miles north of Millen, Geary's men found Camp Lawton, a prison pen situated in a dense pine forest. Until recently the place had held some three thousand Union prisoners who had been moved there from Andersonville, including many 154th New York men. A huge log stockade, surmounted by guardhouses, surrounded a field pocked with holes dug by the prisoners for shelter. "In imagination we could see the emaciated forms of our brothers still peopling these wretched holes in the ground," Alfred Benson wrote bitterly a decade later. Marcellus Darling was one of the first to enter the abandoned stockade, anxiously searching for a sign of his prisoner-of-war brother. All he found was a few unconscious prisoners left behind to die and some wooden and bone spoons he picked up as relics.[36]

Sunday, December 4, 1864. After a 10:00 a.m. start, the 154th made slow time following the wagon train through numerous swamps and covered only about five miles. The caravan crossed Horse Creek and entered Screven County. Cannonading was heard to the north; the men speculated that it marked a cavalry fight or the 14th Corps meeting some opposition. Geary's 1st and 3rd brigades crossed to the eastern side of Crooked Creek, leaving Jones's brigade on the west side to cover the bridge. The 154th camped at dark, and some of the men went on picket. Lieutenant Bird led a foraging party across some poor country, and by the time they returned to the main road, they were far in advance of the division, so they camped and waited until the following morning to rejoin the column.[37]

Monday, December 5, 1864. The 154th set off behind the train at 7:00 a.m., crossed Crooked Creek, and found the Middleground Road to be much better than that of the day before. An hour after starting, the regiment came across Alex Bird and his foragers. The men marched about fourteen miles before encamping at 8:00 p.m. Streams crossed during the day included Little Horse Creek and the South Fork of Little Ogeechee Branch; the troops burned the bridges behind them. The area was a dead level of sandy soil, pine forests, and swamps, but foraging was nevertheless good.[38]

General Williams repeated his injunction against the burning of buildings and warned against setting grass and woods on fire as a particular danger to the ammunition train. He reiterated that foraging was to be done only by authorized parties, now to consist of not less than a hundred men. The fact that Williams had to repeat the same old orders indicates both his desire to see them obeyed and their ineffectiveness.[39]

On the South Fork of Little Ogeechee Branch, Geary's division destroyed the large Zeigler sawmill. A short distance to the east the men came to the Zeigler farm. According to family legend, Israel Zeigler and his slave, Moes, hid food and valuables in a brook that ran through a nearby field; Zeigler then took shelter there himself. His wife, Margaret "Peggy" Zeigler, was sick in bed. Five-year-old Reuben Zeigler, one of eleven children, was sitting atop a gatepost in the front yard when a group of mounted bummers arrived. When the dirty, smelly Yankees ordered the frightened boy to catch a chicken, he scurried under the house and hid behind the chimney, where he remained overnight. Meanwhile the soldiers rousted Peggy Zeigler from her sickbed, swaddled her in the mattress, thrust her through the second-floor bedroom window, and rolled her down the sloping porch roof onto the ground. She survived the fall, apparently unhurt. The soldiers sweet-talked Moes into divulging the hiding place and took all the goods. The last the Zeiglers saw of Moes, he was grinning from the back of a wagon, riding to freedom with the Yankees.[40]

Toward the end of the day, Geary's division passed in succession the properties of H. H. McGee, Jim McGee, Noel Lanier, Dave Lee, and Walter Walker, camping for the night on the last two farms. A century later, H. H. McGee's great-grandson recounted tales of encounters he had heard from his grandmother, a grown woman at the time of the war, tales that were embroidered over the years with legend. It was said a slave housemaid charmed the Yankees and saved the H. H. McGee house from molestation. In this twist on a typical steel magnolia preservation legend, the heroine was transformed into a loyal slave. At Jim McGee's place, the story went, the Yankees saw his framed Masonic diploma hanging in a hallway and stopped their depredations. Noel Lanier reportedly took a potshot at the soldiers from behind his farm's well. The Yankees were going to hang or shoot him, but his wife was "a great diplomat" and talked them out of retaliation. Sherman's orders stipulated that if bushwhackers molested the march, "a devastation more or less relentless, according to the measure of such hostility," should be enforced. If Noel Lanier actually took a potshot at the Yankees, his house would have gone up in flames despite his wife's diplomatic skills.[41]

Although three of Sherman's four corps crossed Screven County, residents reported that the resulting destruction was slight. News of the Yankees' approach caused the usual panic and sent many inhabitants fleeing from their homes. Among them was a minister who returned to his place after the passage of the enemy. "Found all safe and well," he wrote; even abandoned homes were not burned in the area. For the next few days, residents recovered their goods from swamp caches, where they had been picked over by the Yankees without much loss. They had made a mistake by hiding goods for fear their houses would be burned, the preacher admitted. The Yankees "did not do us much harm," he wrote, except by taking readily found horses, mules, and hogs.[42]

A Confederate colonel who was home on leave reported that only four or five houses were burned in all of Screven County. The Yankees had targeted certain homeowners—a man who hunted escaped Union prisoners with bloodhounds, another who barricaded roads in the army's advance, and a foolhardy fellow who shot the first soldier to approach his house. Sherman's men left the county's inhabitants with enough provisions to tide them over, the colonel maintained, had they not subsequently been overrun by Joseph Wheeler's Confederate cavalry. Wheeler lacked a supply system of his own and, like Sherman, depended on the land for sustenance. To the rebel colonel, Wheeler's men were worse than the Yankees; they "filled the whole country with terror."[43]

An unidentified refugee in Screven County commented on the depredations of Wheeler's cavalry in a letter to the *Countryman*. Widely reputed to be "the greatest horse thieves in the country," Wheeler's men "never acted worse than they have recently." While the Yankees were burning and destroying property in one part of the county, the writer alleged, Wheeler's troopers were stealing horses and mules in another. Remarking on this letter, Joseph Turner wrote, "The whole land mourns, on account of Wheeler's cavalry. Here in middle Georgia, they are dreaded fully as much, if not more, than the yankees."[44]

On this night of December 5 the 154th rested only forty-eight miles from Savannah. In recent days the men had entered a different landscape. The rich soil of central Georgia gave way to sandy, swampy terrain covered in pine forests, with relatively less to offer foragers. In this countryside, the march was about to enter a new phase.[45]

To the Sea

Tuesday, December 6, 1864. On a warm day, the regiment marched at 8:00 a.m. toward Springfield. The roads were good in the forenoon, but swampy terrain, destroyed bridges, tangles of timber left by the enemy, and skirmishing by the advance slowed the afternoon's trek. Proceeding at a moderate pace and resting often, the 154th made about nine miles during the day, entered Effingham County, and camped near the Lanier farm on a rainy night.[1]

Wednesday, December 7, 1864. The men started at 7 o'clock on a wet morning. General Geary assigned each company, regiment, and brigade a specific number of wagons to accompany. At one point two dozen wagons sank to their beds in the mud of the wretched road. Plantations were small and widely scattered in a vast pine forest, so foraging was poor. When the caravan crossed Turkey Branch, the roads improved. After covering about nine miles, the regiment camped at 8:00 p.m. about a mile north of Springfield and thirty miles from Savannah.[2]

Near the regiment's campsite was the Zettler farm. Elvy E. Zettler later recalled enemy misbehavior—her mother revealing the location of some blackberry wine under threats of arson, a bummer stealing an armful of dresses for his black "wench," a sarcastic philanthropist presenting the family with a worthless Confederate bill—but she also acknowledged kind and conscientious Yankees who acted ashamed of their unruly comrades. "Not a soldier offered any violence to us," she admitted, "or even used insulting language." Her brother Berrian M. Zettler remembered the desolated farm—the empty smokehouse, corncrib, and sugar, syrup, and rice houses, the denuded potato banks and gardens, the detected subterranean caches and swampy hiding spots, the abandoned quarters (all but one of forty slaves had followed the enemy). Although Elvy claimed to have been left with nothing to eat but the legendary dropped corn, she added that a soldier gave the family some hardtack and they were left with some peas, rice, and scavenged meat. The Yankee camps also yielded lots of cowhides, which they cured into leather, and fat, which they rendered into tallow. In Elvy Zettler's memory, meeting the enemy was less horrible than the fear of facing the Yankees had been.[3]

According to a secondhand UDC account, Jane Newton Burke remembered but a single kind Yankee on her family's Effingham County plantation. He took a shine to a two-year-old girl, who reminded him of his own toddler daughter; he embraced her and left packages of provisions for her.[4]

Twice this day the 154th New York was struck by tragedy. Sergeant Charles H. Brown of Company F died at the division hospital of congestive intermittent fever. And about two miles north of Springfield, Private Jesse D. Campbell of Company D accidentally shot himself. His comrades buried him on the spot. When the regiment reached Savannah, news was sent to the two men's families. Brown's company comrade Private Edson D. Ames sent the sergeant's meager belongings home in a cigar box.[5]

Thursday, December 8, 1864. Geary's division took the advance of the 20th Corps. The 154th marched at 6:30 a.m. and passed through the Effingham County seat, Springfield, which Mervin Barber described as "a few old buildings and a small court house." This day's march was slow. The pioneers cleared away obstacles left by the enemy and constructed miles of corduroy road by cutting logs and laying them side by side in the mud. After a slog of eleven miles, the regiment camped at 4:00 p.m. near the Conaway property. Some skirmishing was heard far to the front, but Major Warner observed that the Confederates were offering "little opposition as yet."[6]

Back in western New York, this day's issue of the *Cattaraugus Freeman* wondered why Sherman had not been supplied with carrier pigeons. The government could have heard from him twice a day—a pigeon reportedly could fly from Georgia to Washington in ten hours. Sherman in fact knew the capabilities of carrier pigeons, but he also valued secrecy and sought to avoid publicity. When Georgia newspapers reprinted accounts from northern papers of his army's composition, he was furious.[7]

Friday, December 9, 1864. Following an inspection, the 154th marched at 7:30 a.m. and proceeded at a moderate pace past Zion Lutheran Church and farms owned by descendants of the early Austrian and German settlers known as Salzburgers. The 1st Division led the 20th Corps into Monteith Swamp, skirmished there with an entrenched enemy, and forced their retreat. General Geary ordered Colonel Jones to support the attack, and the brigade marched on the double-quick to the front, only to find the Confederates had retired. On rejoining the division at nightfall, the 154th camped near the Helmey farm, fifteen miles from Savannah.[8]

In a UDC memoir, Jennie Ihly Darnell recollected living with her Salzburger grandparents on their Effingham County farm when the Yankees swept through "like wild Comanche Indians." As an elderly woman, she remained impressed by the foragers' mechanical efficiency in dismantling the barn and outbuildings and emptying them of great quantities of fodder. In true UDC form, she quoted her defiant retorts to Yankee teasers and offered a tribute to the slaves, who she claimed were true and loyal until the war ended and freedom was declared. She wrote proudly of her grandmother's successful ruse in hiding provisions on the second floor of an unused house that lacked a stairwell. She also recalled kind Yankees thwarting pillagers and returning her silk dress, which had been found in a trunk buried in the turkey pen.[9]

A Unionist refugee who had fled his home to escape Confederate conscription officers joined the 20th Corps column in Effingham County, intending to follow it to Savannah. "I have been hunted through swamps month after month," he told the northerners. "My wife and children have been half starved, insulted, and abused, and all because we loved the old flag." Touched by his story, the soldiers took a collection and presented him with a $130 purse. He broke down and cried with gratitude.[10]

Saturday, December 10, 1864. Detailed to accompany the 20th Corps train, Jones's brigade backtracked about two miles and posted guards around the parked wagons. At noon the train lurched forward, the brigade following as rear guard. Throughout the day the distant dull booming of cannon signified the advance had again encountered the enemy. Although bordered by swamps, the roads were good, and in midafternoon the 154th struck the Charleston Railroad at Monteith Station. The regiment was now in Chatham County, only ten miles from Savannah. The wagons turned south on a road running parallel to the destroyed track. At 8:00 p.m. the 154th camped for the night within five miles of the city. A hard rain fell this night.[11]

Sunday, December 11, 1864. The sun emerged for the first time in several days. Following an inspection, the regiment moved a mile north of the road, toward the Savannah River. The division's advance elements skirmished to the accompaniment of distant heavy cannonading. In the afternoon, Jones's brigade was hurried into line in response to a report of the enemy massing in front. For half an hour the men were under artillery fire, but nobody was harmed, and just before dark they moved down the riverbank about a mile and pitched camp three miles from Savannah.[12]

The operational nature of the campaign now changed; the March to the Sea was over, and the siege of Savannah began. Sherman's army stretched from the Savannah River to the Ogeechee. Geary's division formed the left of the line, with Jones's brigade in reserve, its left resting on the high riverbank opposite the upper end of Hutchinson Island, the 154th lined up in some eroded Revolutionary War breastworks. In front of the division stretched an open expanse of rice fields crossed by a wide canal. The enemy had cut a dam and flooded the fields, creating a vast moat of water up to six feet deep, beyond which loomed Fort Hardeman, a large earthwork armed with ten guns and garrisoned by two hundred men, its front bristling with stakes interlaced with iron wire. From the fort the Confederate line, manned by Georgia militia and studded with twenty guns, stretched beyond the flooded fields far to Geary's right. In the far distance Savannah was in plain sight. The city's strongly fortified approaches were weakly defended by approximately ten thousand Confederate troops commanded by Lieutenant General William J. Hardee. Sherman consequently had the opportunity to capture Savannah and Hardee's force as well. He would meet with but partial success.[13]

Four-mile-long Hutchinson Island contained hundreds of acres of rice fields and swampy shores teeming with alligators. A great number of slaves had been left there; some of them canoed to the mainland to join the Yankees. Geary sent a staff officer to reconnoiter the island's upper end; he returned and reported it unoccupied by the enemy. After the 154th bivouacked for the night, Hospital Steward Charles Harry

Matteson and Lieutenants Alex Bird, Dell Ames, and Guy Waterman found a boat and crossed the channel to forage on Hutchinson.[14]

Monday, December 12, 1864. The foragers returned from their island escapade about 1:00 a.m. to find their comrades wide awake, under arms, deployed in line of battle, and expecting to splash across the flooded rice fields in a two-brigade night attack on Fort Hardeman planned by Geary. After the men stood under arms from midnight to 4 a.m., "the matter was abandoned," Major Warner noted with relief, "and we returned to camp." During the day the regiment packed up and moved a few rods closer to the riverbank. Some of the men hid in the undergrowth as sharpshooters, admiring the exotic semitropical foliage and live oaks festooned with Spanish moss. There was considerable shelling from enemy guns during the day, to which the Union forces did not reply, lacking artillery of sufficient caliber.[15]

Geary ordered another reconnaissance of Hutchinson Island; only a few Confederate scouts were found. But this night the enemy moved some troops there. When three members of the 154th subsequently paddled over to forage, a score of rebels suddenly arose on shore, leveled their muskets at the unlucky Yankees, and captured Private Clark E. "Salty" Oyer of Company G, Corporal William P. Haight and Private Delos Peck of Company E, and five blacks, including General Geary's cook.[16]

"We need hardtacks," Francis Bowen commented in his diary. The hearty meals of middle Georgia were a thing of the past; the men were reduced to rations of rice and sorghum and quickly grew tired of the fare. According to postwar reminiscences, Sherman happened to visit the 154th's line during this period and asked the men how they were getting along. One replied that they needed rations. "Aren't you getting plenty of rice?" asked Sherman. The soldier countered that he would just as soon lie on his back and let the sun (or the moon, depending on the telling) shine in his mouth than eat any more rice. Sherman's response to this impertinence went unrecorded.[17]

Tuesday, December 13, 1864. On a cold morning considerable firing erupted in front. During the day a sunken battery was built on the riverbank near the 154th's position and occupied by the four guns of Captain Thomas S. Sloan's Pennsylvania Independent Battery E, covering the approaches up and down river and across Hutchinson Island to the South Carolina shore. Colonel Jones ordered a special sharpshooter company to be formed of the brigade's best marksmen; a sergeant, a corporal, and three privates were to come from the 154th. There was more grumbling about the lack of food. Joshua Pettit reported absolutely "*no rations.*"[18]

In the late afternoon a spherical case shot exploded in camp, wounding Francis Bowen, Zeno Besecker, Private Wellman P. Nichols of Company C, and Captain James Gallagher. Major Warner noted that shell fragments gave others minor injuries, but they went officially unreported. In the postwar years Private John Douglass of Company E, Private Edward G. Herrington of Company F, and Corporal Patrick Foley and Privates John C. Green and Amos McIntyre of Company K claimed minor shrapnel wounds dating from the siege. The last three alleged that their injuries concerned them less than a coffee kettle that was destroyed while perking on a fire. They joked that the Rebs had aimed the shot intentionally, knowing that the coffee was the last they had.[19]

After the wounded were conveyed to the division hospital, the 154th moved its camp about one hundred yards away from the river. General Geary ordered Colonel Jones to send a detachment from the 134th New York to Hutchinson Island. During the night the remainder of the 134th joined them. Geary issued another order: no other parties were to cross the river to the island. Jones was to collect all the boats and scows in the vicinity and put them under guard.[20]

Wednesday, December 14, 1864. The 154th spent a warm day supporting Sloan's battery and picketing the riverbank. At brigade headquarters, Colonel Jones sent the 73rd Pennsylvania to join the 134th New York on Hutchinson Island and ordered Lieutenant Guy Waterman to take command of the sharpshooter company. Skirmishers were advanced at the front, which caused more than the usual shelling. Meanwhile an old ferryboat bulwarked with cotton bales and armed with a single heavy gun steamed upriver and bombarded the Union works from the opposite side of Hutchinson Island, doing some damage and causing considerable confusion but hurting no one in the 154th. The men hugged the earth in the most sheltered spots they could find. The enemy's heavy artillery gave them a decided advantage, Major Warner noted. Welcome news arrived: a Confederate bastion on the Ogeechee

River called Fort McAllister had fallen to a division of the 15th Corps, and communications were consequently opened with the Federal fleet. The magnitude of those events soon became apparent.[21]

Thursday, December 15, 1864. All night long the enemy fortifications threw shot and shell at the Union lines. At dawn the gunboat made another foray and added to the din. Major Warner thought retribution was finally at hand, however; heavy guns from Fort McAllister and the Union fleet were expected to arrive at Geary's division in a few days. Undeterred by the barrage or by Geary's orders, Lieutenant Bird and Captains Benson and Gallagher captured a flat boat that ran ashore and enjoyed a ride on the river. The 154th had monthly inspection and remained in camp until 9:00 p.m., when details were assigned to construct a strong lunette on the left of the front line. The work parties labored all night. During the day, 150 20th Corps wagons started for a new supply base on the Ogeechee River to pick up badly needed rations delivered by the fleet. Nine of the wagons were slated to carry mail—the first the army had received since leaving Atlanta—and the men anxiously awaited their return.[22]

On this day Left Wing commander Slocum wrote to Sherman, suggesting that the entire 20th Corps be sent to the South Carolina side of the Savannah River to seal the only escape route open to Hardee's army. Sherman dismissed Slocum's proposal, expecting troops stationed in coastal Carolina to block Hardee. In the next few days Slocum ordered a 20th Corps brigade to occupy Argyle Island, above Hutchinson Island, and it briefly crossed over into South Carolina, but Hardee's escape route remained open.[23]

"We have got a drove of niggers and wenches that will reach twenty miles, I dare say," exaggerated Gene Graves. Emory Sweetland estimated that 10,000 black refugees were still with the entire army. General Williams calculated that some 6,000 to 8,000 blacks had joined the 20th Corps during the march, but only 2,500 still remained. Contrary to postwar northern mythology, the black population did not flock en masse to the Yankees. The thirty-odd Georgia counties the army entered contained some 150,000 slaves in 1860. Sherman stated that up to 70,000 of them attached themselves to the army at some point during the march, a figure that historian Lee Kennett believes to be vastly inflated. Lloyd Lewis estimated that three-quarters of the blacks turned back after a few days with the army, weary and homesick. Lewis also noted that the 20th Corps, with its contingent of abolitionist easterners, collected almost as many blacks as all the western troops of the Right Wing.[24]

Friday, December 16, 1864. "Rebs shelled us right smart from their gunboat at night," Alex Bird recorded. During the day the fire from both water and land was brisk. Gene Graves noted that the enemy's heavy guns seemed to make the earth tremble. Meanwhile, the famine continued. "This is the fourth day," Mervin Barber noted, "that we have lived on one-half pound of rice a day and roasted acorns from the live oaks." The men nevertheless remained healthy, by and large. First Sergeant Richard J. McCadden of Company G stated that his health was never better; not a man in his company was sick. Morale remained high. "I never saw a more confident army," Sherman declared in a letter to his wife. "The soldiers think I know everything and that they can do anything." A detail of three hundred from Jones's brigade, including members of the 154th, was sent to work on the front line's Fort No. 1. Meanwhile, officers of the 134th New York and 73rd Pennsylvania occupied a Hutchinson Island rice mill as an observation post. Unfortunately, their vision did not extend to the lower end of the island.[25]

Saturday, December 17, 1864. A respite from the constant shelling was made even more enjoyable by the arrival of a large amount of mail. The soldiers were deeply satisfied, First Sergeant George J. Mason of Company K wrote, to "hear from God's country again." Some of the men received packages; Francis Bowen got socks, gloves, and a silk handkerchief from his wife. When Chaplain Norton sat by the fire in front of his tent at sunset to read his letters from home, the enemy opened another cannonade. "I hope soon to write you from the city of *Savannah*," he wrote to his daughter, "but fear that many brave boys will fall ere we enter it." Every hour a detail left the regiment to work on the interior of Fort No. 1. Meanwhile the men fixed up camp, tearing down and realigning their tents and building brush beds.[26]

Sunday, December 18, 1864. Major Warner reported that Hardee had rejected Sherman's demand for Savannah's surrender, "so we must fight for it." The enemy artillery fire, Warner wrote, was "somewhat annoying even when nobody is hurt." With nothing to eat but rice, beef, and acorns, hunger continued to gnaw at the men.[27]

Monday, December 19, 1864. A warm spell continued. The 154th cleaned up camp, worked on Fort No. 1, and picketed the riverbank. The first rations of hardtack, coffee, and sugar finally arrived from the newly established base. The Confederates were unusually quiet until evening, when they unleashed a tremendous barrage from all their batteries, which continued well into the night.[28]

The division and brigade commanders met with General Williams at corps headquarters and discussed tactics to be used in storming the enemy's works. While the officers mulled plans for an assault, the enlisted men wondered whether they would have to make a bayonet charge before the siege could succeed. All communications to Savannah were cut, Marcellus Darling thought, and it would have to be surrendered when supplies ran out. But the Confederates still had an escape route from the city—the route that Slocum had unsuccessfully petitioned Sherman to plug.[29]

Tuesday, December 20, 1864. After another night and day of work, Fort No. 1 was completed. But the labor wasn't over; after returning to camp and fixing up their tents, the men spent the evening working on breastworks. Confederate batteries continued to trouble them. The gunboat again ran upriver to the far side of Hutchinson Island, Major Warner noted, "and made quite a muss among our camps." "One shell burst in the regiment, severely wounding one of the niggers and slightly wounding a few of the men," Alex Bird wrote; the victims' names went unrecorded. Sloan's battery drove the intruder away with a shot through its paddlewheel. During the night, three siege guns were hauled to Fort No. 1 and mounted. An assault loomed a step closer.[30]

Back in Milledgeville, the *Southern Recorder* published an article headlined "Sherman's Run." The Yankees had damaged Georgia's railroads and caused great private loss, the reporter admitted, but their campaign "was not a triumphant march." Sherman was retreating from Atlanta and avoiding any place that offered the least resistance. He would have bypassed Milledgeville, the reporter asserted, had Confederate troops remained there.[31]

Wednesday, December 21, 1864. The camp stirred with excitement at 4 a.m. with news that the Confederates had evacuated Savannah. Overnight, Hardee's troops had crossed a makeshift bridge to the lower end of Hutchinson Island—undetected by Jones's men at the upper end—thence to a smaller island and on to the South Carolina shore, where they traversed the very area on which Slocum had wanted to post the 20th Corps. Sherman had lost the opportunity to capture Hardee's army, but the men in the ranks seemed unaware of the failure. To them, the fall of Savannah was victory enough. Colonel Jones immediately recalled his force from Hutchinson Island and prepared his brigade to march. Within an hour the 154th was on the move at a rapid pace. Up ahead, General Geary met Mayor Richard D. Arnold and some aldermen and accepted the surrender of Savannah. With music ringing in their ears, the men marched into the city with fixed bayonets. At 6:45 they passed the town clock, exultant, wrote Francis Bowen, to be "complete victors of the place."[32]

"Found the city in good condition," wrote Bowen, "with many women and children therein." Well-to-do whites generally kept out of sight, but the poorer whites seemed pleased to see the Yankees. A few Unionists waved handkerchiefs or miniature American flags from balconies or windows. The black residents were ecstatic and gave their liberators a boisterous welcome. "The Yankees entered our peaceful little city in a much more orderly way than I anticipated," wrote Fanny Cohen Taylor, a Confederate soldier's wife, although she reported many robberies of blacks and lower-class whites. Soldiers entered a few homes and demanded food, tobacco, or liquor, a reporter noted, "but these were exceptional cases."[33]

A staff artist for *Harper's Weekly* captured the scene as Geary's division—the only unit of Sherman's army to enter Savannah—marched down Bay Street and assembled at City Hall and the Customs House, where the general delivered a speech to his three brigades. Following the oration Jones's brigade marched south on Bull Street to the large city park, Forsyth Place, beyond which the 154th New York camped on the sprawling city parade ground.[34]

The campaign was over, but old habits were hard to break. Members of the 154th had no sooner entered the city before they looked around to see what was to be had. Alex Bird strolled downtown and found a lot of tobacco. Marcellus Darling found twenty bushels of sweet potatoes in a basement, loaded them into a wagon, and issued them to the men. "They counted it a 'good haul,'" he reported. It was a nice break after a couple weeks of eating rice and hardtack. The taste of sweet potatoes brought back memories of the heyday of the great march.[35]

[7]

Savannah Interlude

THE peaceful occupation of Savannah brought a welcome end to the siege. As the first to enter the city, General Geary's division became the garrison force, the only troops quartered in Savannah proper. The ensuing period turned out to be one of the most pleasant in the 154th New York's nearly three years of service.

Writing to their home folk, the soldiers struggled to describe the momentous march. As Marcellus Darling put it, "There is so much to write about, I can't tell what to mention first." When he got home, he promised his family, he would tell them about "what good times we had." Richard McCadden, on the other hand, stressed that the march was "long and wearisome" but proudly added that he "stood it very well." (Alpheus Williams reported that the 20th Corps marched 305 miles from Atlanta to Savannah.) George Mason simply stated that the army had been "very successful all the way through" and had "done a great deal of damage to the Rebs." Gene Graves exaggerated the last point: "The State of Georgia is completely destroyed." As for the fall of Savannah, John Langhans wrote, "We think here the Rebs are about whipped, for they won't wait to give Sherman battle anymore. They left this place in a great hurry, before fighting at all, and left all their cannons in their forts."[1]

Back in Putnam County, Joseph Turner acknowledged the Yankees' success in the pages of the *Countryman.* Sherman's march "should mantle with the blush of shame the cheek of every Georgian, and every Confederate. We, for one, feel deeply mortified—humbled—chagrined—even degraded." But Turner remained defiant, considering it folly to think that Sherman had subjugated the Georgians. "The effects of that march will not be half so disastrous as many of our people seem to think," he argued. "Our cause is not lost. Our army and our people will rally again."[2]

For several days after arriving in Savannah, the 154th worked at setting up camp on the parade ground south of Forsyth Place. Geary ordered his division to take what lumber it needed, wherever it could be found, to erect huts. "Boards and fences are being snatched high and dry for tenting," Francis Bowen wrote; the regiment's horse and mule teams hauled load after load to the campsite. The men had honed their hut-building skills in Virginia, Tennessee, and Atlanta, and with an abundance of supplies they now constructed their most homelike shanties ever, full of comfortable domestic touches. Andrew Blood and two comrades shared a snug hut outfitted with bunks and furnished with stools, a table, shelves to hold their tin plates and cups, and a brick fireplace outfitted with an oven. As regimental shantytowns rose on the parade ground and elsewhere in Savannah, the face of the "Forest City" was transformed. Taking a walk, Fanny Cohen Taylor "was surprised to see what these wretches had done in the way of making themselves comfortable. All of our squares built up with wooden houses, so that I scarcely recognized the streets."[3]

The soldiers were short of blankets and heat was welcome on chilly winter nights. They constantly took firewood wherever they could find it. Such thefts forced Fanny Cohen Taylor to bed early on cold nights. Wooden structures, among them the slave auction stands in front of the courthouse, were torn down to feed the campfires. Stoves were eagerly sought because they burned wood slower than fireplaces.[4]

For the most part, the men were amply provisioned during their stay in Savannah. Pork, hardtack, coffee, and sugar were staples. On a couple of occasions in January 1865, they complained of being on half rations. In the meantime, they purchased extra food from civilians or the commissary department. Many of them enjoyed a plentiful local delicacy, oysters. The mollusks were so popular that the 2nd Division provost marshal regulated their price at one dollar per bushel.[5]

Most of the men survived the campaign in good health, but a number took sick in Savannah. When smallpox broke out in the city, the 154th passed a resolution barring any outside blacks from entering camp. When the regiment departed Savannah, sixteen hospitalized men were left behind. During the early days of the Carolinas campaign, several other sick men were sent back to the city. In the meantime, the regiment's medical corps returned to full strength when Surgeon Dwight W. Day and a new assistant surgeon, George H. Bosley, arrived at Savannah.[6]

"It is probable but not certain that we are to remain and garrison the town," Major Warner wrote the day after arriving in Savannah. "General Geary expects to be military governor. Hope we may stay." Two weeks later Marcellus Darling voiced the same hope, confessing, "It is much better to lay in camp with plenty of rations than to be marching all around over the whole Confederacy."[7]

One reason for the men's reluctance to leave was their appreciation of Savannah, which they described as a splendid city. They especially admired the attractive monuments in the squares, the grand fountain in Forsyth Place, and the handsome live oak, sycamore, and magnolia trees. They were able to overlook the wartime shabbiness that had dulled Savannah's elegance—abandoned houses and stores, tumble-down fences, decayed sidewalks and wharves, and streets littered with dead horses and mules. While most of the men succumbed to Savannah's charms and hoped to stay, some naysayers found life in the city to be dull. "Garrisoning Savannah has about played out for the 2nd Division," Francis Bowen wrote less than three weeks into the occupation. He considered such duty demoralizing.[8]

When General Sherman famously presented President Lincoln with Savannah as a Christmas gift, he estimated that the city contained about 25,000 bales of cotton. The total turned out to be 38,500 bales. Warehouses were full of cotton, John Langhans noted; every day he went to the riverfront to watch ships load with it and depart for the North. Emory Sweetland wrote that there was a motion before the House of Representatives to award Sherman's army the proceeds from the sale of Savannah's cotton—much as prize money was distributed in the naval service—which could amount to three hundred dollars per man. In fact, the Senate considered such a measure, but nothing came of it; the government appropriated the proceeds. Sherman's men had to content themselves with a joint congressional resolution thanking them "for their gallant conduct in their late brilliant movement through Georgia."[9]

Much more than cotton was captured in Savannah. A lengthy addendum to Geary's official campaign report listed public property his division seized in the city, from steamboats, railroad trains, and heavy artillery pieces to cartridge boxes, bullet molds, and currycombs. Geary also estimated the amounts of "property and supplies appropriated or destroyed" by his division during the march, including livestock, foodstuffs, cotton bales, cotton gins, mills, and factories—noting that the totals, as given in the returns of his quartermaster and commissary officers, excluded the gleanings of bummers. The general calculated his men had destroyed twenty-six and a half miles of railroad, together with bridges, trestles, water tanks, cordwood, and the like.[10]

Geary established his headquarters office in the Central Railroad Bank building, next to the U.S. Customs House on Bay Street. His orders, published in the public press, divided the city into eastern and western districts, split by Bull Street. Every 2nd Division regiment was assigned to patrol a designated area to keep the peace and to guard public and private property. No citizens were to be arrested, except for misdemeanors. Tattoo was to be beaten throughout the city at eight o'clock in the evening, followed by taps at nine, after which all enlisted men found on the streets without a proper pass were to be arrested. Citizens desiring to leave Savannah to go to the rebel lines had to apply for permission at Geary's headquarters. Those destitute of provisions could apply for relief at the city store, where they would receive supplies upon the order of Mayor Richard Arnold. In other orders, Geary regulated trade by civilians and sutlers and sought to quell extortion and price gouging, directed citizens and soldiers to keep city streets and sidewalks swept clean and free of offal, and threatened vandals with arrest and hard labor.[11]

In postwar reminiscences, Savannahians accused the Yankees of heinous vandalism in a city cemetery. According to a UDC account (based on stories about the narrator's friend's grandmother), when rumors circulated that the approaching Yankees desecrated graves, some residents dug up their family plots in Colonial Cemetery and moved the coffins out of town as a precaution. Other postwar writers alleged that treasure-seeking bummers ransacked many of Colonial's graves and vaults, opening coffins, scattering bones and skulls, and robbing jewelry and gold fillings from corpses. According to local lore, when the Yankees left Savannah, residents gathered toppled headstones and attached them to the cemetery's rear wall.[12]

On Christmas day some of the best singers serenaded their comrades with carols. Edgar Shannon and Marcellus Darling enjoyed a holiday feast of oysters, butter, and rice pudding; Mervin Barber had nothing but a cold johnnycake. The men were rowdy on New Year's Eve and fired salutes the next day. Later in January they were mustered for pay and issued new clothing. They celebrated news of Thomas's defeat of Hood at Nashville and the fall of Fort Fisher in North Carolina, which would eventually lead to the capture of Wilmington, the Confederacy's last major open seaport. They also welcomed a report that Colonel Patrick Jones had been promoted to brigadier general, but they were disappointed when he departed for the North on sick leave and the disliked Colonel George Mindil assumed command of the 2nd Brigade by seniority.[13]

Sherman reviewed his four corps in Savannah on different days. The 20th Corps paraded last, on December 30. Sherman inspected Geary's division on Liberty Street that morning, and at noon the troops broke into column and marched before the general on Bay Street. The soldiers retained the precision they had mastered on the Army of the Potomac's drill fields. "It is said the 20th Corps has won the prize," Major Warner remarked. Corps commander Alpheus Williams boasted, "Hundreds of officers have told me it was the finest and most splendid review they ever saw." Elite white women claimed in postwar memoirs to have ignored the parades. "Everyone's shutters were tightly closed," asserted Eleanor Kinzie Gordon. But she admitted that her two young daughters stood on chairs to watch the reviews through the parlor window blinds. One of them was the future founder of the Girls Scouts of America, Juliette Gordon Low.[14]

Union soldiers printed two newspapers, the *Loyal Georgian* (which was subsumed after three issues by the *Savannah Republican*) and the *Savannah Daily Herald*. Members of the 154th enjoyed sending copies home as examples of "the Yankee spirit in Savannah," as Marcellus Darling put it. City residents scorned the papers. When the *Loyal Georgian* declared Savannah had been redeemed and regenerated, Fanny Cohen Taylor wrote, it was "the first time I had a hearty laugh since the Goths had been among us." Many years after he sold newspapers as a youth at the parade ground encampments, a Savannah man recalled winning customers with his honesty. When soldiers asked if he was for the Union or a rebel, he replied, "I'm a rebel, sir!"[15]

"The boys are dancing," Francis Bowen noted in his diary on the night of January 4, 1865, "and the darkies are jigging and patting and singing." By now, the ex-slaves were considered part of the 154th's regimental family. In a postwar reminiscence, Sergeant Major William A. Farlee recalled a facetious muster-in ceremony to initiate these black cooks, servants, and pioneers as "official" members. The candidate was put on a blanket or tarpaulin gripped by a ring of soldiers. At a shouted command, the inductee was tossed and tumbled for a while, after which he was declared to be a member of the regiment in good standing.[16]

Blanket tossing was a favorite amusement, whether the bouncer was black or white. Sergeant Fergus Elliott of the 109th Pennsylvania recorded tremendous cheering in the 154th's camp in his diary on January 20, 1865. "They were amusing themselves by tossing up niggers in a blanket with no regard for sex, as the cheering greatly increased when one of the softer sex was tossed." Regimental veterans remembered blanket tossing was used occasionally as a mild punishment. A sergeant was sentenced to a session on the blanket when he was found guilty of stealing firewood. Three black women who entered the regiment's camp in violation of the smallpox-induced ban on outsiders were punished with a tossing.[17]

Not all of the soldiers' amusements were so innocent. Brothels were plentiful in Savannah; a Union sentinel guarded each. On duty in January 1865, Mervin Barber recorded "a good deal of disturbance at the houses of ill fame." The *Savannah Republican* railed against the disgraceful scenes at one "den of infamy" on Abercorn Street, where disgusting exhibitions appalled passersby and shameless officers mingled in the vulgar crowd.[18]

On the second day in the city Alex Bird noted, "The regiment all got pretty drunk." Drunkenness was prevalent in the army, wrote Emory Sweetland. "There are but very few in our regiment that do not get tight about as often as they can get liquor, and I scarcely know anyone that does not smoke or chew tobacco, and generally both." Citing excessive drinking among officers, Colonel Mindil banned the sale of whiskey to members of the brigade and promised prompt punishment for intoxication.[19]

Soldiers also found innocuous amusements. Edgar Shannon wasted two dollars on a theatrical performance that he deemed no better than a schoolchildren's production. After a crowd of rowdy soldiers rioted at a theater, requiring two regiments to restore order, General Geary ordered a brief curtailment of "exhibitions or amusements of any kind." It was a pity that so many soldiers and civilians should be deprived of public amusement because of "the ungentlemanly bearing of a few men," the *Savannah Republican* lamented. A later order banned public dances "or any other kind of amusements" without a special permit from the provost marshal. No license was to be granted to "any exhibition of a low order."[20]

Religion kept some men on the straight and narrow. While other men played cards, Levi Bryant assured his wife, he read his Bible and prayed for his family. In more than a month at Savannah, Chaplain William Norton preached to the regiment only once. Instead, together with United States Christian Commission clergymen, he conducted daily services in city churches, where Yankee soldiers and southern civilians mingled peacefully. On New Year's Day, General Sherman and many of his soldiers, including Major Warner and other members of the 154th, attended the Independent Presbyterian Church on Bull Street. Two Sundays later Warner attended a church densely crowded with soldiers. Job Dawley also went to church that day and wished he knew a woman to sit with.[21]

Details were occasionally sent to work on immense fortifications outside the city, but for the most part, the 154th New York did provost duty in Savannah. About forty-five men formed squads every morning in front of the city and county jail and were assigned to patrol neighborhoods and to guard houses, stores, and warehouses. Special orders sent details to fatigue duty on the wharf and to guard duty at the "Pest Hospital." Colonel Jones ordered the men of his brigade to dress and equip themselves in the best possible manner, with clean weapons, blackened shoes, and bright brasses. Colonel Mindil ordered the regimental commanders to outfit their men with tin 20th Corps star badges. The soldiers polished their muskets for afternoon dress parades, which attracted citizen spectators. They policed the city proudly, "strutting up and down the street," observed a chaplain, "pregnant with their own importance and superiority."[22]

Sherman was quartered in Savannah and lauded the peace kept by the White Star division. "No city was ever occupied with less disorder or more system than this of Savannah," Sherman boasted on New Year's Eve, adding that "women and children of an hostile people walk its streets with as much security as they do in Philadelphia." That same day he wrote to Grant, "The people here seem to be well content as they have reason to be, for our troops have behaved magnificently. You would think it is Sunday, so quiet is everything in the city day and night." Still, the self-described "Vandal Chief" acknowledged the inhabitants' enmity and fear of his men: "They regard us just as the Romans did the Goths and the parallel is not unjust. Many of my stalwart men with red beards and huge frames look like giants."[23]

According to Sherman's staff officers, the "giants" were gentle in Savannah. The good conduct of Geary's men was apparent, Major

Hitchcock asserted, and lauded by the citizens. Unlike Emory Sweetland, Hitchcock had seen only two drunken soldiers in the city, and both of them were being escorted to the guardhouse. Acting aide-de-camp Major George W. Nichols painted a peaceful picture of ladies strolling city streets in perfect confidence and security and children playing in the squares. In his memoirs, Sherman recalled Savannah as placid. Women daily flocked to hear army bands at guard mountings, dress parades, and reviews; schools were open; the churches were full every Sunday; and markets for provisions and wood were established to cater to the general population, regardless of race or political persuasion. Sherman concluded, "I doubt if Savannah, either before or since, has had a better government than during our stay."[24]

Nichols lauded Geary's work as military governor of Savannah, praising the general as hospitable, sensible, discreet, firm, effective, and popular with the citizens. "No city was ever kept in better order. Clean streets, careful and well-instructed guards, perfect protection of property, and a general sense of comfort and security, indicate the executive capacity and the good judgment of the general." Residents admitted the city had never been so well ordered and safe in peacetime. A Confederate captain who visited under a flag of truce found Savannah to be "as orderly as could possibly be, guards being stationed at almost every house to prevent the people [from] being molested."[25]

The *Savannah Republican* attributed the city's quiet to an amiable partnership between occupiers and occupied. The soldiers' excellent discipline had imposed order where violence threatened. Few outrages had occurred considering the numbers of soldiers and inhabitants in town. Occasional "departures from decorum" were "exceptions to the general good conduct." Friendly visits took place between civilians and soldiers, the paper observed, without any threats or cut throats. "It will pass into history to the credit of both parties that one has used victory with moderation, while the other has evinced philosophical resignation to that which was inevitable."[26]

Savannah residents were surprised by the arrival of Geary's division. Startled by the news, Jane Wallace Howard dressed and ran downstairs to find a column of troops marching down her street. Troops tramping around a square wakened one woman, while another was aroused by her black maid's cries of Yankees thick as bees. The rebel departure was so quiet that the first many residents knew of it was that morning's sight of blue-clad soldiers.[27]

Marcellus Darling estimated that about sixteen thousand of the twenty thousand civilians in Savannah were women and children. Unlike the ill-fated Atlantans, Savannahians were not forcibly expelled from their city; Sherman gave them the option of staying or leaving. Only about two hundred chose to depart. George Mason noted a war weariness among those who remained. Most of them took an oath of allegiance to the United States, he reported (although how many actually did is uncertain). To Edgar Shannon, the residents were "bitter as slaves towards us and would like to see every man of us sunk." There were some Unionists in the city, Charles Abell observed, but "as a general thing the people are Rebs, and the *women* more so than the men." They had as much respect and admiration for Yankees as for the devil. When the soldiers strung United States flags over certain streets, some women refused to walk beneath them. Many women wore black during the occupation, as if in mourning.[28]

"I am acquainted with a few females now," Job Dawley reported, "but it does not seem much like the North." Patriotic Confederate women avoided the Yankees as much as possible. In a UDC account, Mary Cheves West stated that female relatives and friends cloistered themselves in her home. Numerous soldiers called at the front door but were turned away. When bummers attempted to steal some hay, West's mother immediately sent a note to Sherman requesting protection. In response, two staff officers moved in with the family, and Sherman himself stopped by for an awkward visit.[29]

Fanny Cohen Taylor kept a diary of her "gloomy life" during the occupation, when she was "dreadfully depressed." She spent her saddest Christmas ever and bemoaned a New Year's Day surrounded by enemies. When a Confederate surgeon visited her family, Taylor called it the first pleasurable moment she had since the vandals entered the city. At another get-together she and her guests "abused the Yankees to our hearts content." Taylor rejected any conciliatory feelings toward the enemy. "If we are conquered," she wrote, "I see no reason why we should receive our enemies as our friends and I never shall do it as long as I live."[30]

Savannah women had awaited the arrival of Sherman's army with fears of rape stoked by lurid rumors and newspaper tales. The general good conduct of Geary's men put such fears to rest. Most women made their antipathy toward the Yankees clear, but icy hostility sometimes melted in the warmth of romance. Major Nichols of Sherman's staff noticed enlisted men lounging with fair damsels on doorsteps and officers snuggling with ringlet-haired maidens on carriage rides. There was, he wrote, "a delightful *entente cordiale* between the officers and ladies." Most southern women resisted romantic entanglements with the enemy as unpatriotic, however, and those who consorted with the Yankees faced ostracism. Love between northern soldier and southern belle certainly blossomed in postwar literature. Nichols started the trend in an 1866 novel, and the theme became a staple in fiction about Sherman's campaigns. These romances—symbolizing reunion and reconciliation between the two sections—were popular in the North but inspired a backlash from southern women writers, who criticized intersectional love affairs and preferred to depict the Yankees as cads.[31]

Savannah's food supplies were precariously low when the city fell; the residents depended on a monotonous diet of rice and seafood. Sherman ordered Mayor Richard Arnold and the aldermen (who continued their civic functions) to distribute captured provisions and army rations to the destitute. Relief supplies shipped from the North augmented the handouts. The provisions "were *very much* needed by a great many poor," wrote Charles Abell; the residents "owe a great deal more to the Yankees than I guess they like to acknowledge." Indeed, Elizabeth Mackay Stiles sneered, "They think they are so liberal, giving us food, and they stole more from one plantation than the whole of New York subscribed." In her opinion the rations were insufficient, and she suspected blacks received more than whites. Abell thought corrupt civilian committees distributed proportionally more to the rich than to the poor. Some Savannah women refused to accept the enemy's aid. Mayor Arnold was more grateful; he later reported that the donated supplies and government rations fed the city until the end of the war and two months beyond.[32]

Despite the assistance, Savannahians struggled to get by. When the formerly prosperous Mrs. G. W. Anderson found herself penniless, former slaves shared food with her family, and she slaughtered some poultry and a pet calf and hoarded some rice and flour. All in all, she reported, "We have made out very well." Countless residents made money selling food and other goods to the soldiers. "These Yankees all want something sweet," a woman remarked, "and we want some greenbacks." The soldiers paid well for whatever the citizens offered. Cakes and pies were sure sellers. A Savannah man later recalled his little sisters selling sacks of roasted peanuts from their stoop to passing soldiers. William A. Pigman remembered peddling dozens of boxes of cigars to the Yankees as a boy. Some white women resorted to selling their fine dresses and ball gowns to black women.[33]

Savannah's black residents were as delighted with the Yankees' arrival as the whites were despondent. A black Baptist minister, the Reverend James Simms, remembered, "The cry went around the city from house to house among our race of people, 'Glory be to God, we are free!'" A white woman listened morosely as a young black girl jumped up and down below her window, singing loudly, "All the rebel gone to hell, now Par Sherman come." Black joy fed white disgust. "Poor deluded creatures," sniffed Elizabeth Mackay Stiles, "with all their suffering they consider themselves in Seventh Heaven—freedom and laziness is such a boon."[34]

White Savannahians were dismayed by how quickly their black chattels embraced freedom. The morning Geary's division entered the city, Caroline A. N. Lamar's slave William decamped to the Yankees. On information he provided, soldiers removed great quantities of spirits from the Lamar house. A day later, Fanny Cohen Taylor's house slave departed, "anxious to enlist in the Federal service." "You can form no conception of the utter demoralization of the servants," wrote Mrs. G. W. Anderson; many families were left without a single slave. She appended a lengthy list of "petted servants" that had deserted her, and she expected others to follow. Blacks from the countryside had flocked to the city and, she worried, "must plunder for a living." She feared for the result if Savannah was left without proper policing.[35]

Most slaves, even those thought to be loyal, fled to the Yankees. Some voiced bitterness at the treatment they had endured from whites; others were magnanimous in forgiving their former masters. For their part, whites were alternately hurt, angry, and befuddled by the betrayal. In a letter to her husband, Caroline Lamar listed defectors among their slaves. The laundress left without a word, leaving her work undone. Of four other women, only one promised to stay briefly; the other three decamped. White women suddenly found themselves performing unfamiliar household tasks. Fanny Cohen Taylor darned her own stockings for the first time in her life.[36]

When Geary's division arrived in Savannah, Jane Wallace Howard noted the soldiers and the blacks appeared to be "on the most intimate terms—a perfect equality prevails." Another woman claimed the Yankees mistreated the blacks, searching their houses, stealing from them, and cursing, abusing, and insulting the females. Army officers often set blacks to menial labor, while black criminals were sentenced to toil in the streets wearing a ball and chain. Some ex-slaves refused to work for either white civilians or the Yankees. Sarah Gordon deplored the sight of blacks "just loafing around doing nothing, when before they were active, happy, and always at work. They seem to think that their liberty consists in lounging around, with hands in their pockets, looking up at the trees." "Poor deluded creatures," wrote Caroline Lamar. "The streets are just filled with them. Sherman says he cannot care for the poor whites, much less the Negroes; they must take care of themselves."[37]

Sherman, no particular friend to blacks, later asserted in his memoirs, "No army ever did more for that race than the one I commanded in Savannah." The military took steps to feed the many black refugees arriving in the city, but it was accused of discriminating against them in the distribution of relief supplies. Furthermore, hundreds of miserable blacks were shipped to South Carolina's Sea Islands, which were already teeming with refugees. On January 16 Sherman issued his famous special order setting aside a lengthy swath of those lands for black settlement, granting each family forty acres. Savannah's black community generally received the order with enthusiasm, and a mass exodus to the islands ensued after Geary's division left the city. But when the war ended, the federal government betrayed black settlers when ex-Confederates successfully reclaimed the lands.[38]

Stopping at a house to see if he could buy some food, Corporal George Brown of Company A met a light-skinned family of former slaves, including an attractive teenaged girl. They offered to bake Brown a hoecake, and while they worked, they told him how they had aided escaped Union prisoners. When Brown offered to pay for the food, they refused his money. Back at his hut, Brown declared to his tent mate, Andrew Blood, that he had been a Democrat but was now an abolitionist. He could no longer support a party that would leave enslaved the beautiful young lady he met that day.[39]

During the regiment's stay in Savannah, Charles Abell informed his home folk that he had formed an acquaintance with the Harris family. When he visited them, it made him feel more at home than he had "since I left that *dear roof.*" The husband and father had deserted the family, but Mrs. Harris was a kind and good woman. "Many of the ladies are bitter Rebs," Abell wrote, "but she is (at heart) true to the old banner." Abell felt that passing an evening chatting with Mrs. Harris was much more advantageous than spending his time and money at museums or theaters.[40]

For their part, white Savannahians reported encounters with Yankees both good and bad. Jane Wallace Howard and her sister baked pumpkin pies and sold them to the soldiers, netting fifteen dollars in greenbacks. Inspired by their success, the girls' cousins baked cakes and sent a young boy out to sell them, with disastrous results. Soldiers threw the lad to the ground, broke his tray, and ate the cakes. Fifteen-year-old Theodore Basch reported that soldiers stripped his father's store of its goods before guards were posted. A postwar reminiscence told of Mrs. Fritz Steckle, an ethnic steel magnolia. When three Yankees invaded her home and threatened to rip open her feather mattress in a search for gold, Mrs. Steckle defied the miscreants and shamed them into leaving.[41]

"Frown down every act of discourtesy and violence," the *Savannah Republican* exhorted the soldiers, "and by your personal example you can defeat and put to shame the few ruffians that must ever be found in armies." The good behavior of Savannahians, it added, entitled them to courteous treatment. Perhaps more effective than newspaper harangues were actual punishments. Years after the war a man recalled a vivid boyhood sight on the parade ground: as a sentence for some crime, a soldier was strapped naked to a cannon.[42]

Savannahians found Geary's men to be generally well behaved. "The city is very quiet," an aunt wrote to her niece, "the soldiers very respectful." "The Federal officers are very polite," Mrs. G. W. Anderson wrote, "and even kind." Even in their postwar reminiscences, Savannah women acknowledged the enemy's general decency. Mary Bond wrote, "We found they were not as terrible as we had expected." A postwar tale told of a South Carolina woman who entered the city to search for her husband, a desperately ill exchanged prisoner. She found him in a hospital and secured his release. Then she went to Geary, who provided her with a pass through the lines, boat transportation home, an ambulance ride to the wharf, and a soldier to help them on board. She never forgot the Yankees' help and sympathy.[43]

Young Savannah white boys occasionally received gifts from the soldiers. One lad, fascinated by the drummers in the square opposite his home, was thrilled when one of the musicians promised him a drum. "He is so excited and happy that he would not go back to Confederate days for any consideration," his mother wrote. South of the 154th's campsite was an area where the army's horses and mules were corralled. A Yankee took William Pigman there and told him to help himself to any animal he wanted. Pigman brought home a mule, but his father made him sell it when it began gnawing on the family's fence. Another boy who received a horse from a Yankee officer was devastated when his father rode the animal and it died.[44]

Old habits proved hard to break. William Pigman's family had some fowl in their yard that were irresistible to the soldiers, who climbed the fence and took some birds. Pigman's family reported the thefts to an officer, who assigned a guard to protect the remaining poultry. Conversely, a northern journalist was surprised to see chickens pecking corn in the streets and asked an officer why the birds went unharmed. The army had lived on chickens all the way from Atlanta, the officer replied. "We have had roast chicken, fried chicken, and stewed chicken, till we are tired of it."[45]

Many Savannah families were ambivalent about housing Yankee officers. Sheltering the enemy was distasteful, but the security and rental income was welcome. In the end they had no choice, and the intrusions were tolerated with relatively good humor, if a bit strained. A Union general roomed at Fanny Cohen Taylor's home, and her hostility evaporated in the face of his consideration. Caroline Lamar's parlor housed two quiet, orderly, and respectful surgeons. Seeking protection, Mary Bond rented a room to two gentlemanly captains, one of whom secured rations for her family. Alex Bird dined at a Tattnal Street boardinghouse but unfortunately left no account of his interactions with the occupants.[46]

Descendants of Anne Flood handed down a poignant story of kindness between enemies. Flood was sixteen years old and alone during the occupation; her mother was dead and her father was a prisoner of war. When a young soldier knocked on her door one night and asked for something to eat, the terrified girl initially refused. Then she changed her mind and told him to wait in the yard. A few minutes later she set a tin plate bearing a large sandwich on the stoop. "Thankee, Ma'am," came a call from the darkness. "For all he knows, it could be poisoned," Flood thought as she closed the door. A while later she opened the door to retrieve her plate. On it sat a small tin of condensed milk.[47]

In the end, Savannahians realized that compared with their fellow Georgians, they had been fortunate. "General Sherman's troops have treated the citizens and private property well here," admitted Eleanor Kinzie Gordon. Thinking of her friends who had fled the city on Sherman's approach, Elizabeth Mackay Stiles wrote, "No woman would have gone had we known as much as we do now." Learning of the Yankees' benign rule in Savannah, a Confederate officer wrote, "I am rejoiced to hear that General Sherman's policy toward our people is marked with humanity and kindness."[48]

As 1865 opened, Geary's men were uncertain whether they would stay in Savannah or leave on another campaign. "I would prefer to remain here but it will make no great difference," Major Warner wrote on January 9. "It is better for the morale of the men to go than to stay." Six days later Warner wrote, "It is pretty certain that General Geary is to leave here and that we are to go with him." The same day, Chaplain Norton informed his daughter that he was expecting to leave on another campaign. "I rather dread it," he wrote; he expected worse weather and more opposition than on the previous march.[49]

The enlisted men resigned themselves to leaving Savannah. "Sherman ain't a-going to let his army lay still," Levi Bryant observed; the general would "shove them right along this winter." Marcellus Darling told his family they would soon hear more of Sherman's movements. Emory Sweetland anticipated more fighting: "I am afraid that we shall have to give the Rebs some hard knocks this spring before that they will cave in."[50]

While the rank and file speculated, their commander completed his plans. Before Savannah fell, Grant had ordered Sherman to man a small coastal base and transport the bulk of his army by water to the Virginia front. Sherman did not vigorously argue Grant's plan, but he hoped to capture Savannah before the transfer occurred. After the city fell, Sherman urged a march overland to join Grant, suggesting, "I could go on and smash South Carolina all to pieces." Grant then changed his mind and gave Sherman permission to march through the Carolinas. A relieved Sherman voiced his philosophy to the army's chief of staff, Major General Henry W. Halleck. The Federal forces were fighting a hostile people as well as hostile armies, and he intended to make all civilians, "old and young, rich and poor, feel the hard hand of war." The march through Georgia had "a wonderful effect in this respect," as would a movement through the Carolinas. His army was "burning with an insatiable desire to wreak vengeance upon South Carolina," he wrote. "I almost tremble at her fate, but feel that she deserves all that seems in store for her."[51]

As a new campaign loomed, both commander and army continued to share a bold assurance. "This army has a confidence in itself that makes it almost irresistible," Sherman boasted to Grant. To his father-in-law Sherman declared of his soldiers, "They will march to certain death if I order it," knowing that he labored not to lose lives in vain. "Every officer and man with me thinks he would be lost unless I am at hand," Sherman informed his brother. "I hear the soldiers talk as I ride by—'There goes the old man. All's right.'" To his wife Sherman bragged, "The soldiers manifest to me the most thorough affection, and a wonderful confidence." The men believed he had been everywhere in the South and exclaimed, "The 'Old Man' must be 'omnipresent' as well as omnipotent."[52]

With his plans approved, Sherman set his army in motion. By January 17 the 1st and 3rd divisions of the 20th Corps had left Savannah's outskirts and crossed into South Carolina. That day a regiment of Brigadier General Cuvier Grover's division of the 19th Corps, newly arrived from Maryland, camped adjacent to the 154th New York, set to relieve the regiment on its departure. Geary ordered his division to be ready to move on January 20, but the appointed time came and went uneventfully. The roads near the Savannah River were under water and impassable. After several days of rain, the weather broke, the mud dried, and orders arrived on January 25 to be ready to march the next morning. That evening the orders were countermanded; the next day, they were reissued. "There is not much doubt this time with regard to our going tomorrow," Major Warner wrote. He was right.[53]

Savannahians regretted the impending departure of Geary's division. "The citizens are bound to have us stay," Gene Graves wrote. "They have sent a petition to Washington to that effect." The document praised Geary as an urbane gentleman, uniformly kind to the citizens, who had done all he could to protect them and their property from insult and injury. The petitioners pleaded unanimously that he be allowed to remain as commandant. But Geary's White Stars were bound to leave; Savannah's citizens would have to get used to Grover's troops. When that became obvious, the city council passed resolutions thanking Geary for great judgment in the conduct of his business and promising to forever remember him as a high-toned gentleman and a chivalrous soldier. Geary reciprocated with an order thanking the mayor and aldermen and citizens in general for their cordial acquiescence and assistance.[54]

Facing a new campaign, Geary's men wondered how it would compare with the march through Georgia. "If we have as good a time on this [campaign] as we did on the other," wrote Almon Deforest Reed, "I shall be satisfied pretty well." Edgar Shannon had a prophetic vision of what was to come. "When it is cold and muddy," he told his sweetheart, "you sit by your fire and think of me in the mud up to my knees."[55]

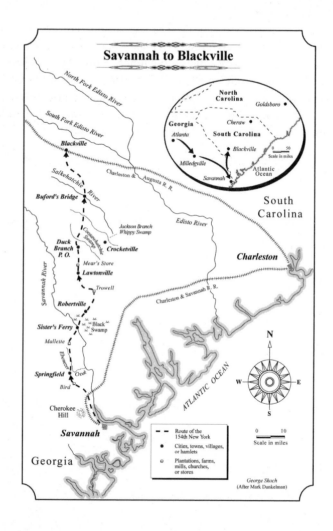

Savannah to Blackville

North Fork Edisto River

South Fork Edisto River

Blackville

Salkehatchie River

Charleston & Augusta R. R.

Buford's Bridge

Jackson Branch
Whippy Swamp

Coosawhatchie
Swamp

**Duck
Branch
P. O.**

Crocketville

Mear's Store

Lawtonville

Trowell

Edisto River

Robertville

Sister's Ferry

Mallette

Black
Swamp

Savannah River

Charleston & Savannah R. R.

Springfield

Ebenezer Creek

Bird

Cherokee
Hill

Savannah

Georgia

South
Carolina

Charleston

ATLANTIC OCEAN

North
Carolina

Goldsboro

Georgia

Cheraw

South Carolina

Atlanta

Blackville

Milledgville

Savannah

Atlantic
Ocean

0   50
Scale in miles

N

W   E

S

- - - Route of the
        154th New York

• Cities, towns, villages,
   or hamlets

▫ Plantations, farms,
   mills, churches,
   or stores

0   10
Scale in miles

*George Skoch
(After Mark Dunkelman)*

[8]

To Lexington Court House

*F*riday, January 27, 1865. The 154th New York, shouldering 131 muskets, left Savannah at eight o'clock on a chilly morning. "The boys felt well," recorded Alex Bird, "and we marched out beyond Cherokee Hill." During the day the frozen road thawed into mud. Marching ahead of the wagon train, the regiment made good time and encamped before nightfall near the Charleston and Savannah Railroad twelve miles from Savannah, on wet ground Major Lewis Warner deemed "the worst place I ever encamped in."[1]

The regiment would work with the wagon train frequently in this campaign. The 2nd Division caravan consisted of 159 wagons (each pulled by a six-mule team) and 33 ambulances (each drawn by two horses). Cargo included rations, fodder for the animals, and ammunition. Except when marching as advance or rear guard, the troops gave the train the road and marched alongside. Each brigade, regiment, and company was assigned a number of wagons to accompany. Thirteen pack mules were allotted to each regiment, and others were used at headquarters; altogether, the division harnessed more than two hundred mules. Each brigade had a pioneer company of about thirty soldiers and a tool wagon equipped with axes, spades, and picks. A pioneer company of seventy-five black men marched with the advance guard to repair the road. On this day Geary's men accompanied the trains of the entire 20th Corps and Left Wing headquarters—in all, about three hundred wagons. The 1st and 3rd divisions had already crossed the Savannah River into South Carolina; two weeks would pass before the corps would be reunited.[2]

Mary Cheves West recalled the departure of Geary's men from Savannah in negative terms in her postwar UDC memoir, describing them as a motley, plunder-laden crowd that left behind disorder, chaos, and dead horses. But wartime Savannah residents missed Geary and his well-behaved troops. They disliked the new commandant, Cuvier Grover, who banished the wives of Confederate soldiers from the city and instituted other unpopular measures. The situation worsened, in white Savannahians' eyes, when black troops arrived in March 1865 to garrison the city.[3]

Saturday, January 28, 1865. The march resumed at 6:00 a.m. over frozen ground. Poor roads ran through level, swampy terrain that Emory Sweetland, a new diarist with an eye for local flora, described as timbered with pines, palmettos, giant cacti, and cypresses whose limbs were hung with Spanish moss. During the day the regiment marched about thirteen miles, entered Effingham County for the second time, and camped about 3:00 p.m. in a pinewoods on the plantation of Maria Bird, a widow whose son was colonel of a Georgia cavalry regiment.[4]

Sunday, January 29, 1865. The 154th moved out at seven o'clock on a cold morning as guard to the ammunition wagons. The convoy made slow progress over bad roads, passing through Springfield about 10 a.m. Since the regiment saw it on the way to Savannah the previous month, the village had been mostly destroyed and its live oaks cut down for firewood by Joseph Wheeler's Confederate cavalry. Beyond Springfield, the men corduroyed the road through swamps bordering Ebenezer Creek. After covering about ten total miles, they camped in midafternoon on Judge Mallette's plantation.[5]

The return to long-distance marching under heavy loads was hard on some soldiers; Levi Bryant confessed that he was very lame. Details were ordered to guard the wagon train through the night, although, as Major Warner noted, no enemy had been seen. News arrived that a large fire broke out in Savannah near midnight on January 27 and spread to an arsenal, causing a massive explosion and raging until daylight. Geary's men would have better controlled the blaze, thought Private David S. Jones of Company K: "I guess the citizens wish the White Stars back again."[6]

"Have not seen but six houses that were occupied since leaving Savannah," Emory Sweetland noted. One of them, just beyond Ebenezer Creek, was the home of Unionist Christopher F. Reisser, his wife, Charlotte, and their seventeen children. A small foraging party had visited the family during the March to the Sea and gathered a modest stock of supplies. Now Geary's division and a division of the 14th Corps stripped the rich farm bare in about half an hour. "They was thick as bees," Charlotte Reisser remembered in a Southern Claims Commission affidavit. "Some was taking and some were not taking," she added, but "all took an interest in it some way."[7]

Monday, January 30, 1865. The weather warmed, and the men enjoyed a quiet rest in camp. Before they could cross the flooded Savannah River, a pontoon bridge had to be laid, the boggy road on the opposite shore had to be corduroyed, and torpedoes planted by the enemy (in the mode of modern land mines) had to be detected and dug. The pioneers tackled those tasks, and a detail from the 154th was sent to help.[8]

Tuesday, January 31, 1865. The regiment remained in camp on another nice day. Some of the men were assigned to picket duty. Back in Savannah, Private John I. Snyder of Company D died at an army hospital. Sixteen days earlier the eighteen-year-old recruit had been admitted with a case of the measles; he recovered only to be stricken with remittent fever. Snyder was initially buried in Savannah's Laurel Grove Cemetery; in the postwar years he was reinterred in South Carolina's Beaufort National Cemetery.[9]

Wednesday, February 1, 1865. Colonel George Mindil reviewed and inspected the 2nd Brigade and found it to be "in splendid order for the field." The 154th relocated its camp in the afternoon of another warm day. Across the Savannah River in South Carolina, Lieutenant Winfield S. Cameron of Company B, serving on General Pap Williams's staff, carried a dispatch to Sherman. Years later Cameron recalled the encounter. Sherman insisted Cameron join him for supper, during which the general regaled the lieutenant with stories. He told of hearing a soldier say, "There comes Uncle Billy. I have known him these four years and he's got the same stump of a cigar in his mouth he had when I first knew him." Sherman laughed heartily at the quip, and Cameron left headquarters charmed by his chatty commander.[10]

Thursday, February 2, 1865. A cloudy morning portended a storm. The men passed time by fixing up their tents. One of the recruits composed a letter to his hometown newspaper. "It is uncertain how long we shall remain here," he wrote; the regiment could march the next day or in a month. He predicted the enemy would defend potential destinations to the best of their ability. "But," he boasted, "Sherman's head is too long and too well filled for them Johnnies." The men expected hard fighting. "We are ready for the worst," he asserted, "if it only benefits the country." Emory Sweetland guessed that the regiment would start in a day or two on a raid to Augusta, and he looked forward to it. "The boys fare better when detached and sent on raids," he opined, "and they like it pretty well." A large amount of mail arrived in camp on this day, causing the usual excitement. Major Warner received his well-earned commission as lieutenant colonel, but some time would pass before he was mustered in at that rank.[11]

Friday, February 3, 1865. Intermittent rain fell during the day. Some of the men watched a horse race. Emory Sweetland paid fifty cents to have his laundry done. Someone in camp killed a five-foot-long rattlesnake. A number of sick men were sent back to Savannah, among them Francis Bowen, suffering from a kidney ailment. All in all, the 2nd Division hospital sent some twenty-five sick soldiers to the city, six of them smallpox patients. This day ended with an aggravation. Just before nightfall, the regiment received an order to pack up and move to a location near division headquarters. They had no sooner done so than they were ordered back to their original location, where they pitched their tents and endured a wet night.[12]

Saturday, February 4, 1865. Soon after daylight the men struck their tents and marched through fog and rain to Sisters Ferry, where they waited until noon to cross the Savannah River into South Carolina. Gunboats and steamers bobbed in the water as the men tramped over a pontoon bridge into Beaufort District. They moved upriver about two miles to a landing and halted for dinner. Wagons were loaded with rations for the campaign, and the men were issued three days' worth. Then they took up the march on a terrible road through a swamp. The entire way had to be corduroyed; stands of timber offered plenty of material for the pioneers. The weather cleared and warmed, but the roads remained wretched. The men slogged to within a mile and a half of Robertville and camped just after dark. The 154th was assigned to picket duty overnight.[13]

The first state to secede from the Union and the place where the war began would now feel the wrath of Sherman's men. The troops felt "extreme bitterness" toward South Carolinia and were "eager to commence the punishment of 'original secessionists,'" wrote the *New York Herald*'s David Conyngham, who was again with the army. General Geary put it bluntly in a letter to his wife: "The state is doomed to utter destruction." General Sherman was aware of his men's mood. "The whole army is crazy to be turned loose in [South] Carolina," he wrote. He believed that the state deserved punishment and that northerners and southerners alike would rejoice to see it devastated as Georgia had been. Sherman told a South Carolinian Unionist refugee, however, that he would not enter the state bent on destruction but to vindicate the government's power. In her postwar UDC memoir, Mary Cheves West claimed Sherman promised to desolate South Carolina. Northerners had urged him to burn and destroy everything in the state, she quoted him as saying, and he would not leave a house standing.[14]

Sunday, February 5, 1865. Major Warner supervised a work party building a road for the trains through three miles of the Black Swamp. The men toiled in the mud until noon, when they returned to camp. The pickets were called in and the regiment marched at 2:00 p.m., covering seven miles at a rapid pace over good roads on a warm day and camping before sunset. The route ran through Robertville, which originally consisted of about twenty houses and a Baptist church. "But the smoking ruins and bare chimneys tell a sad tale of war," Emory Sweetland observed. "The church is all that is left of this once handsome village."[15]

Among the Robertville residents who fled the Yankees' approach was Nancy Bostick DeSaussure. Late in life she wrote that before she left she set daguerreotypes of her Pennsylvania schoolmates on her mantel, hoping some Yankee would recognize a relative and spare her house. When she finally returned, a single fence was all that was left standing in the entire village. The Baptist church, intact when the 154th New York passed through, had also been burned.[16]

Geary's division camped this night at a crossroads near Thomas Trowell's plantation. In the bushes near the big house were found the corpses of three Union soldiers. Local blacks testified that Trowell had pointed out the Yankees to some Confederate cavalrymen, who shot them in cold blood. Geary had the victims buried and Trowell's house and property destroyed and held Trowell to be tried as accessory to murder. Trowell's fate went unrecorded in the general's report.[17]

Monday, February 6, 1865. Assigned to accompany the train as rear guard, the 154th did not move until 11:00 a.m. Drizzle fell most of the raw day. Although the roads ran through swamps, they were passable. About two hours into the march the regiment went by a plantation that—unlike its neighbors—had not been harmed because the occupants had the Stars and Stripes flying from a window. It was illegal to possess a United States flag in the Confederacy, so this banner presumably had been hidden away for three years. The march continued through the ruins of Lawtonville, which had been totally destroyed by Union troops. The regiment made good time, covering about thirteen miles before halting near E. R. Mears's store and pitching camp soon after dark on a wet night. "A very good country through here," Emory Sweetland noted, "but looking rather desolate with buildings and fences destroyed." Nearly all the structures had been burned, Major Warner wrote; only their tall chimneys survived. Even some of them were torn down.[18]

Lore handed down by Lawtonville's Rhodes family celebrated a once wealthy planter who preserved his composure in the midst of ruin. As a signer of South Carolina's secession ordinance, George Rhodes feared for his life at the hands of Sherman's men, so he and his family packed up their valuables and fled the army's approach. When they returned, they found all the plantation's buildings burned except a carriage house, in which they camped while a modest home was built. The impoverished Rhodes did not become bitter and resentful, his descendants claimed. Rather, he "continued to love and serve his family, his church, and his community" and spent his later years "enjoying his books and his memories," watching the sunset over his broad fields as he sipped his after-dinner peach brandy.[19]

Tuesday, February 7, 1865. A 6:00 a.m. order to march was countermanded, and the men were instructed to remain in camp until further notice. Two hours later they got under way in a cold drizzle, grumbling about the disagreeable weather and the horrible roads. As the column slogged through ten miles of deep mud, passing through the ruins of Duck Branch Post Office, Geary put six hundred pioneers to work.

Some laid corduroy in waist-deep water where the road dipped into Coosawhatchie Swamp while others constructed a footbridge. During the day the 2nd Division entered Barnwell District. In the afternoon it grew colder. Camp was made an hour after darkness fell. Not all was bleak this day. The foragers were successful and the men ate well, a welcome mail reached the regiment, and many black families rejoiced to reach the army.[20]

In their later years, area ex-slaves recalled the awe of encountering Sherman's hordes. There were thousands of them, Henry Pristell remembered, thick as weeds and as closely aligned as panels on a fence. They killed all the livestock and poultry on the plantation— and barbequed meat over a flaming fence—but they did not burn the houses of blacks or whites, he asserted, or harm anyone physically. Isaiah Butler was about ten when the Yankees arrived. The first thing they did, he recalled decades later, was to shoot a goat in the barn's loft. Then they tore up everything and burned the big house, but they treated the blacks well and left the slave quarters standing.[21]

Fifteen-year-old Silvia Chisolm was enslaved on the same plantation as Butler. As an old woman, she attributed the burning of the big house to the absence of its owners, who had fled the Yankees' advance. With white males largely absent, Lucy Daniels recollected, "the women had to pile up four or five in one house to protect they selves." But white women who sought shelter with neighbors consigned their abandoned homes to the flames. Former slaves asserted that the homes of the wealthy were burned whether abandoned or not (excepting those of doctors and preachers), while those of poor whites were spared. Some wealthy white women installed poorer neighbors in their houses to protect the structures, Phoebe Faucette recalled, but the soldiers saw through the ruse.[22]

Emory Sweetland wrote that Sherman's army destroyed "most of the private homes" in South Carolina. Abandoned houses were always burned, David Conyngham reported, and occupied homes often met the same fate—"few escaped; and the country was converted into one vast bonfire." Contrary to those assertions, house burning in South Carolina generally moderated as the campaign wore on.[23]

Wednesday, February 8, 1865. The march commenced at 6:00 a.m. on a clear, cold, windy day. Owing to the muddy roads and sluggish trains, the men made slow progress in the forenoon, covering twelve miles that took them across Jackson Branch of Whippy Swamp. At brigade headquarters, Colonel Mindil issued an order condemning straggling and wandering and warned that Union soldiers had been found murdered in the woods. Undeterred, Alex Bird meandered miles away from the main column to Crocketville, where he found nothing standing but the church. Meanwhile, the main column crossed the Salkehatchie River and the adjoining swamp at Buford's Bridge, a series of small bridges with intervening causeways more than half a mile long. Just before sunset the regiment encamped on the northern bank, where the enemy had been forced from fortifications by a flanking maneuver. The men were now eighteen miles south of Blackville, a village on the Charleston and Augusta Railroad.[24]

In a memoir, Confederate army veteran M. M. Brabham recalled his return to Buford's Bridge about two months after Geary's division was there. The Yankees had burned many homes in the neighborhood, and his father and uncle had moved in with his grandmother. Brabham was surprised to find the large clan enjoying three meals a day. The river and streams were teeming with more fish than residents had ever known. That summer, Brabham recalled, the white people "loafed and fished" and directed the remaining blacks in planting crops. New houses arose, and the residents began their recovery from the Yankees' ravages.[25]

On this night Alex Bird wrote in his diary, "Took a double shuffle on a piano." Symbols of social and cultural respectability, pianos frequently met degraded ends at the hands of Sherman's men. "I have often witnessed the ludicrous sight of a lot of bearded, rough soldiers capering about the room in a rude waltz, while some fellow was thumping away unmercifully at the piano, with another cutting grotesque capers on the top-board," wrote reporter David Conyngham. "When they got tired of this saturnalia, the piano was consigned to the flames, and most likely the house with it." Did that happen to the piano Bird danced on, or the house it sat in? He did not say.[26]

Pianos served as musical props in a set of postwar legends that could be called "dramatic piano interludes." Not surprisingly, these stories involve women, the main customers of pianos, piano lessons, and sheet music in the South. Residents along the 154th New York's path related several such tales in the postwar years, indicating they were probably widespread elsewhere along the trail of Sherman's army. Some dramatic piano interludes tell of reconciliation, others of confrontation, and still others of homes preserved as southern women serenaded Yankee soldiers over the keyboard.[27]

One tale involved a piano in the big house of a Blackville-area plantation. When the Yankees approached the place, it was said, all the white males fled, leaving twelve-year-old Kathleen Rosa Tobin in charge of the premises. As bummers swarmed the house, a Yankee officer ordered her to play the piano. Frightened, she struck up the only tune she could think of: "Dixie." The bummers broke out in cheers. The officer called her a brave little rebel and asked what she wanted as a reward. She replied that her mother was very sick upstairs and requested that the house not be burned. The soldiers were immediately ordered out, a guard was posted, "and the old plantation home of the Tobins was spared—a monument of white along the great black trail of ruin."[28]

Thursday, February 9, 1865. After a clear, cold night, the men marched at 6:00 a.m. toward Blackville. The 2nd Brigade was in the lead, and the regiment made good time on better roads over rolling, well-timbered countryside with fewer swamps at a higher elevation. "Passed some nice plantations with good buildings today," noted Emory Sweetland. "A good deal of forage was obtained." Alex Bird returned from his ramble mounted on a mule and bearing sweet potatoes and sorghum. A few flakes of snow fell around noon, the first the men had seen all winter. The regiment halted and pitched camp at 3:30 p.m. within three-quarters of a mile of Blackville, where Geary's division was to rendezvous with the rest of the 20th Corps.[29]

Roughly ten miles east of the main column's line of march stood Forest Home plantation. According to family legend, a group of bummers ransacked the big house, stuffing silver into pillowcases and slashing family portraits (a favorite target). One soldier hacked up a mattress so violently he emerged from the house sneezing and covered in down. Fifteen-year-old John Henry Jennings was heartbroken when a bummer rode off on his favorite horse. In his later years, Jennings refused to discuss the war and remained suspicious of all northerners. He could not blame the Yankees for destroying Forest Home, however, because the big house escaped the torch.[30]

Friday, February 10, 1865. The regiment marched at 7:00 a.m. about a quarter mile and camped on the main road leading into Blackville, expecting to remain while the entire 20th Corps converged. But at noon the 154th was ordered to fall in and moved into a field near the corps train, taking position to guard it. Major Warner posted pickets on the two roads in the regiment's front. General Geary and his 1st and 3rd Brigades departed in the afternoon, leaving Mindil's brigade with the wagons. General Sherman rode into Blackville during the day. Emory Sweetland estimated the town's population at about five hundred. "Most of the place is destroyed," he wrote. "The troops are busily engaged in destroying the railroad."[31]

Preservation tales have been attached to least three antebellum homes that survived the destruction in Blackville. Simon Brown's house was reportedly spared when his wife waved a Masonic flag from the second-story porch, attracting the attention of a sympathetic officer. According to family lore, the home of Dr. William H. Hagood was set afire, but faithful slaves extinguished the blaze and saved the place. Dr. James O. Hagood's house was torched, his grandson related, but it was saved by a young boy who climbed upon the roof, pretended that he was simpleminded, refused to come down, "and insisted upon helping the soldiers *to put the fire out.*" By appearing to be dimwitted, the boy outwitted the Yanks.[32]

When the Yankees arrived at the Blackville home of the Molonys, a family tale relates, they found an old black nanny rocking a white baby in a chair on the front porch. Unbeknownst to the soldiers, the woman was sitting atop a side of meat. When the Yankees left, all the Molony family had to subsist on was the meat saved by the nanny and the proverbial dropped corn left behind by the enemy. ("Picking up dropped corn left by the Federals was an action repeated throughout all of South Carolina," stated a modern-day chronicler, "as many family histories attest.") The dropped corn is but one of two legendary motifs in the Molony story. Along the route of the 154th New York, several old family tales told of women sitting on barrels, beds, or trunks to conceal valuables from thieving Yankees. These stories (also collected in modern versions by Elissa Henken) are legends wherein crafty southern women outwit the Yankees using a simple ruse with biblical origins. In a story from Genesis, Laban searched his daughter Rachel's tent, looking for idols she had stolen from him. Rachel had hidden them in camel trappings and sat atop them, successfully concealing them from her father.[33]

Saturday, February 11, 1865. After a clear, cold night, the regiment marched at 7:00 a.m. as guard to the train and four hours and eight miles later arrived at Duncan's Bridge on the South Fork of the Edisto River. The men camped on the south bank, ate dinner, and watched the engineers and pioneers assemble a pontoon bridge for the passage of the trains, which crossed throughout the night. The Edisto was divided into seven streams, Emory Sweetland noted, "all of which our troops bridged in a few hours."[34]

About two and a half miles north of Blackville the column passed near the Healing Springs Baptist Church and the waters for which it was named. According to local lore, when news of the spring's curative powers spread among the Yankees, soldiers detoured off the main road to fill canteens and barrels with Healing Springs water. The elixir reportedly calmed them, and as a result, wrote a local historian, "the Federals were not as destructive around the springs as in neighboring Blackville."[35]

Perhaps the Yankees in a Boylston family legend had imbibed the soothing water. In this tale, a Yankee officer and four men appeared at the home of Austin and Polly Boylston, near Duncan's Bridge. Expecting their arrival, Polly had baked cornbread and fried ham. The Boylstons fed the five Yankees, and they departed without doing any harm to the house, although they emptied the barn of corn and wheat. Compared with other folks in the region, the Boylstons felt fortunate in incurring such small losses.[36]

Sunday, February 12, 1865. At daybreak the regiment led the brigade across the South Fork of the Edisto River into Orangeburg District and splashed through a swamp. About 1:00 p.m. the column reached Jeffcoat's Bridge on the Edisto River's North Fork, having marched thirteen miles. The enemy had burned the bridge and was in some force across the river. Geary's division was at the head of the reunited 20th Corps. The general threw a couple of his advance regiments across the stream to drive the Confederates away. When night fell, the engineers rebuilt the bridge. The regiment camped near the property of W. Williams. Emory Sweetland reported an unusual aspect of the day's march: "Have not seen a building burned today." As the men moved deeper into South Carolina's high country, arson was diminishing.[37]

Houses still went up in flames, however. About five miles west of the 154th's campsite, the house Emma Porter and her family shared with a neighbor was burned. Almost six decades later, Porter related her ordeal to a newspaper reporter. She told hide-and-seek stories in which some goods went undetected but a disloyal slave revealed the location of others. She told of blacks scaring the white folks with rumors of Yankee atrocities—the opposite of what typically happened. She also related two sitting-women tales. In the first, as the house fire erupted, her aunt sat atop a mound of meat piled on the floor. The Yankees ordered her to move, but she refused. Finally they forced her away and took the meat. In a more typical tale, Porter sat on a trunk wielding a poker outside the burning house. Unbeknownst to the enemy, the trunk contained a treasure—her brother's Confederate uniform. When an officer taunted her, Porter responded defiantly and sang a song. The trunk and its cherished contents were saved.[38]

Monday, February 13, 1865. Awakened at daybreak with news that the enemy had fled, the men were ordered to fall in and advance at once. They crossed the North Fork of the Edisto River into Lexington District and halted for breakfast to the sounds of skirmishing by the advance. The afternoon was spent waiting for the other two divisions to pass with their trains, after which Geary's men fell in at dusk and continued the northward march. They made about five miles through hilly country before encamping for the night near the Jeffcoat and M. Liart properties. Three decades after the war, Winfield Cameron could still picture the smoke-smudged men cooking their meals in split canteens. David Jones thought the thick smoke rising from pitch pine campfires resembled steam from a teakettle. The soldiers created vaster clouds of smoke by torching South Carolina's pine forests. The days were gloomy with dense smoke, reported David Conyngham, and at night the tall pines were transformed into hissing, screeching pillars of fire.[39]

Tuesday, February 14, 1865. The march resumed in the direction of Lexington Court House at 8:00 a.m. on a cold, dreary day. After an eight-mile tramp, the men bivouacked at a crossroads at 2:30 p.m., just as it began to rain. Then the temperature dropped and coated everything in ice. General Geary said the region was inhabited by poor whites and offered scanty forage; Major Warner reported bounty. The previous day, corps commander Pap Williams had ordered that all foraging parties consist of at least fifty men, commanded by a commissioned officer who would keep them well in hand and prevent them from plundering houses. Geary told his brigade and regimental commanders that he considered small, unauthorized foraging parties—bummers—to be stragglers.[40]

Wednesday, February 15, 1865. The regiment was on the road to Lexington Court House at seven o'clock on a wet morning. By noon the ice coating the trees had melted. Geary's division led the corps, unencumbered by the wagons for a change. The 2nd Brigade followed the 1st. Around noon, near Congaree Creek, the latter skirmished with some Confederate cavalry, said (correctly) to be Major General Wade Hampton's troops, transferred from Virginia. Hampton's men partially burned the bridge over the creek; the division pioneers quickly rebuilt it. Pushing on, Geary's men prevented the destruction of the bridge at Red Bank Creek. The 154th marched to within a mile and a half of Lexington, where it encamped at 2:30 p.m., having covered approximately twelve miles. While the regiment went into bivouac, Geary's 3rd Brigade, accompanied by the general, proceeded into Lexington and drove the enemy from the village. It was quite a pretty place, Geary reported; private property was strictly protected by his troops, and no houses were burned. What Geary did not mention was that Kilpatrick's cavalry had previously put the torch to Lexington. A southerner passed through the town two weeks later and described it as a blackened ruin.[41]

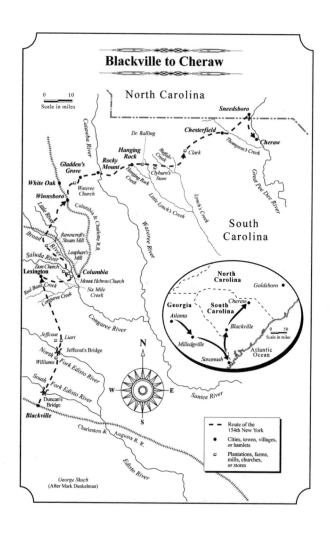

Blackville to Cheraw

0   10
Scale in miles

North Carolina

Sneedsboro

Dr. Ralling

Catawba River

Chesterfield   *Cheraw*

Hanging Rock

Rocky Mount

Gladden's Grove

Buffalo Creek

Clark

Thompson's Creek

Clyburn's Store

Hanging Rock Creek

White Oak

Wateree Church

Winnsboro

Columbia & Charlotte R.R.

Little River

Little Lynch's Creek

Lynch's Creek

Great Pee Dee River

South Carolina

Wateree River

Ravencroft's Steam Mill

Broad River

Saluda River

Leaphart's Mill

Zion Church

Lexington   *Columbia*

Mount Hebron Church

Red Bank Creek

Six Mile Creek

Congaree Creek

Congaree River

[inset map]

North Carolina

Goldsboro

Georgia   South Carolina   *Cheraw*

Atlanta

Blackville

Milledgville

0   50
Scale in miles

Savannah

Atlantic Ocean

Jeffcoat   *Liart*

Jeffcoat's Bridge

North Fork Edisto River

Williams

South Fork Edisto River

Duncan's Bridge

Blackville

Charleston & Augusta R.R.

Santee River

N

W   E

S

Edisto River

[legend]

– – – Route of the 154th New York

● Cities, towns, villages, or hamlets

▫ Plantations, farms, mills, churches, or stores

George Skoch
(After Mark Dunkelman)

To Winnsboro

*T*hursday, February 16, 1865. The regiment marched eastward at 8:00 a.m. toward Columbia, South Carolina's capital. The division was assigned to escort the corps train, and three men were detailed to each wagon. The road ran adjacent to a new railroad under construction and supposedly situated, Emory Sweetland noted, "to be secure from interruption by Sherman's Vandals." After covering six miles, the soldiers camped near Six Mile Creek, five miles west of Columbia, and built breastworks to guard their rear against Wade Hampton's cavalry. "It is reported that the Fifteenth Corps are in our front," Major Lewis Warner noted, "they having arrived opposite the city last evening." That the 15th Corps was closer to the capital than the 20th was significant.[1]

Friday, February 17, 1865. The 154th was ordered to march northwest to Zion Church, a ford on the Saluda River, at nine o'clock on a mild morning that gradually turned hot. The men moved slowly for about five miles, passed Mount Hebron Methodist Church and the Sons of Temperance hall, halted at Leaphart's Mill, and went into camp at dusk on or near the Leaphart plantation. According to family lore, the big house went undamaged except for a minor vandalism: an officer shattered the mantel in the parlor when a slave was slow to respond to his commands. All day long, the roadside woods were afire. By evening, heavy winds swirled clouds of dust into the smoke. Word arrived that a division of the 15th Corps had occupied Columbia. The Left Wing was not to enter the city but skirt it to the east. Thus it happened that the 20th Corps missed witnessing the cataclysm that erupted there this night.[2]

Saturday, February 18, 1865. The 2nd Division was ordered to be ready to march at the head of the corps at 6:30 a.m., but two hours passed before the column moved out. The men crossed the Saluda River on a pontoon bridge near Zion Church and tramped north about seven miles. "All the buildings on the road today were burned," Emory Sweetland noted. He counted fifty-four prisoners whom the division had picked up on the march. Camp was made at Ravencroft's Steam Mill, fifteen miles from Columbia. Major Warner reported the capital's fate: "Columbia was nearly all burned to the ground last evening by the drunken soldiers of the Fifteenth Corps. Loss of life said to be heavy." Drunken (and revengeful) soldiers, burning cotton, and high winds indeed combined to create a major conflagration, but the reports Warner heard were exaggerated. Although about one-third of the city burned, enough housing stock remained to shelter all the inhabitants. Rumors of many fatalities were incorrect; no civilians died, but two Union soldiers were killed while suppressing the riot. The great fire and chaos that swept Columbia were awful enough to be long and bitterly remembered as the apex of Yankee destruction in South Carolina. As Richard McCadden commented, "Many's the home was made desolate in one short day, for the city was full of inhabitants."[3]

General Slocum ordered that supplies be rapidly collected and economically used, six days' worth be kept constantly on hand, surplus tents and baggage be burned or abandoned to free up wagon space, and all disabled horses and mules be shot. Furthermore no refugees, white or black, were to accompany the columns. The mobs of blacks that routinely flocked to the army in Georgia were henceforth to be discouraged in the Carolinas.[4]

Sunday, February 19, 1865. Following the usual rotation, the 2nd Division, which had led the corps the previous day, now joined the trains at the rear. Consequently Geary's men did not move until 1:30 p.m. and only made four miles over hilly terrain and bad roads before camping for the night, guarding the approaches to the wagons. At 9:00 p.m. the 154th was again ordered into line and marched behind the train to the bank of the Broad River, pitching the day's second camp at midnight. Then the regiment was detailed for picket duty. General Slocum issued another order prohibiting unauthorized foraging ahead of the army and threatening arrest and severe punishment to anyone found in front of the advance guard. Orders notwithstanding, Mervin Barber crossed the river and seized bacon and burned cotton, returning to the regiment the next day.[5]

Monday, February 20, 1865. As rear guard to the train, the 154th crossed the Broad River on a pontoon bridge at 2:00 p.m. and entered Fairfield District. Soon the column came to the Greenville and Columbia Railroad, which other troops were demolishing. After a march of about seven miles, during which they forded the Little River, the men halted at 8:00 p.m. and camped. They were enjoying a stretch of good weather, and foraging yields were plentiful.[6]

Six-year-old James M. Smith and his family lived on a farm between the Broad and Little rivers. In his later years he related that every animal on the place was confiscated but for a single chicken that ran under the house out of reach—the lone remaining animal of numerous family legends. The family benefited because of a staple of legend: when Smith's father gave an officer the Masonic sign of distress, the Yankee drove plunderers from the house and provided the family with rations. The Smiths also scavenged the enemy's leavings, which included scraps of meat and the fabled dropped corn, subsisting on the gleanings for the next three weeks.[7]

Postwar legends came to account for the survival of other plantation big houses in the area. One was reportedly spared when a family member (presumably female) soothed Yankee officers with music in another dramatic piano interlude. Yankees were said to have threatened to hang a wealthy and elderly homeowner when he refused to reveal the hiding place of his silver, but his daughter interceded and saved her father and the big house by divulging the location. A more modest preservation was recalled at a third plantation, where a young girl hid her favorite doll under a pile of leaves. A Yankee found the treasure and hung it on a clothesline. Another postwar tale celebrated an area resident who was seized on his plantation, escorted to 20th Corps headquarters, and astonished his captors with his aggressive vituperation and plucky bombast, wishing every blue-bellied son of a bitch who followed Sherman would breakfast in hell. After listening with amusement to the man's tirade, General Williams had him sent home.[8]

"Fairfield district is wealthy," reported David Conyngham. In her later years, ex-slave Rosa Starke related the luxuries of her owner's Fairfield plantation: grounds adorned with gardens, terraces, orchards, an apiary, and a fishpond; acres planted in sweet potatoes, watermelons, and strawberries; a room in the four-room smokehouse filled with brown sugar; the thirty-room big house outfitted with expensive carpets, linens, china, barrels of wine and liquor, and a mint's worth of silver. Starke recalled the result when Sherman's men encountered this opulence. "The Yankees come set all the cotton and the gin-house afire. Load up all the meat; take some of the sugar and shovel some over the yard; take all the wine, rum, and liquor; gut the house of all the silver and valuables, set it afire, and leave one thousand niggers cold and hungry, and our white folks in a misery they never has got over to the third generation of them."[9]

Tuesday, February 21, 1865. Once again the 2nd Division took the lead. The march began at 6:00 a.m. over an excellent road through beautiful, rich countryside. At noon, fourteen miles later, the column reached the Fairfield District seat, Winnsboro, from which rose a cloud of smoke visible two miles away. Bummers were setting fires. General Slocum ordered Geary's 1st Brigade, commanded by Colonel Ario Pardee Jr., to double-quick into town and extinguish the flames. Generals Slocum, Williams, and Geary joined Pardee's men in the work. Years later a local man stated that the fire started in a warehouse and spread up and down Congress Street until it reached brick buildings. According to reporter David Conyngham (attributed to Winnsboro residents), rabid secessionist Jane Lauderdale set fire to her home instead of having it fall into Yankee hands—and that was the spark that fired the town. However the conflagration started, the Yankees stopped it. While some of Pardee's men extinguished blazes, others removed the contents of endangered houses into yards. When all the fires were out, the 1st Brigade was detailed to guard the town.[10]

At the request of Winnsboro's mayor, Geary assigned two members of his provost guard as safeguards, and they organized some citizens into a provisional police force, drove bummers out of town, and preserved order as best they could. The mayor had a note from Wade Hampton pledging that any Federal safeguards would be protected from arrest or injury if overtaken by his troops. True to Hampton's word, when a detachment of his men entered Winnsboro the next day, they treated the two Yankees with courtesy and let them go unmolested, with the heartfelt thanks of a crowd of citizens.[11]

When the 154th New York and the rest of Mindil's brigade arrived in Winnsboro, the men drew some coffee and had dinner. Then they moved onto the Columbia and Charlotte Railroad and spent the rest of the day destroying the track leading north out of town, twisting iron rails around the stone hitching posts in front of fine homes. General Sherman, who had been accompanying the Right Wing, rendezvoused with the 20th Corps in Winnsboro on this day. He would remain with the Left Wing until it reached Cheraw, some seventy miles northeast, where the entire army would congregate to cross the Great Pee Dee River.[12]

Emory Sweetland judged Winnsboro to be "the largest and handsomest place" he had seen in South Carolina. He thought it contained about eighteen hundred inhabitants; Geary pegged the population at twenty-five hundred. Sweetland referred to the fire in his diary but neglected to mention any destroyed dwellings. Cotton warehouses were burned, he wrote, "but all other buildings were strictly guarded." He added a sad exception: "About dark a church near us was fired by some miscreant and burned to the ground."[13]

Less than two months later the *Winnsboro News* carried a shocking story of a mob of profane Yankee arsonists exhuming a coffin from a graveyard and setting it upright so its occupant faced the burning Episcopal church, while others dragged the sanctuary's organ into the yard and played tunes to accompany the saturnalia. In the postwar decades, Winnsboro women added lurid details to this story. All agreed that the coffin contained the remains of a Confederate officer who had died in town just days before. One woman heard that the drunken Yankees carried the corpse into the church, dressed it in the minister's vestments, placed it in the pulpit, and surrounded it with cheers as they torched the building. This secondhand storyteller admitted that she could not vouch for the truth of her tale.[14]

Some two dozen houses burned in Winnsboro, the *News* reported. Rich and poor, young and old, black and white, arch secessionist and Union loyalist—all suffered Yankee insults and depredations alike, the paper charged. It cited shocking cases of abuse of the elderly, including a nonagenarian white woman who was carried outside on her deathbed to watch her home burn. The "demons of destruction" accompanied their misdeeds with a sordid stream of foul language, cursing everyone they came across. "Fairfield presents a melancholy spectacle," the *News* concluded, one that "a barbarous, uncivilized enemy only can produce."[15]

In a letter written after the Yankees' departure, Winnsboro's Margaret McMaster described a mixture of malicious and kind acts on their part. While soldiers ripped down curtains and rummaged through clothing in her house, others helped to move furniture outside and several climbed a ladder and poured water over the roof, saving the dwelling from catching fire. When McMaster's mother pleaded with a bummer to leave the family something to eat, he reminded her of the July 1864 burning of Chambersburg, Pennsylvania, by Confederate raiders and commented, "It is not our lookout whether you starve or not."[16]

A wealth of postwar legends emerged from the Yankees' occupation of Winnsboro. Family tales absolved Jane Lauderdale of David Conyngham's arson charge. It was said that the Yankees thoroughly plundered the Lauderdale house before they set it ablaze. In one account, Lauderdale struck the familiar pose of the southern mother in Sherman's wake, kneeling in the street to pick up dropped corn to feed her hungry children. Before the Yankees came, neighbors recalled, Lauderdale was wealthy; after their visit she was impoverished, her home and shop in ashes. Within three months, however, she opened a new store.[17]

The headmistress of a Winnsboro girls' seminary, Catharine Ladd, figured in a postwar tale in which a sympathetic Yankee officer removed a Masonic chart from her home and had his men bury it in the garden for safekeeping—an odd twist on the usual hide-and-seek stories, with Yankees seeking to deceive Yankees. Ladd and the officer then hurried to the Masonic Hall, where she rescued the Masonic jewels from the blazing building. Contrary to tradition, however, Ladd's Masonic connections did not save her home from being burned.[18]

Katharine Theus Obear was twelve when the Yankees came to Winnsboro. By noon of this Tuesday it seemed as if her family was doomed from nearby fires, she recalled in old age. But Geary's men extinguished the blazes, rounded up stragglers, posted kind and respectful guards, and brought order to the town. The few positive experiences paled beside the terror, however, of streets and vacant lots filled with homeless families, of items salvaged from burning homes destroyed by brutal soldiers, of Yankees stealing out of sheer meanness. Many residents had nothing to eat but cowpeas and hominy made from the legendary dropped corn. Winnsboro seemed stripped of civilization itself, without groceries, horses, mules, vehicles, railroads, or telegraphs—just desperate people.[19]

One of the homeless families that huddled on Winnsboro's streets was that of fourteen-year-old Isabelle Wolfe. In a postwar memoir, she related the ordeal in vivid detail. When snarling, swearing bummers battered down the doors and ransacked the house, Wolfe darted screaming into the street and encountered a Yankee general, who instructed a captain to accompany her and restore order. The captain found the house in flames. As soldiers carried carpets, mirrors, and a piano from the doomed building, the Wolfes moved a safe distance away and joined a group of similarly stricken neighbors. That night the frightened group huddled while drunken soldiers roamed the town unchecked. But the captain who had helped the Wolfes earlier again came to their rescue. The single kind Yankee found lodgings for the family, stored their piano in a guarded warehouse, and provided them amply with food.[20]

Julia A. Tyler related a familiar legend in a UDC memoir. She and her sister were staying with a cousin in Winnsboro when bummers ransacked the house. They smashed the women's trunks to pieces and tossed the contents downstairs. Only one trunk survived—the one on which Tyler sat. A Yankee asked her what was in it. Nothing they would care for, she replied, "and surely they would leave one for me to sit on since they had broken up all the chairs." The bummers left the trunk alone, and the sitting woman thus saved the family silver.[21]

According to legend, one Winnsboro family fastened its shutters and bolted its doors, hoping their house would appear to be deserted and escape harm. But a smoking chimney betrayed the illusion, and bummers broke in and ransacked the place. Among their plunder were two Cornish hens, pets of a daughter. The girl begged the Yankees to spare the birds. In response, they took the hens into the yard, threw them into the air, and shot them dead.[22]

In a memoir for her grandchildren, Margaret Crawford Adams told of sharing a house on Winnsboro's outskirts with eight other families when the enemy arrived. She hoped to appease them with a tableload of food, but it vanished along with the plates and utensils and the table itself. A hundred rascals crowded the house, searching rooms, breaking open doors, closets, drawers, and trunks, and bellowing like a herd of cattle. When the main column arrived, an officer belatedly assigned the house a safeguard. A young soldier sat for the rest of the day by a bedridden sick woman, caring for her and wiping her fevered face. An officer arrested a soldier who tried to set fire to the kitchen. When the Yankees finally left, Winnsboro residents emerged to swap shocking tales of old men repeatedly hanged to force them to reveal hidden treasure, of women who scolded soldiers and so were tied in chairs in their yards to watch their houses burn. In Adams's memory, the passage of the army was a "horrible nightmare" from which people awoke to find themselves destitute. "The Confederacy seemed suddenly to have changed," she wrote; "a glory had passed from it, and, without acknowledging it, we felt the end was near."[23]

Major General William Tecumseh Sherman, "Uncle Billy" to his men.
Library of Congress.

Corporal John Langhans of Company H, 154th New York, the author's great-grandfather. *Author's collection.*

As major and lieutenant colonel, Lewis D. Warner commanded the regiment on both marches and kept a detailed diary. *Courtesy of the William C. Welch Collection at the U.S. Army Military History Institute, Carlisle Barracks, Pa.*

Union army wagons near the railroad depot (at right) in Atlanta,
photographed by George N. Barnard in November 1864.
Library of Congress.

The Georgia state capitol at Milledgeville, where Sherman's
soldiers reveled and ransacked.
Harper's Weekly, January 7, 1865.

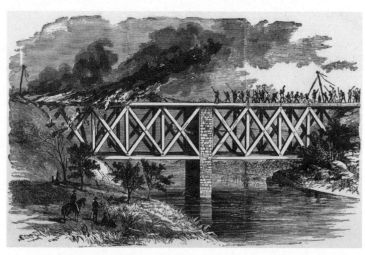

Colonel Patrick Henry Jones's brigade destroying the railroad
bridge over the Ogeechee River on November 30, 1864.
Frank Leslie's Illustrated Newspaper, January 14, 1865.

The fountain in Forsyth Place, Savannah, looking toward the parade ground,
site of the regiment's camp. Photographed by Samuel A. Cooley in 1865.
Library of Congress.

General Sherman reviewing troops on Bay Street in Savannah, drawn by William Waud. The Custom House is at right; the building just beyond (under the flag) was General John White Geary's headquarters.
Library of Congress.

Winnsboro, South Carolina, where the 154th New York destroyed the railroad and twisted iron rails around stone hitching posts in front of fine residences.
Harper's Weekly, April 1, 1865.

The 154th New York burned the courthouse (at right) in
Chesterfield, South Carolina, on March 4, 1865.
Harper's Weekly, April 1, 1865.

The regiment camped on the grounds of the United States Arsenal at
Fayetteville, North Carolina, on the night of March 12, 1865; army
engineers destroyed the complex the following morning.
Harper's Weekly, April 1, 1865.

Corporal Job B. Dawley of Company K was killed by the Confederates after
his capture near Speights Bridge Post Office in Greene County,
North Carolina, on March 26, 1865.
Author's collection.

To Sneedsboro

*W*ednesday, February 22, 1865. The 154th New York spent much of the day destroying the railroad near Winnsboro, while the remainder of the 2nd Brigade continued the job up to White Oak Station. At 3:00 p.m. Major Lewis Warner reported to 1st Brigade commander Colonel Ario Pardee, and the 154th accompanied Pardee's men northward over seven miles of rough country, camping after dark at Wateree Church. The rest of the 2nd Brigade followed and bivouacked nearby.[1]

Decades after the war, ex-slave Anne Broome recollected that the Yankees galloped onto her Fairfield District plantation, asked for wine, and ordered the blacks to sing and cook a dinner before burning the outbuildings and the big house. Former slave Jim Henry cited a familiar reason that the Yankees did not burn anything at the Winnsboro plantation of Confederate general John Bratton: Bratton was a high-degree Mason. (Bratton family tales told of Yankees tearing out the big house's stairway and riding horses through its hall but made no mention of Masonry.) Amie Lumpkin recalled pleading successfully with the Yankees to spare her white folks' house. She also recollected seeing soldiers throw explosive balls against houses to set fires, but there is no evidence of Sherman's men using such incendiary devices.[2]

Two Fairfield District ex-slaves recalled Yankees being humbled. As a joke, a Yankee pulled the beard of Charlie Robinson's master, Joe Beard. But his captain scolded the smart aleck, who slunk away in shame. Abe Harris said a torch-bearing Yankee threatened to burn his bedridden elderly master alive if he did not turn over his riches. "Burn and be damned," the master replied, thus saving the big house—and on this occasion, taking the legendary role usually allotted to female hotspurs.[3]

A UDC remembrance by the granddaughter of Margaret Daniel Durham offered another proud resistance tale. Learning that Durham, the widowed mistress of a White Oak area plantation, had three sons in the Confederate army, the Yankees threatened to cut off her head and stick it on a gatepost. Durham declared it would be a kindness. Chastened by her bravery, an officer sent her meals from camp.

Durham fondly remembered her slave Uncle Jake, who refused when threatened with death to reveal a cache of buried meat and silver. But his terrified daughter revealed the hiding place, and the Yankees dug up the loot. From that time on, the holes were left unfilled to commemorate Uncle Jake's loyalty. Another Durham tale echoed the familiar stories of slashed portraits. A large map of the United States was mounted in the hall of the big house. Using his bayonet, a bummer cut South Carolina out of the map with such force that he carved the state's outline into the plaster behind it. "Old woman," he exclaimed to Durham, "that is the way we intend to wipe South Carolina off the map." Durham's granddaughter never tired of hearing this story and viewing the scarred wall.

Like so many other southern women, Margaret Durham told her descendants that she scavenged dropped corn to feed her children. She also passed down a tale of a cow that was taken by the Yankees but managed to escape and return home. Escaped cow stories are another legendary motif in southern tales of Sherman's marches. Cows are well known for returning home, of course—but not after escaping from a butchering enemy and traveling great distances, as in these legends.[4]

In another UDC memoir, Rebecca A. Bates related that she and her family, on the advice of a trusted but frightened old slave, fled their home west of Winnsboro and sought sanctuary at the nearby home of her grandmother. It was a futile move. The "Blue Jackets" burned their abandoned house and ransacked their refuge. Bates said that a kindly Irish Yankee brought the hungry family a ham and instructed them to hide it. While many southerners disparaged the enemy's ethnic troops, this Irishman was Bates's single kind Yankee.[5]

Mrs. R. E. Ellison reported no such kindness in a UDC memoir composed fifty years after the Yankees invaded her Winnsboro-area childhood home. On the contrary, she charged that the enemy deliberately attempted to starve helpless women and children by spitting and mixing soap into food to create an inedible glop. By hiding her sheet music in the garret, Ellison avoided a dreaded dramatic piano interlude. Meanwhile, when the Yankees repeatedly threatened to burn the big house, a loyal slave interceded and managed to save it.[6]

In a particularly far-fetched UDC tale's dramatic piano interlude, sixteen-year-old Mary Ellison's mother ordered her to play every old song she knew when the Yankees arrived at the family manse outside Winnsboro. As the soldiers climbed the veranda steps and reached the door, the strains of one sentimental tune after another halted their captain. Determined to overcome his weakness, he stepped across the threshold only to be stopped yet again by the melody of "Home, Sweet Home." At that the shamefaced officer wiped a tear from his eye and ordered his men to depart. Mary played until they were out of sight. "Then she collapsed, sobbing in her mother's arms."[7]

A family preservation legend celebrated the steel magnolia mistress of a Winnsboro-area plantation. When a Yankee general ordered her to reveal the whereabouts of hidden silver, she refused. He threatened to burn down her house. "If you do," she replied, "you will burn me and baby, too." The contrite general ordered that she not be harmed and threatened to shoot any man who set fire to her house.[8]

Southerners delighted in relating postwar tales of Yankee thievery. (In contrast, they claimed with considerable exaggeration that Confederate soldiers were better disciplined and always respected private property.) Legends depicted Sherman and his men as superplunderers who insatiably lusted for gold and silver and systematically stole them, dividing the spoils according to rank, with Sherman getting a disproportionately large share. Thousands of Yankees, Jennie Ihly Darnell charged in her UDC memoir, "were suddenly placed on Easy Street; the acknowledgement was made by many of them." Stories were told of steamships and trains hauling loads of stolen loot to the North. No doubt some soldiers carried pilfered silver cups and spoons home at the end of the war. But Sherman's men stripped to light loads on the march. For every silver trinket that a Yankee put in his knapsack, he discarded a pile of loot by the roadside. For his part, Sherman admitted in his memoirs to one act of vandalism during the two marches. Sleeping on the floor of an abandoned house on a bitter cold night in South Carolina, he rekindled a fire with a wrecked bedstead and an old mantel clock.[9]

In Anna E. McCants's UDC account, her widowed mother refused to vacate her Winnsboro-area big house when bummers threatened to burn it, and another valorous steel magnolia foiled a villainous gang of thugs. Then, as so often happens in family legends, bad Yankees were followed by good. An older soldier entered the desolate home and took pity on the widow huddled with her two small children. When this single kind Yankee tried to pat Anna on the head, however, she recoiled as if he was a viper, repelled by the prospect of a bluecoat's touch.[10]

In a long and elaborate memoir that historian Mark Grimsley has deemed "private myth making at work," Winnsboro plantation mistress Grace Pierson Beard portrayed herself as a pistol-packing steel magnolia who thwarted thieving Yankees and saved her big house. She also described a wrenching moment when an officer who bore a striking resemblance to her Confederate soldier husband entered the house. Mistaking the Yankee for his father, Beard's young son ran to him, climbed on his knee, called him Pa, and showed off his new booties. In response, the officer stroked the boy's curls and murmured in his ear. The sight infuriated Beard. "I felt as if my baby was everlastingly polluted," she wrote. Like Anna McCants and other southerners, Beard considered the mere touch of a Yankee to be contaminating.[11]

Thursday, February 23, 1865. Having rejoined the 2nd Brigade, the 154th Regiment marched at 6:30 a.m. via Gladden's Grove to Rocky Mount Post Office, site of a Revolutionary War skirmish, where it crossed the Catawba River on a pontoon bridge into Lancaster District and tramped two more miles before camping at 8:00 p.m. Sixteen miles of rough country were covered during the day. In his ledger book, a Gladden's Grove storekeeper listed eleven houses burned along the main road between Winnsboro and Rocky Mount and seven spared. At the Catawba, the men had an arduous time wrestling the wagons down and up the steep, slippery, two-hundred-feet-high clay riverbanks. A long stretch of good weather had ended with an afternoon downpour, and wagons wallowed in mud up to their axles, horses floundered, and cannon carriages stuck fast. After General Sherman crossed the Catawba with the 20th Corps, the swollen river swept away the pontoon bridge, stranding the 14th Corps on the west bank. That night Charles Abell started a letter to his family. "We are making a desolation of South Carolina," he wrote, adding, "We have made rapid progress towards the land of freedom and Abe Lincoln's proclamations." Mervin Barber's diary entry recorded grim news from the army grapevine: eighteen Union soldiers had been found hanging from trees with their throats cut, wearing signs labeled "Death to foragers." The victims, some of Kilpatrick's cavalrymen, had been slain by their captors two days earlier about thirty miles northwest of the 154th's position.[12]

A postwar newspaper account of Mr. F. B. Lumpkin of Rocky Mount combined two common legendary motifs, that of the Masonic tie and that of the wealthy old white man hanged to reveal hidden treasure. The Yankees had a hard time stringing the three-hundred-pound Lumpkin up. When they eased him down to catch his breath, he flashed the Masonic distress signal, and one of the Yankees rescued him from his fate. Why Lumpkin did not signal from the first went unexplained.[13]

Mrs. J. R. Reid remembered taking to a single room with her family when the Yankees looted their Rocky Mount–area home. The bummers spoke respectfully about her father to the white folks but cursed him as a damned old rebel to the blacks. One Yankee tormented her mother by donning a suit belonging to Reid's absent brother. On the other hand, some decent Yankees comforted Reid's weeping sister and restrained a particularly savage comrade. One kind soldier gave the family a bushel of cornmeal and suggested it would be safe beneath the bed in a woman's room—especially if the woman was seated on the bed. In Reid's memory, not only were the Yankees cognizant of the sitting-woman trick, but they suggested it to southern women.[14]

"Yards were cleared of dogs," recalled a Rocky Mount resident. The soldiers adopted some dogs as pets, along with cats, goats, squirrels, and harmless snakes. Roosters were kept for cockfights. But Sherman's men generally killed dogs. Bloodhounds—known to track fugitive slaves and escaped Yankee prisoners of war—were universally shot, and the slaughter evolved to include most dogs, whose remains joined the carcasses of livestock littering the countryside. "Such was the wholesale destruction of this animal life," wrote a Georgian, "that the whole region stunk with putrefying carcasses, and earth and air were filled with innumerable turkey buzzards fattening upon their thickly strewn death feasts."[15]

A Rocky Mount–area former slave named Violet Guntharpe alleged in her later years that starvation followed in the Yankees' desolate wake. "Lots of the children die, as did the old folks, while the rest of us scour the woods for hickory nuts, acorns, cane roots, and artichokes, and seine the river for fish." In Guntharpe's opinion, only the worst blacks followed the army. "The balance settle down with the white folks and simmer in their misery all through the spring time, 'til plums, mulberries, and blackberries come, and the shad come up the Catawba River."[16]

Friday, February 24, 1865. Mindil's brigade did not move until 10:00 a.m. as it took the rear on a wet morning. After sloshing through the mud for about three and a half miles of rough and rocky countryside, the men halted at sunset. Then they fell in behind the wagons and moved a mile and a half before camping for the night. Their diary entries complained about the miserable weather and roads and predicted hard times to come.[17]

Saturday, February 25, 1865. The regiment remained in camp on another rainy day. Major Warner feared "hard work and slow progress before we reach our destination." Thomas Spiking returned to the regiment; after his capture in Georgia and imprisonment in South Carolina, he had been paroled on February 10 at Wilmington, North Carolina.[18]

Sunday, February 26, 1865. The regiment moved at 7:00 a.m. in charge of twenty-five wagons. The rain had ceased and the sun had reappeared, but the roads remained impassable and had to be corduroyed. Emory Sweetland spotted an unlikely laborer carrying rails: 20th Corps commander Alpheus Williams. Despite the conditions—wagons that wandered off the corduroy sank three feet into the muck—the terrain was less hilly, and the men made good progress through a poor countryside. They crossed a portion of Kershaw District, reentered Lancaster District, reached Hanging Rock Post Office on Hanging Rock Creek at 2:30 p.m., and encamped after covering about ten miles. Nearby, the huge eponymous boulder marked the site of another Revolutionary War skirmish. The 154th was assigned to picket duty during the warm, pleasant night.[19]

Monday, February 27, 1865. Early orders to march were countermanded, and the regiment remained on picket until 2:00 p.m., when it was ordered to change camp. The men packed up, fell in, forded Hanging Rock Creek, moved about three miles through thinly populated and poorly cultivated country, and camped at the top of a ridge on Dr.

Ralling's farm. The mud had been drying up fast in the warm weather, but rain fell all night. General Geary forbade pillaging by brigade foraging parties; only needed supplies were to be taken. Any foragers who committed cowardly or cruel acts were to be dismounted and returned to the ranks. On this evening Major Warner noted, "Our foragers came in pretty well loaded and the men have enough to eat." He put some noncommissioned officers on guard as punishment for straggling.[20]

Tuesday, February 28, 1865. The 2nd Brigade marched at the head of the corps at 6:30 a.m. Rain fell all morning, and the men stopped near Little Lynch's Creek to corduroy the muddy road so the trains could follow. In all, nine miles of fine country were traversed before the regiment camped at 1:00 p.m. at Clyburn's Store, two miles beyond the creek. The bimonthly muster for pay was made, and Lewis Warner was mustered in as lieutenant colonel. Rebel prisoners reported—accurately, it turned out—that Wilmington, the Confederacy's last major seaport, had fallen to Union troops.[21]

Wednesday, March 1, 1865. As rear guard to the entire corps train, the regiment did not move until 1:00 p.m. and marched only eight miles in as many hours, crossing Buffalo Creek and Lynch's Creek, whereupon the men entered Chesterfield District. Camp was pitched at 9:00 p.m. about two miles from Lynch's Creek. The roads were very good, but the slow pace was inevitable at the tail end of the column. The regiment passed few plantations in this hardscrabble countryside of rolling hills, pinewoods, and white sandy soil that was thinly settled by poor whites, but Lieutenant Bird and a small mounted foraging party found plenty nevertheless and dined this night "like princes." They would not rejoin the regiment for two days. Colonel Mindil noted that the typical Carolina planter kept little flour on hand and breadstuffs were consequently scarce. Consequently he ordered a special brigade detail to seize mills and to grind readily found wheat and corn into flour and meal. As a result, his brigade never had less than half rations of breadstuffs during the campaign.[22]

Thursday, March 2, 1865. The 2nd Brigade was still in the rear with the train when the regiment moved at 8:00 a.m. in charge of sixteen wagons. They made about nine miles before dinner, halting near Big Black Creek while a bridge was built. Just before dark they camped there, near the Clark farm. A drizzle fell most of the day, but the roads were in fine shape through a thinly populated region of poor land and stunted pines. For the first time in South Carolina, Mervin Barber was assigned to safeguard a house.[23]

Friday, March 3, 1865. Leading the 2nd Division, the 154th New York got under way at 6:30 on a rainy morning that yielded to a damp, foggy afternoon. The men crossed Big Black Creek and made slow progress over bad roads through swamps and small streams, corduroying much of the way, before reaching Chesterfield Court House about 9:00 p.m. Emory Sweetland admired the village's handsome brick courthouse and jail. When the 20th Corps' advance had entered Chesterfield the previous day, an artist for *Harper's Weekly* had sketched troops milling around the courthouse.[24]

Northern sources disagreed on Chesterfield's size. David Conyngham described it as a paltry town of six houses, while Emory Sweetland compared it to his five-hundred-person hometown. Sweetland's assessment was probably the more accurate. In addition to the courthouse, the village housed workshops, mills, a foundry, and a factory. Black residents outnumbered whites five to one. Less than two weeks after Abraham Lincoln's November 1860 election as president, Chesterfield had been the site of South Carolina's first secession meeting. At its conclusion, a banner inscribed "Immediate State Action" was carried from the courthouse and tacked to a large red oak across the road. There it remained, according to local lore, when General Sherman reached the village.[25]

This night the 154th was detailed for picket duty. A report reached camp that the Confederates had evacuated Cheraw, the head of navigation on the Great Pee Dee River, a dozen miles to the east and the army's objective point. The Right Wing had indeed driven the Confederates out of Cheraw, where it would cross the river. The Left Wing, however, would move upriver to a crossing in North Carolina.[26]

At a Chesterfield female seminary Major Nichols of Sherman's staff asked a boarding student why she had not fled to her distant and safe home. "What is the use?" the girl replied. "Your people go everywhere; you overrun the state; and I am as well off here as at my father's house." According to a postwar UDC recollection, a Chesterfield widow would have agreed. She was on her way home with her sick son when she ran into a group of bummers nine miles out of town. The Yankees stole her horse and left her and the boy sitting in their buggy in the cold rain.[27]

Saturday, March 4, 1865. Early in the morning a brief shower dissipated as the 154th New York returned from picket duty and regrouped in Chesterfield. On this day the regiment acted as rearguard to the division train, at the tail end of Geary's column; consequently it did not move out until about 1:00 p.m. Before leaving the village, the men burned the courthouse and jail. All the district's public records, some of them predating the Revolutionary War, were destroyed in the courthouse fire. The blaze left a bitter legacy. "Everyone involved with local history in this state knows the heartache that the phrase 'burned county' conjures up," wrote a modern-day historian, citing Chesterfield District as a particularly severe case, long rued by genealogists.[28]

The loss of the courthouse itself (one of four South Carolina county courthouses destroyed by Union forces) was lamented, for the 1826 structure was the work of the architect and engineer Robert Mills, a native South Carolinian and one of the first professionally trained American architects, who designed public works and buildings throughout the country during a long and productive career. His most famous work, the Washington Monument, remained unfinished in 1865, almost a decade after his death. The Chesterfield courthouse was one of fourteen that Mills designed in his native state.[29]

Was the firing of the courthouse a spontaneous act, or was it ordered? Members of the regiment admitted to the arson in their writings but added no details. Colonel Warner mentioned the fire in his diary but not in his official report. No one up the chain of command—Mindil, Geary, or Williams—mentioned it in their reports, either. One Chesterfield legend alleges that the courthouse was doomed when Sherman saw the secession banner. He was so enraged by it, a twentieth-century commentator wrote, that he immediately ordered the courthouse to be fired, posting guards to prevent the building's contents from being removed or the blaze from being extinguished. A UDC account alleged that Sherman entered and exited Chesterfield by the light of burning buildings, including the courthouse and jail. These stories, typical in damning Sherman personally, do not jibe with the timing of events. The general entered Chesterfield Court House with advance elements of the 20th Corps on March 2 and departed on

March 3, the day before the 154th New York burned the courthouse.[30]

In recent years the Chesterfield courthouse fire was commemorated in a painting, from which prints were made to benefit the local historical and genealogical society. The artist based her image on the *Harper's Weekly* woodcut of the courthouse, adding flames bursting from the upper portion of the structure into a cloud of black smoke and a bucket brigade (that ironically resembles Yankee soldiers) making a futile attempt to extinguish the blaze.[31]

Ellen Chapman's UDC memoir stated that the Yankees burned her family's house. A recent county history asserts that much of Chesterfield was burned, but a UDC memoir by Mrs. H. D. Tiller said that occupied homes escaped the torch. The Yankees twice fired her barn, but both times she extinguished the blaze. Looking back, Tiller marveled at how quickly the area recovered from prostration to plenty. She benefited from a hog, whose story echoes the legendary motif of the escaped cow. The hog was so thin, the Yankees laughed at it—but they took it anyway. Some three weeks later, the hog returned to Tiller's place "fat and slick."[32]

According to another UDC memoir, the home of a Chesterfield woman was pillaged—bummers took her patchwork quilts to use as saddle blankets—but escaped the flames. For three days after the enemy passed, she was without food. Without provisions, went another UDC tale, Chesterfield residents were forced—in a variation of the familiar dropped corn legend—"to pick up peas where the horses were fed." A twentieth-century Chesterfield historian switched the story back to dropped corn and—in a variant—mentioned another family that survived on nothing but apples.[33]

Generations of Chesterfield families have handed down preservation legends. One told of bummers thwarted by a faithful slave in their efforts to torch a half-built house. In another, a smart-aleck bummer asked a rural woman to push her last bale of cotton out where he could burn it. According to a descendant, this steel magnolia told him to move it himself or burn it where it was. The bummer laughed and spared the cotton bale and the house. In an unusual hide-and-seek story, a family's silver escaped discovery buried in a stable but was inexplicably forgotten until uncovered years later by pawing horses.[34]

The 154th New York made slow progress after leaving Chesterfield Court House, hampered by roads that ran through quicksand and crossed Thompson's Creek and several other streams. Andrew Blood got ahead of the advance guard while foraging and was arrested. After a march of about ten miles, camp was made about 9:00 p.m. near Sneedsboro, Anson County, North Carolina, about a dozen miles up the Great Pee Dee River from Cheraw. In the previous three decades, many of Sneedsboro's residents had fled its exhausted soil. In this forsaken place on this particular night Colonel Warner's thoughts turned several hundred miles to the north. "Today is undoubtedly a great day at Washington," he noted in his diary—Abraham Lincoln had been inaugurated for his second term as president.[35]

Warner also reflected on the arrival in North Carolina. "Whether the wholesale destruction of property will be continued as we advance remains to be seen," he wrote. "I hope a better spirit will prevail. North Carolina has shown considerable Union sentiment during the war and I believe a proper course by our army"—here he chose an ironic metaphor—"would cause the slumbering fire to burst into a flame, which could not be quenched."[36]

The regiment suffered another fatality this day. Joseph Moyer, the expert honey hunter, died of measles at the 2nd Division hospital. At his home in Allegany, Cattaraugus County, Moyer left a wife and two young daughters.[37]

Sunday, March 5, 1865. The 14th Corps was said to be laying a pontoon bridge over the nearby Pee Dee. Guessing they would cross the river after the 14th did, the men whiled away the day in camp. Andrew Blood was released from arrest at noon. Mervin Barber attended an evening prayer meeting.[38]

In his diary entry, Colonel Warner jotted some reflections. "We are now in North Carolina, leaving the other state behind, and also our mark, which it will take years to obliterate. Sherman will long be remembered, as was Attila, as the scourge of God to Carolina." Later in the month, other members of the regiment looked back on the march through the Palmetto State. "You well say desolation marked our tracks," Richard McCadden wrote, "for we scarcely left a house, barn, or pigpen standing for over 100 miles, or you must say in the state." James Clements wrote bluntly, "We have not left anything for the Rebs. We have just stripped South Carolina." From army headquarters, Sherman offered his own perspective: "South Carolina has had a visit from the West that will cure her of her pride and boasting."[39]

[11]

Cheraw

onday, March 6, 1865. Although the 14th Corps and Kilpatrick's cavalry eventually would cross the Pee Dee near Sneedsboro, problems in assembling the pontoon bridge delayed the movement. Consequently the 20th Corps was ordered to return to South Carolina to cross the river at Cheraw. The 154th New York tramped south over a plank road at 7:00 a.m., covered roughly fourteen miles, and reached Cheraw at about 1:00 p.m. Mervin Barber described it as one square mile in size and filled with military stores and munitions. Cheraw also warehoused a large amount of cotton and household goods sent from the low country for safekeeping. "It is a pleasant-looking town," granted reporter David Conyngham (generally a harsh critic of southern municipalities), "with near two thousand inhabitants." Others estimated the population at up to four thousand, including many refugees. Just downstream from the charred remains of Cheraw's covered bridge (burned by the retreating Confederates), army engineers threw a pontoon span across the Pee Dee. The 2nd Division began to cross about 4:00 p.m., but because of an accident to the bridge, the 154th did not cross until 8:00 p.m. On the eastern bank the regiment entered Marlboro District and marched four miles through fine country, camping at 10:00 p.m. at Smith's Mill on Wolf Creek.[1]

Emory Sweetland recorded destruction in Cheraw in his diary. "The public buildings and stores have been burned and many dwelling houses were blown down this morning by the explosion of an immense amount of ammunition captured from the Rebs." The fleeing Confederates had dumped tons of powder and artillery shells in a gully near the riverfront, and careless Union soldiers had accidentally ignited the pile. In postwar memoirs, Cheraw women claimed the enemy deliberately set off the blast. In any event, the resulting explosion killed and wounded several soldiers, injured a number of civilians, stampeded animals, demolished much of the business district, and caused damage a good distance beyond.[2]

Susan Bowen Lining was cooking in her family's apartment in a hospital when the blast erupted. Ten days later she described the result in a letter. The pan she was holding flew from her hand as things were hurled from one side of the room to the other and her screaming young son clung to her. No one in her family was hurt, but every window in the place was shattered, shutters were blasted from their hinges, and plaster fell from ceilings and walls. Years later, in a UDC reminiscence, Laura Prince Inglis related secondhand family stories about the panicked residents rushing into the streets after the blast. Among them were her feeble octogenarian grandmother (carried by two slaves), her mother and sisters, and an infant brother. Tales of the throng of terror-stricken residents reminded her of accounts of citizens fleeing doomed Pompeii.[3]

The explosion "shook the town badly," General Sherman recalled in his memoirs. He had expected to find nothing more in Cheraw than a place to cross the Pee Dee, so he was delighted to discover the immense stockpiles of enemy war matériel. As it turned out, Cheraw equaled Columbia and Fayetteville, North Carolina, as the most important supply depots captured during the campaign. While the military stores were thoroughly destroyed, Sherman funneled three-quarters of his infantry through the town with minimal damage to private homes, other than those leveled by the explosion.[4]

In the postwar decades, preservation myths evolved to account for Cheraw's survival. In one, the mayor rode out and surrendered the town to Sherman, thereby saving his constituents from the torch. The relater of this myth also speculated that Cheraw might have been spared so that its homes could house Yankee officers. In another tale, the five-year-old daughter of one of the town's Roman Catholics begged Sherman as a fellow Catholic to spare Cheraw, winning his acquiescence. This story ignores the fact that Sherman was not a Catholic, although his wife and children were.[5]

Members of the 154th New York did some sightseeing during their seven-hour layover in Cheraw. A number of them were drawn to St. David's Episcopal Church. According to postwar southern accounts, Yankees removed the pews to hold a dance and used the pulpit as a bandstand, but the 1768 landmark was otherwise unharmed. The

154th men seemed most interested in St. David's cemetery, where they sought the graves of Revolutionary War generals Francis Marion and Thomas Sumter. (The famous "Swamp Fox" was the namesake of Francis Marion Bowen and other members of the regiment.) They were disappointed to find that the heroes' graves were nothing but small, unmarked brick vaults. Mervin Barber thought the crumbling mounds were a disgrace. Richard McCadden nevertheless chipped a piece of brick from one tomb and sent it home as a memento. But the men were mistaken—neither Marion nor Sumter was buried in Cheraw; the vaults held the remains of two British officers. Locals had most likely fooled the Yankees into thinking otherwise.[6]

Some members of the regiment must have engaged in less innocent pursuits than visiting historic graveyards during the Cheraw stopover. "Every house in the town was entered," Susan Bowen Lining wrote, "and each family robbed of everything in the form of provisions, silver, jewelry, clothing, and what they could not carry off they destroyed by fire or the axe." Lining escaped this plundering herself, however; Yankee sentinels guarded her rooms at the hospital. Three of her slaves fled to the enemy, one carrying a valise full of the family's clothing, linens, and silver tablespoons. For two weeks, until they were able to hire a servant girl, the Linings were forced to cook their own meals, wash their own clothes, haul their own water, and cut their own firewood. Those experiences, Lining concluded, would never be forgotten.[7]

Cheraw women repeatedly voiced bitter memories in postwar reminiscences. In a UDC account, Mrs. H. W. Scott compared the Yankees to swarming locusts, devouring, desecrating, and destroying everything in their path, pillaging and burning shops, setting fire to library books, violating the sanctity of homes, slashing oil paintings, stealing jewelry and silver plate, taking food from innocent children, and frightening mothers with their insolence—to name but "some of the indignities perpetrated by Sherman and his miserable hoard of men."[8]

Virginia C. Tarrh described the plundering of Cheraw in a turn-of-the-century compilation of South Carolinian women's reminiscences. Crowds of bummers found all the valuables her household had buried. Officers and enlisted men occupied rooms in her house, while the backyard swarmed with rogues who smashed up furniture and china. She recalled peeking out of her windows—never daring to stare boldly—to watch neighbors' carriages carry away bacon and black women. For several days after the Yankees departed, Tarrh recalled, all the white folks had to eat was what their ex-slaves shared with them, the blacks having received food from the enemy.[9]

In her later years, Laura Prince Inglis told her war stories repeatedly. A favorite was a tale about a heavy, padlocked chest. When a Yankee officer asked what it contained, Inglis's mother said she had no idea. He called her a liar; she suggested that he see for himself. For more than an hour the Yankees struggled to open the chest, cursing over their lack of success. Finally they split it open with an ax. To their great disgust, it was tightly packed with religious magazines.[10]

According to a friend, some of Inglis's recollections were "quite lurid." Certain topics were taboo, she said, "because Southern ladies would never disclose such public humiliation." Inglis left indelicate tales out of her written memoirs, but in private she told about two young women forced to "partially disrobe and play the piano for Yankee soldiers"—a particularly shocking dramatic piano interlude. She was less reticent about the dance allegedly held in St. David's Church, at which the Yankees' partners were, scandalously, "the only available women—*women of color!*"[11]

The Reverend Dr. John Bachman, guardian to a group of women on a plantation about six miles south of Cheraw, described Yankee sexual debauchery in a letter purportedly written six months after their passage. After chasing all the black men away from the slave quarters, Bachman charged, the "libidinous, beastly barbarians" assaulted the black women in "scenes of licentiousness, brutality, and ravishment that have scarcely had an equal in the ages of heathen barbarity." Officers forced a white woman to strip to see if she had valuables hidden under her dress. Meanwhile waves of bummers robbed, vandalized, threatened, and beat blacks and whites alike, including Bachman himself. Although a handful of Yankees saved the big house from fire, their comrades looked on idly, unconcerned whether it burned or not. Summing up, Bachman condemned Sherman's men as cruel, ruthless, inhuman barbarians who systematically tortured the weak and unarmed. Jefferson Davis endorsed this searing indictment and gave it a wide readership when he published Bachman's letter in his 1881 memoirs.[12]

In her memoir, Harriet Powe Godfrey called the Yankee occupation her idea of hell. She and her baby had been sent from her father's plantation the mile or two into Cheraw, the idea being she would be safer in town. There her wedding ring was stolen, and a bummer adorned his mule with her bridal veil. Other Godfrey tales incorporated legendary motifs. Yankee officers forced her to play and sing in a dramatic piano interlude. When the enemy torched her father's big house, faithful slaves extinguished the flames not once but four times. For several days, she claimed, her family subsisted on the ubiquitous diet of dropped corn picked up in deserted Yankee camps, until friends succored them with food and clothing.[13]

Several other Cheraw families handed down legends with familiar motifs. A guinea fowl that flew into a tall pine to avoid the potshots of bummers was the lone remaining animal on one family's home place. Like so many others, they claimed to have scraped up grains of dropped corn for sustenance. According to Mrs. C. E. Jarott's UDC reminiscence, her family picked rice and peas from the Yankees' footprints to sustain themselves for several days. When an escaped cow returned home, the delighted family enjoyed milk and butter more than they ever had before. Jarrott's fondest memory was of hide-and-seek. She hid her jewelry and gold and silver coins in her little tin lunch can and buried it three times before she was satisfied with the hiding place, which went undetected. The tin is now in the Museum of the Confederacy in Richmond, Virginia.[14]

In a UDC tale by Mrs. J. S. Hartzell (retold in more recent years by a Cheraw schoolteacher), a refugee in Cheraw sent a note to General Sherman, begging him for cows to provide milk for some babies. In response, Sherman cruelly sent a dry cow. But that night a cow escaped from the Yankees, swam the Pee Dee, and returned to the father of one of the hungry infants, thus saving the starving babies.[15]

Hartzell also told two stories of loyal slaves. When the Yankees strung Aunt Patty up by her thumbs and held pistols to her head to force her to divulge the hiding place of her mistress's silver, she obstinately refused and the treasure was never found. She was rewarded in the postwar years with a house and ten acres of land. Meanwhile Daddy Granville joined the Yankee ranks, apparently in earnest. He asked for permission to take charge of some captured horses, and the Yankees readily agreed. Every night Granville slipped away with a few horses and returned the animals to their owners. The faithful slave continued this work until the army reached Fayetteville, North Carolina, where, "having done all that he could for his people," he left the Yankees and returned home.[16]

Hartzell's opinion of the Yankees was entirely negative. In Cheraw, she wrote, Sherman's men "committed every outrage then known to so-called civilized warfare." Not all Cheraw residents agreed. Elizabeth M. Godfrey recalled that the Yankees treated the town's women and children very respectfully, although they were sometimes rude in speech. In her UDC memoir, Henrietta Buchanan remembered the occupation as remarkably peaceful. Cheraw was well patrolled day and night, and the troops were under good control. No one that she heard of was harmed or subjected to "personal indignities," although after the army moved on, stragglers committed robberies. Most families lost their silver, Buchanan noted, and the town was stripped of food, but the residents did not starve and felt that they had much to be thankful for.[17]

Hundreds of miles away, in General Robert E. Lee's army in Virginia, Captain John C. Evans worried about his family when he heard rumors of Cheraw's occupation. "You can't imagine my anxiety about you at this time," he wrote to his wife on March 5. Eleven days later he was under the impression that Cheraw had been entirely destroyed. "What are my poor dear ones suffering now?" he wondered. "If I could only know that you are all alive and suffered no bodily harm, I would be so glad, but here I am without one word from you." He closed with a plaintive plea: "God in mercy preserve my dear family."[18]

Throughout the Confederate armies, soldiers like Evans fretted about their loved ones in the afflicted states. They bemoaned the devastation wreaked by Sherman's army in Georgia, and their despair deepened during the march through the Carolinas. A Georgian in Lee's army regretted having to serve in Virginia while the Yankees overran his home state: "I had rather fight for those that I love." A South Carolina soldier conceded the Yankees had the upper hand and declared, "I would like to hear of some terms of peace before they run clear over us." Inspecting Confederate soldiers' letters seized in South Carolina, reporter David Conyngham found them all to be desponding. General Lee, worried about sagging morale and increasing desertions by his Georgians and Carolinians, blamed the situation in part on demoralizing correspondence from home. "The state of despondency that now prevails among our people is producing a bad effect upon the troops," Lee wrote in February 1865. "Desertions are becoming very frequent and there is good reason to believe that they are occasioned to a considerable extent by letters to the soldiers by their friends at home."[19]

Within weeks after Sherman's army left Cheraw, surrendered Confederate soldiers returned home to help the community in its struggle to recover. Time eventually healed the land's scars, but the demise of slavery, the ancient "peculiar institution" and the Confederacy's cornerstone, left a legacy of racial bitterness and mistrust that haunted the South and daunted its progress for a century and more. Three years after the Yankees marched through Cheraw, Josephine Pritchard remarked on the downfall of the white elite. "It would grieve you to see how our rich planters are reduced," she informed a friend. A mutual acquaintance was reduced to living in a small summer home—the big house had been burned—and his wife and his sons did the work formerly done by slaves. Another planter had died owing Pritchard substantial amounts of money, a debt that would have been paid if not for emancipation, for he had been rich in slaves.[20]

Tuesday, March 7, 1865. The ground was white with frost when the march commenced at 6:00 a.m. toward Rockingham, North Carolina. The 2nd Brigade led the 20th Corps. Thirteen miles later, at 1:00 p.m., the 154th New York reached the Wilmington, Charlotte, and Rutherford Railroad one mile west of Station 103 and four miles east of Rockingham. The early stopping time would allow the corps' rear to catch up and camp at a reasonable hour. Before bivouacking, the men tore up three-quarters of a mile of track and twisted up a pile of new iron rails. During the day the 154th crossed from Marlboro District, South Carolina, into Richmond County, North Carolina. Just before leaving the former, the regiment passed a turpentine factory. (The men noted that Carolinians tapped pines for turpentine like they tapped maples for sap at home.) The advance had set fire to this factory, and the blaze was spectacular. Thousands barrels of melting, flaming rosin ran across a road into a swamp.[21]

This time the regiment left South Carolina for good. Just as Sherman and his men had threatened, the state had suffered much worse than Georgia. House burning had increased dramatically but was far from universal. With Columbia's glaring exception, residential arson had gradually diminished as Sherman's men marched from the Savannah River to the Pee Dee. Early on, entire villages like Robertville and Lawtonville were burned to the ground. After the Columbia conflagration, the army appeared sated with torching houses. Soldiers extinguished the fires set by bummers in Winnsboro. Cheraw suffered from the explosion but escaped arson. As the army moved north through the upcountry, fewer rural houses were burned (with the exception of unoccupied homes). Other buildings, however, were torched throughout the state. According to a Fairfield District resident, only four ginhouses and a single gristmill were left standing in that entire county.[22]

Ninety years after the march, historian Richard H. McMaster assessed its effects on Fairfield District. Even its remotest sections saw hostile troops, he noted, from entire divisions down to small groups of stragglers. "The county was swept pretty clean of food, forage, and animals," McMaster wrote, "but less than half of the plantation homes were burned." In his appraisal, the most destructive Yankees belonged to the Right Wing and Kilpatrick's cavalry, who were the most ruthless of all. (Rumor had it that Kilpatrick's men carried matches in their saddlebags.) McMaster admitted that Carolinians also suffered greatly at the hands of Confederate soldiers, who foraged as thoroughly as the Yankees. Joseph Wheeler's cavalry had a particularly bad reputation as looters. Former slave Manda Walker, from a plantation near Wateree Church, remembered Wheeler's men as "just as hard and wolfish as the Yankees."[23]

Fairfield District residents were fortunate, McMaster asserted, that Henry Slocum's Left Wing marched through the county's wide central corridor. "This command happily had no stomach for burning family dwellings," McMaster wrote. He attributed the Left Wing's leniency to Slocum. Fairfield residents gratefully considered Slocum a humane commander, similar to Revolutionary War generals who had maneuvered benignly in the district. They even compared him favorably to admired Confederate generals.[24]

Twentieth Corps commander Alpheus Williams shared Slocum's lenient attitude and likewise issued orders against plundering. But Williams admitted, "The soldiers quietly took the matter into their own hands. Orders to respect houses and private property not necessary for subsistence of the army were not greatly heeded. Indeed, not heeded at all." Williams was often painfully touched by "the distressed and frightened condition" of the elderly and children in the army's wake. High-ranking officers discouraged vandalism, noted David Conyngham, but it was seldom punished. There were no informers, so the generals knew little of what occurred. Conyngham was aware of only one or two punishments for theft. One of them involved the stern

General Geary, who caught a captain plundering a house, relieved him of his sword, and ordered him to be tied up behind a wagon.[25]

Gene Graves offered a view from the ranks on the devastation in South Carolina and the simple reason for it. "The boys destroyed everything they could lay their hands on in that state, for that was the first to go out of the Union and they remembered it. It is the worst looking country I ever saw. There is not a building standing, nor a fence. It is all laid to waste." Graves exaggerated, but he made his point. The destruction in South Carolina far exceeded that in Georgia.[26]

Now General Slocum issued an order to the Left Wing, reminding his command that North Carolina, one of the last states to secede, was home to many Unionists. "It is to be hoped," he wrote, "that every effort will be made to prevent any wanton destruction of property, or any unkind treatment of citizens."[27]

Days after the passage of Sherman's army, Elizabeth Allston passed through Cheraw. "We were never out of the sight of dead things," she recalled years later in a memoir, "and the stench was almost unbearable." She saw dead horses, cows, and hogs as evidence of an effort to starve the inhabitants. In a formerly abundant country of small farms, the two-room houses were all tightly shut up, with no signs of life. In Allston's memory, the wake of Sherman's army "was like the path stripped by a tornado, narrow but complete destruction in it." Now the tornado touched down in the Old North State.[28]

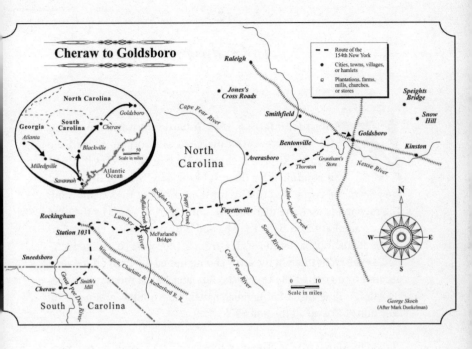

Cheraw to Goldsboro

Route of the
154th New York
Cities, towns, villages,
or hamlets
Plantations, farms,
mills, churches,
or stores

North Carolina
Georgia
South Carolina
Goldsboro
Cheraw
Atlanta
Blackville
Milledgville
Savannah
Atlantic
Ocean
Scale in miles
0   50

Raleigh
Jones's
Cross Roads
Smithfield
Speights
Bridge
Snow
Hill
Goldsboro
Bentonville
Kinston
Cape Fear River
North
Carolina
Averasboro
Grantham's
Store
Thornton
Neuse River
Rockingham
Rockfish Creek
Puppy Creek
Fayetteville
Little Coharie Creek
South River
Buffalo Creek
Station 103½
Lumber River
McFarland's
Bridge
Sneedsboro
Wilmington, Charlotte & Rutherford R. R.
Cape Fear River
Cheraw
Smith's
Mill
Great Pee Dee River
South   Carolina

N
W   E
S

0   10
Scale in miles

George Skoch
(After Mark Dunkelman)

To Goldsboro

*W*ednesday, March 8, 1865. A hard rain was falling when the 154th New York marched at 1:00 p.m. toward the Lumber River in Richmond County, North Carolina, and it continued for the rest of the day. The 2nd Brigade, at the rear of the corps, had to wait for the passage of the wagon train. The men made no more than six miles over terrible roads by the time they camped at 10:00 p.m. They passed only one house. Ordered to moderate their behavior in North Carolina, they were so inclined anyway. Levi Bryant thought the army should not be too hard on the state because of its numerous Unionists. But later in the month he noted, "North Carolina ain't a-faring much better" than South Carolina, "only they don't burn up all the houses."[1]

Thursday, March 9, 1865. The march began at 6:30 a.m.; the regiment remained at the rear of the column with the train. Rain began falling in the afternoon, and by night the soldiers were drenched by the heaviest downpours of the season. They corduroyed the road for much of ten miles before camping near the Lumber River at 8:00 p.m. under miserable conditions. During the day the men saw only two houses.[2]

Friday, March 10, 1865. The regiment was ordered to move at 6:30 on a gloomy morning. After a brief noontime hailstorm, the weather cleared. The 154th led the division across the Lumber River at McFarland's Bridge and entered Cumberland County, making slow progress over awful roads running through swamps. Most of the way had to be corduroyed. Confederate scouts were active on the column's left flank; a 2nd Brigade bummer was shot near the line of the march. The regiment sloshed six miles, camped at Buffalo Creek, and was ordered to do picket duty.[3]

Saturday, March 11, 1865. The weather cleared overnight, and a nice day seemed to be in the offing. While the 1st and 3rd divisions moved forward unencumbered, Geary's division was ordered to accompany the entire corps train. The 154th was assigned as rear guard. The regiment followed the rumbling wagons across a pontoon bridge over Rockfish Creek, both sides of which were bordered with swamps, and crossed several smaller streams. Geary's men had to corduroy several miles of road to get the train through, but being at the rear of the column, the 154th escaped that labor. Enemy cavalry crowded close to the column's left flank, and fighting was reported at the front. Despite the adverse conditions, the men covered about fourteen miles. They did not camp, however, until 4:00 a.m. on March 12, near Puppy Creek. "Our brigade foragers found a barrel of whiskey," Alex Bird reported, "and most everybody was drunk."[4]

Far from the regiment, at an army hospital in Beaufort, North Carolina, one of the recruits, Private Willard H. Crosby of Company D, died of edema. He had been hospitalized in Savannah in January suffering from kidney disease. He left a wife and two young daughters at home in Ashford, Cattaraugus County. Forty-seven days after her husband died, Charlotte Crosby gave birth to a son and named him for his late father.[5]

Sunday, March 12, 1865. After falling asleep at 4:30 a.m., the men were awakened at 7 a.m. and ordered to march an hour later. They did not get off, however, until noon of a pleasant day. Once again the 2nd Brigade was at the rear of the column. This time the men marched on a plank road, which was in generally good condition. At dark the regiment entered Fayetteville and moved to a commanding hill called Haymount in the city's west end, where it camped on the grounds of the United States Arsenal, General Sherman's headquarters. The men expected to remain for a day before crossing the Cape Fear River. They found Fayetteville to be an attractive town, strongly fortified and housing a large amount of arms and stores. Most of the estimated four thousand inhabitants appeared to have Unionist sentiments, and hundreds expressed a desire to accompany the army. The town was well guarded to prevent ravages by the soldiers.[6]

Communications with Union forces at Wilmington were opened when a tugboat sent up the Cape Fear by Major General Alfred H. Terry arrived carrying dispatches for Sherman. For the soldiers, the connection to the seacoast meant an opportunity to write to their loved ones, and they acted on it immediately. Their letters departed in a small steamboat, which accompanied the tug back to Wilmington before heading north.[7]

Summarizing the "grand, successful march" through the Carolinas, Charles Abell informed his parents, "The country was beautiful and quite wealthy, but war 'where we have been' has made it a desolation." He added a prediction. "Spring will either show another long stride downhill of Lee's army, or *Sherman gets one almighty thrashing.*" Emory Sweetland told his wife of the arduous marching through swamps and mud; he estimated that the roads had been corduroyed for half the distance from the Savannah River. Any stories from rebel sources of Sherman's defeat were "all *bosh,*" he assured her. The campaign was a complete success, causing the Confederacy irreparable losses and hastening the end of the war. Carolinians were despondent and wished peace on any terms. "If [Jefferson] Davis does not give up soon," Sweetland predicted, "Sherman's great army will join Grant's army at Richmond and compel a peace."[8]

In diary entries, fifteen-year-old Malinda B. Ray contradicted Sweetland's appraisal of Carolinian morale. Before the army took control of Fayetteville, bummers looted the Ray home and encouraged a mob of blacks and poor whites to plunder her father's store. (Poor people were delighted with the Yankee occupation, she noted with disgust.) But after a captain and a squad of soldiers arrived to safeguard the house, the family was not troubled again. Ray was surprised that the Yankees she met were cultivated gentlemen. In the end, however, she remained unmoved by their decency. "If the Yankees imagine [that] in depriving us of our clothes, jewelry, and even our food, they are taking away our spirit they are greatly mistaken," she declared. Her Confederate resolve was strengthened by her contact with the enemy. She hoped that Confederate soldiers would die on the battlefield rather than return home subject to such a foe.[9]

Josephine Bryan Worth was a schoolgirl when the Yankees entered Fayetteville. Years later, in a UDC memoir, she too marked the difference between the bummers and the main army. The former rapidly ransacked her house; the latter assigned the place a safeguard. Worth also remembered the army's third element: its surreal flotsam, a stream of wagons, cattle, sheep, and camp followers, among them blacks in carriages heaped high with looted furniture and other goods.[10]

Fayetteville women harshly condemned the bummers' behavior in other postwar reminiscences. Alice Campbell described bummers chopping pianos, furniture, and painted portraits to bits with axes, smashing china and glassware, and emptying barrels of flour and molasses onto velvet carpets. "There was no place, no chamber, trunk, drawer, desk, garret, closet, or cellar that was private to their unholy eyes," wrote a woman who lost all her clothing but what she wore. Alice Mallett remembered that the only food bummers left for her family was some meat they thought might be poisoned.[11]

Sarah Ann Tillinghast added legendary motifs to her memoir of Yankee depredations. Seeking to save something edible for her household, she filled a bucket with flour and molasses and told an aunt to sit on it and guard it. The sitting-woman ruse worked. That evening three families dined on the pail's contents and the lone remaining animal, a chicken saved by a slave.[12]

Factories, banks, warehouses, stores, a newspaper office, and a handful of houses were burned in Fayetteville. The Yankees used churches as barracks and left them tattered and filthy, their Bibles and hymnals mutilated and inscribed with obscenities. Hundreds of the town's remaining horses and mules were rounded up and shot. Years later, citizens recalled random acts of cruelty, as when a Yankee forced a man to strip in the street. Josephine Bryan Worth remembered that the soldiers were fond of giving children and young ladies items stolen from their neighbors. Like many southern women, she was annoyed by the enemy's lack of manners. They luxuriated in rocking chairs or stretched out on carpets in front of their tents, blocking the sidewalks and forcing women to walk around them in the street, subject to their impudent stares.[13]

Monday, March 13, 1865. The soldiers passed the morning washing their clothes and watching the engineers batter down the thick masonry walls of the massive arsenal complex, a gated compound of barracks, storehouses, shops, magazines, and rifle factory, anchored at the corners by tall, octagonal towers. When the walls collapsed, the roofs fell with a deafening crash. The piles of rubble were set on fire, detonating shells stored in underground bomb proofs and sending black smoke spiraling skyward while soldier onlookers cheered and army bands played. Frightened residents watched the spectacle feeling helpless but were grateful that the Yankees protected private property in the vicinity; only one house next to the rifle factory was consumed. Years later, Fayetteville folks recalled the arsenal's destruction with sadness. Its handsome buildings had been the town's showplace and pride.[14]

Surrounded by army and naval officers on a Fayetteville hotel balcony, Sherman reviewed the 20th Corps. "My army is as united and cheerful as ever," the general boasted, "and as full of confidence in themselves and their leaders as ever." Two gunboats from Wilmington swayed in the water as the 154th crossed a pontoon bridge over the Cape Fear River. The men marched about two miles before camping for the night beside the plank road leading to North Carolina's capital, Raleigh.[15]

Tuesday, March 14, 1865. The regiment enjoyed a day of rest. Rations were issued, and it was reported that transports carrying army stores were on the way upriver. The men continued to launder and to write letters; they hoped that mail would reach them before they left the vicinity the next day. Back at the Cape Fear, the 2nd Division hospital shipped its patients north by steamers. Also aboard were white refugees who had joined the column during the march.[16]

Black refugees were gathered in a large camp at Fayetteville. North Carolina contained "more niggers than you can shake a stick at; great, fat, lazy fools," wrote Levi Bryant. He no longer considered himself to be an abolitionist, "for it is first a nigger, then a mule, and then a soldier—and the soldier is used worse than any of them." John Langhans, on the other hand, was impressed by the welcome the army received from blacks. "The Rebs had told the darkies we would kill them all, but they were all glad to see us," he reported. "They stood in crowds of ten to thirty all along the road." But with army policy discouraging the practice, Carolinian blacks did not flock to the Yankees as numerously as their counterparts had in Georgia. General Geary stated that some five hundred blacks followed the 2nd Division, most of them women and children. Colonel Mindil reported only thirty-two black refugees with the 2nd Brigade. Blacks whose freedom predated the war called such newly liberated slaves "Sherman Cutlooses." Now Sherman in fact cut them loose. He ordered the throng of black refugees to march to Wilmington, accompanied by two hundred of his men.[17]

Decades later, area blacks recalled their encounters with the Yankees for WPA interviewers. To Louisa Adams, it seemed like the soldiers were "popping out of the ground" when they suddenly appeared at her Richmond County plantation. Slave John C. Becton recalled a bummer catching a shoat on his Fayetteville area plantation, cutting off a hindquarter, and telling him to carry it to his mother, which he did by dragging it on the ground. He also remembered the Yankees routinely called blacks "Johnnie, Dinah, Bill, and other funny names." Sarah Louise Augustus remembered Sherman's men saying that "if they had to come again they would take the babies from the cradles." When the soldiers told the blacks they were free, they "became so excited they began to shout and pray. I thought they were all crazy."[18]

A rumor buzzed in camp that the enemy was in force with artillery support some fifteen miles away, behind the South River. "We may have to fight our way through yet," Lieutenant Colonel Lewis Warner observed. General Geary notified his command that it would be detached to escort the corps train when the army moved forward the next day. This routine assignment turned out to be of great consequence.[19]

"Some of our boys were chased by the Rebs and nearly captured," Alex Bird noted in his diary. Almost thirty years later, Sergeant Charles A. McIntosh of Company C recalled how he and Sergeant Major William Farlee ran into trouble near the Cape Fear River about eight miles from the regiment's camp. As they gathered sweet potatoes in a barnyard, yelling and shooting alerted them to rebel cavalrymen chasing a Yankee along the nearby road. Farlee dashed for his horse, jumped a gate in the farm lane, and made his getaway. McIntosh's mule balked at the gate and he was taken prisoner. The Confederates marched him to a field where he joined a group of thirty other captive bummers. At dark their guards started the Yankees marching. When the Confederates crossed a stream on a log bridge, forcing the Yankees to splash through the water, McIntosh darted beneath the span undetected. He then made his way to a shanty housing some blacks, and one of the occupants offered to guide him back to the army. The two traveled a long way through a swamp, evading a Confederate picket post along the way. "I was a hard looking customer when I got back in our lines," McIntosh remembered. "We got in camp about midnight."[20]

Wednesday, March 15, 1865. "Army ordered to strip for a fight," Colonel Warner noted. The Confederates were said to occupy Sherman's next objective, Goldsboro. As Geary had indicated the previous day, while the 1st and 3rd divisions moved ahead, the 2nd Division remained behind to escort the 20th Corps train. When the 154th New York moved at 4:00 p.m., however, it was in charge of the cavalry's train. Rain was falling, and the men made only six miles over wretched roads before halting at 4:00 a.m. on March 16. "This slow movement is very fatiguing to the men, especially in the night," Warner observed. The stop-and-go pace made for "a tedious night."[21]

Thursday, March 16, 1865. After a brief rest the weary soldiers ate some breakfast and slept for a couple of hours. Then they got up and moved the cavalry's wagons about four miles to join the main train. After dinner they relaxed until dark, when the march resumed in the rain. It took the men all night to wrestle the wagons two miles over the execrable road. Geary's division was now guarding the trains of the entire 20th Corps, the cavalry division, and the engineers, plus the pontoon train—a total of almost eleven hundred wagons. As onerous as the duty was, it kept the men away from danger, for while the White Stars dragged wagons through the mud, the 20th Corps' 1st and 3rd divisions, a division of the 14th Corps, and Kilpatrick's cavalry fought a battle at Averasboro, suffering about seven hundred casualties. The Confederates, who lost approximately five hundred men, abandoned their lines in the night. As a consequence of the fighting, Geary was ordered to send empty wagons and ambulances to the front, together with a number of ammunition and supply wagons.[22]

Friday, March 17, 1865. All night the soldiers pushed mud-caked wagons over almost impassable roads in disagreeable weather. In the morning they laid corduroy for the train to bump over. In the afternoon they crossed the South River on a makeshift span of poles and logs. On the opposite shore they entered Sampson County and were pleased to find a better road and better weather. They tramped three miles and pitched camp. After being up two nights in a row with scarcely anything to eat, they were exhausted and hungry. After a good supper, they immediately went to sleep.[23]

Saturday, March 18, 1865. The march got under way at 6:30 a.m., with the 154th leading the brigade and in charge of the first forty wagons of the train. The weather was fine and the roads were drying up quickly. But once again the soldiers had to corduroy most of the way, and progress was consequentially slow. They covered no more than three miles as low, swampy terrain gave way to fine, thickly settled countryside. Shortly after crossing Little Coharie Creek, they halted at sunset. After setting up camp, they were issued some badly needed new shoes and detailed for overnight picket duty. "If we meet no enemy," Colonel Warner mused in his diary, "I hope that not many days will elapse before we are in a permanent camp."[24]

Sunday, March 19, 1865. The regiment marched at 7:00 a.m. in the rear of the brigade but in advance of the train. A clear and uncommonly still morning led to an uncomfortably warm afternoon. The entire brigade corduroyed the road, which was lined with pines, perfect material for the work. Heavy artillery firing was heard to the front and left—the rest of the Left Wing was fighting at Bentonville. Geary received orders to follow a new road toward Goldsboro, about twenty-five miles distant. The 154th moved three miles in that direction and camped at nightfall. About 11:00 p.m. the regiment was ordered to march at midnight as escort to the 20th Corps headquarters train bound for the front. The men knew a heavy engagement had been waged that day, but the result was unknown. They expected a battle on the morrow.[25]

Monday, March 20, 1865. Shortly after midnight the regiment started on its mission. The men moved about a mile, and the order was countermanded. They returned to camp and were detailed to relieve another regiment on picket duty. Meanwhile, in response to an urgent message from Sherman, Geary's 1st and 3rd brigades marched to the front, where preparations were being made for an attack the next day at Bentonville. The 2nd Brigade, together with the engineer and pontoon regiments, was left in charge of the train. When daylight broke, the 154th's pickets were drawn in, the wagons were packed up and parked as close together as possible, and the regiment built entrenchments around the train. About noon a staff officer arrived with an order from Geary: the train was to proceed to Goldsboro by the most direct road. But the men did not move until 9:00 p.m.; they were still slogging over bad roads at midnight.[26]

Tuesday, March 21, 1865. When the regiment camped at 3:00 a.m. at Thornton's plantation, a report circulated that the enemy had retired from the Left Wing's front. After a few hours of sleep the men were on the move again at 8:00 a.m. They marched about seven miles over much improved roads and halted while a bridge was built. The tramp resumed at 4:00 p.m. in a heavy rain, and they covered only one more mile before camping at dark at Grantham's Store. Heavy cannonading was heard to the left in the evening, the final shots at Bentonville. Although General Joseph E. Johnston's Confederate army retreated, the battle was inconclusive. The road to Goldsboro was now open for Sherman's army, but it had failed to destroy the enemy.[27]

During the day troops under General Alfred Terry crossed the road in the 154th's front, having journeyed inland from Wilmington. Terry's command formed part of Major General John M. Schofield's Army of the Ohio, which at this point joined Sherman's army. Among Terry's regiments was the 112th New York, a Chautauqua County unit raised in tandem with the 154th during the summer of 1862 and organized at the same camp. Now, two and a half years later, members of the two regiments enjoyed a reunion. When a 112th man complained to Edson Ames that his regiment had not received mail in seven days and had been on half rations, Ames proudly replied that the 154th had not received mail in seventy days and foraged for its rations.[28]

Wednesday, March 22, 1865. The regiment marched toward the Neuse River at eight o'clock on a cool morning. As the day warmed, clouds of dust swirled in high winds. The men made about nine miles and parked the train about three miles from Goldsboro, where the wagons were expected to remain for the present and a temporary corps depot and hospital were to be established. A group of Confederate prisoners passed by. "They looked awful," wrote Levi Bryant, "ragged and dirty and half-starved."[29]

Sherman's army rendezvoused around Goldsboro, ending the campaign by uniting with Schofield's Army of the Ohio, establishing a base, and reopening communications with the north. "The army has been successful and accomplished its objective and more," stated Edgar Shannon, but more work remained to be done. While most of Sherman's men enjoyed a rest, the 154th New York would be active for several more days. Until the railroad between Kinston and Goldsboro was repaired, wagons had to haul supplies from the former to the latter. Colonel Warner expected the regiment would accompany the train the roughly thirty miles to Kinston the next day. Every available wagon was being unloaded for the purpose. Warner estimated the round trip would take five days. He had no idea that the mundane assignment would lead to tragic consequences.[30]

[13]

Killings in Greene County

Thursday, March 23, 1865. At 6:00 a.m. the 154th New York and the 109th Pennsylvania, under the overall command of Lieutenant Colonel Lewis Warner, headed toward Kinston as escort to two hundred wagons. The day was pleasant, the roads were good, and most of the men rode in the empty vehicles. The convoy crossed the Neuse River into Wayne County, passed through Goldsboro, and headed down river into Lenoir County. Richard McCadden thought Goldsboro seemed like "a nice little town," but Edgar Shannon described it as antiquated. After a twenty-mile trip, the men camped at sunset eight miles from Kinston. Some of them took advantage of the fine countryside and foraged good dinners.[1]

Edgar Shannon predicted that Goldsboro would "make a poor show after Sherman's army gets out of it." But General John Schofield's men occupied the town and protected it from Sherman's vandals. In a memoir initially published in 1866, Cornelia Phillips Spencer recalled crowds of refugees pouring into Goldsboro daily seeking food and shelter, having fled from the army's path through the countryside. Most of them arrived on foot, having no other means of transportation. The number of carriages, buggies, and wagons collected by the Yankees astonished Spencer. Those they had no use for were burned or broken up.[2]

In another postwar reminiscence, J. M. Hollowell recalled how bummers tormented the Wayne County countryside. In one instance, they stripped a woman and her small children of food except a bit of cornmeal and a jug of sorghum—but they dropped dripping wads of tobacco into the jug. According to Hollowell, most of the pillaging took place within a few miles of Goldsboro. The Yankees hesitated to go farther into the countryside unless in heavy force, for fear of roving bands of Confederate bushwhackers. His memory was accurate. At this late stage of events, bummers were perhaps in more peril than ever before.[3]

Friday, March 24, 1865. The march resumed at 6:00 a.m. The men passed through Kinston, crossed the Neuse River, and proceeded about two miles down river to a landing, where they loaded wagons with supplies. Eight companies of the 154th accompanied full wagons to Kinston and spent the night; the other two companies remained behind to load more wagons. The men found Kinston full of refugees seeking government rations. During the day, Brigadier General Patrick H. Jones returned to the regiment after his lengthy convalescence in the North.[4]

Saturday, March 25, 1865. Eight companies headed for Goldsboro at 6:00 a.m.; the two companies at the landing would reach Kinston this evening and follow a day behind the others. Many of the men had ridden in the wagons from Goldsboro to Kinston. Now they walked, repairing the roads where necessary. Camp was made about eight miles from Goldsboro.[5]

The regiment again suffered a death when Private Joel W. Woodruff of Company G succumbed to edema at Goldsboro. He had been hospitalized at Savannah and still suffered during the Carolinas campaign; bloated with dropsy, he either marched at will without his musket or rode in an ambulance. On this Saturday he lay down in his hospital tent and expired within minutes. Woodruff left a widow and four children at his East Otto, Cattaraugus County, home.[6]

During this day parties of bummers, accompanied by black followers, slipped away from the 154th to see what could be found. About three decades later the participants related what happened. One group headed north on confiscated horses into Greene County, toward Snow Hill. Two women waved a United States flag to attract them to a large white house, where the patriarch possessed documents, signed by a Federal general, attesting he was a Unionist. He regaled the Yankees with stories, and the ladies treated them to a dramatic piano interlude. The expedition was off to a good start.

At the next house the bummers captured a Confederate lieutenant and a private. Private Norman H. Hugaboom of Company K confiscated the officer's sword. After filling wagons and carts with plenty of edibles, the Yankees escorted their captives to the vicinity of Snow

Hill and turned them over to a detachment of the 12th New York Cavalry. A captain of the 12th noticed Hugaboom's sword, and after some words between the two he had the young private arrested and tied to his horse. The captain told the other bummers to turn in their personal mounts and return with the vehicles to their command. He also warned that a detachment of rebel cavalry was in the vicinity. Then he and his squad rode away with the hapless Hugaboom in tow. What seemed at the time a misfortune to Hugaboom would turn out to be a lucky break.

Corporals Nelson Fisk and Esley Groat of Company G somehow managed to remain mounted, Fisk on a roan horse, Groat on a mule. The other bummers were now on foot. The cavalry troopers had scarcely departed when a group of Confederate horsemen galloped down the road, firing as they came. The Yankees scattered into the woods, leaving behind two wounded black companions. In the panic, the foragers' carts overturned and strewed the road with food.

Groat kicked his mule and galloped off after the 12th New York men. Fisk hopped from his roan, tossed away some plundered jewelry, and crawled under a pile of brush. Privates Asa S. Wing and Jeremiah Houck of Company G darted into the bushes; Houck found his way to a nearby barn. Meanwhile, the Confederates fanned out and captured Corporal Zadock H. Fales of Company I, Private Thomas Murray of Company G, and Charles McIntosh, nabbed for the second time within two weeks. A Confederate threatened to shoot Fales, who reportedly replied like a steel magnolia: "Shoot and be damned." Almon Deforest Reed somehow escaped. When the enemy vanished, he spotted Fisk hiding in the brush heap and motioned to him, whereupon three Confederates rose from their own hiding places and captured the two Yankees.

Then the 12th New York cavalrymen—perhaps alerted by Esley Groat—galloped back onto the scene, sending the enemy fleeing with their prisoners. That night Jeremiah Houck appeared in camp "looking wild" after his close call. Meanwhile Asa Wing, after separating from Houck and watching the capture of his comrades, set off on foot for Goldsboro. Eventually he fell in with another fugitive Yankee, but before long a squad of Confederate cavalry captured and immediately robbed the two bummers.[7]

Thinking he was about to be captured, Nelson Fisk threw away the incriminating breastpin and pair of earrings he had stolen from some southern woman. Conscience prevented some members of the regiment from plundering. Levi Bryant explained to his wife why he did not send her any presents: "The horsemen can ride on in the advance of the troops and stop at the houses and get what they want, and when the troops come up they post a guard at the door and let no one in. And I never had face enough on me to go into a house and step up to a young girl and demand her rings or blow out her brains. And I thank God for the heart I have. It is not so hard as some I find. When I can stoop to rob the women of their little keepsakes, I must have my heart hardened, and case hardened first. So if you want me to send you such presents I must come home and let your father case-harden my old heart." Not all the men obeyed such scruples, of course. General Geary admitted, "That acts of pillage and wrong to defenseless inhabitants were committed by foragers when not under the eye of their officers we had daily evidence."[8]

Sunday, March 26, 1865. The eight companies marched at 6:00 a.m. and reached Goldsboro three and a half hours later, having rapidly covered fourteen miles. At noon they found the 20th Corps camped on the north side of the Neuse, where they reunited with the 2nd Brigade. After dinner they laid out a camp in the woods and started to fix it up. They were delighted to receive mail, the first they had seen since leaving Sisters Ferry, Georgia. Edgar Shannon assured his girlfriend, "I was very glad to hear from you after so long a campaign, out by ourselves all alone." He received ten letters in all and delighted in reading them. "For an hour or two I was back in Cattaraugus with those I love, instead of here in the army." Dell and Edson Ames received sad news from home: a young brother had died. After the difficulties of the campaign, Edson wrote, "then to get such bad news, it almost makes me sick."[9]

More of the 154th's foragers ran into trouble in the Greene County hinterlands. Like the other group of bummers, Sergeant Andrew G. Park and Private Joseph Cullen of Company B, Sergeant Harrison Coe of Company F, Sergeant George Bailey and Corporal Job B. Dawley of Company K, and two black companions had struck off from the regiment on March 25. They had stolen a carriage and a single rig and the horses to drive them and stuffed the vehicles with eggs, butter, and other treats. On this Sunday evening they stopped near Speights Bridge Post Office, about twelve miles northwest of Snow Hill, and requested supper at the home of the Williams family. While the meal was being prepared, a squad of blue-clad horsemen rode up and surrounded the house. The bummers assumed the intruders were Union troops until they began taking potshots through the windows.[10]

The attackers were a squad of the 6th Georgia Cavalry commanded by Second Lieutenant James Jasper O'Neill. Only twenty years old, O'Neill was a hardened veteran who had previously served in an infantry regiment and survived wounding and captivity. He and the 6th Cavalry had plagued Sherman's men (and local civilians) during the marches through Georgia and the Carolinas in hard and dangerous service. Yankee bullets dismounted him five times, O'Neill stated in a UDC memoir, but he escaped serious wounds. He commanded a squad of secret scouts who dressed in blue to fool the enemy, enabling them to capture unsuspecting Yankees in broad daylight. Now he and his men had the drop on the Yankees in the Williams house.[11]

O'Neill strode across the veranda to the front door, fired his pistol, and shouted for the occupants to surrender. From inside, Joseph Cullen fired a shot that clipped whiskers from O'Neill's throat. A general fusillade followed, with the Confederates shooting into windows and the Yankees returning fire from inside. One of the Georgians was hit in the hand, and one of their horses was shot. From the cover of the house the bummers drove the enemy away.

Expecting them to return any minute, the five Yankees mounted horses and headed down the road, followed by their two black companions driving the vehicles. About three-quarters of a mile away, they crossed a deep creek on a plank bridge (presumably Contentnea Creek at Speights Bridge). George Bailey suggested they stop to tear up the planks and throw them in the creek to impede pursuit. His companions unwisely vetoed his advice. Soon O'Neill and his men, "yelling like devils," caught up with the fleeing bummers. Four or five "Rebs" galloped by Andrew Park to fire at the carriages, which were careening down the road at "full chisel." They soon overtook the vehicles and brought them to a halt, capturing the two blacks. At the same time another Georgian drew his horse abreast of Park and demanded his surrender. Park obeyed and handed over his weapon. The Confederate ordered him to hand over his money, and Park turned over his cash and trinkets.

Another Confederate rode up to Park without a word and fired his revolver at the helpless bummer, who simultaneously threw himself forward onto his horse's neck. The shot burned a hole in Park's overcoat and cut the drawstring of his drawers at the small of his back, but he was unhurt. When Park demanded to be treated as an unarmed prisoner of war, the Georgian replied that all bummers should be killed, that they had no business plundering Confederate citizens. When Park said that they were foraging for provisions in accordance with orders, the Confederate responded, "Damn you, we do not take any prisoners of war—no time to fuss with them." He cocked his revolver and took aim at Park. Then he reconsidered. He would spare Park, whose exchange would free a Confederate from a northern prison camp. "Turn around and go with me damn lively," he ordered. Park and his captor rode a short distance and met up with Joseph Cullen and George Bailey, both of them now prisoners in the hands of the Georgians. The entire party continued a short distance and came to a sudden halt.

Sprawled motionless in the road were the bodies of Harrison Coe and Job Dawley. Standing nearby were Jasper O'Neill and the rest of his men. Joe Cullen asked O'Neill for permission to see if the two were alive. O'Neill assented, and Cullen approached the still bodies. Both men were dead. Coe had been shot point-blank in the chest, Dawley in the back. Cullen opened Dawley's shirtfront, excised the fatal bullet from under the skin of the young man's chest, and pocketed it. When Andrew Park asked O'Neill for permission to bury Dawley and Coe, O'Neill curtly refused. The top of the ground was too good for them, the Georgian declared. In O'Neill's eyes, the two dead bummers had gotten what they deserved.

A year after the incident, Park swore he witnessed O'Neill murder his two comrades, but decades later he stated that he first saw Dawley and Coe "not five minutes after they were shot." The exact circumstances of their deaths remain uncertain. Did they resist capture or antagonize their captors? Were they caught carrying plundered loot? Or were they executed in cold blood? The answers died with the principals involved.

Leaving the corpses of Coe and Dawley behind, the Georgian cavalrymen marched their prisoners northwest toward the town of Wilson. A half mile up the road, the Confederates took Cullen, Park, and Bailey into the woods, intending to hang them. The guards lined the prisoners up with their backs against a gigantic fallen tree and threatened to shoot anyone who moved. By then, Jasper O'Neill had recognized Joe Cullen as his assailant at the Williams house. "Damn you,"

O'Neill exclaimed, "you are the fellow who shot me, and I'll have you anyway." Cullen stared at the incensed lieutenant for a moment before he calmly stated that if they wished to hang him, he would die like a soldier. For a moment all was silent. Impressed by Cullen's bravery, O'Neill dropped his threat and the three bummers were herded away.

In the following weeks Cullen, Park, Bailey, and the previous day's captives were shipped from place to place in the collapsing Confederacy: from Wilson to Raleigh, Salisbury, and Charlotte, North Carolina, and to Chester, Spartansburg, and Newberry Court House, South Carolina, where they were paroled. They then proceeded to Washington, Georgia, and took a train to Augusta, where with the war over they were "turned loose," as Charles McIntosh put it, "to make our way to Savannah the best way we could." From Savannah the men were shipped to New York City, where they were mustered out in June and July 1865.

After he returned home, Andrew Park contacted Laura Coe, Harrison Coe's young widow, and John M. Dawley, Job Dawley's brother and a fellow veteran of the 154th New York. Park provided Mrs. Coe with an affidavit to support her claim for a widow's pension, and in 1866 she and her three-year-old daughter were awarded a stipend of eight dollars per month. Park presented John Dawley with a grisly relic of his brother's death—the bullet Joe Cullen had extracted from Job Dawley's chest.[12]

Edgar Shannon reported the capture of Park and the others about two weeks after the incident. "We don't know whether the rebels killed them or not," Shannon noted. "We hope they may come out all right." A week later Chaplain William Norton stated that the missing men were still in the enemy's hands "we suppose." When word of Dawley's death reached the regiment a month later, his Company K comrade David Jones wrote, "He was one of the best boys in the regiment." Marcellus Darling described Dawley in his memoir as "a brave and good soldier as ever wore a uniform, my dear good friend." Darling stated that Dawley had been "shot down in cold blood. I can see him standing and never flinching, when they shot him, as others escaping reported he did." Until Park reported it, Coe's fate remained unknown. The two corpses apparently were never recovered. Dawley's family erected a cenotaph to his memory in his hometown of Perrysburg, Cattaraugus County. It stated that Job was twenty years, two months, and ten days of age when he was killed. Coe died at age twenty-five.[13]

The killing of Coe and Dawley was not an isolated incident. In a patch of woods Colonel George Mindil found the corpse of a 20th Corps soldier who had been shot through the chest and his pockets rifled. A local black told Mindil that a squad of Confederate cavalry had killed ten captured Yankees on the same day that Coe and Dawley were shot. In response, General Geary issued an order banning unauthorized foraging expeditions. "This order is rendered necessary," he explained, "from the fact that small parties of men are known to have been sent out and captured."[14]

Nor were Coe and Dawley the only victims of the 6th Georgia Cavalry. A dozen Yankee prisoners had reportedly been executed by members of the 6th near Sandersville during the March to the Sea. When the war ended, the regiment's commander, Colonel John R. Hart, was under arrest for permitting his men to murder a captain of a New York regiment and a civilian in April 1865 at Wilson, North Carolina—the same town through which Coe and Dawley's surviving comrades had been herded during their peripatetic captivity. Coe and Dawley had the misfortune to fall into the hands of a ruthless bunch in the 6th Georgia Cavalry, an outfit whose crimes were condoned, if not ordered, by its officers.[15]

[14]

Victory

ON Monday, March 27, 1865, for the first time in many days, the 154th New York did not have to march. The men built quarters, policed camp, and drew three days' rations. With the supply line secure, food was again plentiful, but foraging parties nevertheless went out on consecutive days to increase the abundance. Looking around, the men were unimpressed by the dull landscape around Goldsboro, with its ubiquitous pines and their tar, pitch, and turpentine works.[1]

"The campaign seems to have closed for the present," wrote Lieutenant Colonel Lewis Warner, "and we are promised a season of rest and supplies preparatory to another and a final campaign, which I trust is to close up this long and tragic war." The troops were sadly in need of clothing, having worn out their uniforms and shoes. No two men seemed to be dressed alike; many wore civilian garb pillaged during the march, including women's hats and bonnets. General Sherman described his troops as "dirty, ragged, and saucy." But within two weeks, new uniforms and soap and water transformed the army's appearance, and Sherman watched the men "strut about as proud as young chicken cocks, with their clean faces and bright blue clothes."[2]

With the campaign over, commanding officers wrote their official reports. As was his custom, General Geary added commentary to his day-by-day summary of the march. The march through the Carolinas, he declared, while generally similar to the March to the Sea, was much more laborious and a thorough test of the soldiers' endurance and morale. They had marched greater distances—435 miles by his count—and surmounted greater natural obstacles during a more inclement season than they had on the Georgia march. Nevertheless, their spirit had remained "confident and buoyant," and their self-belief and trust in Sherman had never wavered.[3]

Geary presented statistical tables enumerating the immense amounts of foodstuffs and animals his division foraged from the countryside and the railroads, fence rails, cotton, resin, and mills it destroyed, all of which he valued at almost $3 million. He figured his men had constructed sixty miles of corduroy road. Colonel Mindil estimated the 2nd Brigade had traversed nearly five hundred miles and corduroyed at least fifteen miles of road. He also calculated the amounts of food his men had foraged and consumed. More than a hundred horses and mules had been added to the brigade's herds and fared well on tons of fodder, all but a small part of it gathered from the countryside. "Considering the distance traveled, the severity of the march, and the hard labor performed on the roads," Mindil concluded, "the troops arrived in camp in good health and excellent spirits."[4]

While the commanders wrote their reports, the enlisted men penned letters home. Wrote Charles Abell to his parents, "Sherman and his *band* of 'thieves and robbers,' as we have been styled by the Southern press, [are] marching through the life-giving portion of the great Southern Confederacy, and great men have estimated that he will be in operating distance of Grant in less than a month more after he starts again. . . . With those two armies acting in conjunction, what will the Gray Backs do? They will crawl worse than their namesakes, and, I dare say, find it too hot for comfort. The silver lining of that black cloud is truly coming into view, and what a glorious rejoicing—I will not attempt to describe—when we *come marching home.*"[5]

In a letter to his sweetheart, Edgar Shannon contrasted the plenty enjoyed by the army with the suffering of the Carolinians. "We have had some gay times and some that were not so gay—occasionally in a swamp ten miles long; I was going to say as many miles in depth, but I thought you might think I was lying. Then again [we] had good roads, splendid foraging, and lots to eat. Chickens and turkeys until I got sick of it, fresh pork and sweet potatoes, jellies and all such luxuries, honey on every side. But if we lived well, someone else must suffer. I tell you that some of the people in North and South Carolina must suffer. I have seen families who in times of peace could look over their thousands of acres and count their gold by thousands, who after our army passed through had not a mouthful to eat, or a quilt to cover them. I have pitied them, but such things are the result of war, and I think they will hesitate next time ere they urge a rebellion."[6]

The Carolinas segment of Sherman's great march was over, but campaigning remained to be done. For the 154th New York, there was one more tragedy yet to endure. It occurred on March 30, 1865, when the enemy killed Private Charles Terett of Company C, who was on detached duty as an orderly at 20th Corps headquarters. Another orderly described the occurrence to Colonel Warner. Somewhere between Goldsboro and Snow Hill, apparently, an unidentified officer and the two orderlies encountered some Confederates. Shots were fired and Terett fell from his horse, "to all appearances dead." His corpse was left in the hands of the enemy. The 154th's hospital steward, Charles Harry Matteson, later heard that Terett's throat was cut and a sign was pinned to his uniform. (Such signs often read "Death to Foragers.") Terett—whose army bounty and pay had gone to the support of his family—left his parents and six younger siblings destitute on a hardscrabble farm in Potter County, Pennsylvania.[7]

To the delight of the members of the 154th, Brigadier General Patrick H. Jones assumed command of the 2nd Brigade on March 30, relieving the disliked Colonel Mindil. Jones presented each member of his old regiment with a new pair of socks and a lump of sugar. Mindil, who had long lobbied for a promotion to brigadier general, received that rank by an honorary brevet and was temporarily appointed to General Slocum's staff. When Colonel Ario Pardee fell ill and went north for medical treatment in April, Mindil took his place in command of the 1st Brigade.[8]

On March 28, 1865, Slocum's Left Wing, consisting of the 14th and 20th Corps, was officially designated the Army of Georgia. An unwelcome change occurred on April 2, when Major General Joseph A. Mower, a division commander in the 17th Corps, replaced Alpheus Williams at the head of the 20th Corps. Mower was a favorite of Sherman's, who had promised him a promotion. The rank and file of the 20th Corps regarded the switch as unfair to Pap Williams. Sherman later admitted that "it may have seemed unjust to replace him at that precise moment," but Williams gracefully acquiesced to the change.[9]

Mower reviewed the 2nd Division on April 5, and that day Geary gave a heartfelt speech as he presented the division and its three brigades with a set of splendid silk flags. Such pomp and pageantry was fleeting. Charles Abell predicted that a final campaign would be "the last great struggle of right over wrong, of Union over secession, of life nationally over national death." Levi Bryant thought Sherman's army would join Grant to capture Richmond, "and then I guess the rebellion is dead." But Sherman had to contend with Joseph Johnston before he could turn his attention to Virginia. No one had an inkling of the drama that would be witnessed in the next few weeks.[10]

The whirlwind of extraordinary events began on April 6, when news reached Goldsboro by telegraph that Richmond had fallen. When the regiment got the news, the men surrounded General Patrick Jones and gave three cheers for him, for the Union, and for their old comrades of the Army of the Potomac. Then they celebrated—some by getting drunk—until 1 a.m. While bands played patriotic airs, the men improvised an accompaniment by igniting tin cans and wagon wheel hubs filled with gunpowder, causing thunderous blasts. After "a long night of deaths and desolation to our beloved country," Emory Sweetland wrote, "the war-worn and weary soldiers can now see the dawning of peace and better days." Gene Graves was unconcerned that Lee's army might be headed toward North Carolina. "I think Sherman could eat them in one mouthful," he declared. "They had better keep away from the White Stars, for the Rebs dread them more than any other two corps in the army."[11]

The 154th New York broke camp on April 10 and led the brigade through Goldsboro and out the road toward Smithfield. The following morning the regiment encountered the enemy and took a few potshots at the retreating Rebs in its last skirmish of the war. None of the men were hurt. That afternoon they reached Smithfield, where they apparently chose to ignore the orders urging moderation in North Carolina (and the imminent end of the war). The men, as Charles Abell noted, "*gutted* the place as usual."[12]

April 12, 1865, brought glorious news. That morning the men were eating breakfast when distant shouting was heard. The hubbub approached their position in the person of General Geary, who sparked the enthusiasm as he slowly rode down the line and spoke to the troops. When he reached the 154th's position and announced the surrender of Lee to Grant, the men threw their hats in the air and shouted their joy. Would Johnston follow Lee's example? "If not," wrote Chaplain William Norton, "we will, with the blessing of Heaven, soon grind him to powder."[13]

That day the 154th New York and the 73rd Pennsylvania set off with the division train for Raleigh. Emory Sweetland noted that very little property was disturbed. The regiment reached North Carolina's capital on April 14 and went into camp behind the insane asylum, situated on a high hill in the city's western outskirts. The institution's superintendent was greatly distressed by the Yankees' presence, but his patients were unconcerned. Certain inmates amused the soldiers with Union speeches and songs. The asylum drew many visitors, among them Generals Sherman, Mower, and Williams.[14]

Confederate soldiers had spread "great yarns" about Sherman's men among Raleigh's populace, John Langhans noticed. He heard a boy remark, "Why, I have stood here all this time and seen the Yankees pass, but I have not seen one with any horns on yet." In a memoir, Raleigh's Kate McKimmon recalled that the Yankees looked fat and sleek, presenting a stark contrast to the Confederates, who two days before had passed through footsore, ragged, and hungry. Raleigh had clean streets and many homes reflecting wealth, Charles Abell observed. "It don't look so demoralized as most of the towns and cities we have passed through." Emory Sweetland thought the inhabitants appeared to be quite loyal. Kate McKimmon reported that the Yankees did no plundering in the capital.[15]

When news arrived on April 16 that Johnston would surrender to Sherman, the regiment got joyfully drunk. But Sherman bungled the ensuing negotiations by offering terms too wide ranging and liberal for political acceptance in the North. As a storm of criticism broke over the general, the government rejected his pact. Members of the 154th did not comment on the controversy in their surviving letters or diaries, but their admiration for Sherman never wavered. In the meantime, on April 17, shocking news arrived: President Lincoln had been assassinated in Washington. The sad tidings "cast a gloom over the whole army," Charles Abell wrote, "and made many an eye flash vengeance." Raleigh was triple guarded, he noted, to prevent the men from laying it as low as Columbia. If there was to be another battle, Abell thought, Sherman's heartsick and furious men would take no prisoners in retaliation for the assassination.[16]

Sherman reviewed the 20th Corps in Raleigh on April 22, 1865. The city, Colonel Warner boasted, "never witnessed a greater military assemblage." Sherman's pride in his army remained palpable. "I will challenge the world," he declared, "to exhibit a finer looking set of men, brawny, strong, swarthy." Three days later, the 154th marched for Jones's Cross Roads. Johnston surrendered to Sherman on April 26, accepting the same terms that Grant had offered Lee. The news traveled after dark from brigade headquarters to the regiment's camp, accompanied by General Jones's compliments and some commissary department whiskey. One by one the officers mounted a stump and made speeches to a cheering audience. The celebration lasted beyond midnight. The regiment returned to Raleigh two days later, and that night fireworks dazzled the sky.[17]

On April 30 the 154th New York broke camp and led the brigade through Raleigh on its way north to Washington. The ensuing march was mostly made in stifling heat and parching dust and proved to be one of the toughest of the regiment's entire service, averaging eighteen miles a day. The men believed they were engaged in a foolish race between the 20th and 14th Corps, instigated by higher-ups who had bet on the outcome. Thousands of Army of Georgia men fell out along the way, hundreds became ill, and dozens died of heat prostration. Including this march of 280 miles, the regiment covered roughly 1,020 total miles from Atlanta to Savannah to Washington. In his later years, John Langhans stressed to his grandchildren that he walked all the way, the only hint of hardship and tedium in the family legend.[18]

Civilians feared the approach of Sherman's men, whose reputation preceded them. Virginians applied for guards to protect their property. But their fears were unfounded. "The march was as orderly as it would have been through our own country," Emory Sweetland reported. "Nothing taken or destroyed. The inhabitants appeared friendly." In the area of Richmond, Sherman's men encountered soldiers of the Army of the Potomac. Charles Abell heard one declare, "Sherman's men don't care for bayonets or bullets, but wherever they take a notion to go, they just go." Some of the easterners dreaded Sherman's reputedly rough and ruthless men.[19]

On May 11, 1865, the 154th marched through Richmond in cadenced step, with drums beating and colors flying. In passing the residence of Robert E. Lee, the regiment snapped a marching salute to its old foe. North of the city the men crossed peaceful countryside until they reached their old Chancellorsville battleground and the nearby Wilderness and Spotsylvania battlefields. The entire area was a vast graveyard; acres of shattered trees loomed over ground strewn with bones and skulls. "Great was the destroying power of war," reflected David Jones on viewing the forlorn landscape, "but Virginia has suffered nothing like South Carolina." Glad to put the battlefields behind them, the men finished their last long march on May 19 at Cloud's Mills, near Alexandria, Virginia.[20]

A final celebration awaited the soldiers in Washington—the Grand Review of the Union armies before President Andrew Johnson, other government officers, foreign dignitaries, and an immense crowd of citizens. The capital was crowded with out-of-town visitors, including a contingent from Cattaraugus County. The black mourning crepe that had draped public and private buildings since Lincoln's assassination was replaced with bunting and bouquets for the victory parades. The Army of the Potomac was reviewed on May 23, 1865; Sherman's army marched the following day. The contrast between the two forces was striking. Sherman's westerners were not as well dressed or as spit-and-polished as the easterners, although they tried to clean up as best they could—General Geary outfitted every man in his division with a pair of white gloves. Onlookers noticed that the famous marchers took a stride from two to four inches longer than their eastern counterparts. Folks also noted that the eastern regiments of the 20th Corps now resembled their western comrades. The audience delighted in the ax-wielding pioneers, chicken-laden foragers, and black cooks, teamsters, and hangers-on interspersed between regiments. The review was a triumph for Sherman's men—they marched as well as their eastern rivals, if not better. "It was a great time," John Langhans, recently promoted to corporal, informed his brother. "I wish you could have seen us that day." Spectators crowded the sidewalks, housetops, and even the trees along the route and greeted Sherman's men with waving handkerchiefs, garlands of flowers, and thunderous cheers and applause. "All that was lacking," wrote Richard McCadden, "was our much loved President [Lincoln] to review us, but alas! He is gone."[21]

After parading through Washington, the men bivouacked beside a railroad near Bladensburg, Maryland. Celebrations continued in the 154th's camp. Two days after the Grand Review, Governor Reuben E. Fenton paid a visit to the 20th Corps and made a speech to the New York State troops. On May 30, Fenton returned to the 154th's camp to present the regiment with a new stand of colors. Among the battle honors painted on the state flag were "Savannah" and "Campaign of the Carolinas."[22]

Two days before the 154th New York was mustered out, Corporal

Langhans summed up the months he had spent marching with Sherman's army. "It is just nine months ago today when we left East Otto," he reflected on June 9, 1865. "When we then looked ahead it looked rather dark, but things look better now. Since then we have made a great circle in the United States and have seen many a hard day or night, but still I have seen lots of good times and I have had lots of fun. I would not have missed this chance for one thousand dollars."[23]

[15]

The Most Enjoyable Campaign of the War

JOHN LANGHANS would not have missed marching with Sherman for a thousand dollars. No doubt the Georgians and Carolinians he encountered along the way would have paid that sum (if they had it) to escape the experience. The devastation Sherman's men inflicted on the land was eventually mended. The damage they left on the southern psyche was apparently permanent, evident in the myth of the marches' utter devastation. Traveling through Dixie in the late 1980s, V. S. Naipaul found Civil War memory to be both a religion and a wound for white southerners, with Sherman their rampant bête noire. Naipaul claimed to have read about the general in newspapers or heard about him on television on a daily basis. Seeking a historical parallel, he wondered if Hannibal had been similarly remembered in Italy a century after his invasion.[1]

Southerners who lived and suffered along the 154th New York's route likewise looked to history for comparisons to Sherman. In her memoir, Decatur's Mary Gay dubbed him "the Nero of the nineteenth century," leader of "the most ruthless, Godless band of men ever organized in the name of patriotism—a band which, but for a few noble spirits who, by the power of mind over matter, exerted a restraining influence, would not have left a Southerner to tell the tale of fiendishness on its route to the sea." Gay thus multiplied the legendary single kind Yankee into a few saints of restraint who by some psychic power prevented their evil comrades from committing genocide. Nero would have glorified in Sherman's relentless mode of warfare, agreed the daughter of Winnsboro schoolmistress Catherine Ladd, but "a Washington or a Lee would have shrunk in terror."[2]

Before they fled Milledgeville, members of the Georgia legislature branded Sherman's men "dastardly and cowardly Hessians," evoking the German mercenaries hired by the British in the Revolutionary

War, known for their harsh treatment of civilians. This charge also fit with the southern stereotype of the Yankee army as largely composed of foreigners. To Winnsboro's Margaret Crawford Adams, Sherman was like Alaric, the Visigoth king who sacked Rome—but even the barbarian Alaric spared churches, "while this modern Goth burned them."[3]

Echoing the wartime rumors of horned Yankees, southerners cast Sherman and his men as demonic. Milledgeville newspaper editor Seth Broughton wrote, "If an army of Devils, just let loose from the bottomless pit, were to invade the country they could not be any worse than Sherman's army." Guy McKinley, a young boy when his Milledgeville area home was overrun, declared as an elderly man, "If the Devil appointed old Sherman 'to make war Hell,' he knew what he was about and sent his worthiest agent." Decades after bummers looted his family's South Carolina plantation and long after the general was dead, John Henry Jennings wryly remarked, "Old Sherman is no longer marching, but he is still burning!"[4]

Martha Amanda Quillin acidly described Sherman as "his most Christian majesty." To her, the day the army passed through Decatur was one that would "*never* be *forgotten*" and "the most miserable of all my life." She marveled at surviving the torture to which her mind and body were subjected. One year later, the effects were still to be felt. "This is now the poorest country in the world," Quillin declared, "and we are homeless wanderers in the desert." No wonder that she concluded, "No one I hope will ever expect me to love Yankees."[5]

Turnwold plantation escaped serious damage during the March to the Sea, and Joseph Addison Turner often described his encounters with the Yankees in humorous terms. But two weeks after Geary's division passed, Turner reflected bitterly on the experience. A mob of savage Yankees ("and Europeans") had surrounded his family with pistols and torches. His frightened children had clung to him weeping. He had ordered his wife to her room and begged her to stay there, fearful lest she should blurt something "which might cause the hyenas to insult her." Thousands upon thousands of other southerners had endured similar indignities. They could hardly be expected to love their tormentors and persecutors or to look favorably on reunion with the Yankees. The chances of reconciliation seemed impossible. Turner quoted a Putnam County resident whose house had been looted by the Yankees: "I always did hate them. Since I have seen them, I hate them more than ever. They are the meanest, lowest, FILTHIEST creatures in all the world. . . . I hope the last one of them will be killed."[6]

Some African Americans who encountered Sherman's army kept negative memories of the experience. "A holy war they called it," stated Thomas Campbell, formerly a slave near Winnsboro, "but they and Wheeler's men was a holy terror to this part of the world, as naked and hungry as they left it." Black lives had been as badly disrupted as white lives. Violet Guntharpe, once a slave in Rocky Mount, summarized the upheaval seventy years after Sherman came. Blacks were not ready for the changes wrought by the war, she declared. They had no education, no land, and no livestock with which to set up housekeeping. Before the war, blacks had good log cabins, milk from cows, meat and grease from fattened hogs, wool and cotton for clothing, and horses and mules to cultivate corn, "but when them Yankees come and take all that away, all us had to thank them for was a hungry belly, and freedom. Something us had no more use for then, than I have today for one of them airplanes I hears flying round the sky."[7]

"We cannot say that we are living as well as we did before the war," Fairfield District resident John Palmer wrote in 1866, "but we 'accept the situation' and are doing the best we can." To Palmer and other whites, the biggest hurdle to overcome was not the ruin sown by Sherman's army but the new racial relations engendered by the demise of slavery, with their economic and social ramifications. The whites had made contracts with the blacks, and for the time being the former were satisfied with the conduct of the latter. But Palmer considered cotton production by free black labor to be "a most fearful agricultural experiment" and considered the outcome doubtful. Southerners of both races would endure a tormented century resolving the consequences of black freedom.[8]

Travelers in the postwar South remarked on the destruction and bitterness bred by the marches. In the summer of 1865, journalist John T. Trowbridge toured the vanquished Confederacy and wrote a book about his experiences. In Atlanta he found "ruins and rubbish, mud and mortar and misery," but the city had begun its remarkable rise from the ashes. Streets were rapidly rebuilding, and there were more stores than ever before. Traversing Georgia, Trowbridge listened to stories of looted homes, slaughtered livestock, plundered provisions, the flight of inhabitants, the running off of slaves, of men hung to make them give up their money, and of kind Yankee officers who placed safeguards to protect property. Riding on a roughly repaired railroad, he was fascinated by the twisted iron littering the landscape. A former Confederate officer complained that Sherman was "the great robber of the nineteenth century" who "stripped our people of everything," but another veteran rebel officer stated the army "generally behaved very well" in Georgia.[9]

Trowbridge found evidence of amplified destruction in South Carolina, whose residents extended their hatred from Sherman's army to the federal government and northerners in general. Only in the Palmetto State was Trowbridge "treated with gross personal insults" as a northerner. Entering North Carolina, he reported an immediate improvement in conditions. Still, in Raleigh the governor exclaimed to him, "Of all the malignant wretches that ever cursed the earth, the hangers-on of Sherman's army were the worst. It can't be expected that the people should love a government that has subjected them in this way."[10]

Englishman John H. Kennaway toured the South at Sherman's suggestion in the autumn of 1865 and found a ravaged land of dismantled and untenanted plantations and neglected and overgrown fields. Once gaily dressed ladies were now depressed to wear plain clothes, perform menial tasks, and support themselves, their house servants and field hands having vanished. It was no surprise that Yankee plundering was deeply resented, Kennaway observed, for southerners claimed to have conducted a civilized and principled war. Comparing the conduct of Sherman's men in Georgia and South Carolina, he wrote, "If in their first march they carried whips, here they were armed with scorpions." A gloomy South Carolinian told Kennaway that residents were bearing their trials bravely but the ruin was so widespread and the efficacy of free black labor so uncertain that it would take at least a half century for the South to recover.[11]

In 1867 the naturalist John Muir set off on a long botanical excursion that took him through Georgia's Screven and Effingham counties. One evening he arrived at the home of a wealthy cotton planter who was scouring rust from cotton-gin saws, which he had submerged in his millpond to save from Sherman's men. "If Bill Sherman should come down now without his army," the planter growled, "he would never go back."[12]

Ironically, when Sherman himself toured the South in 1879 and stopped in Atlanta and Savannah, he met with a polite, if not warm, reception. But when the general returned to Atlanta two years later, he was received coolly. In the end, only one other Yankee general was as reviled by southerners: Benjamin F. Butler, who Confederates called "Beast" (for his notorious insult to the women of New Orleans) and "Spoons" (for his alleged theft of their silverware). In Sherman's opinion, southerners were fortunate that he, scourge though he was, had commanded the great marches rather than Butler.[13]

The passage of decades did not diminish contempt for Sherman in the South. As folklorist Elissa Henken observed, vanquished southerners, smarting from wartime hardships and postwar humiliation, concentrated their hatred on the man whose troops had brought the war to their homes, "that Devil Sherman," whose "name has become an epithet and analogy of opprobrium; no worse could be said of a person." In the totally destructive marches of southern myth, the general naturally plays the chief villain.[14]

On Memorial Day in 1903, more than a decade after his death, a monument to Sherman was dedicated at Fifth Avenue and Fifty-ninth Street in New York City. The sculpture by Augustus Saint-Gaudens depicts the mounted general following the winged figure of Victory. Beneath his striding horse's hooves is a broken pine branch—the only allusion in the grouping to the shattered South that Sherman left behind. When South Carolinian Anna Key Bartow first saw the monument, she proposed in verse some changes to ensure its accuracy. Victory's face should be veiled and her palm branch bound with rue, Bartow suggested; Sherman's horse should trample dead mothers and starved babies, and the general should carry a torch to blaze his trail. The sculpture also needed a background of lone chimneys, deserted gateways, tottering walls, crumbled hearths, and circling vultures. And it lacked an inscription—"War is Hell."[15]

The memories never ceased to fester. "We seemed to have lost all that life was worth living for," Margaret Crawford Adams informed her grandchildren in relating the poverty and degradation engendered by Sherman's marches. In a 1916 Winnsboro newspaper article, an anonymous author wrote, "It is not the cause that the opposing side fought for so much that still rankles in our Southern hearts, but the villainous means by which the end was gained." In a 1926 magazine article titled "Marching through Georgia Sixty Years After," a native Georgian mentioned Sherman only once and made a single reference to his men as a "devastating and irresistible boll-weevil army." Sherman's ruthlessness was most ungentlemanly, the Georgian populist Thomas E. Watson wrote a year later, but most effective. Had Confederate generals waged a similarly destructive war, "the result of the conflict might have been different."[16]

By Watson's time, southern hatred of Sherman was a cliché. Writers could not resist citing it in books about the region. If you dared to mention Sherman's name in Georgia or the Carolinas, William J. Robertson suggested in 1927, "seek cover first, and then if escape is not blocked, leave the section immediately for the North." Sherman incarnated "all the hated qualities of the 'damned Yankee.'" Indeed, the sins of Sherman the father had been visited upon his Yankee sons, Virginius Dabney reported in 1942. Northerners were regarded in some southern circles as Sherman's "spiritual descendants," as ruthless in their personal and business relationships as the diabolically efficient general.[17]

By the time of the Civil War centennial, an element of entrepreneurship had crept into the South's Sherman hatred. Thomas D. Clark reported in 1961 that southerners expected the four-year centennial observance to provide an enormous cash harvest as a major tourism draw. Sherman's notorious silver thieves "are now almost warmly remembered in the South," Clark wrote; the "once-hated freebooters have all but become sentimental characters in this day when every place a hundred years old is a potential tourist attraction." Nowhere was the dichotomy of both reviling and preserving Sherman's memory more evident than in Atlanta, which, observed B. C. Hall and C. T. Wood, "has fed off its martyrdom ever since Sherman burned it down in 1864."[18]

By the early twenty-first century, some southern Sherman hatred was tinged with camp. In 2004 a community club in Bartow, Georgia (the former Spier's Turnout on the Georgia Central Railroad), published a cookbook titled *Sherman Didn't Burn Our Recipes*. The name implies that Sherman burned everything else in Bartow, but the book's cover includes a photograph of a grand Bartow home built in 1860, which escaped the flames to serve present-day travelers (including the author) as a bed and breakfast. A 20th Corps officer reported destroying the Spier's Turnout station house, but an illustration in the book depicts the still-standing depot, which dates from 1859. In naming its cookbook after Sherman, the club felt compelled to add a disclaimer: "We do not recognize him as one of our favorite hometown heroes."[19]

To some modern-day southerners, Sherman hatred is more of a tradition than a deeply felt passion. When journalist Christopher Dickey returned to his native South in July 2008 to gauge the political scene as a historic presidential election neared, he chose to retrace "the deepest scar in the country—the blazing track of total war" left by Sherman's army. But Dickey found memories of the war to be largely irrelevant in modern Dixie. Citing the hobbyists who reenact the battles and camps of Johnnie Reb and Billy Yank far removed from the grave circumstances of their nineteenth-century prototypes, Dickey concluded, "Today the troubling inheritance of the Civil War has been turned into family entertainment."[20]

While southerners compared Sherman to Nero, Alaric, and Satan, and his army to their legions, northerners lionized the general and his men and elevated their marches to legendary status. Sherman was amused to be compared to history's renowned captains. On New Year's Day 1865, when he was toasted in Savannah and compared to Caesar and Hannibal, he joked that those two were small potatoes, never having read the *New York Herald* or been photographed. A year later he noted, "According to some enthusiasts, Hannibal, Alexander, and Napoleon fall below my standard." He claimed to laugh at such flatteries, but he enjoyed reporting them. His reputation spanned the globe. Writing to his wife from Savannah, he boasted of praise the March to the Sea had won in England and France. When he visited Havana in November 1866, he found the Cubans knowledgeable about "El Grande Marcha." Touring Europe in 1872, Sherman was showered with accolades. Twenty years after the marches, his mail remained full of requests from admirers for autographs, photographs, and wartime relics.[21]

To the generations since the Civil War, the March to the Sea has been as securely linked with Sherman's name as his famous (but misquoted) saying "War is hell." The march through Georgia captured the public imagination; the Carolinas campaign did not. Sherman deemed the Carolinas march "far more difficult and important," as he declared at Goldsboro in March 1865. Nine months later he wrote, "The march to the sea seems to have captivated everybody, whereas it was child's play compared with the other." In his memoirs he declared that the Carolinas march was ten times more important than that through Georgia. The latter was simply a "shift of base" from Atlanta to Savannah, he explained, while the Carolinas campaign—more difficult owing to terrain, weather conditions, and length—had brought about the capture of important cities and supply depots. Echoing Sherman, military analyst B. H. Liddell Hart characterized the Carolinas campaign as "the greatest march in modern history," citing the army's rapid transit of "intensely difficult terrain" while opposed by "a galaxy of Confederate generals and their great allies, Generals Winter and Mud."[22]

But posterity, including Union veterans and their families, remembered the March to the Sea. Its cachet was captured in Henry Clay Work's 1865 song "Marching through Georgia." This rollicking tune was not the only ditty inspired by the march, but it was by far the most popular. To Sherman's veterans, it was an anthem. At the 154th New York's annual reunion in 1891, a band closed the proceedings with a rendition. At the 1892 reunion, a glee club sang it. A year later, a mixed quartet sang it, the veterans joining heartily in the rousing refrain: "Hurrah! hurrah! we bring the jubilee! Hurrah! hurrah! the flag that makes you free! So we sang the chorus from Atlanta to the sea, while we were marching through Georgia." Georgians, of course, despised the tune. The state's UDC department launched a campaign to ban it from the nation's school songbooks. Sherman loathed it, too, but he could not escape it. Whenever he arrived at a function featuring music, the band was sure to blare Work's song.[23]

Other artists embraced the March to the Sea's romance. The National Academy of Design's 1865 exhibition featured paintings depicting the campaign by Thomas Nast and Felix Octavius Carr Darley. That same year Darley produced a drawing titled "On the March to the Sea." Made into an engraving, this depiction became the iconic image of the march, with its railroad destruction, burning barns, foraging, and blacks fleeing to freedom. Herman Melville celebrated the march in his 1866 poem "The March to the Sea," describing how "Sherman's miles of men" conquered nature and the feeble opposition of the enemy in a laughing frolic, although not without consequences: "For behind they left a wailing, A terror and a ban, And blazing cinders sailing, And houseless households wan, Wide zones of counties paling, And towns where maniacs ran."[24]

Like the general public, 154th New York veterans romanticized the Georgia march at the expense of the Carolinas campaign. "Was not the March to the Sea the most fascinating scene in all the great drama of our home war?" asked Alfred Benson in 1874, noting the campaign already had "the tinge of romance." Benson contrasted the march's uncertain beginning with its bright outcome. "That which promised to be the most perilous undertaking of the war turned out to be almost a holiday march, and with its zest of freshness and novelty, the most enjoyable campaign of the war." Marcellus Darling remembered it in his later years as simply "a picnic all the way."[25]

Charles McKay in his memoir described the March to the Sea as a campaign of "daring conception, brilliant execution, and triumphant finale," "one of the greatest in history," attributing its success to "the ablest man in genuine generalship that the war produced." By the time the army neared Savannah, McKay recalled, Sherman's men felt invincible. "Having the fullest confidence in our commander, we were now inspired with the utmost confidence in ourselves, and looked with almost disdain upon any force that the Confederates could bring against us." McKay's assessments fit perfectly into the emerging northern myth.[26]

In 1914, Alex Bird came across his old army diaries and arranged to have the March to the Sea entries published in his local newspaper during the campaign's fiftieth anniversary. It would bring back memories to his old comrades, Bird wrote, "and may be of some interest to some of their children and to others." Tellingly, the next year he did not bother to publish his diary of the Carolinas campaign.[27]

Perhaps the Carolinas campaign never achieved the luster of the Georgia march in the memories of Union veterans and the northern public because of its grubbier nature—the often gloomy weather, the slogging through mud, the endless labor of corduroying roads and wrestling with stuck wagons. "You have been writing about the nice times you have had at the parties and dances," John Langhans wrote to his brother at the end of the war. "But never mind, I shall make all that up. Maybe I was laying in some mud hole about those times in South Carolina, but that is all forgotten now." Memories of devastated and charred South Carolina also must have dampened any glorification.[28]

Like their commander, however, the men realized the magnitude of their achievement in the Carolinas. Edgar Shannon summarized it when the regiment reached Goldsboro: "Once more we have got where we can see out after a two months' campaign through the enemy's country, without a base and but very few rations except what we foraged on the country, an enemy continually in our front and rear, a great number of rivers, swamps without number. I think there is not such another march on record."[29]

"The people of the South was much surprised when they see us marching through there," John Langhans wrote, "for they thought we never could do it." Sherman himself voiced mild astonishment at his accomplishment. " I can hardly realize it," he confessed to his wife from Savannah, "for really it was easy, but like one who has walked a narrow plank, I look back and wonder if I really did it." He referred, of course, to the March to the Sea; the more difficult Carolinas campaign was yet to come.[30]

"The Reb generals in the west are no match for old Sherman," Emory Sweetland wrote at Goldsboro as the war was ending. "He is probably the best general that the war has brought forth." At Raleigh a few weeks later, Charles Abell wrote, "When danger is near, I like to see Billy Sherman near." Uncle Billy's men idolized him for the rest of their lives. To Charles McKay, writing in the early years of the twentieth century, his former commander was "the immortal Sherman." According to my father, John Langhans "always said that Sherman was a great general." Amos McIntyre paid tribute to his old commander by naming his first-born child William Tecumseh Sherman McIntyre.[31]

The soldiers realized that they had marched to fame with their general. On the eve of leaving Savannah for the Carolinas campaign, Emory Sweetland compared the magnitude and sweep of his army career to that of his brother, who had spent most of his service in hospitals and the Veteran Reserve Corps. Sweetland mused that his brother would most likely return home without seeing much of the war or the world, while "I am likely to have the United States pretty well mapped over and to have visited all the principal cities in the Union, also the great battlefields, and seen all the great generals in the army." He poignantly added, "Sometimes I have seen a little more than I wanted to for a short time."[32]

To their deaths, declared Lloyd Lewis, Sherman's men "would carry the thought of these marching days and feasting nights as life's highest tide." Veterans of the 154th New York basked in the warmth of the memories and the praise of their contemporaries. At the regiment's annual reunions in the late nineteenth and early twentieth centuries, orators lauded the men's role in the marches. One politician assured the old soldiers that the world had never ceased to admire Napoleon's remarkable exploits, but considering the March to the Sea, "we may well say that the American army is deserving a place in history as prominent as that of the famous army of Napoleon." The veterans in turn bequeathed pride to their descendants. When Stephen Welch's granddaughter was a little girl, she would "stick out her chest and announce that her grandfather had marched with Sherman to the sea." When she grew and learned more about what happened in the march, however, her pride diminished.[33]

The pride of Sherman's veterans never sagged. Historian Joseph Glatthaar summed up the attitude of Sherman's army at the war's end: "There were no apologies now, nor would there ever be, for what they had done in the heat of war to the people of Georgia and the Carolinas. There was only immense pride in being part of a very special body of men." Veterans of the 154th New York expressed that pride in a turn-of-the-century compilation of biographical sketches of Cattaraugus County veterans. John Langhans's sketch stated, "While on the March to the Sea, he was detailed to forage with 50 men, and was always successful in his expeditions." "His hard service was on the March to the Sea," stated the account of Private Joseph Putnam of Company H; "he endured privations of the camp and dangers of the field with the courage and determination of a faithful soldier." According to Stephen Welch's sketch, "Not until the welcomed peace had come did the tried veterans of 'Old Billie's' army, who had followed him 'to the sea' and marched with him through the Carolinas, receive their well-earned discharge." None of the sketches alluded to the devastation the veterans had wrought on the marches.[34]

Even after they died, the veterans marched with Sherman. Former private Truman Hinman of Company B was remembered with this headline in his 1934 obituary: "Civil War Veteran Who Marched with Sherman from Atlanta to the Sea Dies at Home at East Randolph." Hinman's service is further known to the ages in the inscription carved into his headstone: "Sherman's March to the Sea and through the Carolinas to Washington and the Grand Review." When my great-grandfather died in 1929, the headline in his obituary fixed him forever as one of Uncle Billy's boys: "JOHN LANGHANS, CIVIL WAR VETERAN, DIES. Was Corporal In Old 154th and Was on Famous March with Shreman [*sic*] to Sea."[35]

John Langhans and his comrades of the 154th New York would have agreed with Herman Melville: "It was glorious glad marching / That marching to the sea."[36]

[16]

Don't Bring Any Matches!

I N September 1864 the 154th New York tramped into Atlanta as
rear guard to its brigade. In January 2007 I crawled into the city
as part of a massive traffic jam on Interstate 75. Of all the places
the regiment passed through while marching with Sherman, Atlanta more than any other has been transformed beyond recognition.
The genesis of that transformation, of course, was the fiery destruction
of much of the city on the eve of the March to the Sea. As Atlanta's
postwar resurrection accelerated in the twentieth century and the city
mushroomed into today's sprawling metropolis, the 154th's campsites
disappeared. By comparing Civil War and modern-day maps, I located
them as best I could.[1]

Nothing at the sites evoked 1864. The approximate location of the
regiment's first camp in Atlanta, at today's intersection of Trinity Avenue and Memorial Drive SW, is surrounded by seven-story state office
buildings near the junction of two interstate highways and their jumble
of entrance and exit ramps. The abandoned Confederate fort in which
the 154th camped on its second night in the city is now a hilltop school
in the residential Grant Park neighborhood. The sites of the two Mc-
Donough Road camps are now submerged beneath the approach roads
and parking lots of the Turner Field baseball stadium. Modern Atlanta
does resemble its Civil War predecessor in one aspect, I found. When
members of the 154th occupied the city, they discovered a large number of transplanted northerners among its populace. Ever since, Atlanta has lured northern immigrants. In the 1880s, a sizable population
of Union veterans founded an active Grand Army of the Republic post
in the city. When I attended a meeting of the Atlanta Civil War Round
Table as a guest, eight of my ten tablemates were native Yankees.[2]

As I headed east from Atlanta through suburbia and exurbia to the
rural countryside, the sense of following in the 154th New York's foot-

prints strengthened. That afternoon I traversed the first of many dirt roads I would follow on the regiment's trail. By the time I reached Savannah, my car was splattered with red mud. Traveling on back roads for miles, passing nothing but woods and fields and the occasional homestead, I took in landscapes similar to those seen by the soldiers. Wartime scenes came to mind when I encountered a wandering cow in the middle of a road near the Ogeechee River, or passed a flock of turkey buzzards feasting on a carcass near South Carolina's Black Swamp, or crossed the Salkehatchie River at Buford's Bridge and found the pine woods on fire. In Effingham County, Georgia, I came to the intersection of the Low Ground and Horsepen roads; the latter was named for a place where locals had hidden their livestock from the Yankees. When I first came to a cotton field, near Bartow, Georgia, I picked three bolls as a souvenir, as my great-grandfather John Langhans had done more than a century before.

If it was impossible to visualize occupied Atlanta, it was easy to imagine wartime Savannah. An immense cargo port now covers the position held by Jones's brigade during the siege, but the city's old core has been preserved largely intact. Standing on the parade ground extension of Forsyth Park, I pictured the 154th's camp of tent-covered shanties. Walking around the historic district, I passed many of the same houses the soldiers saw when they patrolled those streets during the occupation. One evening I had dinner in the first-floor restaurant and visited the second-floor tattoo parlor in the old Central Railroad Bank building, where Geary had his headquarters. Watching freighters, tugs, and excursion boats ply the Savannah River reminded me of my great-grandfather's daily visits to the wharf to watch the shipping.

On February 4, 2007, my itinerary jibed with the 154th's when I visited Sisters Ferry 142 years to the day after the regiment crossed the Savannah River there into South Carolina. While I had managed to follow the regiment's route almost exactly in Georgia, I ran into occasional difficulties in the Carolinas. No accessible roads seemed to follow the 154th's path through the Black Swamp in Jasper County, South Carolina, or the Sand Hills Game Land in Scotland County, North Carolina. Looking for the site of McFarland's bridge on the Lumber River in North Carolina, I got lost in a maze of sandy logging roads. Still, many sites were easily found. In Cheraw I visited the cemetery at St. David's Church and viewed the British officers' graves that had fooled members of the regiment. In Fayetteville I sketched a steel "Ghost Tower" that offered a skeletal replica of one of the old United States Arsenal's corner towers. An expert guide accompanied me around the Speights Bridge area of Greene County, North Carolina, where Harrison Coe and Job Dawley were captured and killed.

Stories of the marches came alive for me while visiting certain sites. Standing by Diannah Dally's grave in a family cemetery near the Alcovy River, I visualized the surrounding countryside on the November 1864 night when the Dally farm was covered with the tents and campfires of Geary's division. (I visited several family, churchyard, and municipal cemeteries whose well-tended neatness reflected a touching southern reverence for ancestors.) At Westover plantation, where Lee Jordan's overseer plied Geary's officers with wine in the big house, the current occupant treated me to a delightful lunch. Sketching the Park's Mill house, I remembered the tale of the faithful slave who supposedly beat out flames on the rooftop and saved the place from destruction.[3]

Wondering where James Denham's shoe factory had been located, I inspected a Putnam County road map and noticed a Denham Road running off Tanyard Road. On the Denham Road I found Denham Tire, and there I was pleased to learn that the proprietor was James Denham's great-great-great-grandson. He put me in touch with a relative who lives in the old Denham place, and the next day I toured the house and outbuildings and a large field, at the edge of which stood a tall chimney—all that was left of the shoe factory after its destruction by Geary's men. Throughout the South, lone chimneys—called "Sherman's sentinels"—are said to be survivors of Yankee arson, no matter how far they are from the line of the march. The Denham smokestack, however, is a true landmark of the March to the Sea's destruction.[4]

Exploring the big house at Turnwold plantation, I recalled Joseph Addison Turner's encounters with bummers. In a parlor at Forest Grove plantation that appeared unchanged since the Civil War, I gazed at the glass-domed artificial flowers that a forager had threatened to destroy—a relic that is the Georgian family's equivalent of my cotton bolls. At the Jones plantation's cemetery at Birdsville, I wondered about Sidney Jones and her dead twins. At the Zeigler homestead in Screven County, I peered through the second-floor window through which Peggy Zeigler reputedly was thrust to roll down the porch roof onto the ground. In addition to historic homes, I saw antebellum plantation smokehouses, commissaries, springhouses, privies, dovecotes, and slave quarters. The current property owners graciously welcomed me and seemed pleased to show me around; some had copied materials to share with me. When the owner of one historic property was unable to meet me, he told me that the gate at the road and the back door to the house would be open and I could make myself at home, an extraordinary example of southern hospitality. When I made the appointment to meet the owner of the Denham homestead, he quipped, "Don't bring any matches!"

All along the 154th New York's route I sketched and photographed antebellum homes, which belied the mythology of unrestrained burning by Sherman's army. Social Circle, Madison, Milledgeville, Savannah (famously), Winnsboro, Cheraw, and Fayetteville all have notable historic districts containing many prewar buildings. Those towns pitch their historic districts to attract so-called heritage tourism, with varying degrees of success. In promotional materials, for example, Madison calls itself "the town Sherman refused to burn." I took photos of twenty-five homes and three churches that were standing when the 154th New York passed through Madison—and there were many more that I missed. Over the years, numerous legends have evolved that purport to explain why the town was spared. Folklorist Elissa Henken heard that Madison escaped the torch because Sherman had a sweetheart there, or he went drinking with the mayor, or the mayor's lovely daughter dissuaded the general, or the town's women cooked a fried chicken dinner for the general and his men, or the town was saved owing to its sheer beauty. Legends of Sherman personally sparing Madison overlook the fact that the general did not enter the town. Despite the lack of a conflagration in Madison, I dined at a local restaurant that offered "Sherman's Fire Chicken Wings."[5]

In memory, William Tecumseh Sherman still stalks the South. He must have been an omnipresent being to have committed all the acts of arson and vandalism with which he is charged. Everywhere I went I encountered Sherman stories. A Georgian told me several jokes in which braver and wilier Confederates bested the hapless general and his men. (It was evident that the storyteller had a genuine dislike of Yankees, but we managed to keep our discussion amicable.) Watching a brief video at a Georgia historical society museum, I was amused to see Sherman incongruously portrayed by an actor with dyed red hair, a sizable paunch, and a thick southern drawl. A South Carolina woman told me that Sherman had the floor of a local church reinforced so he could stable his horses therein. I said it was the first time I had heard of Sherman doing something constructive in the South. (Elissa Henken notes that legends of evil men stabling horses in churches date from the Middle Ages.) At a South Carolina historical site, a costumed guide told me an antebellum house had been spared from burning because the inhabitants shared the Masonic bond with General Sherman; he was surprised when I told him the tale must be spurious. A North Carolinian related that Sherman tied his horse to a favorite tree in front of the ancestral home; the horse disfigured the tree by eating the top off of it. Alas for the tale's veracity, Sherman had never come near the place. As stories were handed down through the generations, actions by many mounted Yankees wearing shoulder straps had no doubt been attributed to Sherman. Who makes the more colorful character in a family story—an unknown second lieutenant, or General Sherman himself?[6]

By prearrangement, I spoke about my project in seven towns along the way—Social Circle, Milledgeville, and Bartow, Georgia; Winnsboro, Chesterfield, and Cheraw, South Carolina; and Snow Hill, North Carolina. My appearances were well publicized in newspapers and radio spots and generally drew audiences of twenty to fifty people. Most of the attendees were white; only a handful of blacks turned out. (One black Georgian told me that many African Americans felt it was best to leave the past in the past.) In Milledgeville—where a newspaper specified me as a "Yankee historian"—I spoke in the old state capitol's reconstructed legislative chamber, where a convention had passed the ordnance of secession in 1861 and Sherman's men had mock-voted the state back into the Union in 1864. In Chesterfield I spoke in the old courthouse, which had replaced the one burned by the 154th New York in 1865.[7]

My talks described how family stories and relics had inspired my interest and led to my plan for a book. I explained my search for southern source material and read accounts pertaining to the audience's locale. I got lots of laughs when I told how my first attempt to follow the marches had been sabotaged by chiggers. Although I had random conversations about the campaigns with folks I met on the road, the question-and-answer periods after my talks yielded the most interesting and fruitful discussions. Attendees were primarily interested in the marches' destruction, wondering, for example, how widespread was the burning of homes.

In Georgia I generally encountered a curiosity that was free of apparent rancor and even lapsed on occasion into humor. I was told that when the board of the Historic Preservation Society of Social Circle considered my lecture proposal, a member joked, "Can we hang him?" In South Carolina, however, a deep-seated resentment toward Sherman and his army was evident, and jests were not to be heard. When a lengthy discussion ensued after my talk in Chesterfield, I was told in no uncertain terms that the southern side of the story of the marches had not made it into the history books, that it was much worse than generally portrayed, and that folks in Sherman's wake were left with nothing. People starved to death, I was told; babies starved to death. One of the attendees later e-mailed me the most lurid family legend I encountered—that of a woman well off the march's path who was gang-raped and left dead by a pack of bummers. After I spoke at the public library in Cheraw, staffers told me they had received complaints about my appearance from the local Sons of Confederate Veterans camp. The librarians thought the protests were silly and suggested that the SCV members attend my lecture and let their opinions be known. As it turned out, their camp was meeting on the same night, so a potential confrontation was averted.

The South "is still burying its Civil War dead," historian David Goldfield observed. He added, "For some, and their numbers are not as small as one would think, the old myths are still operative." I expected to encounter the opposition of neo-Confederates, as modern-day devotees of the Confederacy are often called. They are, after all, the spiritual, if not the lineal, descendants of the Sons of Confederate Veterans and the UDC and the old Ku Klux Klan and equally as passionate in upholding the righteousness of the Lost Cause and the Redemption. As Goldfield put it, neo-Confederates band together "not so much to learn history as repeat it." The most extreme of these "southern nationalists," or "southrons"—most of them conservative, white males—advocate a separate southern nation, much as their philosophical forebears did in 1860 and 1861. They resent the criticism, ridicule, and perceived superiority of northerners. "Some southerners will take it very personally," Goldfield notes; "it is not only their history but themselves under attack, for how can you separate one from the other?" They cling devotedly—and increasingly desperately—to the tenets of the Lost Cause and the alleged righteousness of overthrowing Reconstruction.[8]

The so-called neo-Confederates seem to be a distinct minority among today's southerners. Their narrow definition of southern heritage excludes too many of their fellow citizens in Dixie. In general, the southerners I met considered Sherman's marches remote enough to be considered objectively, untainted by the prejudices of the past. In some circles, old shibboleths have given way to historical curiosity. Many of the folks I met were unaware of the fact that the stories they have heard all their lives are legends. Every individual and audience I spoke with dropped any hostility and voiced approval when I stressed that I wanted to include the southern side of the story in this book. Making that promise, I received their compliments and encouragement. Whether they approve of the result is up to them to decide. Whether my great-grandfather and other veterans of the 154th New York would approve of including the southerners' stories with their own is altogether another question—but in the end, it seems to me, it is a simple matter of justice.

Acknowledgments

At its roots, this book is a vast collaborative effort. In my decades of study of the 154th New York, I have had the good fortune to connect with more than 1,100 descendants of members of the regiment, who have kindly shared with me a large archive of the soldiers' wartime letters and diaries. I thank them all with all my heart for helping me produce a life's work in this and my previous books. Special thanks go to those listed in the bibliography for providing the essential materials to tell the regiment's side of the story. My thanks also go to the archivists and librarians at the various repositories that yielded regimental materials.

Following the 154th's route through Georgia and the Carolinas, I received much friendly help. My deep appreciation goes to all along the way who provided materials, stories, insights, and inspiration. Without their kindness, this book could not have been written. In Georgia, I benefited from the assistance of Mike Brubaker, research manager, and Staci Sullivan, Cherokee Garden Library director, Kenan Research Center, Atlanta History Center, Atlanta; Richard Cloues, Historic Preservation Division, Georgia Department of Natural Resources, Atlanta; Valerie Lyons, Atlanta Civil War Round Table, Atlanta; Charlie Crawford, Georgia Battlefields Association, Atlanta; Andy Phydras, military records archivist, Georgia Archives, Morrow; Paul K. Graham, archivist, DeKalb History Center, Decatur; Dally descendant Mary Jo Whitley, Social Circle; her son Thomas Y. Whitley Jr., Jersey; Bob Bailes, Historic Preservation Society of Social Circle; Dina and Pierre Glardon, Rutledge; Marshall W. "Woody" Williams, Madison; Linda Naples, Uncle Remus Regional Library, Morgan County Branch, Madison; Jim and Sylvia Moon, Swords; Pete and Elaine Sutherland of the Park house, Buckhead; Denham descendants Jim Denham of Denham Tire and Auto Repair and Brannen Sanders at the Denham homestead, Eatonton; Denham descendant Cason Ellis, St. Simons Island; Turnwold owner William Harrington Jr., Atlanta; Thulia Bramlett at Westover, Milledgeville; Grant Gerlich, executive director, Old

Capital Museum, Milledgeville; Jim Turner, director, and Matt Davis, assistant curator of education, Old Governor's Mansion, Milledgeville; Kathe Fuller, Milledgeville; Warthen descendants Lyle Lansdell and her mother, Sarah Lansdell, of Forest Grove, Sandersville; Mary Alice Jordan, Washington County Historical Society, Sandersville; Hubert and Patsy Jordan of Magnolia Mornings, Bartow; Leroy Lewis, Jefferson County Historical Society, Louisville; Bob Hammond, curator, Burke County Museum, Waynesboro; Jesse Stone, president, Burke County Genealogical Society, Waynesboro; Jones descendant Mary Franklin Andrew, Birdsville; Steve Earl Burke, Millen; Bill Giles, park manager, Magnolia Springs State Park, Millen; Dr. John K. Derden, East Georgia College, Swainsboro; Zeigler descendant Dianne W. Kinsey, Atlanta, and her mother, Patricia Ann Zeigler, Sylvania; Betty Ford Renfro, secretary, Historic Effingham Society, Springfield; Norman V. Turner, Springfield; John Duncan, Savannah; Robert K. Weber, Special Collections librarian, and Stephany Kretchmar, library assistant, Georgia Historical Society, Savannah; and Lawrence Nix, Sister's Ferry, Effingham County. Special thanks go to Hugh T. Harrington of Milledgeville, who deserves an extra accolade for his constant and valued help.

My helpers in South Carolina included Betty Jean Miller, Barnwell; the staff of the Barnwell Public Library; Harry Quattlebaum and his mother, Myrtle Quattlebaum, Blackville; Terri Mull, Blackville Public Library; Ray Miller, Blackville; Horace Harmon, director, and Mike Spears, historical interpreter, Lexington County Museum, Lexington; Linda Malone, archivist, Fairfield Archives and History, Thomas Woodward Chapter, South Carolina Daughters of the American Revolution, Winnsboro; Sharon F. Corey, Glenn Perdue, and Brent Davis of the Chesterfield District Chapter, South Carolina Genealogical Society, Chesterfield; Margaret Collins Dotson, Chesterfield; Patsy Brock Leviner, Wallace; Sarah C. Spruill, Cheraw Visitors Bureau, Cheraw; Rev. Allen L. Usher, Cheraw; and Dr. Larry E. Nelson, Francis Marion University, Florence.

In North Carolina I received assistance and support from Rhonda L. Williams, local and state history library associate, Cumberland County Public Library, Fayetteville; Terry L. Beckwith, reference librarian, and Rhonda Konig, local history librarian, Wayne County Public Library, Goldsboro; Mike Edge, Greene County Museum, Snow

Hill; 154th New York descendant Dr. William V. Burlingame, Hillsborough; and historian Gerald J. Prokopowicz of East Carolina University, Greenville.

In corresponding with southern repositories I was aided by John O'Shea, Special Collections librarian, Reese Library, Augusta State University, Augusta, Georgia; Shawn McCauley, Research Services assistant, Manuscript, Archives, and Rare Book Library, and Naomi L. Nelson, coordinator for Research Services, Robert W. Woodruff Library, Emory University, Atlanta, Georgia; Laura Botts, head of Special Collections, Jack Tarver Library, Mercer University, Macon, Georgia; Henry G. Fulmer, curator of manuscripts, South Caroliniana Library, University of South Carolina, Columbia; Gloria Beiter, research consultant, and Karen Stokes, archivist, South Carolina Historical Society, Charleston; Elizabeth B. Dunn, Research Services librarian, Rare Book, Manuscript, and Special Collections Library, Duke University, Durham, North Carolina; Matthew Turi, manuscripts reference librarian, and Elizabeth McAuley, information and communications specialist, Wilson Library, University of North Carolina, Chapel Hill.

Several journalists helped spread the word by printing articles about my quest in their newspapers: Adrea Miller of the *Walton Tribune,* Monroe, Georgia; Pam Beer and Hugh Harrington of the *Baldwin Bulletin* and Alexander Cain of the *Union-Recorder,* Milledgeville, Georgia; Jessica Newberry of the *News and Farmer/Jefferson Reporter,* Louisville, Georgia; and the *Cheraw Chronicle and Chesterfield Advertiser,* Cheraw, South Carolina.

Michael Knight, Reginald Washington, Jill M. Abraham, and Jack House assisted me, through correspondence and in person, at the National Archives in Washington, D.C. The Reference Team at the National Register of Historic Places, a branch of the National Park Service in Washington, also provided help. While doing research in Washington, I had the pleasure of once again staying with my old friend Christopher L. Ford and his wife, Michelle, and son, Wesley, at their Fairfax, Virginia, home. I also enjoyed a reunion with old friend Robert S. Sherman and his wife, Diana, at their home in Oakton, Virginia.

On occasion I pitched questions to historians who have specialized in Sherman's campaigns, and helpful answers came from Anne J. Bailey, Georgia College and State University, Milledgeville; Albert Castel, Hillsdale, Michigan; Lee Kennett, Pleasant Garden, North Carolina;

John F. Marszalek, Giles Distinguished Professor Emeritus, Mississippi State University, Starkville; Noah Andre Trudeau, Washington, D.C.; and Stanley Weintraub of Newark, Delaware.

Some widely scattered people offered help in various ways. Richard Cofer of Brooksville, Florida, descended from a member of the 6th Georgia Cavalry, shared valuable sources on that regiment. Ed Burton of Stilwell, Kansas, shared the memoir of his ancestor Fannie Burton Mobley of Social Circle. David Slay of Texas Christian University, Fort Worth, Texas, got me going on my southern research by providing relevant citations from his bibliography of Georgia Civil War manuscripts. William Marvel of South Conway, New Hampshire, notified me of the misidentified Job B. Dawley letter at Yale. Robert F. Hancock, senior curator of the Museum of the Confederacy in Richmond, Virginia, answered a question for me. Bill Spiking of Lees Summit, Missouri, shared copies of the pension file of his great-great-granduncle, Pvt. Thomas D. Spiking Jr., which revealed Spiking's capture during the march through Georgia. I greatly enjoyed playing my Dobro in jam sessions in Milledgeville with singer and guitarist Liam Kelly of Blacksburg, Virginia, and in Cheraw with singer, guitarist, and songwriter Larry Spears, with his wife, Kay, as our captive audience. Roger L. Vance, group editorial director of the Primedia History Group, granted permission to reprint a portion of my article "Death to All Foragers" from *American History* magazine, relating to the fates of the bummers in Greene County, North Carolina, in March 1865.

This is the third of my books that T. Michael Parrish, editor of the series Conflicting Worlds: New Dimensions of the American Civil War, has ushered into print. My thanks to him for his assistance and support over the years and especially during the lengthy and (for me) difficult course of this project. My thanks too to the outside reader, who prodded and pushed me to utilize the sources correctly and to write what I believe is the right book, and to Grace Carino for her thorough copyediting. For any mistaken facts or interpretation, I alone am responsible.

My parents, Harold and Irene Dunkelman, encouraged my early efforts in historical research and other endeavors. Both died when I was a young man, my mother in 1967 and my father in 1972. In the years since, my aunt Floris Dunkelman Sarver of Getzville, New York, has been a wonderful surrogate parent to my sister, Amy Dunkelman Rowland, and me—loving, kind, wise, and supportive. My living link to John Langhans, our ancestor who was proud to be one of Uncle Billy's boys, she has always inspired me with her passion for our family's history. I am pleased to dedicate this book to her with my deepest love and sincerest gratitude. Finally, I simply could not do what I do without the love and support of my wife, Annette, and our son, Karl. I send them my love.

Notes

INTRODUCTION

1. "Interview with Dad," undated typed transcript of author's interview with Harold J. Dunkelman, author's collection.

2. John Langhans to Julius Langhans, October 21, November 5, 1864; January 22, April 29, May 28, June 9, 1865, John Langhans Letters, Floris Sarver Collection, Getzville, N.Y.

3. William T. Sherman, *Memoirs of General William T. Sherman, by Himself,* 2 vols. (1875; reprint, Bloomington: Indiana Univ. Press, 1957); Lloyd Lewis, *Sherman: Fighting Prophet* (New York: Harcourt, Brace and Co., 1932), 465 (quotations).

4. Lewis, *Sherman,* 434–57; Edward Caudill and Paul Ashdown, *Sherman's March in Myth and Memory* (Lanham, Md.: Rowman and Littlefield, 2008), 68.

5. William Alan Blair, ed., *A Politician Goes to War: The Civil War Letters of John White Geary* (University Park: Pennsylvania State Univ. Press, 1995), 217; Franklin M. Garrett, *Atlanta and Environs: A Chronicle of Its People and Events* (Athens: Univ. of Georgia Press, 1969), 1:649; 2 Kings 25:8–17, KJV.

6. Morrison H. Heckscher, curator, Department of American Decorative Arts, Metropolitan Museum of Art, to author, May 1, 1986.

7. Margaret Mitchell, *Gone with the Wind* (New York: Macmillan, 1937), 436–45, 458–70; Caudill and Ashdown, *Sherman's March in Myth and Memory,* 100–104, 131–32; Jim Cullen, *The Civil War in Popular Culture: A Reusable Past* (Washington: Smithsonian Institution Press, 1995), 65–107; Tara McPherson, *Reconstructing Dixie: Race, Gender, and Nostalgia in the Imagined South* (Durham, N.C.: Duke Univ. Press, 2003), 47–65; Sarah E. Gardner, *Blood and Irony: Southern White Women's Narratives of the Civil War, 1861–1937* (Chapel Hill: Univ. of North Carolina Press, 2004), 234–50.

8. Gaines M. Foster, *Ghosts of the Confederacy: Defeat, the Lost Cause, and the Emergence of the New South* (New York: Oxford Univ. Press, 1987), 4–6; David Goldfield, *Still Fighting the Civil War: The American South and Southern History* (Baton Rouge: Louisiana State Univ. Press, 2002), 15–16, 18–22, 25, 27–28, 34; Harry S. Stout, *Upon the Altar of the Nation: A Moral History of the Civil War* (New York: Viking, 2006), 429; Paul F. Paskoff, "Measures of War: A Quantitative Examination of the Civil War's Destructiveness in the Confederacy," *Civil War History* 44 (March 2008): 36–39, 55, 58.

9. Bill King, "Nelson Charms at Omni," *Atlanta Constitution,* July 24, 1978, B-1.

10. Author to William Graves, Expeditions Editor, National Geographic Magazine, September 8, 1980.

11. William Graves, Senior Assistant Editor, National Geographic Society, to author, September 22, 1980.

12. Noah Andre Trudeau, *Southern Storm: Sherman's March to the Sea* (New York: Harper, 2008); John F. Marszalek, *Sherman's March to the Sea* (Abilene, Tex.: McWhiney

Foundation Press, 2005); Anne J. Bailey, *War and Ruin: William T. Sherman and the Savannah Campaign* (Wilmington, Del.: Scholarly Resources, 2003); Jim Miles, *To the Sea: A History and Tour Guide of the War in the West, Sherman's March across Georgia and through the Carolinas, 1864–1865* (Nashville: Cumberland House, 2002); William R. Scaife, *The March to the Sea* (Atlanta: Published by the author, 1989), 20; Burke Davis, *Sherman's March* (New York: Random House, 1980); Richard Wheeler, *Sherman's March* (New York: Thomas Y. Crowell, 1978); John G. Barrett, *Sherman's March through the Carolinas* (Chapel Hill: Univ. of North Carolina Press, 1956); Earl Schenck Miers, *The General Who Marched to Hell: Sherman and the Southern Campaign* (New York: Dorset Press, 1951); Caudill and Ashdown, *Sherman's March in Myth and Memory*, 71, 78, 169.

13. Anne J. Bailey, *The Chessboard of War: Sherman and Hood in the Autumn Campaigns of 1864* (Lincoln: Univ. of Nebraska Press, 2000); Lee Kennett, *Marching through Georgia: The Story of Soldiers and Civilians during Sherman's March* (New York: HarperCollins, 1995); Charles Royster, *The Destructive War: William Tecumseh Sherman, Stonewall Jackson, and the Americans* (New York: Alfred A. Knopf, 1991); Caudill and Ashdown, *Sherman's March in Myth and Memory*, 77, 83–84; James Reston Jr., *Sherman's March and Vietnam* (New York: Macmillan, 1984); Victor Davis Hanson, *The Soul of Battle: From Ancient Times to the Present Day, How Three Great Liberators Vanquished Tyranny* (New York: Free Press, 1999), 405; Caleb Carr, *The Lessons of Terror: A History of Warfare against Civilians: Why It Has Always Failed and Why It Will Fail Again* (New York: Random House, 2002), 10, 141; Caudill and Ashdown, *Sherman's March in Myth and Memory*, 70, 170–73.

14. B. H. Liddell Hart, *Sherman: Soldier, Realist, American* (New York: Dodd, Mead and Co., 1929); James M. Merrill, *William Tecumseh Sherman* (Chicago: Rand McNally, 1971); Charles Edmund Vetter, *Sherman: Merchant of Terror, Advocate of Peace* (Gretna, La.: Pelican Publishing Co., 1992); John F. Marszalek, *Sherman: A Soldier's Passion for Order* (New York: Free Press, 1993); Michael Fellman, *Citizen Sherman: A Life of William Tecumseh Sherman* (New York: Random House, 1995); Stanley P. Hirshson, *The White Tecumseh: A Biography of William T. Sherman* (New York: John Wiley and Sons, 1997); Lee Kennett, *Sherman: A Soldier's Life* (New York: HarperCollins, 2001); Charles Bracelen Flood, *Grant and Sherman: The Friendship That Won the Civil War* ((New York: Farrar, Straus and Giroux, 2005); Edward G. Longacre, *Worthy Opponents: William T. Sherman and Joseph E. Johnston; Antagonists in War—Friends in Peace* (Nashville, Tenn.: Rutledge Hill Press, 2006); Caudill and Ashdown, *Sherman's March in Myth and Memory*, 66–86.

15. Rachel Sherman Thorndike, *The Sherman Letters: Correspondence between General and Senator Sherman from 1837 to 1891* (New York: Charles Scribner's Sons, 1894); M. A. DeWolfe Howe, *Home Letters of General Sherman* (New York: Charles Scribner's Sons, 1909); Brooks D. Simpson and Jean V. Berlin, eds. *Sherman's Civil War: Selected Correspondence of William T. Sherman, 1860–1865* (Chapel Hill: Univ. of North Carolina Press, 1999). On Sherman as a writer, see Edmund Wilson, *Patriotic Gore: Studies in the Literature of the American Civil War* (New York: Farrar, Straus and Giroux, 1977), 174–218; Stout, *Upon the Altar of the Nation*, 371; and Caudill and Ashdown, *Sherman's March in Myth and Memory*, 94.

16. Caudill and Ashdown, *Sherman's March in Myth and Memory*, 91–123, 133; Cynthia Bass, *Sherman's March* (New York: Villard Books, 1994); John Jakes, *Savannah, or,*

A Gift for Mr. Lincoln (New York: Dutton, 2004); E. L. Doctorow, *The March* (New York: Random House, 2005), 9–10, 61–62.

17. Joseph T. Glatthaar, *The March to the Sea and Beyond: Sherman's Troops in the Savannah and Carolinas Campaign* (New York: New York Univ. Press, 1985), 175, 183; Caudill and Ashdown, *Sherman's March in Myth and Memory,* 79.

18. Mark H. Dunkelman, *Brothers One and All: Esprit de Corps in a Civil War Regiment* (Baton Rouge: Louisiana State Univ. Press, 2004), 268–69; George K. Collins, *Memoirs of the 149th Regiment New York Volunteer Infantry* (1891; reprint, Hamilton, N.Y.: Edmonston Publishing, 1995), v–vi, 286–318; Adin B. Underwood, *The Three Years' Service of the Thirty-third Mass. Infantry Regiment, 1862–1865* (1881; reprint, Huntington, W. Va.: Blue Acorn Press, 1993), vii–ix, 234–88; Mark H. Dunkelman and Michael J. Winey. *The Hardtack Regiment: An Illustrated History of the 154th Regiment, New York State Infantry Volunteers* (East Brunswick, N.J.: Fairleigh Dickinson Univ. Press, 1981), 123–40; George W. Conklin, *Under the Crescent and Star: The 134th New York Volunteer Infantry in the Civil War* (Port Reading, N.J.: Axworthy Publishing, 1999), 211–31; James S. Pula, *The Sigel Regiment: A History of the 26th Wisconsin Volunteer Infantry, 1862–1865* (Campbell, Calif.: Savas Publishing, 1998), 276–304.

19. Charles W. McKay, "'Three Years or during the War,' with the Crescent and Star," in *The National Tribune Scrap Book,* 121–60 (n.p., n.d.); Marcellus Warner Darling, *Events and Comments of My Life* (n.p., n.d.), unpaginated; Alfred W. Benson, untitled reminiscence of the March to the Sea, Kansas State Historical Society, Topeka (hereafter cited as Benson reminiscence); Dunkelman, *Brothers One and All,* 257, 260, 266–67.

20. Edwin Dwight Northrup Papers, #4190, Department of Manuscripts and University Archives, Cornell University, Ithaca, N.Y. (hereafter cited as Northrup Papers); Dunkelman, *Brothers One and All,* 269–75.

21. Langhans to Julius Langhans, June 9, 1865.

22. John M. Gibson, *Those 163 Days: A Southern Account of Sherman's March from Atlanta to Raleigh* (New York: Coward-McCann, 1961); Katharine M. Jones, *When Sherman Came: Southern Women and the "Great March"* (Indianapolis: Bobbs-Merrill, 1964); Jacqueline Glass Campbell, *When Sherman Marched North from the Sea: Resistance on the Confederate Home Front* (Chapel Hill: Univ. of North Carolina Press, 2003). See also Caudill and Ashdown, *Sherman's March in Myth and Memory,* 78–79; Lisa Tendrich Frank, "Bedrooms as Battlefields: The Role of Gender Politics in Sherman's March," in *Occupied Women: Gender, Military Occupation, and the American Civil War,* edited by LeeAnn Whites and Alecia P. Long (Baton Rouge: Louisiana State Univ. Press, 2009), 34–35.

23. Laurel Thatcher Ulrich, *Well Behaved Women Seldom Make History* (New York: Alfred A. Knopf, 2007), 50; Goldfield, *Still Fighting the Civil War,* 2.

24. Caudill and Ashdown, *Sherman's March in Myth and Memory,* 5, 37.

25. Ibid., 1–3, 5, 38–39, 45–62, 89, 90, 105, 180–83. For an example of the myths represented as history, see Wolfgang Schivelbusch, *The Culture of Defeat: On National Trauma, Mourning, and Recovery* (New York: Metropolitan Books, 2003), 57, 61–62.

26. Mark Grimsley, *The Hard Hand of War: Union Military Policy toward Southern Civilians, 1861–1865* (Cambridge: Cambridge University Press, 1995), 208.

27. Ibid., 174, 185, 190–91, 204, 219–23, 225; Mark Grimsley, "'Thieves, Murderers, Trespassers': The Mythology of Sherman's March," people.cohums.ohio-state.edu/

grimsley1/myth/myth.htm. See also Grimsley's "The Long Shadow of Sherman's March," people.cohums.ohio-state.edu/grimsley1/dialogue/long_shadow.htm.

28. Elissa R. Henken, "Taming the Enemy: Georgian Narratives about the Civil War," *Journal of Folklore Research* 40, no. 3 (September–December 2003): 289–307; Caudill and Ashdown, *Sherman's March in Myth and Memory*, 174–75. See also Janice Hume and Amber Roessner, "Surviving Sherman's March: Press, Public Memory, and Georgia's Salvation Mythology," *Journalism and Mass Communication Quarterly* 86, no. 1 (Spring 2009): 119–37.

29. Henken, "Taming the Enemy," 302–5; McPherson, *Reconstructing Dixie*, 75, 152; Dixon Hollingsworth, ed., *The History of Screven County, Georgia* (Dallas, Tex.: Curtis Media Corporation, 1989), 39.

30. Medora Field Perkerson, *White Columns in Georgia* (New York: Rinehart, 1952), 61–62; Caudill and Ashdown, *Sherman's March in Myth and Memory*, 168.

31. Rev. J. A. W. Thomas, *A History of Marlboro County, with Traditions and Sketches of Numerous Families* (1897; reprint, Baltimore: Regional Publishing Co., 1978), 287–88; Marion Little Durden, *A History of Saint George Parish, Colony of Georgia, Jefferson County, State of Georgia* (Swainsboro, Ga.: Magnolia Press, 1983), 80. During the Civil War, South Carolina called its future counties districts.

32. Caudill and Ashdown, *Sherman's March in Myth and Memory*, 147–75.

33. Reston, *Sherman's March and Vietnam*, 65–129; Jerry Ellis, *Marching through Georgia: My Walk with Sherman* (New York: Delacorte Press, 1995); Ross McElwee, *Sherman's March: A Meditation on the Possibility of Romantic Love in the South during an Era of Nuclear Weapons Proliferation*, 1986, DVD by First Run Features, 2004; McPherson, *Reconstructing Dixie*, 127–40; C. Peter Wagner, "Healing the Land: The Power to Heal the Past," *Prayer Track News* 5, no. 2 (April–June 2006): 1, 7; "Finding Cump," home. gwi.net/~timuse/findingcump.htm; Anne J. Bailey to author, October 18, 19, 2005; Tony Horwitz, *Confederates in the Attic: Dispatches from the Unfinished Civil War* (New York: Pantheon Books, 1998), 282–319; Caudill and Ashdown, *Sherman's March in Myth and Memory*, 138–39, 172–74.

34. Victoria E. Ott, *Confederate Daughters: Coming of Age during the Civil War* (Carbondale: Southern Illinois Univ. Press, 2008), 14–15, 36–37, 74–75, 99, 101; Frank, "Bedrooms as Battlefields," 45–46, 48, 201n11.

35. Ott, *Confederate Daughters*, 130–32, 136–37, 157–63; Goldfield, *Still Fighting the Civil War*, 97; Stout, *Upon the Altar of the Nation*, 429.

36. Gardner, *Blood and Irony*, 54, 72, 79, 80, 82–85, 112; Caroline E. Janney, *Burying the Dead but Not the Past: Ladies' Memorial Associations and the Lost Cause* (Chapel Hill: Univ. of North Carolina Press, 2008), 170–71.

37. Karen L. Cox, *Dixie's Daughters: The United Daughters of the Confederacy and the Preservation of Confederate Culture* (Gainesville: Univ. Press of Florida, 2003), 1–3, 28–32, 93–96, 101–6, 110–11; Janney, *Burying the Dead but Not the Past*, 167–74; Gardner, *Blood and Irony*, 117–20; Goldfield, *Still Fighting the Civil War*, 98; W. Fitzhugh Brundage, *The Southern Past: A Clash of Race and Memory* (Cambridge: Harvard Univ. Press, Belknap Press, 2005), 36–37.

38. Gardner, *Blood and Irony*, 120, 123, 127–28, 138; Goldfield, *Still Fighting the Civil War*, 111.

39. Gardner, *Blood and Irony*, 114, 123–28, 138, 158, 166–67; Brundage, *Southern Past*, 15.

40. Gardner, *Blood and Irony,* 120, 160.

41. "Reminiscences of Mrs. H. W. Scott," in South Carolina Division, United Daughters of the Confederacy, *Recollections and Reminiscences, 1861–1865 through World War I* (n.p., 1990), 1:547–48 (hereafter cited as South Carolina UDC).

42. Henken, "Taming the Enemy," 302; Jones, *When Sherman Came,* 43–44, 331, 332; Ott, *Confederate Daughters,* 137. Mrs. L. F. J., who in writing her memoir preferred to remain anonymous, later remarried and became Mrs. L. F. Harris of Madison, Georgia. Trudeau, *Southern Storm,* 273.

43. Jan Harold Brunvand, *Encyclopedia of Urban Legends* (New York: W. W. Norton, 2001), xxi–xxii, xxviii–xxix, xxxii, 111–13, 193–94.

44. WPA Slave Narrative Project, Federal Writers' Project, United States Work Projects Administration, Manuscript Division, Library of Congress, Washington, D.C. (hereafter cited as WPA).

CHAPTER 1

1. Lewis D. Warner diary, September 2, 1864, Charles H. Warner III Collection, Santa Rosa, Calif.

2. Major Lewis D. Warner's official report in U.S. War Department, *The War of the Rebellion: The Official Records of the Union and Confederate Armies,* 128 vols. (Washington: Government Printing Office, 1880–1901), series I, vol. 38, pt. 2, 253 (hereafter cited as *OR*). All subsequent references are to series I. Warner diary, September 2, 1864; Emory Sweetland to Mary Sweetland, September 4, 1864, Emory Sweetland letters, Lyle Sweetland Collection, South Dayton, N.Y.; Alexander Bird diary, September 2, 1864, Janet Bird Whitehurst Collection, Los Banos, Calif.; McKay, "'Three Years, or during the War,' with the Crescent and Star," 153; Earl B. McElfresh, *Maps and Mapmakers of the Civil War* (New York: Harry N. Abrams, 1999), 189.

3. Horace Smith diary, September 2, 1864, Mazomanie Historical Society, Mazomanie, Wis.; Zeno Besecker interview notes, May 18, 1887, Northrup Papers; James W. Clements to Amanda Clements, September 7, 1864, James W. Clements letters, Judith Wachholz Collection, River Falls, Wis.; Alfred W. Benson diary, September 3, 1864, Kansas State Historical Society, Topeka, Kans.; Marcellus W. Darling to his family, September 19, 1864, Marcellus W. Darling letters, University of Iowa Library, Iowa City, Iowa.

4. Warner diary, September 3, 4, 1864; Bird diary, September 3, 1864; Benson diary, September 3, 1864; Smith diary, September 3, 4, 1864; Darling, *Events and Comments of My Life;* "From the 154th N.Y. Vol.," *Fredonia (N.Y.) Censor,* September 28, 1864, quoting letter of Milon J. Griswold of September 12, 1864; Sweetland to Mary Sweetland, September 4, 1864; Mervin P. Barber diary, September 8, 1864, Paul A. Lockwood Collection, Newark, Ohio; McKay, "'Three Years, or during the War,' with the Crescent and Star," 153.

5. Newton A. Chaffee to A. W. W. Chaffee, September 13, 1864, Gowanda Area Historical Society, Gowanda, N.Y.; Sweetland to Mary Sweetland, September 4, 1864; Darling to his family, September 11, 1864; Addison L. Scutt to his mother-in-law, October 2, 1864, Jerry L. Scutt Collection, Portville, N.Y.

6. *Fredonia Censor,* September 28, 1864, quoting Griswold's letter of September 12, 1864; muster rolls, April 30, August 31, 1864, 154th New York, National Archives, Washington, D.C.

7. Edgar Shannon to Francelia Hunt, September 7, 1864, author's collection; Stephens Mitchell, "Atlanta: The Industrial Heart of the Confederacy," *Atlanta Historical Bulletin* 3 (May 1930): 20–27; Richard M. McMurry, *Atlanta 1864: Last Chance for the Confederacy* (Lincoln: Univ. of Nebraska Press, 2000), 141–42; James Lee McDonough and James Pickett Jones, *War So Terrible: Sherman and Atlanta* (New York: W. W. Norton, 1987), 82–83; Kennett, *Marching through Georgia*, 112–14; Albert Castel, *Decision in the West: The Atlanta Campaign of 1864* (Lawrence: Univ. Press of Kansas, 1992), 69; McKay, "'Three Years, or during the War,' with the Crescent and Star," 153.

8. Muster-in rolls, September 24–26, 1862, and muster rolls, August 31, 1864, 154th New York; Dunkelman and Winey, *Hardtack Regiment*, 198; Dunkelman, *Brothers One and All*, 94.

9. New York [State] Adjutant General, *Annual Report of the Adjutant General of the State of New York for the Year 1904*, serial no. 39 (Albany: Brandow Printing Co., 1905), 1090–1232; muster rolls and descriptive books, 154th New York, National Archives, Washington, D.C.; Sweetland to Mary Sweetland, August 11, 1864; William Charles to Ann Charles, September 24, 1864, William Charles letters, Jack Finch Collection, Freedom, N.Y..

10. Howe, *Home Letters of General Sherman*, 305, 308; Bell Irvin Wiley, *The Life of Billy Yank: The Common Soldier of the Union* (Baton Rouge: Louisiana State Univ. Press, 1993), 284, 343–44; William Marvel, *Mr. Lincoln Goes to War* (Boston: Houghton Mifflin, 2006), 61; Glatthaar, *March to the Sea and Beyond*, 33.

11. Levi D. Bryant to Cornelia Bryant, October 30, 1864, Levi D. Bryant letters, Cornelia Kopp Collection, Reading Center, N.Y.; Dunkelman, *Brothers One and All*, 71.

12. Muster rolls, October 31, 1864.

13. Muster rolls, October 31, December 31, 1864.

14. Mark H. Dunkelman, *Colonel Lewis D. Warner: An Appreciation* (Portville, N.Y.: Portville Historical and Preservation Society, 1990), 1–19; Warner diary, September 22, 1864; Mark H. Dunkelman, "Brigadier General Patrick Henry Jones," *Lincoln Herald* 89, no. 2 (Summer 1987): 71–76; Roger D. Hunt and Jack R. Brown, *Brevet Brigadier Generals in Blue* (Gaithersburg, Md.: Olde Soldier Books, 1990), 416; John G. Zinn, *The Mutinous Regiment: The Thirty-third New Jersey in the Civil War* (Jefferson, N.C.: McFarland and Co., 2005), 5, 13; Smith diary, August 31, 1864; Byron A. Johnston interview notes, January 29, 1893, and undated, Northrup Papers.

15. Blair, *Politician Goes to War*, vii–xxv, 117; Harry Marlin Tinkcom, *John White Geary: Soldier-Statesman, 1819–1873* (Philadelphia: Univ. of Pennsylvania Press, 1940).

16. Charles Elihu Slocum, *The Life and Services of Major General Henry Warner Slocum* (Toledo, Ohio: Slocum Publishing Co., 1913); William F. Fox, "Life of General Slocum," in New York [State], New York State Monuments Commission, *In Memoriam Henry Warner Slocum, 1826–1894* (Albany: J. B. Lyon, 1904), 65–98; Brian C. Melton, *Sherman's Forgotten General: Henry W. Slocum* (Columbia: Univ. of Missouri Press, 2007); Charles W. Abell to his parents, November 3, 1864, Charles W. Abell letters, Jean Schultz Collection, Westford, Vt.; Milo M. Quaife, ed., *From the Cannon's Mouth: The Civil War Letters of General Alpheus S. Williams* (Detroit: Wayne State Univ. Press and the Detroit Historical Society, 1959), 3–11.

17. Hart, *Sherman*, 331; Lewis, *Sherman*, 510; Vetter, *Sherman*, 219–21; Fellman, *Citizen Sherman*, 193–94; Hirshson, *White Tecumseh*, 271; Marszalek, *Sherman*, 259, 281, 287; Kennett, *Sherman*, 98–99.

18. Darling to his family, September 11, 1864; Sweetland to Mary Sweetland, September 7, 1864; Shannon to Francelia Hunt, September 7, 1864, author's collection; Chaffee to A. W. W. Chaffee, September 13, 1864; Smith diary, September 4, 1864; Warner diary, September 11, 12, 1864; William D. Harper diary, September 11, October 3, 1863, Raymond Harper Collection, Dunkirk, N.Y.; Barber diary, November 7, 1864; Bryant to Cornelia Bryant, October 30, November 8, 1864; Langhans to Julius Langhans, November 5, 1864.

19. Bird diary, September 18, 1864; Benson diary, September 2, 18, 1864; Darling to his family, September 11, 19, 1864; Shannon to Francelia Hunt, September 22, 1864; Edgar Shannon letters, Timothy T. Shaw Collection, Cheektowaga, N.Y.; Warner diary, September 18, 1864.

20. Warner diary, September 6, 9, 12, 15, 16, 17, 24, 29, 1864; Barber diary, October 10, November 10, 1864; Harper diary, September 6–November 8, 1864; Clements to Amanda Clements, undated fragment; Bird diary, November 1, 1864; Langhans to Julius Langhans, November 5, 1864; Lewis D. Warner to Nelson Wheeler, October 26, 30, 1864, quoted in W. Reginald Wheeler, *Pine Knots and Bark Peelers: The Story of Five Generations of American Lumbermen* (New York: Ganis and Harris, 1960), 67.

21. Langhans to Julius Langhans, November 5, 1864; *Fredonia Censor,* September 28, 1864, quoting Griswold's letter of September 12, 1864; Abell to his parents, November 3, 1864.

22. Milton D. Scott to William Scott, October 14, 1864, Richard DeBell Collection, Falconer, N.Y.; Harper diary, memorandum; Abell to his parents, November 3, 1864; Smith diary, November 1, 1864; Warner diary, September 21, 1864.

23. Darling to his family, September 19, 1864; Abell to his mother, October 1, 1864; Harper diary, October 12, 1864; Joshua R. Pettit diary, October 12, 1864, Mary C. Ranney Collection, Ellicottville, N.Y.; Jesse D. Campbell to his family, October 23, 1864, Jesse D. Campbell letters, Jesse D. Campbell pension file, National Archives, Washington, D.C..

24. Benson diary, October 6, 1864; George Eugene Graves to Celia Smith, October 16, 1864, George Eugene Graves letters, author's collection; Harper diary, September 8, 9, 10, 27, October 3, 7, 30, 1864; Bird diary, September 17, 1864; Job B. Dawley carte-de-visite inscribed "Atlanta Ga. Oct. 19th/64," author's collection.

25. Scott to William Scott, October 14, 1864; Scutt to his mother-in-law, October 2, 1864; William W. Norton to Frankie Norton, November 3, 1864, William W. Norton letters, author's collection; Langhans to Julius Langhans, November 5, 1864; muster rolls, December 31, 1864; Bryant to Cornelia Bryant, November 8, 1864.

26. Barber diary, September 30, 1864; Pettit diary, September 30, 1864; "Register of Deaths," Company C Descriptive Book; Barber diary, September 10, 1864; Sweetland to Mary Sweetland, November 1, 1864; John R. Neff, *Honoring the Civil War Dead: Commemoration and the Problem of Reconciliation* (Lawrence: Univ. Press of Kansas, 2005), 125–28.

27. Mark H. Dunkelman, "Hurray for Old Abe! Fenton! and Dr. Van Aernam! The 1864 Election, As Perceived by the 154th New York Volunteers," *Lincoln Herald* 98, no. 1 (Spring 1996): 12–22.

28. Dunkelman, *Brothers One and All,* 61–67; Sweetland to Mary Sweetland, September 4, November 12, 1864; Chaffee to A. W. W. Chaffee, September 13, 1864; Shannon to Francelia Hunt, September 7, 1864, author's collection, and September 15, 1864, Shaw Collection; Smith diary, November 1, 1864; Warner diary, November 8, 10, 12, 1864;

Wheeler, *Pine Knots and Bark Peelers*, 66; Bryant to Cornelia Bryant, October 30, 1864; Glatthaar, *March to the Sea and Beyond*, 46–51, 200–202.

29. Dunkelman, "Hurray for Old Abe!" 20; Franklin Ellis, ed., *History of Cattaraugus County, New York* (Philadelphia: L. H. Everts, 1879), 327; Smith diary, November 14, 1864; Henry Van Aernam to John Manley, November 22, 1864, author's collection; William Adams, ed., *Historical Gazetteer and Biographical Memorial of Cattaraugus County, New York* (Syracuse: Lyman, Horton and Co., 1893), 132–33.

30. McMurry, *Atlanta 1864*, 177–78, 180; McDonough and Jones, *War So Terrible*, 319–20; Castel, *Decision in the West*, 543–44.

CHAPTER 2

1. Van Aernam to Amy Melissa Van Aernam, September 9, 1864, U.S. Army Military History Institute, *Carlisle Barracks, Pa.*; Shannon to Francelia Hunt, October 4, 1864, Shaw Collection; Sweetland to Mary Sweetland, October 2, 1864; Scott to William Scott, October 14, 1864; Abell to his mother, October 1, 1864.

2. Wheeler, *Pine Knots and Bark Peelers*, 67–69; Geary's report, *OR*, vol. 44, 266; Warner diary, October 16–20, 23–29, 1864; Harper diary, October 16–19, 23–34, 26–29, 1864; Barber diary, October 16–19, 23–25, 26, 29, 1864; Bird diary, October 23, 26–29, 1864; McKay, "'Three Years or during the War,' with the Crescent and Star," 153; "From Atlanta to the Sea, Tramping with the 154th N.Y. Volunteers," unidentified newspaper clipping, Northrup Papers; *Atlas to Accompany the Official Records of the Union and Confederate Armies* (Washington: Government Printing Office, 1891–95), plate LXXXIII, no. 2 (hereafter cited as *Official Atlas*).

3. Howe, *Home Letters of General Sherman*, 313–14; Sweetland to Mary Sweetland, October 30, 1864; Smith diary, November 14, 1864.

4. Benson diary, September 2, 1864; Shannon to Francelia Hunt, September 7, 1864, author's collection; Clements to Amanda Clements, September 7, 1864; Chaffee to A. W. W. Chaffee, September 13, 1864; McDonough and Jones, *War So Terrible*, 269; Sweetland to Mary Sweetland, September 4, 1864; Barber diary, September 28, 1864; *Fredonia Censor*, September 28, 1864, quoting Griswold's letter of September 12, 1864; Thomas G. Dyer, *Secret Yankees: The Union Circle in Confederate Atlanta* (Baltimore: Johns Hopkins Univ. Press, 1999), 186; Darling to his family, September 19, 1864.

5. Chaffee to A. W. W. Chaffee, September 13, 1864; Castel, *Decision in the West*, 378, 464, 488, 617n41; Stephen Davis, "'A Very Barbarous Mode of Carrying on War': Sherman's Artillery Bombardment of Atlanta, July 20–August 24, 1864," *Georgia Historical Quarterly* 79, no. 1 (Spring 1995): 57, 75–80; Russell S. Bonds, *War Like the Thunderbolt: The Battle and Burning of Atlanta* (Yardley, Pa.: Westholme, 2009), 221–22; Albert Castel to author, November 2, 2005.

6. Van Aernam to Amy Melissa Van Aernam, September 9, 1864, U.S. Army Military History Institute; Clements to Amanda Clements, September 7, 1864; Kennett, *Marching through Georgia*, 114, 127; Castel, *Decision in the West*, 70, 464.

7. "100 Years Old" and "Mrs. Hannah Winship Boutelle," unidentified newspaper clippings; Mary Callaway Jones, "Reminiscence of Mrs. Isaac Winship," 1938, typescript; and "Interesting Sketches of Pioneer Women: Mrs. Isaac Winship," unidentified newspaper clipping, all in Winship-Flourney Family Papers, Kenan Research Center,

Atlanta History Center, Atlanta, Ga.; Charles B. Boatenreiter, "Family Information on John Boutelle," and "Historical Society to Show Pictures of Early Atlanta," unidentified newspaper clipping, June 15, 1945, in Boutelle-Kean Family genealogy file, Kenan Research Center, Atlanta History Center; Thomas H. Martin, *Atlanta and Its Builders: A Comprehensive History of the Gate City of the South* (Atlanta: Century Memorial Publishing Co., 1902), 2:393, 709–12; Van Aernam to Amy Melissa Van Aernam, September 9, 1864, U.S. Army Military History Institute; David P. Conyngham, *Sherman's March through the South* (New York: Sheldon and Co., 1865), 237; Mitchell, "Atlanta," 22; Dyer, *Secret Yankees,* 36.

8. Jones, "Reminiscence of Mrs. Isaac Winship"; "Interesting Sketches of Pioneer Women: Mrs. Isaac Winship"; "100 Years Old"; "Mrs. Hannah Winship Boutelle"; Boatenreiter, "Family Information on John Boutelle"; Van Aernam to Amy Melissa Van Aernam, September 9, 1864, U.S. Army Military History Institute.

9. Henry Van Aernam interview notes, October 17, 1893, Northrup Papers; "Letter from Surgeon Van Aernam," *Cattaraugus Freeman* (Ellicottville, N.Y.), August 18, 1864.

10. Elizabeth F. Smith, ed., *The Reminiscences of James Ormond* (Crawfordville, Fla.: Magnolia Monthly Press, 1966), 16, 20, 21, 26–32; James Ormond to Henry Ward Beecher, January 24, 1876, Kenan Research Center, Atlanta History Center.

11. Smith, *Reminiscences of James Ormond,* 32; General Orders No. 26, September 19, 1864, General Orders and Circular Orders Issued, Second Brigade, Second Division, Twentieth Corps, National Archives, Washington, D.C.

12. Van Aernam interview notes, October 17, 1893.

13. Darling to his family, September 11, 1864.

14. Shannon to Francelia Hunt, September 7, 1864, author's collection, and September 15, 1864, Shaw Collection; Benson diary, September 5, 11, 1864; Clements to Amanda Clements, September 7, 1864.

15. Besecker interview notes, May 18, 1887; Bradford Rowland and Clark E. Oyer interview notes, August 29, 1886, Northrup Papers.

16. Mary Rawson Ray diary, September 3, 1864, Rawson-Collier-Harris Family Collection, Kenan Research Center, Atlanta History Center.

17. Sherman, *Memoirs,* 2:111, 126. On the morality of the expulsion, see Grimsley, *Hard Hand of War,* 186–88, and Stout, *Upon the Altar of the Nation,* 369.

18. *Fredonia Censor,* September 28, 1864, quoting Griswold's letter of September 12, 1864; Darling to his family, September 19, 1864; Smith diary, September 17, 1864.

19. "Persons Sent from Atlanta by Gen. Sherman," *Atlanta Historical Bulletin* 6 (February 1932): 21–32; Chaffee to A. W. W. Chaffee, September 13, 1864; Pettit diary, September 12, 1864; Besecker interview notes, May 18, 1887; Castel, *Decision in the West,* 548–49; Kennett, *Marching through Georgia,* 207–12; Dyer, *Secret Yankees,* 204, 205, 206–7; Shannon to Francelia Hunt, September 22, 1864, Shaw Collection.

20. Shannon to Francelia Hunt, September 15, 1864, Shaw Collection.

21. Mary Rawson Ray diary, September 12, 1864.

22. Mary A. H. Gay, *Life in Dixie during the War* (1897; reprint, Atlanta: DeKalb Historical Society, 1979), 179–82; Sally Sharp Garrison reminiscences, Kenan Research Center, Atlanta History Center.

23. Eleanor Harrison Sheridan, "Atlanta 1864—A Reminiscence," in Georgia Division United Daughters of the Confederacy, *Confederate Reminiscences and Letters,*

1861–1865, 22 vols. (Atlanta: Georgia Division United Daughters of the Confederacy, 1995–2006) 3:103–6 (hereafter cited as Georgia UDC); Winnie Davis Mobley, "War Experience of Miss Neppie Jones," Georgia UDC, 5:54.

24. Smith, *Reminiscences of James Ormond,* 32.

25. Samuel P. Richards diary, September 2, 4, 9, 21, 1864, Kenan Research Center, Atlanta History Center.

26. Carrie Berry diary, August 3, 11, September 2, 10, 13, 26, October 2, 23, 28, 30, December 21, 1864, Kenan Research Center, Atlanta History Center.

27. Richards diary, September 9, 1864; Mobley, "War Experience of Miss Neppie Jones," 3:27.

28. Georgia Narratives, WPA Slave Narrative Project, vol. 4, pt. 4, 128, 130–31 (hereafter cited as WPA Georgia Narratives).

29. Kennett, *Marching through Georgia,* 33, 83; Dyer, *Secret Yankees,* 204–5.

30. Darling to his family, September 11, 1864; Scott to William Scott, October 14, 1864; Sweetland to Mary Sweetland, November 1, 1864; Van Aernam to Amy Melissa Van Aernam, September 9, 1864, U.S. Army Military History Institute; Campbell to his family, October 23, 1864.

31. Sherman, *Memoirs,* 2:113–16, 144, 145, 152, 153–54, 164–66; Ulysses S. Grant, *Personal Memoirs of U. S. Grant* (New York: Charles L. Webster and Co., 1885), 2:348–50, 359.

32. Warner diary, October 30, November 1, 2, 4, 1864; Company A muster roll, December 31, 1864; *Presidents, Soldiers, Statesmen* (New York: H. H. Hardesty, 1899), 1467.

33. Warner diary, November 2, 1864; Darling to his mother, November 4 and 5, 1864; Abell to his parents, November 3, 1864; Smith diary, November 14, 1864; Van Aernam to John Manley, November 22, 1864, author's collection; Sweetland to Mary Sweetland, October 30, November 4, 1864; Norton to Frankie Norton, November 4, 1864.

34. J. Cutler Andrews, *The North Reports the Civil War* (Pittsburgh: Univ. of Pittsburgh Press, 1955), 575, 577, 583, 584, 619–20; Trudeau, *Southern Storm,* ix–x; Noah Andre Trudeau to author, May 4, 2008; George W. Pepper, *Personal Recollections of Sherman's Campaigns in Georgia and the Carolinas* (Zanesville, Ohio: Hugh Dunne, 1866), 209–11; Conyngham, *Sherman's March through the South,* 5, 6, 114, 118, 160–61.

35. Bryant to Cornelia Bryant, November 8, 1864; Warner diary, November 5–11, 1864; Harper diary, November 5, 6, 1864; Barber diary, November 5, 6, 1864; "From Atlanta to the Sea, Tramping with the 154th N.Y. Volunteers"; Darling to his mother, November 5, 1864; Sweetland to Mary Sweetland, November 4, 1864.

36. Sherman, *Memoirs,* 2:72, 174–76; *OR,* vol. 44, 43.

37. Sweetland to Mary Sweetland, November 4, 1864; *Fredonia Censor,* September 28, 1864, quoting Griswold's letter of September 12, 1864; Simpson and Berlin, *Sherman's Civil War,* 699–700, 724; Russell S. Bonds, "Sherman's First March through Georgia," *Civil War Times* 46, no. 6 (August 2007): 30–37.

38. Dyer, *Secret Yankees,* 208–12; Bonds, *War Like the Thunderbolt,* 341, 347–59.

39. Warner diary, November 11, 1864; Barber diary, November 11, 1864; Pettit diary, November 11, 1864.

40. Berry diary, November 12–15, 1864.

41. Warner diary, November 12–13, 1864; Graves to Celia Smith, December 16, 1864; Conyngham, *Sherman's March through the South,* 237; Smith diary, November 14, 1864; Francis M. Bowen diary, November 14, 1864, Ronald Bowen Collection, Brighton, Mich..

42. Mills Lane, ed., *Times That Prove People's Principles: Civil War in Georgia* (Savannah: Beehive Press, 1993), 207; "Atlanta When It Was Left in Ashes," unidentified newspaper clipping, Edda A. Cole scrapbook, Kenan Research Center, Atlanta History Center; Meta Barker, ed., "Atlanta As Sherman Left It: Atlanta Then and Now," *Atlanta Historical Bulletin* 3 (May 1930): 15–20; Scaife, *March to the Sea*, 20; Bonds, *War Like the Thunderbolt*, 363–63, 408–10, 480n45.

43. Warner diary, November 14, 1864.

CHAPTER 3

1. Warner, Blood, Barber, Bowen, and Harper diaries; Graves to Celia Smith, December 16, 1864; *Official Atlas*, plate LXXI, no. 1; Wheeler, *Pine Knots and Bark Peelers*, 69; Georgia Department of Natural Resources, *Georgia Civil War Markers* (Atlanta: Georgia Department of Natural Resources—State Parks, Recreation and Historic Sites Division, 1982), 141 (hereafter cited as *Georgia Civil War Markers*); J. Calvin Weaver, M.D., "One Hundred Years of Medicine in DeKalb County, 1822–1922," typescript, DeKalb History Center, Decatur, Ga. All diary citations are for the date referred to in the text, except where otherwise noted. Major Warner's, Colonel Jones's, and General Geary's official reports are in *OR*, vol. 44, 302–3 (Warner); 295–97 (Jones); and 265–83 (Geary). Times and distances are from Lewis Warner's diary, on which he based his official report. The former Goldsmith farm is today the site of the small city of Pine Lake.

2. Warner diary; Benson reminiscence, 7; Darling, *Events and Comments of My Life*; "From Atlanta to the Sea, Tramping with the 154th N.Y. Volunteers."

3. Clements to Amanda Clements, undated letter fragment; "From Atlanta to the Sea, Tramping with the 154th N.Y. Volunteers"; Graves to Celia Smith, December 16, 1864; Benson diary; Benson reminiscence, 8.

4. Martha Amanda Quillin to her cousin Sallie, November 15, 1865, Davis-Quillin Family Collection, Kenan Research Center, Atlanta History Center, Atlanta, Ga.; Trudeau, *Southern Storm*, 82, 96–97.

5. WPA Georgia Narratives, vol. 4, pt. 2, 298; McPherson, *Reconstructing Dixie*, 44–45.

6. Warner, Barber, Harper, Bowen, and Bird diaries; Warner's report, *OR*, vol. 44, 302; *Official Atlas*, plate LXXI, no. 1; M. A. DeWolfe Howe, ed., *Marching with Sherman: Passages from the Letters and Campaign Diaries of Henry Hitchcock* (New Haven: Yale Univ. Press, 1927), 237; *Georgia Civil War Markers*, 141. Rockdale County was later carved out of the former northwestern portion of Newton County.

7. Benson reminiscence, 15; Warner, Harper, and Bowen diaries.

8. Graves to Celia Smith, December 16, 1864; Benson reminiscence, 14; Wheeler, *Pine Knots and Bark Peelers*, 67.

9. Garrett, *Atlanta and Environs*, 1:647–49.

10. Vernon E. Field, "Memories of the Civil War," typescript, 1984, 2–3, author's collection; WPA Georgia Narratives, vol. 4, pt. 3, 68.

11. George Ward Nichols, *The Story of the Great March* (New York: Harper and Brothers, 1865), 112–15; Conyngham, *Sherman's March through the South*, 321; WPA Georgia Narratives, vol. 4, pt. 4, 170; Elizabeth W. Allston Pringle, *Chronicles of Chicora Wood* (New York: Charles Scribner's Sons, 1922), 221, 232–33; Sarah Ann Tillinghast

memoirs, State and Local History Collection, Cumberland County Public Library, Fayetteville, N.C.; Mary E. Copp Wilbur reminiscence, typescript, Aaron Wilbur Papers, Alexander A. Lawrence Collection, Georgia Historical Society, Savannah, Ga.

12. Omye Howard Graham, "Reminiscence of the Civil War," Georgia UDC, 5:55–56.

13. Tillinghast memoirs; Grace Pierson James Beard, "A Series of True Incidents Connected with Sherman's March to the Sea," manuscript #2799, Southern Historical Collection, Univ. of North Carolina, Chapel Hill, N.C.; B. M. Zettler, *War Stories and School-Day Incidents for the Children* (Springfield, Ga.: Page's Printing Co., 1984), 157–60.

14. South Carolina Narratives, WPA Slave Narrative Project, vol. 14, pt. 4, 259 (hereafter cited as WPA South Carolina Narratives).

15. Pringle, *Chronicles of Chicora Wood,* 223–25, 227, 232; Laura Inglis, "A Reminiscence of Sherman's Raid," South Carolina UDC, 4:305.

16. Warner, Blood, Benson, Bird, and Harper diaries; Geary's report, *OR,* vol. 44, 270; *Official Atlas,* plate LXXI, no. 2; Howe, *Marching with Sherman,* 68; *Georgia Civil War Markers,* 143; Kenneth K. Krakow, *Georgia Place Names: Their History and Origins* (Macon, Ga.: Winship Press, 1999), 3, 38.

17. James A. Mobley, "Atlanta's Headache from Sherman," Georgia UDC, 5:53–54; Anita B. Sams, *Wayfarers in Walton: A History of Walton County Georgia, 1818–1967* (Monroe, Ga.: General Charitable Foundation of Monroe, Georgia, 1967), 189.

18. Durden, *History of Saint George Parish,* 80; E. Bryant, "Over the Ogeechee," typescript, Hubert and Patsy Jordan Collection, Bartow, Ga.

19. Mary Jo (Dally) Whitley to author, April 10, 28, May 9, 2006; Frank, "Bedrooms as Battlefields," 39–40, 44; Campbell, *When Sherman Marched North from the Sea,* 36.

20. Frank, "Bedrooms as Battlefields," 33–45; Foster, *Ghosts of the Confederacy,* 32; Gardner, *Blood and Irony,* 20–21.

21. Williams, Orders, November 17, 20, 1864, *OR,* vol. 44, 484, 503; Grimsley, *Hard Hand of War,* 174–75, 191.

22. "Sherman's March," *Cattaraugus Freeman,* November 17, 1865.

23. Warner, Harper, Bird, and Blood diaries; *Official Atlas,* plate LXXI, no. 2; Conyngham, *Sherman's March through the South,* 245.

24. Blood diary; Benson, reminiscence, 14–15; Rowland, Oyer, and Esley Groat interview notes, undated, Northrup Papers; John F. Wellman, "The Fun in Army Life: Laughable Occurrences in Camp," *Cattaraugus Republican* (Salamanca, New York), September 19, 1902; Maggie Garrett, "Uninvited Guests Enjoy Turkey Dinner at Social Circle, Georgia," Georgia UDC, 5:52–53.

25. Fannie Burton Mobley memoirs, Ed Burton Collection, Stilwell, Kans. The Burton home survives today at 309 West Hightower Trail in Social Circle.

26. Warner, Bird, and Harper diaries; Geary's report, *OR,* vol. 44, 270; "From Atlanta to the Sea, Tramping with the 154th N.Y. Volunteers"; *Georgia Civil War Markers,* 143; *Official Atlas,* plate LXXI, nos. 2, 3; Marshall W. Williams to author, October 8, 2007.

27. *Official Atlas,* plate LXXI, nos. 2, 3; Conyngham, *Sherman's March through the South,* 246; Marshall W. Williams to author, August 9, 2007; Glatthaar, *March to the Sea and Beyond,* 67; Paskoff, "Measures of War," 38, 55, 58.

28. "From Ellen Peck Farrar to Her Cousin Mattie (Mrs. John N. Andrews)," Georgia UDC, 1:224–26.

29. Blood, Bird, Warner, and Harper diaries; Barber diary, November 18, 1864; Warner's report, *OR*, vol. 44, 302; Geary's report, *OR*, vol. 44, 270; *Official Atlas*, plate LXXI, no. 3; "From Atlanta to the Sea, Tramping with the 154th N.Y. Volunteers."

30. Conyngham, *Sherman's March through the South*, 246–48; Bird diary.

31. Jones, *When Sherman Came*, 14–15, 331.

32. Sue Leak Ashford, "A Mason's Guarantee of Protection," Georgia UDC, 5:47.

33. Blood, Bird, Warner, and Harper diaries; Geary's report, *OR*, vol. 44, 270; *Official Atlas*, plate LXXI, no. 3; *Georgia Civil War Markers*, 144.

34. Benson reminiscence, 9–10; Conyngham, *Sherman's March through the South*, 263–64; Lewis, *Sherman*, 438; Glatthaar, *March to the Sea and Beyond*, 137–38; Hirshson, *White Tecumseh*, 256; Vetter, *Sherman*, 247; Davis, *Sherman's March*, 31; Gibson, *Those 163 Days*, 37; Stout, *Upon the Altar of the Nation*, 399.

35. Harper, Bird, Warner, Barber, and Blood diaries; Conyngham, *Sherman's March through the South*, 251; Geary's report, *OR*, vol. 44, 270; *Official Atlas*, plate LXXI, no. 3; *Georgia Civil War Markers*, 144; Krakow, *Georgia Place Names*, 217; "Col. Lee Jordan Dead," *Union Recorder* (Milledgeville, Ga.), January 24, 1899; David B. Warren, "The Jordan Family of Georgia and Their Belter Parlor Furniture," *Magazine Antiques*, December 1998, 830–31.

36. Harper and Blood diaries; Geary's report, *OR*, vol. 44, 270.

37. Morgan County Heritage Book Committee, *Morgan County, Georgia Heritage, 1807–1997* (Waynesville, N.C.: Walsworth Publishing Co., 1997), 227; Louise McHenry Hicky, *Rambles through Morgan County: Her History, Century Old Houses and Churches, and Tales to Remember* (Washington, Ga.: Wilkes Publishing Co., 1971), 25.

38. Company B muster roll, December 31, 1864, and muster-out roll, June 11, 1865.

39. Warner, Harper, Bird, and Blood diaries; Geary's report, *OR*, vol. 44, 270–271; *Official Atlas*, plate LXXI, no. 3.

40. Park's Mill House File, Historic Preservation Division, Georgia Department of Natural Resources, Atlanta, Ga.; Geary's report, *OR*, vol. 44, 270–71; Betty and Dan Turner, "These Old Houses: Park's Mill House," *Lake Oconee (Ga.) Free Press*, September 18, 1989, 5; Karen G. Wood, *The Power of Water: Four Early Mill Sites on Georgia's Oconee River* (n.p., n.d.), 37–44; *Georgia Civil War Markers*, 144–45; Perkerson, *White Columns in Georgia*, 326; Hicky, *Rambles through Morgan County*, 26. When damming of the river created Lake Oconee, the Park house was moved about a mile south to 1511 Wood Road, Buckhead.

41. Katherine Walters, "Denhamville Important in Putnam County's History," *Eatonton (Ga.) Messenger*, April 18, 1991; Katherine Walters, "Denhamville Supplied the Confederacy," *Eatonton Messenger*, April 25, 1991; Katherine Bowman Walters, *Oconee River: Tales to Tell* (Spartanburg, S.C.: Reprint Co., 1995), 140–41, 284, 298–99; Harold S. Wilson, *Confederate Industry: Manufacturers and Quartermasters in the Civil War* (Jackson: Univ. Press of Mississippi, 2002), 209.

42. Geary's report, *OR*, vol. 44, 271; Collins, *Memoirs of the 149th Regiment New York Volunteer Infantry*, 289.

43. Report of Major Nicholas Grumbach, 149th New York, *OR*, vol. 44, 320; "A Daughter to Her Mother," *Countryman*, December 6, 1864, 673; "What Must I Do?" *Countryman*, December 6, 1864, 680; Blood diary; Walters, *Oconee River*, 299; Walters, "Denhamville Supplied the Confederacy."

44. Geary's report, *OR,* vol. 44, 271; Joshua R. Pettit diary.

45. Bowen diary, November 23, 1864; Benson reminiscence, 10–13.

46. Edmund L. Drago, "How Sherman's March through Georgia Affected the Slaves," *Georgia Historical Quarterly* 57, no. 3 (Fall 1973): 366; Glatthaar, *March to the Sea and Beyond,* 63; Bowen diary, November 23, 1864; Blood diary, November 19, 1864; George H. Davidson interview notes, March 8, 1895, Northrup Papers; Oyer interview notes, undated.

47. Mark H. Dunkelman, "Through White Eyes: The 154th New York Volunteers and African-Americans in the Civil War," *Journal of Negro History* 83, no. 3 (Summer 2000): 96–111; Drago, "How Sherman's March through Georgia Affected the Slaves," 364; Benson reminiscence, 10–11.

48. WPA South Carolina Narratives, vol. 14, pt. 1, 151, pt. 4, 23–24; WPA Georgia Narratives, vol. 4, pt. 1, 111, 129–32; Carnice Jennings Groves, *Jennings-McMillan-Faulling-Whaley-Bluer and Other Early Families of South Carolina* (Daytona Beach, Fla: Daytona Beach Community College, 1971), 104; Drago, "How Sherman's March through Georgia Affected the Slaves," 363.

49. WPA Georgia Narratives, vol. 4, pt. 3, 216; WPA South Carolina Narratives, vol. 14, pt. 1, 238–39, pt. 2, 203, pt. 4, 258, 267–68; Drago, "How Sherman's March through Georgia Affected the Slaves," 370, 371.

50. Mrs. C. E. Jarrott, "Mrs. C. E. Jarrott's Reminiscences," South Carolina UDC, 1:502; Mrs. Kirby-Smith Anderson, "Uncle Isaac," Georgia UDC, 22:102–3; Drago, "How Sherman's March through Georgia Affected the Slaves," 363, 366.

51. WPA South Carolina Narratives, vol. 14, pt. 3, 211.

52. Glatthaar, *March to the Sea and Beyond,* 63, 73–74; Campbell, *When Sherman Marched North from the Sea,* 45–46, 66, 120n27; Kennett, *Marching through Georgia,* 291, 306–307. See also Drago, "How Sherman's March through Georgia Affected the Slaves," 370, and Fellman, *Citizen Sherman,* 217, 226.

53. E. Susan Barber and Charles F. Ritter, "Physical Abuse . . . and Rough Handling": Race, Gender, and Sexual Justice in the Occupied South," in Whites and Long, *Occupied Women,* 49–51, 56–62.

54. Sweetland to Mary Sweetland, January 20, 1865.

CHAPTER 4

1. Geary's report, *OR,* vol. 44, 271; Walters, *Oconee River,* 299; Wilson, *Confederate Industry,* 209; "Daughter to Her Mother"; "The Coming of the Yankees," *Countryman,* December 6, 1864, 672; Walters, "Denhamville Supplied the Confederacy."

2. Brannen Sanders, anecdote related to author, January 23, 2007; Walters, "Denhamville Supplied the Confederacy"; "Old 'Denhamville' Tannery Chimney Reflects Rich History of Putnam," undated article from the *Eatonton Messenger,* courtesy of Cay Ellis.

3. Warner, Bird, Harper, and Blood diaries; Geary's report, *OR,* vol. 44, 271; *Official Atlas,* plate LXXI, no. 3; Joseph Addison Turner, *Autobiography of "The Countryman,"* ed. Thomas H. English. (Atlanta: Emory Univ. Library, 1943), 9–18; Paul M. Cousins, *Joel Chandler Harris: A Biography* (Baton Rouge: Louisiana State Univ. Press, 1968), 15, 22, 24, 26, 34, 35, 37, 38, 40, 45, 55; Joel Chandler Harris, *On the Plantation: A Story of a Georgia Boy's Adventures during the War* (Athens: Univ. of Georgia Press, 1980), 13–14,

21–22, 25–26, 32–33, 48, 51–54, 105; "To Georgia Editors and the Hatless," *Southern Recorder* (Milledgeville, Ga.), January 3, 1865; Walters, "Denhamville Important in Putnam County's History"; file #80001225, Turnwold, Putnam County, Ga., National Register of Historic Places, National Park Service, Washington, D.C. See also Lawrence Huff, "'A Bitter Draught We Have Had to Quaff': Sherman's March through the Eyes of Joseph Addison Turner," *Georgia Historical Quarterly* 72, no. 2 (Summer 1988): 306–26.

4. Cousins, *Joel Chandler Harris,* 16, 17, 36, 41, 42, 43, 44; Turner, *Autobiography of "The Countryman,"* 14, 16; Harris, *On the Plantation,* 50; file #80001225, Turnwold, National Register of Historic Places.

5. Gardner, *Blood and Irony,* 17, 19; Martha Caroline Marshall to her brother, December 6, 1864, Walraven Family Papers, Kenan Research Center, Atlanta History Center; "Coming of the Yankees," 671–72.

6. "Letter to Gen. Sherman," *Countryman,* February 7, 1865, 74.

7. "Coming of the Yankees," 672; "The First Five," *Countryman,* December 13, 1864, 690; "Drinking a Yankee's Health," *Countryman,* December 13, 1864, 687.

8. "Coming of the Yankees," 672; "What We Lost," *Countryman,* December 6, 1864, 676; "The Irishman," *Countryman,* December 13, 1864, 698; "We Doesn't Pay," *Countryman,* December 13, 1864, 691; "Wagon Lost," *Countryman,* December 20, 1864, 716.

9. Harris, *On the Plantation,* 227–31.

10. Geary's report, *OR,* vol. 44, 271; "The Yankees at Philadelphia Church," *Countryman,* December 6, 1864, 673.

11. Blood diary, November 20, 1864; Warner, Bird, Harper, and Blood diaries; Geary's report, *OR,* vol. 44, 271; *Official Atlas,* plate LXXI, nos. 3, 4; Robert K. Krick, *Lee's Colonels: A Biographical Register of the Field Officers of the Army of Northern Virginia* (Dayton, Ohio: Morningside House, 1992), 491.

12. Turner, *Autobiography of "The Countryman,"* 19; "Our Guests" and "Slow Come," *Countryman,* November 29, 1864, 664; "Old Sherman's Gone," *Countryman,* December 13, 1864, 692; "Incidents," *Countryman,* November 29, 1864, 664.

13. "The Yankees! The Yankees!" *Countryman,* November 29, 1864, 664; "Coming of the Yankees," 672; "Rumor of Another Invasion," *Countryman,* December 13, 1864, 690; "A Yankee Lie," *Countryman,* December 13, 1864, 691; "A Gin-House Burned," *Countryman,* December 6, 1864, 684.

14. "Letter to Gen. Sherman" (*Countryman*), 74–75.

15. Warner, Bird, Harper, Barber, and Blood diaries; Geary's report, *OR,* vol. 44, 271; *Official Atlas,* plate LXXI, no. 4.

16. "Westover," *Southern Recorder,* January 3, 1865; Warren, "The Jordan family of Georgia and Their Belter Parlor Furniture," 830; file #87000094, Westover, Baldwin County, Ga., National Register of Historic Places, National Park Service, Washington, D.C.; Westover, Baldwin County, Ga., GA-14-31, Historic American Buildings Survey, Prints and Photograph Division, Library of Congress, Washington, D.C.; Conyngham, *Sherman's March through the South,* 251.

17. Conyngham, *Sherman's March through the South,* 251–52; Hume and Roessner, "Surviving Sherman's March," 127–28.

18. James Royal Ladd, "From Atlanta to the Sea," *American Heritage* 30, no. 1 (December 1978): 8; file #87000094, Westover, National Register of Historic Places; "Westover," *Southern Recorder,* January 3, 1865.

19. Louisa Kenan White, "Reminiscences of the Sixties," in Bible Records, Military Rosters and Reminiscences of Confederate Soldiers Copied and Compiled from the Files of The Georgia Division, United Daughters of the Confederacy, 1942, Georgia Archives, Morrow, Ga. This account mistakenly identifies Lee Jordan as his father.

20. Warner, Bird, Harper, Barber, and Blood diaries; Benson reminiscence, 20–22; Fox, "Slocum and His Men," in New York [State], New York State Monuments Commission, *In Memoriam Henry Warner Slocum,* 285; *Georgia Civil War Markers,* 134–35; Hugh T. Harrington, *Civil War Milledgeville: Tales from the Confederate Capital of Georgia* (Charleston, S.C.: History Press, 2005), 87.

21. Clements to Amanda Clements, undated letter fragment; Robert J. Massey, "Georgia Solons 'Skedaddled' before Sherman," *Sunny South* (Atlanta, Ga.), November 11, 1901, 5; "The Yankees in Milledgeville," *Southern Recorder,* December 20, 1864; Harrington, *Civil War Milledgeville,* 47–48, 98; James C. Bonner, "Sherman at Milledgeville in 1864," *Journal of Southern History* 22, no. 3 (August 1956): 277–78.

22. Robert J. Massey, "Sherman in Georgia's Capital," *Sunny South,* November 30, 1901, 5; Jones, *When Sherman Came,* 24–27, 331; Harrington, *Civil War Milledgeville,* 48, 98.

23. Jones, *When Sherman Came,* 27–32, 331.

24. Sister R [Rebecca Ann Harris] to Iverson Louis Harris Jr., December 1, 1864, Iverson Louis Harris Papers, Rare Book, Manuscript, and Special Collections Library, Duke University, Durham, N.C.; Hugh T. Harrington to author, April 13, 2006.

25. Mattie [Hanna] Roberts, "History of Milledgeville, Georgia," Georgia UDC, 7:88, 91, 92.

26. Harper and Warner diaries; Benson reminiscence, 20–22; file #78000958, Barrowville, Baldwin County, Ga., National Register of Historic Places, National Park Service, Washington, D.C.; Guy C. McKinley memoirs, unpaginated typescript, Georgia College and State University, Milledgeville, Ga.

27. Bonner, "Sherman at Milledgeville in 1864," 285; Benson reminiscence, 20–22; "Our City," *Confederate Union* (Milledgeville, Ga.), December 13, 1864; "Letter of a Confederate Surgeon on Sherman's Occupation of Milledgeville," *Georgia Historical Quarterly* 32, no. 3 (September 1948): 232.

28. Sister R [Rebecca Ann Harris] to Iverson Louis Harris Jr., December 1, 1864.

29. Conyngham, *Sherman's March through the South,* 254–55; Benson reminiscence, 20; Darling, *Events and Comments of My Life;* McKay, "'Three Years or during the War,' with the Crescent and Star," 154; Bonner, "Sherman at Milledgeville in 1864," 283, 284, 286–87.

30. Benson reminiscence, 20; Darling, *Events and Comments of My Life;* Oyer interview notes, undated; Conyngham, *Sherman's March through the South,* 256–58; Massey, "Georgia Solons 'Skedaddled' before Sherman"; Harrington, *Civil War Milledgeville,* 52.

31. Sister R [Rebecca Ann Harris] to Iverson Louis Harris Jr., December 1, 1864; "Our City."

32. WPA Georgia Narratives, vol. 4, pt. 2, 306; "Sherman's Army in Milledgeville," *Confederate Union,* December 6, 1864; "Yankees in Milledgeville"; Harrington, *Civil War Milledgeville,* 95; Bonner, "Sherman at Milledgeville in 1864," 280–81, 282, 283; Hugh T. Harrington to author, November 29, 30, 2009. Bonner states two homes were destroyed in Milledgeville, one belonging to a government official.

33. "Sherman's Army in Milledgeville."

34. "Our City."

35. "Yankees in Milledgeville"; "The Food Question," *Confederate Union,* Decem-

ber 6, 1864; "The Duty of the Hour," *Confederate Union,* December 13, 1864; "Supplies Wanted," *Southern Recorder,* January 3, 10, 1865.

36. Barber and Bird diaries; Oyer interview notes, undated.

37. Conyngham, *Sherman's March through the South,* 345–46; Huff, "Seeing Atlanta Shelled," 97; Richard J. McCadden to his mother and brother, March 29, 1865, Ron Meininger Collection, Gaithersburg, Md.; Besecker interview notes, May 18, 1887; "How to Rob Bee-Hives," *Cattaraugus Freeman,* February 16, 1865.

38. Benson reminiscence, 16–17.

39. Wheeler, *Pine Knots and Bark Peelers,* 67–68.

40. Conyngham, *Sherman's March through the South,* 250–51; OR 44, 297.

41. Field, "Memories of the Civil War," 2.

42. Slocum, Orders, November 23, 1864, *OR,* vol. 44, 532; Williams, Circular Order, November 23, 1864, *OR,* vol. 44, 533.

43. Warner diary.

CHAPTER 5

1. Jones, *When Sherman Came,* 30; "Letter of a Confederate Surgeon on Sherman's Occupation of Milledgeville," 231–32.

2. McKinley memoirs.

3. Warner, Blood, Pettit, Bird, Barber, and Harper diaries; Geary's report, *OR,* vol. 44, 272; *Official Atlas,* plate LXXI, no. 5; *Georgia Civil War Markers,* 136. Today the creek's name is spelled Gumm.

4. Gary B. Mills, *Southern Loyalists in the Civil War: The Southern Claims Commission* (Baltimore: Clearfield, 2004), vii–x, 291; *Official Atlas,* plate LXXI, no. 5; Harriet Howard file, Settled Claims, 1877–1883, Southern Claims Commission Records, National Archives, Washington, D.C.

5. Sherman, *Memoirs,* 2:191; Howe, *Marching with Sherman,* 90–91; Trudeau, *Southern Storm,* 236.

6. Benson reminiscence, 18–19; Theodore C. Harns interview notes, undated, Northrup Papers.

7. Warner, Blood, Pettit, Bird, Barber, and Harper diaries; Geary's report, *OR,* vol. 44, 272; *Official Atlas,* plate LXXI, no. 5; Howe, *Marching with Sherman,* 92–93; *Georgia Civil War Markers,* 136.

8. Mary Alice Jordan, ed. *Cotton to Kaolin: A History of Washington County, Georgia 1784–1989* (Sandersville, Ga.: Washington County Historical Society, 1989), 27, 32.

9. Warner, Blood, Bird, Barber, and Harper diaries; Howe, *Marching with Sherman,* 95–100; Warner's report, *OR,* vol. 44, 302–303; Jones's report, *OR,* vol. 44, 295–96; *Official Atlas,* plate LXXI, no. 5; Conyngham, *Sherman's March through the South,* 270.

10. Ella Mitchell, *History of Washington County* (Atlanta: Cherokee Publishing Co., 1973), 65–67.

11. Jones, *When Sherman Came,* 40–44, 332; Gardner, *Blood and Irony,* 185–86.

12. Jordan, *Cotton to Kaolin,* 29–31; Gwen K. Hall, *On the Road to Savannah: The History of General Sherman's March through Washington County, Georgia* (Sandersville, Ga.: Major Mark Newman Camp 1602, Sons of Confederate Veterans, 2000), unpaginated.

13. File #04001556, Forest Grove, Washington County, Georgia, National Register of Historic Places, National Park Service, Washington, D.C.

14. Warner, Blood, Bird, Barber, and Harper diaries; Warner's report, *OR,* vol. 44, 302–3; *Official Atlas,* plate LXXI, no. 5; *Georgia Civil War Markers,* 137.

15. Warner, Bird, Barber, and Harper diaries; H. C. Rodgers to General Williams, November 27, 1864, *OR,* vol. 44, 563; *Official Atlas,* plate LXXI, no. 6; *Georgia Civil War Markers,* 137.

16. Warner, Bird, Barber, and Harper diaries; *Official Atlas,* plate LXXI, no. 6; *Georgia Civil War Markers,* 139; Krakow, *Georgia Place Names,* 15, 210. The name Spier is sometimes spelled Speir; I use the spelling found in Krakow.

17. *Official Atlas,* plate LXXI, no. 6; Percy S. Flippin, ed., "From the Autobiography of Herschel V. Johnson, 1856–1867," *American Historical Review* 30 (January 1925): 311–36; Percy Scott Flippin, *Herschel V. Johnson of Georgia: States Rights Unionist* (Richmond, Va.: Press of The Dietz Printing Co., 1931), 1–3, 7, 24, 56, 69, 84, 121, 131–35, 141–45, 177–97, 221, 317–19, 326–27; Abell to his parents, October 26, 1864; Stanley Weintraub, *General Sherman's Christmas: Savannah, 1864* (New York: Smithsonian Books, 2009), 106–7.

18. Warner, Bird, Barber, and Harper diaries; H. W. Perkins to Geary, November 30, 1864, *OR,* vol. 44, 583; *Official Atlas,* plate LXXI, nos. 6, 7; *Georgia Civil War Markers,* 139; Krakow, *Georgia Place Names,* 17.

19. Benson reminiscence, 19; Sweetland, undated letter fragment, probably December 15, 1864; Darling, *Events and Comments of My Life;* Sherman, *Memoirs,* 2:193.

20. Mrs. S. E. McCroan, "Reminiscences of the Civil War of the '60s," Georgia Archives, Morrow, Ga.

21. Warner diary; Jones's report, *OR,* vol. 44, 296; *Frank Leslie's Illustrated Newspaper,* January 14, 1865.

22. Bird diary; Wellman, "Fun in Army Life"; Trudeau, *Southern Storm,* 380–83.

23. Geary's report, *OR,* vol. 44, 273; Jones's report, *OR,* vol. 44, 296; Warner, Harper, Barber, and Bird diaries; *Official Atlas,* plate LXXI, no. 6; Slave Market, Louisville, Jefferson County, Ga., GA-14–2, Historic American Buildings Survey, Prints and Photograph Division, Library of Congress, Washington, D.C.; Trudeau, *Southern Storm,* 284–85.

24. Durden, *History of Saint George Parish,* 75–79.

25. Jones, *When Sherman Came,* 49–59, 332; Durden, *History of Saint George Parish,* 78–79. Jones refers to the hanging victim by his initial H; Durden identifies him as Judge Holt.

26. Bryant, "Over the Ogeechee."

27. Durden, *History of Saint George Parish,* 79.

28. Warner, Harper, Barber, and Bird diaries; Geary's report, *OR,* vol. 44, 273; Williams, Orders, *OR,* vol. 44, 599; *Official Atlas,* plate LXXI, no. 7.

29. *Presidents, Soldiers, Statesmen,* 1503, 1505; Harns interview notes, undated; "The Boys in Blue of '61, XII," undated clipping from the *Sioux City [Iowa] Journal;* Darling, *Events and Comments of My Life.*

30. Albert M. Hillhouse, *A History of Burke County, Georgia, 1777–1950* (Swainsboro, Ga.: Magnolia Press, 1985), 257.

31. Warner, Harper, Barber, and Bird diaries; Geary's report, *OR,* vol. 44, 274; *Official Atlas,* plate LXXI, no. 7.

32. Warner and Bird diaries; Geary's report, *OR,* vol. 44, 274; file #71000280, Birdsville Plantation, Jenkins County, Ga., National Register of Historic Places, National Park Service, Washington, D.C.; Porter Carswell, "The Romance of Birdsville," *Savannah Morning News Magazine,* June 28, 1964, 6–7; Perkerson, *White Columns in Georgia,*

80–85; Hillhouse, *History of Burke County, Georgia,* 263–66; "William B. Jones," in William B. Jones, M.D., Collection, Georgia Archives, Morrow, Ga; Albert M. Hillhouse, *Nuggets and Other Findings in Burke County, Georgia* (Danville, Ky.: Prompt Printing, 1981), 180–83. Birdsville is today part of Jenkins County.

33. *Georgia Civil War Markers,* 6, 153; Carswell, "Romance of Birdsville," 6–7; Perkerson, *White Columns in Georgia,* 80–85; Nell H. Baldwin and A. M. Hillhouse, *An Intelligent Student's Guide to Burke County (Ga.) History* (Waynesboro, Ga.: Published by the authors, 1956), 66; Lillian Lewis Powell, Dorothy Collins Odom, and Albert M. Hillhouse, *Grave Markers in Burke County, Georgia* (Waynesboro, Ga.: Chalker Publishing Co., 1974), 144–45; Mary Franklin Andrew, interview by author, January 27, 28, 2007. The historical marker is 3.3 miles west of Birdsville on Route 17. No record of the birth of the twins survives; nor are their graves marked in the family cemetery.

34. Washington L. Kilpatrick to James H. Kilpatrick, December 31, 1864, Lyle Lansdell Collection, Carrboro, N.C.; W. L. Kilpatrick, *The Hephzibah Baptist Association Centennial, 1794–1894* (n.p., n.d.), 209–10.

35. Warner diary; Warner's report, *OR,* vol. 44, 303; Geary's report, *OR,* vol. 44, 274; *Official Atlas,* plate LXXI, no. 8; Report from Prisoner of War Records, War Department, November 22, 1890, in Thomas D. Spiking Jr. pension file, National Archives, Washington, D.C.

36. *Georgia Civil War Markers,* 152; Geary's report, *OR,* vol. 44, 274; Benson reminiscence, 21–22; Darling, *Events and Comments of My Life.* Camp Lawton is today the site of Magnolia Springs State Park.

37. Warner, Pettit, Harper, and Bird diaries; Geary's report, *OR,* vol. 44, 275; Geary to H. W. Perkins, December 4, 1864, *OR,* vol. 44, 627; *Official Atlas,* plate LXXI, no. 8. The position of this night's encampment is depicted incorrectly on the map.

38. Warner, Pettit, Harper, and Bird diaries; Geary's report, *OR,* vol. 44, 275; *Official Atlas,* plate LXXI, no. 8; *Georgia Civil War Markers,* 152: Hollingsworth, *History of Screven County,* 38. The Middleground Road is today segmented under different names.

39. Williams, Orders, December 5, 1864, *OR,* vol. 44, 633.

40. Geary's report, *OR,* vol. 44, 275; Dianne W. Kinsey to author, April 17, May 9, 2006. The Zeigler mill and home are misidentified on *Official Atlas,* plate LXXI, no. 8 as "Jigler's," and the mill is misplaced on Little Horse Creek rather than the South Fork of Little Ogeechee Branch.

41. Undated letter of Leon B. McGee quoted in John Ellis Walker, *Genealogy of the Walker Family* (n.p., n.d.); Sherman, *Memoirs,* 2:175.

42. Hollingsworth, *History of Screven County,* 39.

43. Ibid., 39–40; Trudeau, *Southern Storm,* 85.

44. "Letter from Scriven," *Countryman,* January 17, 1865, 22; "Wheeler's Cavalry," *Countryman,* January 24, 1865, 46.

45. Benson reminiscence, 24; McKay, "'Three Years or during the War,' with the Crescent and Star," 154.

CHAPTER 6

1. Warner, Bird, Barber, and Harper diaries; *Official Atlas,* plate LXXI, no. 8.

2. Warner, Bird, Barber, and Harper diaries; Geary's report, *OR,* vol. 44, 275; *Official Atlas,* plate LXXI, no. 9.

3. Zettler, *War Stories and School-Day Incidents for the Children,* 131–33, 157–61.

4. Graham, "Reminiscence of the Civil War," 5:56.

5. Muster rolls, December 31, 1864; Bird diary; Edson D. Ames to his family, March 30, 1865, Carolyn Ames Simons Collection, Phoenix, Ariz.; Alfred W. Benson to Dexter Campbell, December 20, 1864, in Jesse D. Campbell pension file. For details of Campbell's death, see Dunkelman, *Brothers One and All,* 162–63.

6. Warner, Bird, Barber, and Bowen diaries; *Official Atlas,* plate LXXI, no. 10; *Georgia Civil War Markers,* 154.

7. "The Albany Statesman Suggests," *Cattaraugus Freeman,* December 8, 1864; Howe, *Marching with Sherman,* 100–101, 110.

8. Warner, Benson, Bird, and Harper diaries; Geary's report, *OR,* vol. 44, 276; Jones's report, *OR,* vol. 44, 296; *Official Atlas,* plate LXXI, no. 10; Norman V. Turner to author, March 10, 2006.

9. Jennie Ihly Darnell, "Reminiscences of the War between the States," Georgia UDC, 3:73–75.

10. Charles Carleton Coffin, *The Boys of '61: Or, Four Years of Fighting* (Boston: Estes and Lauriat, 1884), 400.

11. Warner, Benson, Bird, Barber, Harper, and Bowen diaries; Jones's report, *OR,* vol. 44, 296; Geary's report, *OR,* vol. 44, 276; *Official Atlas,* plate LXXI, no. 10.

12. Warner, Benson, Bird, Harper, and Bowen diaries.

13. Geary's report, *OR,* vol. 44, 276–77; Warner's report, *OR,* vol. 44, 303; Warner, Barber, and Bowen diaries; *Official Atlas,* plate LXXI, nos. 10, 11; Charles C. Jones Jr., *The Siege of Savannah in December, 1864* (Albany, N.Y.: Joel Munsell, 1874), 75, 78, 79, 80–82, 85–86, 112; Sherman, *Memoirs,* 2:193, 195.

14. Geary's report, *OR,* vol. 44, 277; Bird diary; Conyngham, *Sherman's March through the South,* 289–90.

15. Bird, Warner, Barber, and Harper diaries; Trudeau, *Southern Storm,* 412; Benson reminiscence, 24.

16. Muster rolls, December 31, 1864; Geary's report, *OR,* vol. 44, 277; Bowen diary; Oyer interview notes, undated; Blair, *Politician Goes to War,* 218.

17. Bowen and Harper diaries; Benson reminiscence, 24; McKay, "'Three Years or during the War,' with the Crescent and Star," 154; Darling, *Events and Comments of My Life;* Charles Harry Matteson interview notes, October 6, 1893, Northrup Papers.

18. Warner and Pettit diaries; Geary's report, *OR,* vol. 44, 277–78; Jones's report, *OR,* vol. 44, 296; Circular Order No. 77, December 13, 1864, General Orders and Circular Orders Issued, Second Brigade, Second Division, Twentieth Corps.

19. Warner, Pettit, and Bowen diaries; muster rolls, December 31, 1864; Warner's report, *OR,* vol. 44, 303; Besecker interview notes, May 18, 1887; Edward G. Herrington to E. D. Northrup, September 12, 1886, Northrup Papers; Matteson interview notes, October 6, 1893; Patrick Foley interview notes, undated, Northrup Papers; *Presidents, Soldiers, Statesmen,* 1605.

20. Harper, Warner, and Pettit diaries; Geary's report, *OR,* vol. 44, 277–78; Jones's report, *OR,* vol. 44, 296; Geary, Circular Orders, Number 141, *OR,* vol. 44, 705; Conklin, *Under the Crescent and Star,* 217.

21. Bowen, Bird, Harper, Warner, and Pettit diaries; Special Order No. 135, December 14, 1864, Special Orders Issued, Second Brigade, Second Division, Twentieth Corps,

National Archives, Washington, D.C.; McKay, "'Three Years or during the War,' with the Crescent and Star," 154; Conklin, *Under the Crescent and Star,* 217.

22. Harper, Warner, and Pettit diaries; Sweetland to Mary Sweetland, December 16, 1864.

23. Slocum to Sherman, December 15, 1864, and Sherman to Slocum, December 15, 1864, *OR,* vol. 44, 719–20: Slocum, *Life and Services of Major General Henry Warner Slocum,* 238–41; Sherman, *Memoirs,* 2:204.

24. Graves to Celia Smith, December 16, 1864; Sweetland to Mary Sweetland, ca. December 15, 1864; Williams's report, *OR,* vol. 44, 211; Kennett, *Marching through Georgia,* 289; Lewis, *Sherman,* 439.

25. Bird, Pettit, Warner, Barber, and Harper diaries; Graves to Celia Smith, December 16, 1864; McCadden to his mother and brother, December 16, 1864, Meininger Collection; Jones's report, *OR,* vol. 44, 296; Howe, *Home Letters of General Sherman,* 317.

26. Bird, Bowen, Warner, Harper, and Pettit diaries; George J. Mason to his sister Mary, December 18, 1864, Juliet Mason Collection, Russell, Pa.; Norton to Frankie Norton, December 17, 1864.

27. Warner, Bird, Bowen, Barber, and Harper diaries; Sherman's surrender demand and General William J. Hardee's refusal are in Sherman, *Memoirs,* 2:210–12.

28. Warner, Harper, Pettit, Bowen, Barber, and Bird diaries.

29. Geary's report, *OR,* vol. 44, 279; Robert P. Dechert to Geary, December 18, 1864, *OR,* vol. 44, 749; Darling to his family, December 16, 1864.

30. Geary's report, *OR,* vol. 44, 279; Warner, Harper, Bird, and Pettit diaries; McKay, "'Three Years or during the War,' with the Crescent and Star," 155; James P. Brady, *Hurrah for the Artillery! Knap's Independent Battery "E," Pennsylvania Light Artillery* (Gettysburg, Pa.: Thomas Publications, 1992), 380.

31. "Sherman's Run," *Southern Recorder,* December 20, 1864.

32. Warner and Bowen diaries; Jones's report, *OR,* vol. 44, 297; Geary's report, *OR,* vol. 44, 280; Derek Smith, *Civil War Savannah* (Savannah: Frederic C. Beil, 1997), 187–88, 193–94; Jones, *Siege of Savannah in December, 1864,* 115–17, 142–43, 155.

33. Warner, Harper, Bird, Barber, Bowen, and Pettit diaries; Conyngham, *Sherman's March through the South,* 293; "Savannah," *Savannah Republican,* January 19, 1865; Spencer B. King Jr., ed., "Fanny Cohen's Journal of Sherman's Occupation of Savannah," *Georgia Historical Quarterly* 41, no. 4 (December 1957): 410; Jones, *When Sherman Came,* 92.

34. *Harper's Weekly,* January 14, 1865; Jones's report, *OR,* vol. 44, 297; Warner's report, *OR,* vol. 44, 303; Bowen diary; Jacqueline Jones, *Saving Savannah: The City and the Civil War* (New York: Alfred A. Knopf, 2008), 121, 133.

35. Bird diary; Darling, *Events and Comments of My Life.*

CHAPTER 7

1. Darling to his family, December 16, 1864; Darling to his brother and sister, January 21, 1865; McCadden to his mother and brother, December 16, 1864; Williams's report, *OR,* vol. 44, 210; Mason to his sister Mary, December 18, 1864; Graves to Celia Smith, December 16, 1864; Langhans to Julius Langhans, January 22, 1865.

2. "Sherman," *Countryman,* January 10, 1865, 10.

3. Bowen diary, December 21, 23, 25, 1864; Andrew D. Blood to Wesley Blood, January 1, 1865, Alan D. Henry Collection, Temperance, Mich.; "Savannah," *Savannah Republican,* January 19, 1865; Captain William H. Lambert to Lieutenant Colonel C. W. Assmussen, December 24, 1864, Letters Sent, Second Division, Twentieth Corps, National Archives, Washington, D.C.; "Notes Taken from the Gamble Collection," Lillian Chaplin Bragg Papers, Georgia Historical Society, Savannah, Ga.; Wilbur reminiscence; King, "Fanny Cohen's Journal," 414.

4. Blood to Wesley Blood, January 1, 1865; Bowen diary, December 23, 1864; King, "Fanny Cohen's Journal," 409, 411, 414; "Advance of Civilization," *Savannah Republican,* January 6, 1865; Warner diary, December 24, 1864; Darling to his brother and sister, January 21, 1865.

5. Blood to Wesley Blood, January 1, 1865; Bowen diary, December 22, 1864, January 6, 10, 14, 1865; Shannon to Francelia Hunt, January 25, 1865, Shaw Collection; Job B. Dawley to his brother, January 15, 1865, Civil War Manuscripts Collection (MS 619), Manuscripts and Archives, Yale University Library, New Haven, Conn.; Langhans to Julius Langhans, January 22, 1865: "Notice," *Savannah Republican,* January 10, 1865.

6. Bryant to Cornelia Bryant, January 12, 20, 1865; Bowen diary, December 30, 1864, January 16, February 16, 1865; *Presidents, Soldiers, Statesmen,* 1380–81; Warner diary, January 19, 1865; muster rolls, February 28, 1865.

7. Warner diary, December 22, 1864; Darling to his wife, January 4, 1865.

8. Mason to his sister Mary, December 30, 1864; Langhans to Julius Langhans, January 22, 1865; Blood to Wesley Blood, January 1, 1865; Rhea Cummings Otto, "Forsyth Park Whittled out of a Pine Forest," *Savannah Morning News,* August 6, 1957, clipping in Walter C. Hartridge Collection, Georgia Historical Society, Savannah, Ga.; Adelaide Wilson, *Historic and Picturesque Savannah* (Boston: Boston Photogravure Co., 1889), 183–84; Jones, *Saving Savannah,* 214–15; Smith, *Civil War Savannah,* 231; H. Ronald Freeman, *Sherman Takes Savannah* (Savannah: Freeport Publishing, 2007), 161; Shannon to Francelia Hunt, January 25, 1865, Shaw Collection; Abell to his mother, January 16, 1865; Bowen diary, January 10, 1865.

9. Sherman to President Lincoln, December 22, 1864, *OR,* vol. 44, 783; Alexander A. Lawrence, *A Present for Mr. Lincoln: The Story of Savannah from Secession to Sherman* (1961; reprint, Savannah: Oglethorpe Press, 1997), 211–12; Langhans to Julius Langhans, January 22, 1865; Sweetland to Mary Sweetland, January 20, 1865; "Cotton Captured at Savannah," *Congressional Globe,* 38th Cong., 2nd sess., Senate, January 5, 1865, 112; "The Cotton Captured at Savannah," *Savannah Republican,* January 12, 1865; "Thanks to General Sherman," *Congressional Globe,* 38th Cong., 2nd sess., House of Representatives, January 5, 1865, 116; "Thanks to General W. T. Sherman," *Congressional Globe,* 38th Cong., 2nd sess., Senate, January 6, 1865, 133; "National Vote of Thanks to Our General and His Invincible Army," *Savannah Republican,* January 14, 1865.

10. Geary's report, *OR,* vol. 44, 280–82.

11. Geary, General Orders Number 1, December 23, 1864, *OR,* vol. 44, 796; Geary, General Orders Number 2, December 24, 1864, *OR,* vol. 44, 804–5; "General Orders, No. 1" and "General Orders, No. 2," *Savannah Republican,* December 30, 1864; "General Orders, No. 3," *Savannah Republican,* January 12, 1865; "General Orders, No. 4," *Savannah Republican,* January 10, 1865; "General Orders, No. 5," *Savannah Republican,* January 16, 1865. The former Central Railroad Bank building at 7 East Bay Street today houses

a restaurant on the ground floor and a tattoo parlor above. See David D'Arcy and Ben Mammina, *Civil War Walking Tour of Savannah* (Atglen, Pa.: Schiffer, 2006), 10–11.

12. Frances K. Drew, "A Savannah Reminiscence," Georgia UDC, 8:29–30; Mary A. Wragg Bond, "A Reminiscence of the War," Alexander A. Lawrence Collection, Georgia Historical Society, Savannah, Ga.; Frances Thomas Howard, *In and out of the Lines: An Accurate Account of Incidents during the Occupation of Georgia by Federal Troops in 1864–65* (New York: Neale Publishing Co., 1905), 196; Larry Shields, "Savannah under Sherman," *Savannah Morning News Magazine,* December 20, 1964: 2; D'Arcy and Mammina, *Civil War Walking Tour of Savannah,* 72–75; Freeman, *Sherman Takes Savannah,* 186.

13. Ellis, *History of Cattaraugus County,* 120; Darling, *Events and Comments of My Life;* Barber diary, December 25, 31, 1864, January 1, 1865; Bowen diary, December 31, 1864, January 5, 6, 8, 15, 1865; Warner diary, December 26–31, 1864, January 5, 8, 14, 18, 1865; Sweetland to Mary Sweetland, January 20, 1865.

14. Warner diary, December 30, 1864; Quaife, *From the Cannon's Mouth,* 355; Jones, *When Sherman Came,* 97; "Review of the Twentieth Corps," *Savannah Republican,* December 31, 1864.

15. "Newspaper Change," *Savannah Republican,* December 29, 1864; Wilson, *Historic and Picturesque Savannah,* 182, 183; Lawrence, *Present for Mr. Lincoln,* 215–16; Warner diary, December 26, 1864; Darling to his family, January 4, 1865; *Cattaraugus Freeman,* January 26, 1865; Otto, "Forsyth Park Whittled out of a Pine Forest"; King, "Fanny Cohen's Journal," 413; Jones, *Saving Savannah,* 222–23.

16. Bowen diary, January 4, 1865; William A. Farlee, "Mustering in Colored Troops," account accompanying letter to E. D. Northrup, January 28, 1879, Northrup Papers.

17. "Interview with Dad"; Edward Campbell McDowell, ed., *Diary of Sgt. Fergus Elliott, Co. G, 109th Pa. Vol. Inf., 1865* (n.p., n.d.), January 20, 1865, in Civil War Times Illustrated Collection, U. S. Army Military History Institute, Carlisle Barracks, Pa.; Bowen diary, January 18, 1865; *Presidents, Soldiers, Statesmen,* 1380–81.

18. Lawrence, *Present for Mr. Lincoln,* 214; Freeman, *Sherman Takes Savannah,* 173; Barber diary, January 6, 1865; "More about Amusements," *Savannah Republican,* January 6, 1865.

19. Bird diary, December 22, 1864; Sweetland to Mary Sweetland, January 20, 1865; Circular Order No. 38, January 20, 1865, General Orders and Circular Orders Issued, Second Brigade, Second Division, Twentieth Corps.

20. Shannon to Francelia Hunt, January 25, 1865, Shaw Collection; "No More Amusements," *Savannah Republican,* January 3, 1865; "More About Amusements."

21. Bryant to Cornelia Bryant, January 12, 1865; Bowen diary, January 15, 1865; Warner diary, January 1, 8, 15, 1865; Norton to Frankie Norton, January 4, 1865; "Church Directory," *Savannah Republican,* January 5, 1865; Blood to Wesley Blood, January 1, 1865; Howe, *Marching with Sherman,* 199–200; Howard, *In and out of the Lines,* 192; Job B. Dawley to his brother, January 15, 1865.

22. Langhans to Julius Langhans, January 22, 1865; Harper diary, December 22, 1864–January 3, 1865; Warner diary, December 22, 1864–January 26, 1865; Bowen diary, December 23, 1864, January 2, 8, 1865; Blood to Wesley Blood, January 1, 1865; Bryant to Cornelia Bryant, January 12, 1865; Special Order No. 137, December 24, 1864, and Nos. 15 and 17, January 15, 17, 1865, Special Orders Issued, Second Brigade, Second Divi-

sion, Twentieth Corps; Circular Order Nos. 90 and 93, December 23, 54, 1864, General Orders and Circular Orders Issued, Second Brigade, Second Division, Twentieth Corps; Circular Order No. 39, January 21, 1865, General Orders and Circular Orders Issued, Second Brigade, Second Division, Twentieth Corps; Walter J. Fraser Jr., *Savannah in the Old South* (Athens: Univ. of Georgia Press, 2003), 242 and illustration; Hirshson, *White Tecumseh,* 266–67 (quotation).

23. Howe, *Home Letters of General Sherman,* 322, 326; Simpson and Berlin, *Sherman's Civil War,* 784.

24. Howe, *Marching with Sherman,* 200; Nichols, *Story of the Great March,* 108; Sherman, *Memoirs,* 2:236.

25. Nichols, *Story of the Great March,* 98–99; 107; William Robert Gignillant to his mother, December 26, 1864, Michael Johnson Kenan Papers, Georgia Historical Society, Savannah, Ga.

26. "Quietude of the City," *Savannah Republican,* January 8, 1865; "Savannah," *Savannah Republican,* January 19, 1865.

27. Howard, *In and out of the Lines,* 180–81; Lawrence, *Present for Mr. Lincoln,* 208; Gignillant to his mother, December 26, 1864.

28. Darling to his family, January 4, 1865; Sherman, *Memoirs,* 2:234; Mason to his sister Mary, December 30, 1864; Shannon to Francelia Hunt, January 25, 1865, Shaw Collection; Abell to his sister Stella, January 29, 1865; Abell to his family, January 22, 1865; Bond, "Reminiscence of the War"; Lawrence, *Present for Mr. Lincoln,* 223, 224.

29. Job B. Dawley to his brother, January 15, 1865; Mary Cheves West, "Sherman in Savannah," Georgia UDC, 8:128–30.

30. King, "Fanny Cohen's Journal," 411–15.

31. Lawrence, *Present for Mr. Lincoln,* 167, 198; Nichols, *Story of the Great March,* 108; Ott, *Confederate Daughters,* 57, 64–65, 132–33; Caudill and Ashdown, *Sherman's March in Myth and Memory,* 91, 92, 93, 94, 103, 107, 114, 130; Nina Silber, *The Romance of Reunion: Northerners and the South, 1865–1900* (Chapel Hill: Univ. of North Carolina Press, 1993), 110–18; Gardner, *Blood and Irony,* 57–60, 61–66, 86–87; Schivelbusch, *Culture of Defeat,* 95–96.

32. John P. Dyer, "Northern Relief for Savannah during Sherman's Occupation," *Journal of Southern History* 19, no. 4 (November 1953): 458–62, 464–68, 470–71; Thomas Gamble Jr., *A History of the City Government of Savannah, Ga., from 1790 to 1901* (Savannah: Under Direction of the City Council, 1900), 263–65; Sherman, *Memoirs,* 2:233, 234, 236–37; Bond, "Reminiscence of the War"; Abell to his family, January 22, 1865; Abell to his sister Stella, January 29, 1865; Jones, *When Sherman Came,* 106; Richard D. Arnold, *Letters of Richard D. Arnold, M.D.,* ed. Richard H. Shryock (Durham, N.C.: Seeman Press, 1929), 123; Smith, *Civil War Savannah,* 208–9; Lawrence, *Present for Mr. Lincoln,* 220–22; Jones, *Saving Savannah,* 221–22.

33. Mrs. G. W. Anderson to Mary, January 1, 1865, Confederate Miscellany, Manuscript, Archives, and Rare Book Library, Emory University, Atlanta, Ga.; Lawrence, *Present for Mr. Lincoln,* 228; Edward J. Thomas, *Memoirs of a Southerner, 1840–1923* (Savannah: Published by the author, 1923), 53–54; "Peddled Cigars to Army of Sherman," *Savannah Evening Press,* December 26, 1932; Howard, *In and out of the Lines,* 186; Jones, *Saving Savannah,* 224; Freeman, *Sherman Takes Savannah,* 183.

34. William A. Byrne, "'Uncle Billy' Sherman Comes to Town: The Free Winter of

Black Savannah," *Georgia Historical Quarterly* 79, no. 1 (Spring 1995): 91–92; Jones, *When Sherman Came*, 106, 333.

35. Caroline A. N. Lamar to Charles A. L. Lamar, December 23, 1864, Charles Augustus Lafayette Lamar Family Papers, Georgia Archives, Morrow, Ga.; King, "Fanny Cohen's Journal," 411; Mrs. G. W. Anderson to Mary, January 1, 1865.

36. Byrne, "'Uncle Billy' Sherman Comes to Town," 93, 95, 97; Caroline A. N. Lamar to Charles A. L. Lamar, December 23, 1864; King, "Fanny Cohen's Journal," 415; Ott, *Confederate Daughters*, 84–87.

37. Howard, *In and out of the Lines*, 186; Byrne, "'Uncle Billy' Sherman Comes to Town," 98, 102, 103, 105; Caroline A. N. Lamar to Charles A. L. Lamar, December 23, 1864.

38. Sherman, *Memoirs*, 2:249, 250–52; Byrne, "'Uncle Billy' Sherman Comes to Town," 108, 110–14; Jones, *Saving Savannah*, 219–20.

39. Blood to Wesley Blood, January 1, 1865.

40. Abell to his family, January 22, 1865.

41. Howard, *In and out of the Lines*, 185–86; "Notes Taken from the Gamble Collection," Bragg Papers; "Incidents of War Times Recalled by Mrs. W. H. Sauls," *Savannah Evening Press*, June 18, 1932.

42. "Review of the Twentieth Corps"; Otto, "Forsyth Park Whittled out of a Pine Forest."

43. Aunt L. to Mrs. J. F. Gilmer, January 10, 1865, Alexander A. Lawrence Collection, Georgia Historical Society, Savannah, Ga.; Mrs. G. W. Anderson to Mary, January 1, 1865; Bond, "Reminiscence of the War"; West, "Sherman in Savannah," 129; Jones, *When Sherman Came*, 103, 333.

44. Aunt L. to Mrs. J. F. Gilmer, January 10, 1865; "Peddled Cigars to Army of Sherman"; "Recalls Sherman's Capture of Savannah 75 years Ago," *Savannah Evening Press*, December 25, 1939.

45. "Peddled Cigars to Army of Sherman"; Coffin, *Boys of '61*, 399.

46. King, "Fanny Cohen's Journal," 411–12, 415–16; Thomas, *Memoirs of a Southerner*, 54; Caroline A. N. Lamar to Charles A. L. Lamar, December 23, 1864; Bond, "Reminiscence of the War"; Bird diary, January 11, 12, 1865.

47. Margaret DeBolt, "Dec. 21, 1864: Recalling Sherman's Entry," *Savannah Evening Press*, December 21, 1975.

48. Eleanor Kinzie Gordon to W. W. Gordon, December 29, 1864, Gordon Family Papers, Georgia Historical Society, Savannah, Ga.; Jones, *When Sherman Came*, 107; Lawrence, *Present for Mr. Lincoln*, 213.

49. Warner diary, January 9, 15, 1865; Job B. Dawley to his brother, January 15, 1865; Norton to Frankie Norton, January 15, 1865.

50. Bryant to Cornelia Bryant, January 20, 1865; Darling to his brother and sister, January 21, 1865; Sweetland to Mary Sweetland, January 22, 1865.

51. Sherman, *Memoirs*, 2:205–10, 212–13, 221–27; Grant, *Personal Memoirs*, 2:401–2.

52. Simpson and Berlin, *Sherman's Civil War*, 774, 782, 786, 798.

53. Warner diary, January 15–26, 1865; Geary, Special Field Order, Number 1, *OR*, vol. 47, pt. 2, 95.

54. Graves to Celia Smith, January 22, 1865; "Resolutions," *Savannah Republican*, January 3, 1865; "Major General Geary," *Savannah Republican*, January 25, 1865; "Gen-

eral Orders, No. 6," *Savannah Republican,* January 21, 1865; Gamble, *History of the City Government of Savannah,* 262.

55. Almon Deforest Reed to his sister, January 25, 1865, Donald K. Ryberg Jr. Collection, Westfield, N.Y.; Shannon to Francelia Hunt, January 25, 1865, Shaw Collection.

CHAPTER 8

1. Warner, Barber, Bird, and Blood diaries; Emory Sweetland diary, Lyle Sweetland Collection, South Dayton, N.Y.; Homer A. Ames diary, Carolyn Ames Simons Collection, Phoenix, Ariz.; Warner's report, *OR,* vol. 47, pt. 1, 742; *Official Atlas,* plate LXXX, no. 1, plate LXXXVI, no. 1.

2. Geary's report, *OR,* vol. 47, pt. 1, 681–82, 696.

3. West, "Sherman in Savannah," 130; Lawrence, *Present for Mr. Lincoln,* 238–41; Freeman, *Sherman Takes Savannah,* 198–99; Smith, *Civil War Savannah,* 236–37.

4. Warner, Sweetland, Bird, Blood, and Ames diaries; Sweetland to Mary Sweetland, February 1, 1865; "From Sherman's Army," *Cattaraugus Union* (Ellicottville, N.Y.), February 23, 1865; Geary's report, *OR,* vol. 47, pt. 1, 682; *Official Atlas,* plate LXXX, no. 1, plate LXXXVI, no. 1; Norman V. Turner, *The History of Camp Jack* (Springfield, Ga.: Published by the author, 2002), 3, 9, 11, 12; Krick, *Lee's Colonels,* 420.

5. Warner, Sweetland, Barber, Bird, Blood, Ames, and Bowen diaries; David S. Jones to his brother, January 30, 1865, David S. Jones letters, Clara Jones Collection, Salamanca, N.Y.; Warner's report, *OR,* vol. 47, pt. 1, 743; Geary's report, *OR,* vol. 47, pt. 1, 682; *Official Atlas,* plate LXXX, no. 1, plate LXXXVI, no. 1.

6. Bryant to Cornelia Bryant, January 30, 1865; Jones to his brother, January 30, 1865; Abell to his sister Stella, January 29, 1865; Bird diary; Harper diary, January 27, 1865. For accounts of the fire, see Smith, *Civil War Savannah,* 233–35; Lawrence, *Present for Mr. Lincoln,* 239–40; and Freeman, *Sherman Takes Savannah,* 192–93.

7. Sweetland diary; Christopher F. Riesser [*sic*] Claim, #15214, Southern Claims Commission Records, transcription courtesy of Norman V. Turner.

8. Warner, Sweetland, Barber, Bird, Ames, and Bowen diaries; Geary's report, *OR,* vol. 47, pt. 1, 682.

9. Warner, Sweetland, Barber, Bird, Blood, and Ames diaries; "Register of Deaths" in Company D's Descriptive Book and Company D muster roll, February 28, 1865; "Declaration for an Original Pension of a Father or Mother," November 25, 1887, John I. Snyder pension file, National Archives, Washington, D.C.; Norman V. Turner to author, April 1, 2006.

10. Warner, Barber, Bird, and Ames diaries; Mindil's report, *OR,* vol. 47, pt. 1, 731; Sweetland to Mary Sweetland, February 1, 1865; Winfield S. Cameron interview notes, November 27, 1893, Northrup Papers.

11. Warner diary, September 22, 1864, February 2, 1865; Smith diary, July 4, November 14, 1864; Blood and Ames diaries; Bird diary, February 2, April 9, 1865; "From Sherman's Army," *Cattaraugus Union,* February 23, 1865, quoting an anonymous soldier's letter of February 2, 1865; Sweetland to Mary Sweetland, February 2, 1865.

12. Warner, Sweetland, Barber, Bird, Blood, and Ames diaries; Bowen diary, February 11, 1865; Sweetland to Mary Sweetland, February 1, 1865; "From the 154th Regiment," *Westfield (N.Y.) Republican,* May 10, 1865.

13. Warner, Sweetland, Barber, Bird, Blood, and Ames diaries; Mindil's report, *OR,* vol. 47, pt. 1, 731; *Official Atlas,* plate LXXX, no. 1, plate LXXXVI, no. 2. Jasper and Hampton counties have since been formed from the former Beaufort District. Robertville is spelled Robertsville on the Civil War–era maps.

14. Conyngham, *Sherman's March through the South,* 310; Blair, *Politician Goes to War,* 228; Simpson and Berlin, *Sherman's Civil War,* 762, 771, 776, 803; West, "Sherman in Savannah," 129; statement of Mary Cheves West, June 5, 1909, South Carolina Historical Society, Charleston, S.C.; Stout, *Upon the Altar of the Nation,* 413, 415, 420.

15. Warner, Sweetland, Barber, Bird, and Blood diaries; Sweetland to Mary Sweetland, March 12, 1865; Warner's report, *OR,* vol. 47, pt. 1, 743; Geary's report, *OR,* vol. 47, pt. 1, 683; *Official Atlas,* plate LXXX, no. 2, plate LXXXVI, no. 2. The current Robertville Baptist Church, built circa 1847, was moved to its present location from Gillisonville about 1867. File #72001213, Robertville Baptist Church, Jasper County, S.C., National Register of Historic Places, National Park Service, Washington, D.C.

16. Jones, *When Sherman Came,* 111–12, 333.

17. Geary's report, *OR,* vol. 47, pt. 1, 683, 1229; Alice Rhodes Rogers, *The Thomas Rhodes Family of South Carolina* (Florence, S.C.: Pattillo Printing, 1996), 184.

18. Warner, Sweetland, Bird, Blood, and Ames diaries; Geary's report, *OR,* vol. 47, pt. 1, 683; *Official Atlas,* plate LXXX, no. 2, plate LXXXVI, no. 2; Dyer, *Secret Yankees,* 160; Hirshson, *White Tecumseh,* 279. Ames's diary entries from February 5 to the end of the month are misdated a day early. Lawtonville is today referred to as Lawtonville Crossroads.

19. Rogers, *Thomas Rhodes Family of South Carolina,* 164, 165.

20. Warner, Sweetland, Bird, Blood, and Ames diaries; Mindil's report, *OR,* vol. 47, pt. 1, 731; Geary's report, *OR,* vol. 47, pt. 1, 683; *Official Atlas,* plate LXXX, no. 2, plate LXXXVI, no. 2. Barnwell District is today composed of portions of Allendale, Bamberg, and Barnwell counties.

21. WPA South Carolina Narratives, vol. 14, pt. 1, 155–56, pt. 3, 280–81.

22. Ibid., pt. 1, 200, 238–39, 261, pt. 4, 267–68.

23. Sweetland to Mary Sweetland, March 12, 1865; Conyngham, *Sherman's March through the South,* 310–11.

24. Warner, Sweetland, Bird, Blood, and Ames diaries; Warner's report, *OR,* vol. 47, pt. 1, 743; Geary's report, *OR,* vol. 47, pt. 1, 683; *Official Atlas,* plate LXXX, no. 2, plate LXXXVI, no. 2; Unnumbered Circular Order, February 8, 1865, General Orders and Circular Orders Issued, Second Brigade, Second Division, Twentieth Corps. Buford's is spelled Beauford's on the 20th Corps map and in Mindil's circular order.

25. A. McKay Brabham Jr., comp., *Mizpah: A Family Book, Including "A Family Sketch and Else or Buford's Bridge and Its People," by Rev. M. M. Brabham* (Columbia, S.C.: R. L. Bryan, 1978), 101–3.

26. Bird diary; David B. Thompson, "Confederates at the Keyboard: Southern Piano Music during the Civil War," in *Bugle Resounding: Music and Musicians of the Civil War Era,* ed. Bruce C. Kelley and Mark A. Snell (Columbia: Univ. of Missouri Press, 2004), 106–10; Conyngham, *Sherman's March through the South,* 247.

27. Henken, "Taming the Enemy," 294; Thompson, "Confederates at the Keyboard," 108.

28. Johnson Hagood, *Meet Your Grandfather: A Sketch-Book of the Hagood-Tobin Family* (Charleston, S.C.: Privately printed, 1946), 92–93, 101.

29. Warner, Sweetland, Barber, Bird, Blood, and Ames diaries; *Official Atlas,* plate LXXX, no. 3, plate LXXXVI, no. 3.

30. Groves, *Jennings-McMillan-Faulling-Whaley-Bluer and Other Early Families of South Carolina,* 68–69, 99–101.

31. Warner, Sweetland, Barber, Bird, Blood, and Ames diaries; Geary's report, *OR,* vol. 47, pt. 1, 684; Sherman, *Memoirs,* 2:274.

32. South Carolina National Heritage Corridor, "Blackville Heritage Trail," brochure; Hagood, *Meet Your Grandfather,* 37–38. The Brown house is at 429 Main Street, and the William Hagood house at 3151 Dexter Street.

33. Raymond P. Boylston, *Healing Springs: A History of the Springs and Surrounding Area* (Orangeburg, S.C.: Sandlapper Publishing, 2004), 175–76; Henken, "Taming the Enemy," 297–98; Genesis 31:34–35, KJV.

34. Warner, Sweetland, Barber, Bird, Blood, and Ames diaries; *Official Atlas,* plate LXXX, no. 3, plate LXXXVI, no. 3.

35. Boylston, *Healing Springs,* 4–5, 177.

36. Ibid., 177–78.

37. Warner, Sweetland, Barber, Bird, Blood, and Ames diaries; Geary's report, *OR,* vol. 47, pt. 1, 685; *Official Atlas,* plate LXXX, no. 3, plate LXXXVI, no. 3.

38. Al Brodie Jr., *A History of the Brodie Family, 1754–1993* (Columbia, S.C.: R. L. Bryan, n.d.), 15–16, quoting Nelle Gardner Morgan, "A Reminiscence of Sherman's Raid in South Carolina," an interview with Emma Porter Brodie published in an Orangeburg, South Carolina, newspaper in 1923.

39. Warner, Sweetland, Barber, Blood, and Ames diaries; *Official Atlas,* plate LXXX, no. 3, plate LXXXVI, no. 3; Cameron interview notes, November 27, 1893; Jones to his brother, January 30, 1865; Conyngham, *Sherman's March through the South,* 311. The portion of Lexington District crossed by the 154th is now in Lexington and Richland counties.

40. Warner, Sweetland, Barber, Bird, Blood, and Ames diaries; Geary's report, *OR,* vol. 47, pt. 1, 685; Williams, General Orders Number 4, *OR,* vol. 47, pt. 2, 410; *Official Atlas,* plate LXXX, no. 4, plate LXXXVI, no. 3; Circular Orders No. 15, February 14, 1865, General Orders and Circular Orders Issued, Second Division, Twentieth Corps.

41. Warner, Sweetland, Barber, Bird, Blood, and Ames diaries; Geary's report, *OR,* vol. 47, pt. 1, 685–86; *Official Atlas,* plate LXXX, no. 4, plate LXXXVI, no. 4; Barrett, *Sherman's March through the Carolinas,* 60.

CHAPTER 9

1. Warner, Sweetland, Barber, Blood, and Bird diaries; Geary's report, *OR,* vol. 47, pt. 1, 686; *Official Atlas,* plate LXXX, no. 4, plate LXXXVI, no. 4.

2. Warner, Sweetland, Barber, Bird, and Blood diaries; Geary's report, *OR,* vol. 47, pt. 1, 686; *Official Atlas,* plate LXXX, no. 4, plate LXXXVI, no. 4; file #80003677, Mount Hebron Temperance Hall, Lexington County, S.C., National Register of Historic Places, National Park Service, Washington, D.C.; Lexington County (S.C.) Museum, "The Leaphart/Harman House," brochure. The house was moved to the museum in 2003 and restored in 2005–6.

3. Warner, Sweetland, Barber, Bird, and Blood diaries; Marion Brunson Lucas,

Sherman and the Burning of Columbia (College Station: Texas A&M Univ. Press, 1976), 163–67; McCadden to his mother and brother, March 29, 1865; Mindil's report, *OR*, vol. 47, pt. 1, 731; Geary's report, *OR*, vol. 47, pt. 1, 686; *Official Atlas*, plate LXXX, no. 4, plate LXXXVI, no. 4.

4. Slocum, General Orders Number 6, *OR*, vol. 47, pt. 2, 479.

5. Warner, Sweetland, Barber, Bird, Blood, and Ames diaries; Mindil's report, *OR*, vol. 47, pt. 1, 731; Slocum, General Orders Number 7, *OR*, vol. 47, pt. 2, 488–89; *Official Atlas*, plate LXXX, no. 4, plate LXXXVI, no. 4.

6. Warner, Sweetland, Barber, Bird, and Blood diaries; Mindil's report, *OR*, vol. 47, pt. 1, 732; Geary's report, *OR*, vol. 47, pt. 1, 687; *Official Atlas*, plate LXXX, no. 4, plate LXXXVI, no. 4; Conyngham, *Sherman's March through the South*, 341.

7. "Sherman's Visit to Fairfield. James M. Smith Writes Interestingly of the Destruction of Property by the Union Army," unidentified newspaper clipping, Fairfield Archives and History, Thomas Woodward Chapter, DAR, Winnsboro, S.C.

8. Julian Stevenson Bolick, *A Fairfield Sketchbook* (Clinton, S.C.: Jacobs Brothers, 1963), 221–22, 226, 248; W. J. Elliott, "The Capture of Dr. John Wallace and Mr. Stephen Gibson," in *Fairfield Remembers Sherman,* comp. Linda Malone (Winnsboro, S.C.: Fairfield Archives and History, 2006), 120–24.

9. Conyngham, *Sherman's March through the South,* 341; WPA South Carolina Narratives, vol. 14, pt. 4, 149–50.

10. Warner, Sweetland, Barber, Bird, Blood, and Ames diaries; Reuben R. Ogden diary, Bradley J. Eide Collection, Chesterfield, Va.; Conyngham, *Sherman's March through the South,* 341; Mindil's report, *OR*, vol. 47, pt. 1, 732; *Official Atlas,* plate LXXX, no. 5, plate LXXXVI, no. 4; "Malvern Hill," in Fairfield Chamber of Commerce, "Historic Winnsboro Tour," brochure; "Sherman in Winnsboro," *Winnsboro (S.C.) News and Herald,* March 8, 1910, Fairfield Archives and History. Conyngham mistakenly referred to the woman as Mrs. Lunderdale.

11. Geary's report, *OR*, vol. 47, pt. 1, 687.

12. Blood, Bird, and Sweetland diaries; McKay, "'Three Years or during the War,' with the Crescent and Star," 155; Bird diary; Sherman, *Memoirs,* 2:288.

13. Sweetland diary; Geary's report, *OR*, vol. 47, pt. 1, 687.

14. "The Late Invasion of Fairfield District by Sherman's Army," *Winnsboro News,* April 18, 1865, in Malone, *Fairfield Remembers Sherman,* 6–8; Jones, *When Sherman Came,* 224; Isabelle Wolfe Baruch, "Recollections of Sherman's Raid through South Carolina," in Malone, *Fairfield Remembers Sherman,* 31; Mrs. K. L. Cureton, "How Mrs. Ladd Saved the Masonic Jewels," in Malone, *Fairfield Remembers Sherman,* 70; Katharine Theus Obear, *Through the Years in Old Winnsboro* (Spartanburg, S.C.: Reprint Co., 1980), 68; Bolick, *Fairfield Sketchbook,* 68; David B. Chesebrough, "'There Goes Your Damned Gospel Shop!' The Churches and Clergy as Victims of Sherman's March through South Carolina," *South Carolina Historical Magazine* 92, no. 1 (January 1991): 26–28; "St. John's Episcopal Cemetery," in Fairfield Chamber of Commerce, "Historic Winnsboro Tour," brochure. St. John's Episcopal Church stood at Garden and Fairfield streets.

15. "Late Invasion of Fairfield District by Sherman's Army," 6–8. According to "Yankee Leniency—Yankee Sympathy," *Winnsboro News,* April 6, 1865, in Malone, *Fairfield Remembers Sherman,* 9, twenty-two houses burned in Winnsboro.

16. "Sherman in Winnsboro," *Winnsboro News and Herald,* March 5, 1901.

17. "Dr. David Lauderdale," in Malone, *Fairfield Remembers Sherman,* 64–65; "Sherman In Winnsboro," *Winnsboro News and Herald,* March 5, 1901, in Malone, *Fairfield Remembers Sherman,* 76; David T. Lauderdale, "The Lauderdales," typescript, 1966, Lauderdale Family File, Fairfield Archives and History; "Our Dry Goods Trade," *Winnsboro News and Herald,* November 3, 1886, Lauderdale Family File.

18. Baruch, "Recollections of Sherman's Raid through South Carolina," 24, 26; Cureton, "How Mrs. Ladd Saved the Masonic Jewels," 69–71.

19. Obear, *Through the Years in Old Winnsboro,* 68–71; Jones, *When Sherman Came,* 223–28; Barrett, *Sherman's March through the Carolinas,* 97. The Obear house, on the west side of North Congress Street, is today Winnsboro's Town Hall. "Obear-Williford House," in Fairfield Chamber of Commerce, "Historic Winnsboro Tour," brochure.

20. Baruch, "Recollections of Sherman's Raid through South Carolina," 24–33. Wolfe was the future mother of financier and governmental adviser Bernard Baruch.

21. Julia A. Tyler, "Mrs. Julia A. Tyler's Experience When Sherman's Army Passed through South Carolina," South Carolina UDC, 7:100.

22. Bolick, *Fairfield Sketchbook,* 140–42.

23. Margaret Crawford Adams, "Tales of a Grand-mother or Recollections of the Confederate War Number 2," manuscript, Margaret Crawford Johnson Adams Papers, South Carolina Historical Society; Jones, *When Sherman Came,* 220–23.

CHAPTER 10

1. Warner, Barber, Bird, and Blood diaries; Warner's report, *OR,* vol. 47, pt. 1, 743; Geary's report, *OR,* vol. 47, pt. 1, 687; Geary, Special Field Orders Number 15, *OR,* vol. 47, pt. 2, 518; *Official Atlas,* plate LXXX, no. 5, plate LXXXVI, no. 4; Fox, "Slocum and His Men," 279.

2. WPA South Carolina Narratives, vol. 14, pt. 1, 105, pt. 2, 267, pt. 3, 130–33; "Bratton Place," in Malone, *Fairfield Remembers Sherman,* 134; "Bratton House," in Fairfield Chamber of Commerce, "Historic Winnsboro Tour," brochure. The Bratton House, today known as Wynn Dee, stands at the corner of Bratton and Zion streets.

3. WPA South Carolina Narratives, vol. 14, pt. 2, 242–43, pt. 4, 36–37; "Glances of Retrospection," in Malone, *Fairfield Remembers Sherman,* 37.

4. Lutie Durham, "Incidents of Sherman's Raid in Fairfield County," South Carolina UDC, 3:260–65.

5. Rebecca A. (Mrs. L. B.) Bates, "Reminiscences of Sherman's Raid," South Carolina UDC, 4:252–53.

6. Mrs. R. E. Ellison, "Recollections of the War," South Carolina UDC, 6:90–94.

7. Margery Hall Robinson Borom, "Home, Sweet Home," Georgia UDC, 8:14–15.

8. "Mother Defies and Wins Admiration of Yankee General," in Malone, *Fairfield Remembers Sherman,* 77.

9. Foster, *Ghosts of the Confederacy,* 123; "A Yankee Letter," in Malone, *Fairfield Remembers Sherman,* 138–39; Caudill and Ashdown, *Sherman's March in Myth and Memory,* 24; Darnell, "Reminiscences of the War between the States," 73; Jane Symons Burden, "Reminiscences," Georgia UDC, 2:57–58; Sherman, *Memoirs,* 2:255–56. On page 292, however, Sherman describes his orderly in Cheraw "staggering under a load of

carpets, out of which the officers and escort made excellent tent-rugs, saddle-cloths, and blankets."

10. Anna E. McCants, "That Brought the Tears," South Carolina UDC, 7:96–97.

11. Grimsley, "'Thieves, Murderers, Trespassers'"; Beard, "Series of True Incidents Connected with Sherman's March to the Sea."

12. Warner, Sweetland, Barber, Bird, and Blood diaries; Mindil's report, *OR*, vol. 47, pt. 1, 732; *Official Atlas*, plate LXXX, no. 5, plate LXXXVI, no. 5; Sherman, *Memoirs*, 2:288–89; prefatory comments in Abell to his parents, March 12, 1865; Conyngham, *Sherman's March through the South*, 341–42; Richard H. McMaster, *The Feasterville Incident: Hampton and Sherman* (Washington, D.C.: Published by the author, 1955), 3, 5. Rocky Mount was about four miles south of present-day Great Falls.

13. "Sherman at Rocky Mount," in Malone, *Fairfield Remembers Sherman*, 105–8.

14. "Mrs. J. R. Reid," in Malone, *Fairfield Remembers Sherman*, 101–4.

15. Ibid., 102; "Sherman's Army in the Rocky Mount Section," *Winnsboro News and Herald*, February 8, 1901; Nichols, *Story of the Great March*, 76–77; Conyngham, *Sherman's March through the South*, 314–16; Hirshson, *White Tecumseh*, 259; "A Faithful Dog," *Savannah Republican*, December 31, 1864; Jones, *Siege of Savannah in December, 1864*, 169. Blacks delighted in the killing of tracking dogs. Drago, "How Sherman's March through Georgia Affected the Slaves," 368.

16. WPA South Carolina Narratives, vol. 14, pt. 2, 217.

17. Warner, Sweetland, Bird, and Blood diaries; Warner's report, *OR*, vol. 47, pt. 1, 743; *Official Atlas*, plate LXXX, no. 5, plate LXXXVI, no. 5.

18. Warner, Sweetland, Barber, Bird, Blood, and Ames diaries; Report from Prisoner of War Records, War Department, November 22, 1890, in Thomas D. Spiking Jr. pension file.

19. Warner, Sweetland, Barber, Bird, Blood, and Ames diaries; Geary's report, *OR*, vol. 47, pt. 1, 688; "Sherman's March to Rocky Mount," in Malone, *Fairfield Remembers Sherman*, 109; *Official Atlas*, plate LXXX, no. 5, plate LXXXVI, no. 5.

20. Warner, Sweetland, Barber, Bird, Blood, and Ames diaries; McCadden to his mother and brother, March 29, 1865; Geary's report, *OR*, vol. 47, pt. 1, 688–89; *Official Atlas*, plate LXXX, no. 5, plate LXXXVI, no. 5.

21. Warner, Sweetland, Barber, Bird, Blood, and Ames diaries; *Official Atlas*, plate LXXX, no. 5, plate LXXXVI, no. 5 (which locates Clyburn's Store incorrectly). Today the stream's name is spelled Little Lynches Creek.

22. Warner, Sweetland, Barber, Bird, Blood, and Ames diaries; Warner's report, *OR*, vol. 47, pt. 1, 743; Geary's report, *OR*, vol. 47, pt. 1, 689; Mindil's report, *OR*, vol. 47, pt. 1, 730; *Official Atlas*, plate LXXX, no. 6, plate LXXXVI, no. 5. Lynch's Creek is today called Lynches River.

23. Warner, Sweetland, Barber, and Blood diaries; Geary's report, *OR*, vol. 47, pt. 1, 689; *Official Atlas*, plate LXXX, no. 6, plate LXXXVI, no. 5.

24. Warner, Sweetland, Barber, Bird, Blood, and Ames diaries; Mindil's report, *OR*, vol. 47, pt. 1, 732; Geary's report, *OR*, vol. 47, pt. 1, 689; *Official Atlas*, plate LXXX, no. 6, plate LXXXVI, no. 5; *The Heritage of Chesterfield County, South Carolina, 2004* (Knoxville, Tenn.: Tennessee Valley Publishing, 2004), 5; "The Twentieth Corps Entering Chesterfield, March 2, 1865," *Harper's Weekly*, April 1, 1865.

25. Sweetland diary, March 3, 1865; Conyngham, *Sherman's March through the South*,

342; *Town of Chesterfield, 1670–1970* (n.p., n.d.), unpaginated; *Heritage of Chesterfield County, South Carolina,* 3–4.

26. Warner diary; Larry E. Nelson, "Sherman at Cheraw," *South Carolina Historical Magazine* 100, no. 4 (October 1999): 332, 339–42.

27. Nichols, *Story of the Great March,* 194; "Reminiscences of Mrs. H. W. Scott," 1:548.

28. Warner, Sweetland, Barber, Bird, Blood diaries; Miles Gardner, *Murder and Mayhem in Old Kershaw: And in Nearby Sections of Lancaster, Kershaw and Chesterfield Counties* (Spartanburg, S.C.: Reprint Co., 2004), 49–50; Paskoff, "Measures of War," 48.

29. Blanche Marsh, *Robert Mills: Architect in South Carolina* (Columbia, S.C.: R. L. Bryan, 1970), 3–20, 118–21; Paskoff, "Measures of War," 46.

30. Warner, Sweetland, Barber, Bird, and Blood diaries; Warner's report, *OR,* vol. 47, pt. 1, 743; Mindil's report, *OR,* vol. 47, pt. 1, 732; Geary's report, *OR,* vol. 47, pt. 1, 689; Williams's report, *OR,* vol. 47, pt. 1, 584; William Light Kinney Jr., *Sherman's March—A Review* (Bennettsville, S.C.: Marlboro Publishing Co., n.d.), 199; "Reminiscences of Mrs. H. W. Scott," 1:548; Sherman, *Memoirs,* 2:290; Nichols, *Story of the Great March,* 191, 192, 194, 198.

31. "Courthouse Burned by Sherman," print by Margaret Collins Dotson, author's collection.

32. Ellen Chapman, "Reminiscence of Sherman's Raid," South Carolina UDC, 4:301; *Heritage of Chesterfield County, South Carolina,* 2, 4, 5; Mrs. H. D. Tiller, "Happenings in and around Chesterfield during the War between the States," South Carolina UDC, 10:321–22.

33. "Reminiscences by Members of Stonewall Chapter, U.D.C.," South Carolina UDC, 6:109; "Reminiscences of Mrs. H. W. Scott," 1:548; *Town of Chesterfield,* unpaginated.

34. *Heritage of Chesterfield County, South Carolina,* 4, 175.

35. Warner, Sweetland, Barber, Bird, Blood, and Ames diaries; Mindil's report, *OR,* vol. 47, pt. 1, 732; *Official Atlas,* plate LXXX, no. 6, plate LXXXVI, no. 6; Larry E. Nelson, *Sherman's March through the Upper Pee Dee Region of South Carolina* (Florence, S.C.: Pee Dee Heritage Center, 2001), 24; Mary L. Medley, *History of Anson County, North Carolina, 1750–1976* (Wadesboro, N.C.: Anson County Historical Society, 1976), 123. Today the community is called Old Sneedsboro.

36. Warner diary.

37. Company I muster roll, April 30, 1865; "Claim for Half-Pay Pension of Eunice S. Moyer," May 24, 1865, "Claim for Widow's Pension," March 2, 1866, both in Joseph Moyer pension file, National Archives, Washington, D.C.

38. Warner, Sweetland, Barber, Bird, Blood, and Ames diaries.

39. Warner diary; McCadden to his mother and brother, March 29, 1865; Clements to Amanda Clements, March 27, 1865; Howe, *Home Letters of General Sherman,* 332.

CHAPTER 11

1. Warner, Sweetland, Bird, Blood, and Ames diaries; Warner's report, *OR,* vol. 47, pt. 1, 743–44; Mindil's report, *OR,* vol. 47, pt. 1, 732; Geary's report, *OR,* vol. 47, pt. 1, 690; *Official Atlas,* plate LXXX, no. 6, plate LXXXVI, no. 6; Conyngham, *Sherman's March through the South,* 351; Nelson, "Sherman at Cheraw," 332, 345, 349; Nelson, *Sherman's March through the Upper Pee Dee Region,* 4, 24–25.

2. Sweetland diary; Nelson, "Sherman at Cheraw," 346–47; Inglis, "Reminiscence of Sherman's Raid," 4:305; Henrietta Buchanan, "Sherman's Raid in Cheraw," South Carolina UDC, 4:302; Henrietta Buchanan, "Recollections of Sherman's Halt in Cheraw," South Carolina UDC, 4:398–99.

3. Susan Bowen Lining to her sister, March 16, 1865, South Carolina Historical Society, Charleston, S.C.; Inglis, "Reminiscence of Sherman's Raid," 4:304–5; Nelson, *Sherman's March through the Upper Pee Dee Region,* 34–36.

4. Sherman, *Memoirs,* 2:292; Sweetland diary; Nelson, "Sherman at Cheraw," 347–48, 352; Nelson, *Sherman's March through the Upper Pee Dee Region,* 24.

5. *Heritage of Chesterfield County, South Carolina,* 228; Adeline Godfrey Pringle Merrill, ed., *Life in Cheraw: The Civil War, Harriet Powe Godfrey, and the Town, 1901–1930,* vol. 2 of *All in One Southern Family* (Charleston, S.C.: N.p., 1996), 16A.

6. Barber, Bird, Blood, and Sweetland diaries; McCadden to his mother and brother, March 29, 1865; D. S. Matheson, *History of First Presbyterian Church, Cheraw, S.C.* (n.p., n.d.), 20; Committee of Chapter B of the Woman's Auxiliary, *Old St. David's, Cheraw, South Carolina, 1770–1947* (n.p., n.d.), 17; File #71000761, St. David's Episcopal Church and Cemetery, Chesterfield County, S.C., National Register of Historic Places, National Park Service, Washington, D.C.; St. David's Episcopal Church, Cheraw, Chesterfield County, S.C., SC-112, Historic American Buildings Survey, Prints and Photograph Division, Library of Congress, Washington, D.C.; Sarah C. Spruill, Cheraw Visitors Bureau, to author, February 9, 2006.

7. Lining to her sister, March 16, 1865.

8. "Reminiscences of Mrs. H. W. Scott," 1:547–48.

9. Jones, *When Sherman Came,* 247–50, 337.

10. Laura Inglis, "Cheraw War Incident," South Carolina UDC, 6:111; "Memoirs of Laura Prince Inglis," in Merrill, *Life in Cheraw,* 6–8; Thomasine McCown Haynes, "Memories of Miss Laura Inglis," in Merrill, *Life in Cheraw,* 14–15.

11. Haynes, "Memories of Miss Laura Inglis," 14–15; "Memoirs of Laura Prince Inglis," 7.

12. Jefferson Davis, *The Rise and Fall of the Confederate Government* (Richmond, Va.: Garrett and Massie, 1938), 600–606.

13. Mrs. H. E. Godfrey, "Sherman's Raiders in Cheraw," in Merrill, *Life in Cheraw,* 16–17.

14. D. S. Matheson, "Three Score Years and Ten," autobiography, typescript, Sarah C. Spruill Collection, Cheraw, S.C.; Jarrott, "Mrs. C. E. Jarrott's Reminiscences," 1:503–4, 505; Robert F. Hancock, Senior Curator, Museum of the Confederacy, to author, April 27, 2007.

15. Mrs. J. S. Hartzell, "Incidents of the War around Cheraw, South Carolina," South Carolina UDC, 4:570; Patsy Brock Leviner to author, March 16, 20, 2007.

16. Hartzell, "Incidents of the War around Cheraw, South Carolina," 570–71.

17. Nelson, *Sherman's March through the Upper Pee Dee Region,* 32; Buchanan, "Sherman's Raid in Cheraw," 4:302–3; Buchanan, "Recollections of Sherman's Halt in Cheraw," 4:397–400.

18. John C. Evans to Annie Evans, March 5, 7, 16, 1865, in Merrill, *Life in Cheraw,* 25–28.

19. Bailey, *Chessboard of War,* 173–74; William J. McNeill, "A Survey of Confederate Soldier Morale during Sherman's Campaign through Georgia and the Carolinas,"

Georgia Historical Quarterly 55, no. 1 (Spring 1971): 17–18; Campbell, *When Sherman Marched North from the Sea,* 79–80; Vetter, *Sherman,* 286–87; Conyngham, *Sherman's March through the South,* 307–8; R. E. Lee to Z. B. Vance, February 24, 1865, *OR,* vol. 47, pt. 2, 1270.

20. Josephine Pritchard to Mary Morrison, May 1868, in Merrill, *Life in Cheraw,* 21–22.

21. Warner, Sweetland, Barber, Bird, Blood, and Ames diaries; Graves to Celia Smith, March 29, 1865; Warner's report, *OR,* vol. 47, pt. 1, 744; Mindil's report, *OR,* vol. 47, pt. 1, 732; Geary's report, *OR,* vol. 47, pt. 1, 690; *Official Atlas,* plate LXXX, no. 7, plate LXXXVI, no. 6. The eastern portion of Richmond County traversed by the regiment has since become part of Scotland County.

22. Hirshson, *White Tecumseh,* 286; John D. Palmer to Joseph A. Woodward, March 1, 1866, South Caroliniana Library, University of South Carolina, Columbia, S.C.

23. McMaster, *Feasterville Incident,* 10–12; Graves to Celia Smith, December 16, 1864; WPA South Carolina Narratives, vol. 14, pt. 4, 172.

24. McMaster, *Feasterville Incident,* 10–12. See also R. H. McMaster, "Sherman's Army in Fairfield," in Fitz Hugh McMaster, *History of Fairfield County, South Carolina: From "Before the White Man Came" to 1942* (Columbia, S.C.: State Commercial Printing Co., 1946), 155.

25. Quaife, *From the Cannon's Mouth,* 373–74; Conyngham, *Sherman's March through the South,* 311.

26. Graves to Celia Smith, March 29, 1865.

27. Slocum, General Orders Number 8, *OR,* vol. 47, pt. 2, 719.

28. Pringle, *Chronicles of Chicora Wood,* 237, 240–41.

CHAPTER 12

1. Warner, Barber, Bird, Sweetland, and Blood diaries; Warner's report, *OR,* vol. 47, pt. 1, 744; *Official Atlas,* plate LXXX, no. 7, plate LXXXVI, no. 6; Bryant to Cornelia Bryant, March 28, 1865.

2. Warner, Barber, Bird, Sweetland, and Blood diaries; *Official Atlas,* plate LXXX, no. 7, plate LXXXVI, no. 6; Joyce M. Gibson, *Scotland County Emerging, 1750–1900: The History of a Small Section of North Carolina* (Marceline, Mo.: Walsworth Publishing, 1995), 135. The eastern portion of Richmond County has since been designated as Scotland County.

3. Warner, Barber, Bird, Sweetland, and Blood diaries; Mindil's report, *OR,* vol. 47, pt. 1, 732; Williams to Maj. L. M. Dayton, March 10, 1865, *OR,* vol. 47, pt. 2, 765; *Official Atlas,* plate LXXX, no. 7, plate LXXXVI, no. 6. The eastern half of Cumberland County has since formed Hoke County.

4. Warner, Barber, Bird, Sweetland, and Blood diaries; Geary's report, *OR,* vol. 47, pt. 1, 691; *Official Atlas,* plate LXXX, no. 8, plate LXXXVI, no. 6.

5. "Register of Deaths," Company D Descriptive Book, and Company D muster rolls, February 28, 1864, April 30, 1865, National Archives; Alfred W. Benson deposition, February 19, 1866; memorandum, Adjutant General's Office, Washington, D.C., June 20, 1868; "Claim for Widow's Pension, with Minor Children," August 24, 1868, all in Willard H. Crosby pension file, National Archives, Washington, D. C.

6. Warner, Barber, Bird, Sweetland, and Blood diaries; Sweetland diary, March 13, 1865; Warner's report, *OR*, vol. 47, pt. 1, 744; Geary's report, *OR*, vol. 47, pt. 1, 691; *Official Atlas,* plate LXXX, no. 8, plate LXXXVI, no. 6; Nichols, *Story of the Great March,* 236, 251; Conyngham, *Sherman's March through the South,* 357–58; Sherman, *Memoirs,* 2:294; John A. Oates, *The Story of Fayetteville and the Upper Cape Fear* (Raleigh, N.C.: Contemporary Lithographers, 1981), 279–80; Eliza Tillinghast Stinson, "Taking of the Arsenal," in J. E. B. Stuart Chapter, United Daughters of the Confederacy, *War Days in Fayetteville, North Carolina: Reminiscences of 1861 to 1865* (Fayetteville, N.C.: Judge Printing Co., 1910), 7–8 (hereafter cited as *War Days in Fayetteville*).

7. Sherman, *Memoirs,* 2:295, 299; Abell to his parents, March 12, 1865.

8. Abell to his parents, March 12, 1865; Sweetland to Mary Sweetland, March 12, 1865.

9. Malinda B. Ray diary, 76–80, State and Local History Collection, Cumberland County Public Library, Fayetteville, N.C.

10. Josephine Bryan Worth, "Sherman's Raid," in *War Days in Fayetteville,* 47–56, reprinted in South Carolina UDC, 4:294–300, and in Jones, *When Sherman Came,* 263–70.

11. Jones, *When Sherman Came,* 267, 274, 285; Lucy London Anderson, *North Carolina Women of the Confederacy* (Fayetteville, N.C.: Published by the author, 1926), 40–43; Oates, *Story of Fayetteville and the Upper Cape Fear,* 414–16.

12. Tillinghast memoirs.

13. Jones, *When Sherman Came,* 268, 269, 270, 272, 274, 275, 284; Worth, "Sherman's Raid," 54, 56; Anderson, *North Carolina Women of the Confederacy,* 40–43.

14. Warner, Barber, Bird, Sweetland, and Blood diaries; Sweetland diary, March 14, 1865; *Official Atlas,* plate LXXX, no. 8, plate LXXXVI, no. 7; Nichols, *Story of the Great March,* 251–52; Simpson and Berlin, *Sherman's Civil War,* 825; Jones, *When Sherman Came,* 267–68, 272, 274; Stinson, "Taking of the Arsenal," 8–9; Worth, "Sherman's Raid," 51–52; Oates, *Story of Fayetteville and the Upper Cape Fear,* 280, 283–84, 412.

15. Warner, Barber, Bird, Sweetland, and Blood diaries; Sweetland diary, March 14, 1865; Simpson and Berlin, *Sherman's Civil War,* 825; *Official Atlas,* plate LXXX, no. 8, plate LXXXVI, no. 7.

16. Warner, Barber, Bird, Sweetland, and Blood diaries.

17. Bryant to Cornelia Bryant, March 28, 1865; Langhans to Julius Langhans, June 9, 1865; Geary's report, *OR*, vol. 47, pt. 1, 703; Mindil's report, *OR*, vol. 47, pt. 1, 730; Sherman, *Memoirs,* 2:299–300; Nichols, *Story of the Great March,* 252; Sam Aleckson, *Before the War, and after the Union: An Autobiography* (Boston: Gold Mind Publishing Co., 1929), 36.

18. WPA North Carolina Narratives, vol. 11, pt. 1, 6, 55, 96.

19. Warner diary; Geary, Special Field Orders Number 26, *OR*, vol. 47, pt. 2, 831.

20. Bird diary; Charles A. McIntosh to E. D. Northrup, December 25, 1893, January 21, 1894, Northrup Papers.

21. Warner, Barber, Bird, and Blood diaries; *Official Atlas,* plate LXXX, no. 8, plate LXXXVI, no. 7.

22. Warner, Barber, Bird, and Blood diaries; Geary's report, *OR*, vol. 47, pt. 1, 693; *Official Atlas,* plate LXXX, no. 8, plate LXXXVI, no. 7; Mark L. Bradley, *This Astounding Close: The Road to Bennett Place* (Chapel Hill: Univ. of North Carolina Press, 2000), 16–17; Nathaniel Cheairs Hughes Jr., *Bentonville: The Final Battle of Sherman and Johnston* (Chapel Hill: Univ. of North Carolina Press, 1996), 14–15, 33–34.

23. Warner, Barber, Bird, Sweetland, and Blood diaries; *Official Atlas,* plate LXXX, no. 8, plate LXXXVI, no. 7. South River is sometimes called the Black River.

24. Warner, Barber, Bird, Sweetland, and Blood diaries; Bryant to Cornelia Bryant, March 28, 1865; *Official Atlas,* plate LXXX, no. 9, plate LXXXVI, no. 7.

25. Warner, Barber, Bird, Blood, Sweetland, and Ames diaries; Mindil's report, *OR,* vol. 47, pt. 1, 732; Geary's report, *OR,* vol. 47, pt. 1, 693; *Official Atlas,* plate LXXX, no. 9, plate LXXXVI, no. 7.

26. Warner, Barber, Bird, Blood, Sweetland, and Ames diaries; Mindil's report, *OR,* vol. 47, pt. 1, 729; Warner's report, *OR,* vol. 47, pt. 1, 744 Geary's report, *OR,* vol. 47, pt. 1, 694; Sherman to Geary, March 19, 1865, *OR,* vol. 47, pt. 2, 907; *Official Atlas,* plate LXXX, no. 9, plate LXXXVI, no. 7.

27. Warner, Barber, Bird, Blood, Sweetland, and Ames diaries; Edson Ames to his family, March 30, 1865; Mindil's report, *OR,* vol. 47, pt. 1, 733; *Official Atlas,* plate LXXX, no. 9, plate LXXXVI, no. 7; Bradley, *This Astounding Close,* 24–25; Hughes, *Bentonville,* 229–30.

28. Warner and Bird diaries; Barber diary, March 22, 1865; Sweetland to Mary Sweetland, March 28, 1865; Mason to his sister, March 30, 1865; Ames to his family, March 30, 1865.

29. Warner, Barber, Bird, Blood, Sweetland, and Ames diaries; Warner's report, *OR,* vol. 47, pt. 1, 744; Mindil's report, *OR,* vol. 47, pt. 1, 729, 732–33; *Official Atlas,* plate LXXX, no. 9, plate LXXXVI, no. 7; Bryant to Cornelia Bryant, March 28, 1865.

30. Bird diary; Shannon to Francelia Hunt, March 22, 1865, Shaw Collection; Warner diary; Mindil's report, *OR,* vol. 47, pt. 1, 729.

CHAPTER 13

1. Warner, Barber, Bird, Blood, and Ames diaries; McCadden to his mother and brother, March 29, 1865; Shannon to Francelia Hunt, April 7, 1865, Shaw Collection.

2. Shannon to Francelia Hunt, April 7, 1865, Shaw Collection; Jones, *When Sherman Came,* 291–92, 338.

3. J. M. Hollowell, *War-Time Reminiscences and Other Selections* (Goldsboro, N.C.: Goldsboro Herald, 1939), 42; Bob Johnson and Charles S. Norwood, eds., *History of Wayne County, North Carolina: A Collection of Historical Stories* (Goldsboro, N.C.: Wayne County Historical Association, 1979), 151.

4. Warner, Barber, Bird, Blood, and Ames diaries; Shannon to Francelia Hunt, March 30, 1865, Shaw Collection.

5. Warner, Barber, Bird, Blood, and Ames diaries.

6. Company G muster roll, February 28, 1865, and muster-out roll, June 11, 1865; Company D Descriptive Book and muster roll, February 28, 1865; Commodore P. Vedder affidavit, September 19, 1866, Joel W. Woodruff pension file, National Archives, Washington, D.C.; Jacob M. Vedder interview notes, January 28, 1893, Northrup Papers; Bryant to Cornelia Bryant, March 28, 1865; "Rev. N. F. Langmade," *Capital Herald* (Little Valley, N.Y.), August 10, 1899.

7. Charles A. McIntosh to E. D. Northrup, October 24, 1893; Nelson H. Fisk, Groat, Rowland, and Vedder interview notes, January 27, 1893; Leonard L. Hunt, Joseph Cullen, and Joseph Charlesworth interview notes, February 21, 1893; Charles E. Whitney interview notes, December 27, 1890; Asa S. Wing interview notes, September 7, 1895, all

in Northrup Papers; Mark H. Dunkelman, "Death to All Foragers," *American History* 37, no. 3 (August 2002): 28–35.

8. Bryant to Cornelia Bryant, March 28, 1865; Geary's report, *OR,* vol. 47, pt. 1, 697.

9. Warner, Bird, Blood, and Ames diaries; Bryant to Cornelia Bryant, March 28, 1865; Shannon to Francelia Hunt, March 30, 1865, Shaw Collection; Edson Ames to his family, March 30, 1865.

10. Nelson H. Fisk to E. D. Northrup, October 10, 1893; Andrew G. Park interview notes, March 1, 1893; both in Northrup Papers; Andrew G. Park affidavit, July 28, 1866, Harrison Coe pension file, National Archives, Washington, D.C.; Dunkelman, "Death to All Foragers," 28–35; James M. Creech, *History of Greene County, North Carolina* (Baltimore: Gateway Press, 1979), 337–38, 559, 560. The Williams house was located on present-day Pelletier Road (State Route 1235). It was torn down in the 1990s. A family cemetery under a large magnolia near the site of the house contains the graves of Isaac M. and Elizabeth Williams, quite possibly the house's inhabitants during the Civil War.

11. James Jasper O'Neill service records, Georgia Archives, Morrow, Ga.; "Capt. J. J. O'Neill," *Confederate Veteran* 21, no. 5 (May 1913): 239; J. J. O'Neill, "A Brief History of My Military Career," in Georgia UDC, 9:45–46; "Curtis Green, Leon Junction, Texas," *Confederate Veteran* 2, no. 6 (June 1894): 164; Mamie Yeary, *Reminiscences of the Boys in Gray, 1861–1865* (Dallas, Tex.: Smith and Lamar, 1912), 282–84.

12. Fisk to Northrup, October 10, 1893; Park interview notes, March 1, 1893; O'Neill service records; Andrew G. Park affidavit, July 28, 1866; Dunkelman, "Death to All Foragers," 28–35.

13. Shannon to Francelia Hunt, April 7, 1865, Shaw Collection; "From the 154th Regiment," *Cattaraugus Freeman,* May 4, 1865, quoting letter of William W. Norton, April 14, 1865; Jones to his sister, May 20, 1865; Darling, *Events and Comments of My Life;* "From the 154th Regiment," *Westfield Republican,* May 10, 1865; Job B. Dawley cenotaph, Ruggtown Cemetery, Perrysburg, N.Y.

14. Colonel George W. Mindil to Captain W. T. Forbes, March 29, 1865, Letters Sent, Second Brigade, Second Division, Twentieth Corps; General Orders No. 13, March 28, 1865,General Orders and Circular Orders Issued, Second Division, Twentieth Corps.

15. John B. Walker to A. Porter, June 5, 1865, A. Porter to Q. A. Gillmore, June 17, 1865, John R. Hart to Major Burger, August 2, September 5, 1865, all in John R. Hart Military Records, National Archives, Washington, D.C.; John R. Hart File, Union Provost Marshal's File of Papers Relating to Two or More Civilians, National Archives, Washington, D.C.; Richard J. Cofer to author, November 3, 6, 2007.

CHAPTER 14

1. Warner, Bird, Blood, and Ames diaries, March 27, 1865; McCadden to his mother and brother, March 29, 1865; Shannon to Francelia Hunt, March 30, 1865, Shaw Collection; Abell to his parents, March 28, 1865.

2. Warner diary, March 27, 1865; Sweetland to Mary Sweetland, March 28, 1865; Johnson and Norwood, *History of Wayne County,* 155, 158; Howe, *Home Letters of General Sherman,* 335, 336, 341, 343.

3. Geary's report, *OR,* vol. 47, pt. 1, 695, 698.

4. Ibid., 697–98; Mindil's report, *OR,* vol. 47, pt. 1, 729–30.

5. Abell to his parents, March 28, 1865.

6. Shannon to Francelia Hunt, March 30, 1865, Shaw Collection.

7. Company C muster-out roll, June 11, 1865, and descriptive book; Lewis D. Warner deposition, January 21, 1868, Flora Terett depositions, June 14, 1877, August 31, 1878, Flora Terett affidavit, March 30, 1886, all in Charles Terett pension file, National Archives, Washington, D.C.; Matteson interview notes, October 6, 1893.

8. Geary's report, *OR,* vol. 47, pt. 1, 699; Frederick H. Dyer, *A Compendium of the War of the Rebellion* (1908; reprint, Dayton, Ohio: Morningside Bookshop, 1978), 458; McCadden to his mother and brother, March 29, 1865; Zinn, *Mutinous Regiment,* 214, 222–23; John G. Zinn to author, January 3, 2006.

9. Dyer, *Compendium of the War of the Rebellion,* 257, 458; Geary's report in *OR,* vol. 47, pt. 1, 699; Fox, "Slocum and His Men," 311–12; Sherman, *Memoirs,* 2:333; Quaife, *From the Cannon's Mouth,* 379–80.

10. Warner and Bird diaries; McCadden to his mother and brother, April 5, 1865, Meininger Collection; Abell diary, April 12, 1865; Bryant to Cornelia Bryant, March 28, 1865.

11. Warner diary, April 6, 1865; Shannon to Francelia Hunt, April 7, 1865, Shaw Collection; Davidson interview notes, March 8, 1895; Sweetland to Mary Sweetland, April 10, 1865; Graves to Celia Smith, April 7, 1865.

12. Warner diary, April 10–11, 1865; Abell diary, April 11, 1865.

13. Darling, *Events and Comments of My Life;* "From the 154th Regiment," *Cattaraugus Freeman,* May 4, 1865, quoting letter of William W. Norton, April 14, 1865.

14. Warner diary, April 12–14, 1865; Sweetland to Mary Sweetland, April 15, 1865; Quaife, *From the Cannon's Mouth,* 382; Nichols, *Story of the Great March,* 298. Today the old asylum grounds house the sprawling Dorothea Dix Hospital at 820 South Boylan Avenue.

15. Langhans to Julius Langhans, June 9, 1865; Jones, *When Sherman Came,* 300, 338; Abell diary, April 13, 1865; Sweetland to Mary Sweetland, April 15, 1865.

16. Warner diary, April 15–17, 1865; Abell diary, April 18, 1865.

17. Warner diary, April 22–28, 1865; Howe, *Home Letters of General Sherman,* 339; McKay, "'Three Years or during the War,' with the Crescent and Star," 156.

18. Warner diary, April 30–May 9, 1865; Langhans to Julius Langhans, April 29, 1865; McKay, "'Three Years or during the War,' with the Crescent and Star," 156; Glatthaar, *March to the Sea and Beyond,* 179; "Interview with Dad."

19. Abell diary, May 7, 1865; Sweetland to Mary Sweetland, May 9, 1865.

20. Warner diary, May 11–23, 1865; Darling, *Events and Comment of My Life;* Jones to his sister, May 20, 1865; Abell to his family, May 18, 1865; Langhans to Julius Langhans, May 28, 1865.

21. Warner diary, May 24, 1865; McKay, "'Three Years or during the War,' with the Crescent and Star," 157; Langhans to Julius Langhans, May 28, 1865; McCadden to his mother and brother, May 29, 1865, Meininger Collection; Pettit diary, May 23, 1865; Lewis, *Sherman,* 576; unnumbered Circular Order, May 23, 1865, General Orders and Circular Orders Issued, Second Division, Twentieth Corps.

22. Warner diary, May 25–June 11, 1865; McCadden to his family, May 30, 1865, author's collection; Pettit diary, May 26 and 30, 1865.

23. Langhans to Julius Langhans, June 9, 1865.

CHAPTER 15

1. B. C. Hall and C. T. Wood, *The South* (New York: Scribner, 1995), 154; V. S. Naipaul, *A Turn in the South* (New York: Alfred A. Knopf, 1989), 98–99; Caudill and Ashdown, *Sherman's March in Myth and Memory*, 184.

2. Gay, *Life in Dixie during the War*, 168; Cureton, "How Mrs. Ladd Saved the Masonic Jewels," 69–70.

3. Harrington, *Civil War Milledgeville*, 47; Adams, "Tales of a Grand-mother or Recollections of the Confederate War Number 2."

4. "Sherman's Army in Milledgeville"; McKinley memoirs; Groves, *Jennings-McMillan-Faulling-Whaley-Bluer and Other Early Families of South Carolina*, 108.

5. Quillin to her cousin Sallie, November 15, 1865.

6. "A Mother's Call upon her Son," *Countryman*, December 6, 1864, 673; "Soon Love Us Again," *Countryman*, December 13, 1863, 696; "The Yankees in Eatonton," *Countryman*, January 10, 1865, 16.

7. WPA South Carolina Narratives, vol. 14, pt. 1, 17, pt. 2, 216–17.

8. Palmer to Woodward, March 1, 1866.

9. John T. Trowbridge, *The Desolate South, 1865–1866: A Picture of the Battlefields and of the Devastated Confederacy*, ed. Gordon Carroll (New York: Duell, Sloan and Pearce, 1956), v, vi, 237, 238, 253, 255–56, 257, 260.

10. Ibid., 265–66, 271, 295–98, 303, 306, 312, 313.

11. John H. Kennaway, *On Sherman's Track: Or, the South after the War* (London: Seeley, Jackson, and Halliday, 1867), 7, 42–43, 115–16, 117, 118, 119, 129, 131, 196.

12. John Muir, *A Thousand-Mile Walk to the Gulf*, ed. William Frederic Bade (Boston: Houghton Mifflin, 1916), ix, xix, 60–61.

13. John F. Marszalek, "Celebrity in Dixie: Sherman Tours the South, 1879," *Georgia Historical Quarterly* 66, no. 3 (Fall 1982): 368–83; Kennaway, *On Sherman's Track*, 119; Carol Reardon, "William T. Sherman in Postwar Georgia's Collective Memory, 1864–1914," in *Wars within a War*, ed. Joan Waugh and Gary W. Gallagher (Chapel Hill: Univ. of North Carolina Press, 2009), 230–31.

14. Henken, "Taming the Enemy," 290.

15. Royster, *Destructive War*, 366–71; Caudill and Ashdown, *Sherman's March in Myth and Memory*, 144; Anna Key Bartow, "St. Gaudens' Statue of General Sherman, The Plaza—New York City," South Carolina UDC, 8: 269–70.

16. Adams, "Tales of a Grand-mother or Recollections of the Confederate War Number 2"; "Sherman's Raid Recalled," newspaper clipping datelined Winnsboro, S.C., June 22, 1916, Fairfield Archives and History, Winnsboro, S.C.; Ralph A. Graves, "Marching through Georgia Sixty Years After," *National Geographic* 50, no. 3 (September 1926): 259–311; Thomas E. Watson, *Prose Miscellanies* (Thomson, Ga.: Tom Watson Book Co., 1927), 114.

17. William J. Robertson, *The Changing South* (New York: Boni and Liveright, 1927), 32; Virginius Dabney, *Below the Potomac: A Book about the New South* (New York: D. Appleton-Century Co., 1942), 6.

18. Thomas D. Clark, *The Emerging South* (New York: Oxford Univ. Press, 1961), 142, 143; Hall and Wood, *The South*, 135.

19. Bartow Community Club, *Sherman Didn't Burn Our Recipes: Bartow's Still Cooking* (Bartow, Ga.: Bartow Community Club, 2004), iii, v, illustration between pp. 20 and 21; report of Col. James S. Robinson, commanding Third Brigade, First Division, Twentieth Corps, *OR*, vol. 44, 255.

20. Christopher Dickey, "Southern Discomfort," *Newsweek*, August 11, 2008, 22–32.

21. Henry Davenport Northrop, *Life and Deeds of General Sherman* (Boston: B. B. Russell, 1891), iv–v, vii, 417; Howe, *Home Letters of General Sherman*, 323, 325, 356; Thorndike, *Sherman Letters*, 261, 290, 336, 358.

22. Lewis, *Sherman*, 636; Howe, *Home Letters of General Sherman*, 334, 340; Thorndike, *Sherman Letters*, 260; Sherman, *Memoirs*, 2:221, 306; Hart, *Sherman*, 378.

23. Kennett, *Marching through Georgia*, 320; "Reunion of the 154th," *Ellicottville (N.Y.) News*, August 6, 1891; "Fighting Battles Over," *Cattaraugus Republican*, July 1, 1892; "A Reunion of Veterans," *Cattaraugus Republican*, October 6, 1893; Richard Marius, ed., *The Columbia Book of Civil War Poetry* (New York: Columbia Univ. Press, 1994), 106, 108; Marszalek, *Sherman*, 488; Lewis, *Sherman*, 619–20, 632–33; Reardon, "William T. Sherman in Postwar Georgia's Collective Memory," 238–39; Caudill and Ashdown, *Sherman's March in Myth and Memory*, 140–41.

24. Mark E. Neely Jr. and Harold Holzer, *The Union Image: Popular Prints of the Civil War North* (Chapel Hill: Univ. of North Carolina Press, 2000), 227, 228; Hennig Cohen, ed., *The Battle-Pieces of Herman Melville* (New York: Thomas Yoseloff, 1963), 120–23, 258.

25. Benson reminiscence, 2, 25; Darling, *Events and Comments of My Life*.

26. McKay, "'Three Years or during the War,' with the Crescent and Star," 154.

27. Alex Bird, "March to the Sea With the 154th N.Y. Vols.," *Ellicottville (N.Y.) Post*, November 25, December 2, 9, 16, 1914.

28. Langhans to Julius Langhans, May 28, 1865.

29. Shannon to Francelia Hunt, March 22, 1865, Shaw Collection.

30. Langhans to Julius Langhans, June 9, 1865; Simpson and Berlin, *Sherman's Civil War*, 785, quoting letter of December 31, 1864.

31. Sweetland to Mary Sweetland, April 10, 1865; Abell to his family, April 29, 1865; "Act of Heroism," *Ellicottville Post*, July 4, 1906 (quoting Charles McKay); McKay, "'Three Years or during the War,' with the Crescent and Star," 143; "Interview with Dad"; *Presidents, Soldiers, Statesmen*, 1605; McIntyre's great-granddaughter Barbara King to author, September 6, 2005.

32. Sweetland to Mary Sweetland, January 25, 1865.

33. Lewis, *Sherman*, 457; Stout, *Upon the Altar of the Nation*, 398–99; "Hon. C. D. Davie's Address at the Reunion of the 154th and Co. I and H of the 37th N.Y. Vols. at West Salamanca Aug. 29th, 1890," *Ellicottville News*, September 25, 1890; transcript of tape-recorded reminiscences of Nellie Eva Welch Gatlin, Krista Shackleford Collection, Bladenboro, N.C.

34. Glatthaar, *March to the Sea and Beyond*, 186; *Presidents, Soldiers, Statesmen*, 1501, 1346, 1429, 1503, 1592.

35. "Truman H. Hinman," *Jamestown (N.Y.) Post Journal*, February 12, 1934; Truman H. Hinman headstone, East Randolph Cemetery, East Randolph, N.Y., photograph courtesy of Marlynn Olson Ray, Penn Run, Pa.; *Ellicottville Post*, September 25, 1929, 1.

36. Cohen, *Battle-Pieces of Herman Melville*, 120.

CHAPTER 16

1. Except where noted, this account is drawn from the journals of my trip.

2. Reardon, "William T. Sherman in Postwar Georgia's Collective Memory," 232.

3. Goldfield, *Still Fighting the Civil War,* 32; file #87000094, Westover, National Register of Historic Places; Westover, Baldwin County, Ga., GA-14-31, Historic American Buildings Survey. Westover's original big house was destroyed by fire in 1954 and has since been replaced by a reproduction erected on the historic foundation.

4. Caudill and Ashdown, *Sherman's March in Myth and Memory,* 179–80.

5. Henken, "Taming the Enemy," 295; Madison Welcome Center, "The Town Sherman Refused to Burn," brochure. See also Brian C. Melton, "'The Town That Sherman Wouldn't Burn': Sherman's March and Madison, Georgia, in History, Memory, and Legend," *Georgia Historical Quarterly* 86, no. 2 (Summer 2002): 201–30; Hume and Roessner, "Surviving Sherman's March," 119, 125–29. On heritage tourism, see McPherson, *Reconstructing Dixie,* 40–44, 96–101.

6. Henken, "Taming the Enemy," 293.

7. Hugh Harrington, "Yankee Historian to Visit and Discuss Gen. Sherman," *Baldwin Bulletin* (Milledgeville, Ga.), January 18, 2007: 5.

8. Goldfield, *Still Fighting the Civil War,* 298–305; McPherson, *Reconstructing Dixie,* 106–14; Reardon, "William T. Sherman in Postwar Georgia's Collective Memory," 242.

Bibliography

Manuscript Sources
Private Collections

Abell, Charles W., Letters and diary. Jean Schultz Collection, Westford, Vt.

Ames, Edson D., Letters. Carolyn Ames Simons Collection, Phoenix, Ariz.

Ames, Homer A., Letters and diary. Carolyn Ames Simons Collection, Phoenix, Ariz.

Barber, Mervin P., Diary. Paul A. Lockwood Collection, Newark, Ohio.

Bird, Alexander. Diary. Janet Bird Whitehurst Collection, Los Banos, Calif.

Blood, Andrew D., Diary and letter, January 1, 1865. Alan D. Henry Collection, Temperance, Mich.

Bowen, Francis M., Diary and letter. Ronald Bowen Collection, Brighton, Mich.

Bryant, E. "Over the Ogeechee." Undated typescript. Hubert and Patsy Jordan Collection, Bartow, Ga.

Bryant, Levi D., Letters. Cornelia Kopp Collection, Reading Center, N.Y.

Charles, William. Letters. Jack Finch Collection, Freedom, N.Y.

Clements, James W., Letters. Judith Wachholz Collection, River Falls, Wis.

Dawley, Job B., Carte-de-visite. Author's collection.

Field, Vernon E. "Memories of the Civil War." Typescript, 1984. Author's collection.

Gatlin, Nellie Eva Welch. Transcript of tape-recorded reminiscences. Krista Shackleford Collection, Bladenboro, N.C.

Graves, George Eugene. Letters. Author's collection.

Harper, William D., Diary. Raymond Harper Collection, Dunkirk, N.Y.

"Interview with Dad." Undated typed transcription of author's interview with Harold J. Dunkelman. Author's collection.

Jones, David S., Letters. Clara Jones Collection, Salamanca, N.Y.

Kilpatrick, Washington L., Letter, December 31, 1864. Lyle Lansdell Collection, Carrboro, N.C.

Langhans, John. Letters. Floris Sarver Collection, Getzville, N.Y.

Mason, George J., Letters. Juliet Mason Collection, Russell, Pa.

Matheson, D. S. "Three Score Years and Ten." Autobiography, typescript. Sarah C. Spruill Collection, Cheraw, S.C.

McCadden, Richard J., Letters. Author's collection.

McCadden, Richard J., Letters. Ron Meininger Collection, Gaithersburg, Md.

Mobley, Fannie Burton. Memoirs. Ed Burton Collection, Stilwell, Kans.

Norton, William W., Letters. Author's collection.

Ogden, Reuben R., Diary. Bradley J. Eide Collection, Chesterfield, Va.

Pettit, Joshua R., Diary. Mary C. Ranney Collection, Ellicottville, N.Y.

Reed, Almon Deforest. Letter, January 25, 1865. Donald K. Ryberg Jr. Collection, Westfield, N.Y.

Scott, Milton D., Letter, October 14, 1864. Richard DeBell Collection, Falconer, N.Y.

Scutt, Addison L., Letter, October 2, 1864. Jerry L. Scutt Collection, Portville, N.Y.

Shannon, Edgar. Letter, September 7, 1864. Author's collection.

Shannon, Edgar. Letters. Timothy T. Shaw Collection, Cheektowaga, N.Y.

Sweetland, Emory. Letters and diary. Lyle Sweetland Collection, South Dayton, N.Y.

Van Aernam, Henry. Letter, November 22, 1864. Author's collection.

Warner, Lewis D., Diary. Charles H. Warner III Collection, Santa Rosa, Calif.

Repositories

Atlanta History Center, Atlanta, Ga.
Kenan Research Center
    Carrie Berry diary
    Boutelle-Kean genealogy file
    Edda A. Cole scrapbook
    Davis-Quillin Family Collection
    Sally Sharp Garrison reminiscences
    James Ormond letter, January 24, 1876
    Ormond Family genealogy file
    Rawson-Collier-Harris Family Collection
    Samuel P. Richards diary
    Walraven Family Papers
    Winship-Flourney Family Papers

Cornell University, Ithaca, N.Y.
Edwin Dwight Northrup Papers, #4190, Department of Manuscripts and University Archives

Cumberland County Public Library, Fayetteville, N.C.
State and Local History Collection
    Malinda B. Ray diary
    Sarah Ann Tillinghast memoirs

DeKalb History Center, Decatur, Ga.

J. Calvin Weaver, M.D. "One Hundred Years of Medicine in DeKalb County, 1822–1922." Typescript.

Duke University, Durham, N.C.
Rare Book, Manuscript, and Special Collections Library
    Iverson Louis Harris Papers

Emory University, Atlanta, Ga.
Manuscript, Archives, and Rare Book Library
    Confederate Miscellany
        Mrs. G. W. Anderson letter, January 1, 1865

Fairfield Archives and History, Thomas Woodward Chapter DAR, Winnsboro, S.C.
Newspaper articles
Lauderdale Family File

Georgia Archives, Morrow, Ga.
Bible Records, Military Rosters and Reminiscences of Confederate Soldiers Copied and Compiled from the files of The Georgia Division, United Daughters of the Confederacy, 1942
William B. Jones, M.D., Collection
Charles Augustus Lafayette Lamar Family Papers
Mrs. S. E. McCroan reminiscences
James Jasper O'Neill service records

Georgia College and State University, Milledgeville, Ga.
Guy C. McKinley memoirs

Georgia Department of Natural Resources, Atlanta, Ga.
Historic Preservation Division
    Park's Mill House File

Georgia Historical Society, Savannah, Ga.
Lillian Chaplin Bragg Papers
Gordon Family Papers
Walter C. Hartridge Collection
Michael Johnson Kenan Papers
Alexander A. Lawrence Collection
    Aaron Wilbur Papers

Gowanda Area Historical Society, Gowanda, N.Y.

Newton A. Chaffee letter, September 13, 1864

Kansas State Historical Society, Topeka, Kans.
Alfred W. Benson diary and untitled reminiscence of the March to the Sea

Library of Congress, Washington, D.C.
Manuscript Division
    United States Work Projects Administration
        Federal Writers' Project
            WPA Slave Narrative Project
                Georgia Narratives
                North Carolina Narratives
                South Carolina Narratives
Prints and Photograph Division
    Historic American Buildings Survey
        Slave Market, Louisville, Jefferson County, Ga., GA-14–2
        St. David's Episcopal Church, Cheraw, S.C., SC-112
        Westover, Baldwin County, Ga., GA-14–31

Mazomanie Historical Society, Mazomanie, Wis.
Horace Smith diary

National Archives, Washington, D.C.
Alfred W. Benson letter, Jesse D. Campbell pension file
Jesse D. Campbell letters, Jesse D. Campbell pension file
Harrison Coe pension file
Willard H. Crosby pension file
Descriptive books, 154th New York
General Orders and Circular Orders Issued, Second Brigade, Second Division,
    Twentieth Corps
General Orders and Circular Orders Issued, Second Division, Twentieth Corps
John R. Hart military records
Letters Sent, Second Brigade, Second Division, Twentieth Corps
Letters Sent, Second Division, Twentieth Corps
Joseph Moyer pension file
Muster rolls, muster-in rolls, and muster-out rolls, 154th New York
Regimental Orders, 154th New York
John I. Snyder pension file
Southern Claims Commission Records
    Barred and Disallowed Case Files, 1871–1880
    Settled Claims, 1877–1883
Special Orders Issued, Second Brigade, Second Division, Twentieth Corps

Thomas D. Spiking Jr. pension file
Charles Terett pension file
Union Provost Marshal's File of Papers Relating to Two or More Civilians
Joel W. Woodruff pension file

National Park Service, Washington, D.C.
National Register of Historic Places Files

South Carolina Historical Society, Charleston, S.C.
Margaret Crawford Johnston Adams Papers
Susan Bowen Lining letter, March 16, 1865
Mary Cheves West statement (undated)

University of Iowa Library, Iowa City, Iowa
Marcellus W. Darling letters

University of North Carolina, Chapel Hill, N.C.
Southern Historical Collection
Grace Pierson James Beard. "A Series of True Incidents Connected with Sherman's March to the Sea." Manuscript #2799.

University of South Carolina, Columbia, S.C.
South Caroliniana Library
    John D. Palmer letter, March 1, 1866

U.S. Army Military History Institute, Carlisle Barracks, Pa.
Edward Campbell McDowell, ed. *Diary of Sgt. Fergus Elliott, Co. G, 109th Pa. Vol. Inf., 1865.* N.p., n.d. In Civil War Times Illustrated Collection.
Henry Van Aernam letters

Yale University Library, New Haven, Conn.
Manuscripts and Archives
    Civil War Manuscripts Collection (MS 619)
        Job B. Dawley letter

Published Sources
Newspapers

Atlanta Journal and Constitution
Baldwin Bulletin, Milledgeville, Ga.
Capital Herald, Little Valley, N.Y.
Cattaraugus Freeman, Ellicottville, N.Y.

Cattaraugus Republican, Salamanca, N.Y.
Cattaraugus Union, Ellicottville, N.Y.
Confederate Union, Milledgeville, Ga.
Countryman, Turnwold Plantation, Putnam County, Ga.
Eatonton (Ga.) Messenger
Ellicottville (N.Y.) News
Ellicottville (N.Y.) Post
Fayetteville (N.C.) Observer
Frank Leslie's Illustrated Newspaper
Fredonia (N.Y.) Censor
Harper's Weekly
Jamestown (N.Y.) Post Journal
Lake Oconee (Ga.) Free Press
Olean (N.Y.) Times
Savannah Evening Press
Savannah Morning News
Savannah Republican
Sioux City (Iowa) Journal
Southern Recorder, Milledgeville, Ga.
Sunny South, Atlanta, Ga.
Union Recorder, Milledgeville, Ga.
Westfield (N.Y.) Republican
Winnsboro (S.C.) News and Herald

Public Documents

Congressional Globe, Washington, D.C.

Brochures

Fairfield Chamber of Commerce. "Historic Winnsboro Tour."
Lexington County (S.C.) Museum, "The Leaphart/Harman House."
Madison Welcome Center. "The Town Sherman Refused to Burn."
South Carolina National Heritage Corridor. "Blackville Heritage Trail."

Books, Essays, and Articles

Adams, William, ed. *Historical Gazetteer and Biographical Memorial of Cat-taraugus County, N.Y.* Syracuse: Lyman, Horton and Co., 1893.
Aleckson, Sam. *Before the War, and after the Union: An Autobiography.* Boston: Gold Mind Publishing Co., 1929.
Anderson, Lucy London. *North Carolina Women of the Confederacy.* Fayette-ville, N.C.: Published by the author, 1926.

Andrews, J. Cutler. *The North Reports the Civil War.* Pittsburgh: Univ. of Pittsburgh Press, 1955.

Arnold, Richard D. *Letters of Richard D. Arnold, M.D.* Edited by Richard H. Shryock. Durham, N.C.: Seeman Press, 1929.

Atlas to Accompany the Official Records of the Union and Confederate Armies. Washington: Government Printing Office, 1891–95.

Bailey, Anne J. *The Chessboard of War: Sherman and Hood in the Autumn Campaigns of 1864.* Lincoln: Univ. of Nebraska Press, 2000.

———. *War and Ruin: William T. Sherman and the Savannah Campaign.* Wilmington, Del.: Scholarly Resources, 2003.

Baldwin, Nell H., and A. M. Hillhouse. *An Intelligent Student's Guide to Burke County (Ga.) History.* Waynesboro, Ga.: Published by the authors, 1956.

Barber, E. Susan, and Charles F. Ritter. "Physical Abuse . . . and Rough Handling": Race, Gender, and Sexual Justice in the Occupied South." In *Occupied Women: Gender, Military Occupation, and the American Civil War,* edited by LeeAnn Whites and Alecia P. Long, 49–64. Baton Rouge: Louisiana State Univ. Press, 2009.

Barker, Meta, ed. "Atlanta as Sherman Left It: Atlanta Then and Now." *Atlanta Historical Bulletin* 3 (May 1930): 15–20.

Barrett, John G. *Sherman's March through the Carolinas.* Chapel Hill: Univ. of North Carolina Press, 1956.

Bartow Community Club. *Sherman Didn't Burn Our Recipes: Bartow's Still Cooking.* Bartow, Ga.: Bartow Community Club, 2004.

Bass, Cynthia. *Sherman's March.* New York: Villard Books, 1994.

Blair, William Alan, ed. *A Politician Goes to War: The Civil War Letters of John White Geary.* University Park: Pennsylvania State Univ. Press, 1995.

Bolick, Julian Stevenson. *A Fairfield Sketchbook.* Clinton, S.C.: Jacobs Brothers, 1963.

Bonds, Russell S. "Sherman's First March through Georgia." *Civil War Times* 46, no. 6 (August 2007): 30–37.

———. *War Like the Thunderbolt: The Battle and Burning of Atlanta.* Yardley, Pa.: Westholme, 2009.

Bonner, James C. "Sherman at Milledgeville in 1864." *Journal of Southern History* 22, no. 3 (August 1956): 273–91.

Boylston, Raymond P. *Healing Springs: A History of the Springs and Surrounding Area.* Orangeburg, S.C.: Sandlapper Publishing, 2004.

Brabham, A. McKay, Jr., comp. *Mizpah: A Family Book, Including "A Family Sketch and Else or Buford's Bridge and Its People," by Rev. M. M. Brabham.* Columbia, S.C.: R. L. Bryan, 1978.

Bradley, Mark L. *This Astonishing Close: The Road to Bennett Place.* Chapel Hill: Univ. of North Carolina Press, 2000.

Brady, James P. *Hurrah for the Artillery! Knap's Independent Battery "E," Pennsylvania Light Artillery.* Gettysburg, Pa.: Thomas Publications, 1992.

Brodie, Al, Jr. *A History of the Brodie Family, 1754–1993.* Columbia, S.C.: R. L. Bryan, n.d.

Brundage, W. Fitzhugh. *The Southern Past: A Clash of Race and Memory.* Cambridge: Harvard Univ. Press, Belknap Press, 2005.

Brunvand, Jan Harold. *Encyclopedia of Urban Legends.* New York: W. W. Norton, 2001.

Byrne, William A. "'Uncle Billy' Sherman Comes to Town: The Free Winter of Black Savannah." *Georgia Historical Quarterly* 79, no. 1 (Spring 1995): 91–116.

Campbell, Jacqueline Glass. *When Sherman Marched North from the Sea: Resistance on the Confederate Home Front.* Chapel Hill: Univ. of North Carolina Press, 2003.

"Capt. J. J. O'Neill." *Confederate Veteran* 21, no. 5 (May 1913): 239.

Carr, Caleb. *The Lessons of Terror: A History of Warfare against Civilians: Why It Has Always Failed and Why It Will Fail Again.* New York: Random House, 2002.

Carswell, Porter. "The Romance of Birdsville." *Savannah Morning News Magazine,* June 28, 1964, 6–7.

Castel, Albert. *Decision in the West: The Atlanta Campaign of 1864.* Lawrence: Univ. Press of Kansas, 1992.

Caudill, Edward, and Paul Ashdown. *Sherman's March in Myth and Memory.* Lanham, Md.: Rowman and Littlefield, 2008.

Chesebrough, David B. "'There Goes Your Damned Gospel Shop!' The Churches and Clergy as Victims of Sherman's March through South Carolina." *South Carolina Historical Magazine* 92, no. 1 (January 1991): 15–33.

Clark, Thomas D. *The Emerging South.* New York: Oxford Univ. Press, 1961.

Coffin, Charles Carleton. *The Boys of '61: Or, Four Years of Fighting.* Boston: Estes and Lauriat, 1884.

Cohen, Hennig, ed. *The Battle-Pieces of Herman Melville.* New York: Thomas Yoseloff, 1963.

Collins, George K. *Memoirs of the 149th Regiment New York Volunteer Infantry.* 1891. Reprint, Hamilton, N.Y.: Edmonston Publishing, 1995.

Committee of Chapter B of the Woman's Auxiliary. *Old St. David's, Cheraw, South Carolina, 1770–1947.* N.p., n.d.

Conklin, George W. *Under the Crescent and Star: The 134th New York Volunteer Infantry in the Civil War.* Port Reading, N.J.: Axworthy Publishing, 1999.

Conyngham, David P. *Sherman's March through the South.* New York: Sheldon and Co., 1865.

Cousins, Paul M. *Joel Chandler Harris: A Biography.* Baton Rouge: Louisiana State Univ. Press, 1968.

Cox, Karen L. *Dixie's Daughters: The United Daughters of the Confederacy and the Preservation of Confederate Culture.* Gainesville: Univ. Press of Florida, 2003.

Creech, James M. *History of Greene County, North Carolina.* Baltimore: Gateway Press, 1979.

Cullen, Jim. *The Civil War in Popular Culture: A Reusable Past.* Washington: Smithsonian Institution Press, 1995.

"Curtis Green, Leon Junction, Texas." *Confederate Veteran* 2, no. 6 (June 1894): 164.

Dabney, Virginius. *Below the Potomac: A Book about the New South.* New York: D. Appleton-Century Co., 1942.

D'Arcy, David, and Ben Mammina. *Civil War Walking Tour of Savannah.* Atglen, Pa.: Schiffer, 2006.

Darling, Marcellus Warner. *Events and Comments of My Life.* N.p., n.d.

Davis, Burke. *Sherman's March.* New York: Random House, 1980.

Davis, Jefferson. *The Rise and Fall of the Confederate Government.* Richmond, Va.: Garrett and Massie, 1938.

Davis, Stephen. "'A Very Barbarous Mode of Carrying on War': Sherman's Artillery Bombardment of Atlanta, July 20–August 24, 1864." *Georgia Historical Quarterly* 79, no. 1 (Spring 1995): 57–90.

Dickey, Christopher. "Southern Discomfort." *Newsweek* 152, no. 6 (August 11, 2008): 22–32.

Doctorow, E. L. *The March.* New York: Random House, 2005.

Drago, Edmund L. "How Sherman's March through Georgia Affected the Slaves." *Georgia Historical Quarterly* 57, no. 3 (Fall 1973): 361–75.

Dunkelman, Mark H. "Brigadier General Patrick Henry Jones." *Lincoln Herald* 89, no. 2 (Summer 1987): 71–76.

———. *Brothers One and All: Esprit de Corps in a Civil War Regiment.* Baton Rouge: Louisiana State Univ. Press, 2004.

———. *Colonel Lewis D. Warner: An Appreciation.* Portville, N.Y.: Portville Historical and Preservation Society, 1990.

———. "Death to All Foragers." *American History* 37, no. 3 (August 2002): 28–35.

———. "Hurray for Ole Abe! Fenton! and Dr. Van Aernam! The 1864 Election, As Perceived by the 154th New York Volunteers." *Lincoln Herald* 98, no. 1 (Spring 1996): 12–22.

———. "Through White Eyes: The 154th New York Volunteers and African-Americans in the Civil War." *Journal of Negro History* 83, no. 3 (Summer 2000): 96–111.

Dunkelman, Mark H., and Michael J. Winey. *The Hardtack Regiment: An Illustrated History of the 154th Regiment, New York State Infantry Volunteers.* East Brunswick, N.J.: Fairleigh Dickinson Univ. Press, 1981.

Durden, Marion Little. *A History of Saint George Parish, Colony of Georgia, Jefferson County, State of Georgia.* Swainsboro, Ga.: Magnolia Press, 1983.

Dyer, Frederick H. *A Compendium of the War of the Rebellion.* 1908. Reprint, Dayton, Ohio: Morningside, 1978.

Dyer, John P. "Northern Relief for Savannah during Sherman's Occupation." *Journal of Southern History* 19, no. 4 (November 1953): 457–72.

Dyer, Thomas G. *Secret Yankees: The Union Circle in Confederate Atlanta.* Baltimore: Johns Hopkins Univ. Press, 1999.

Ellis, Franklin, ed. *History of Cattaraugus County, New York.* Philadelphia: L. H. Everts, 1879.

Ellis, Jerry. *Marching through Georgia: My Walk with Sherman.* New York: Delacorte Press, 1995.

Fellman, Michael. *Citizen Sherman: A Life of William Tecumseh Sherman.* New York: Random House, 1995.

"Finding Cump." home.gwi.net/~timuse/findingcump.htm.

Flippin, Percy S., ed., "From the Autobiography of Herschel V. Johnson, 1856–1867." *American Historical Review* 30 (January 1925): 311–36.

———. *Herschel V. Johnson of Georgia: States Rights Unionist.* Richmond, Va.: Press of the Dietz Printing Co., 1931.

Flood, Charles Bracelen. *Grant and Sherman: The Friendship That Won the Civil War.* New York: Farrar, Straus and Giroux, 2005.

Foster, Gaines M. *Ghosts of the Confederacy: Defeat, the Lost Cause, and the Emergence of the New South.* New York: Oxford Univ. Press, 1987.

Frank, Lisa Tendrich. "Bedrooms as Battlefields: The Role of Gender Politics in Sherman's March." In *Occupied Women: Gender, Military Occupation, and the American Civil War,* edited by LeeAnn Whites and Alecia P. Long, 34–35. Baton Rouge: Louisiana State Univ. Press, 2009.

Fraser, Walter J., Jr. *Savannah in the Old South.* Athens: Univ. of Georgia Press, 2003.

Freeman, H. Ronald. *Sherman Takes Savannah.* Savannah: Freeport Publishing, 2007.

Gamble, Thomas, Jr. *A History of the City Government of Savannah, Ga., from 1790 to 1901.* Savannah: Under Direction of the City Council, 1900.

Gardner, Miles. *Murder and Mayhem in Old Kershaw: And in Nearby Sections of Lancaster, Kershaw and Chesterfield Counties.* Spartanburg, S.C.: Reprint Co., 2004.

Gardner, Sarah E. *Blood and Irony: Southern White Women's Narratives of the Civil War, 1861–1937.* Chapel Hill: Univ. of North Carolina Press, 2004.

Garrett, Franklin M. *Atlanta and Environs: A Chronicle of Its People and Events.* Athens: Univ. of Georgia Press, 1969.

Gay, Mary A. H. *Life in Dixie during the War.* 1897. Reprint, Atlanta: DeKalb Historical Society, 1979.

Georgia Department of Natural Resources. *Georgia Civil War Historical Markers.* Atlanta: Georgia Department of Natural Resources—State Parks, Recreation and Historic Sites Division, 1982.

Georgia Division United Daughters of the Confederacy. *Confederate Remi-*

niscences and Letters, 1861–1865. 22 vols. Atlanta: Georgia Division United Daughters of the Confederacy, 1995–2006.

Gibson, John M. *Those 163 Days: A Southern Account of Sherman's March from Atlanta to Raleigh.* New York: Coward-McCann, 1961.

Gibson, Joyce M. *Scotland County Emerging, 1750–1900: The History of a Small Section of North Carolina.* Marceline, Mo.: Walsworth Publishing, 1995.

Glatthaar, Joseph T. *The March to the Sea and Beyond: Sherman's Troops in the Savannah and Carolinas Campaign.* New York: New York Univ. Press, 1985.

Goldfield, David. *Still Fighting the Civil War: The American South and Southern History.* Baton Rouge: Louisiana State Univ. Press, 2002.

Grant, Ulysses S. *Personal Memoirs of U. S. Grant.* 2 vols. New York: Charles L. Webster and Co., 1885.

Graves, Ralph A. "Marching through Georgia Sixty Years After." *National Geographic* 50, no. 3 (September 1926): 259–311.

Grimsley, Mark. *The Hard Hand of War: Union Military Policy toward Southern Civilians, 1861–1865.* Cambridge: Cambridge University Press, 1995.

———. "The Long Shadow of Sherman's March." people.cohums.ohio-state. edu/grimsley1/dialogue/long_shadow.htm.

———. "'Thieves, Murderers, Trespassers': The Mythology of Sherman's March." people.cohums.ohio-state.edu/grimsley1/myth/myth.htm.

Groves, Carnice Jennings. *Jennings-McMillan-Faulling-Whaley-Bluer and Other Early Families of South Carolina.* Daytona Beach, Fla: Daytona Beach Community College, 1971.

Hagood, Johnson. *Meet Your Grandfather: A Sketch-Book of the Hagood-Tobin Family.* Charleston, S.C.: Privately printed, 1946.

Hall, B. C., and C. T. Wood. *The South.* New York: Scribner, 1995.

Hall, Gwen K. *On the Road to Savannah: The History of General Sherman's March through Washington County, Georgia* (includes Glenda Ruth Cheatham Johnson, *The Brown House*). Sandersville, Ga.: Major Mark Newman Camp 1602, Sons of Confederate Veterans, 2000.

Hanson, Victor Davis. *The Soul of Battle: From Ancient Times to the Present Day, How Three Great Liberators Vanquished Tyranny.* New York: Free Press, 1999.

Harrington, Hugh T. *Civil War Milledgeville: Tales from the Confederate Capital of Georgia.* Charleston, S.C.: History Press, 2005.

Harris, Joel Chandler. *On the Plantation: A Story of a Georgia Boy's Adventures during the War.* Athens: Univ. of Georgia Press, 1980.

Hart, B. H. Liddell. *Sherman: Soldier, Realist, American.* New York: Dodd, Mead and Co., 1929.

Henken, Elissa R. "Taming the Enemy: Georgian Narratives about the Civil War." *Journal of Folklore Research* 40, no. 3 (September–December 2003): 289–307.

The Heritage of Chesterfield County, South Carolina, 2004. Knoxville, Tenn.: Tennessee Valley Publishing, 2004.

Hicky, Louise McHenry. *Rambles through Morgan County: Her History, Century Old Houses and Churches, and Tales to Remember.* Washington, Ga.: Wilkes Publishing Co., 1971.

Hillhouse, Albert M. *A History of Burke County, Georgia, 1777–1950.* Swainsboro, Ga.: Magnolia Press, 1985.

———. *Nuggets and Other Findings in Burke County, Georgia.* Danville, Ky.: Prompt Printing, 1981.

Hirshson, Stanley P. *The White Tecumseh: A Biography of William T. Sherman.* New York: John Wiley and Sons, 1997.

Hoehling, A. A. *Last Train from Atlanta.* New York: Thomas Yoseloff, 1958.

Hollingsworth, Dixon, ed. *The History of Screven County, Georgia.* Dallas, Tex.: Curtis Media Corporation, 1989.

Hollowell, J. M. *War-Time Reminiscences and Other Selections.* Goldsboro, N.C.: Goldsboro Herald, 1939.

Horwitz, Tony. *Confederates in the Attic: Dispatches from the Unfinished Civil War.* New York: Pantheon Books, 1998.

Howard, Frances Thomas. *In and out of the Lines: An Accurate Account of Incidents during the Occupation of Georgia by Federal Troops in 1864–65.* New York: Neale Publishing Co., 1905.

Howe, M. A. DeWolfe. *Home Letters of General Sherman.* New York: Charles Scribner's Sons, 1909.

———, ed. *Marching with Sherman: Passages from the Letters and Campaign Diaries of Henry Hitchcock.* New Haven: Yale Univ. Press, 1927.

Huff, Lawrence. "'A Bitter Draught We Have Had to Quaff': Sherman's March through the Eyes of Joseph Addison Turner." *Georgia Historical Quarterly* 72, no. 2 (Summer 1988): 306–26.

Hughes, Nathaniel Cheairs, Jr. *Bentonville: The Final Battle of Sherman and Johnston.* Chapel Hill: Univ. of North Carolina Press, 1996.

Hume, Janice, and Amber Roessner. "Surviving Sherman's March: Press, Public Memory, and Georgia's Salvation Mythology." *Journalism and Mass Communication Quarterly* 86, no. 1 (Spring 2009): 119–37.

Hunt, Roger D., and Jack R. Brown. *Brevet Brigadier Generals in Blue.* Gaithersburg, Md.: Olde Soldier Books, 1990.

Jakes, John. *Savannah, or, A Gift for Mr. Lincoln.* New York: Dutton, 2004.

Janney, Caroline E. *Burying the Dead but Not the Past: Ladies' Memorial Associations and the Lost Cause.* Chapel Hill: Univ. of North Carolina Press, 2008.

J. E. B. Stuart Chapter, United Daughters of the Confederacy. *War Days in Fayetteville, North Carolina: Reminiscences of 1861 to 1865.* Fayetteville, N.C.: Judge Printing Co., 1910.

Johnson, Bob, and Charles S. Norwood, eds. *History of Wayne County, North Carolina: A Collection of Historical Stories.* Goldsboro, N.C.: Wayne County Historical Association, 1979.

Jones, Charles C., Jr. *The Siege of Savannah in December, 1864.* Albany, N.Y.: Joel Munsell, 1874.

Jones, Jacqueline. *Saving Savannah: The City and the Civil War.* New York: Alfred A. Knopf, 2008.

Jones, Katharine M. *When Sherman Came: Southern Women and the "Great March."* Indianapolis: Bobbs-Merrill, 1964.

Jordan, Mary Alice, ed. *Cotton to Kaolin: A History of Washington County, Georgia, 1784–1989.* Sandersville, Ga.: Washington County Historical Society, 1989.

Kennaway, John H. *On Sherman's Track: Or, the South after the War.* London: Seeley, Jackson and Halliday, 1867.

Kennett, Lee. *Marching through Georgia: The Story of Soldiers and Civilians during Sherman's March.* New York: HarperCollins, 1995.

———. *Sherman: A Soldier's Life.* New York: HarperCollins, 2001.

Kilpatrick, W. L. *The Hephzibah Baptist Association Centennial, 1794–1894.* N.p., n.d.

King, Spencer B., Jr., ed. "Fanny Cohen's Journal of Sherman's Occupation of Savannah." *Georgia Historical Quarterly* 41, no. 4 (December 1957): 407–16.

Kinney, William Light, Jr. *Sherman's March—A Review.* Bennettsville, S.C.: Marlboro Publishing Co., n.d.

Krakow, Kenneth K. *Georgia Place Names: Their History and Origins.* Macon, Ga.: Winship Press, 1999.

Krick, Robert K. *Lee's Colonels: A Biographical Register of the Field Officers of the Army of Northern Virginia.* Dayton, Ohio: Morningside, 1992.

Ladd, James Royal. "From Atlanta to the Sea." *American Heritage* 30, no. 1 (December 1978): 4–11.

Lane, Mills, ed. *Times That Prove People's Principles: Civil War in Georgia.* Savannah: Beehive Press, 1993.

Lawrence, Alexander A. *A Present for Mr. Lincoln: The Story of Savannah from Secession to Sherman.* 1961. Reprint, Savannah: Oglethorpe Press, 1997.

"Letter of a Confederate Surgeon on Sherman's Occupation of Milledgeville." *Georgia Historical Quarterly* 32, no. 3 (September 1948): 231–32.

Lewis, Lloyd. *Sherman: Fighting Prophet.* New York: Harcourt, Brace and Co., 1932.

Longacre, Edward G. *Worthy Opponents: William T. Sherman and Joseph E. Johnston; Antagonists in War—Friends in Peace.* Nashville, Tenn.: Rutledge Hill Press, 2006.

Lucas, Marion Brunson. *Sherman and the Burning of Columbia.* College Station: Texas A&M Univ. Press, 1976.

", ""]

Malone, Linda, comp. *Fairfield Remembers Sherman.* Winnsboro, S.C.: Fairfield Archives and History, 2006.

Marius, Richard, ed. *The Columbia Book of Civil War Poetry.* New York: Columbia Univ. Press, 1994.

Marsh, Blanche. *Robert Mills: Architect in South Carolina.* Columbia, S.C.: R. L. Bryan, 1970.

Marszalek, John F. "Celebrity in Dixie: Sherman Tours the South, 1879." *Georgia Historical Quarterly* 66, no. 3 (Fall 1982): 368–83.

———. *Sherman: A Soldier's Passion for Order.* New York: Free Press, 1993.

———. *Sherman's March to the Sea.* Abilene, Tex.: McWhiney Foundation Press, 2005.

Martin, Thomas H. *Atlanta and Its Builders: A Comprehensive History of the Gate City of the South.* Atlanta: Century Memorial Publishing Co., 1902.

Marvel, William. *Andersonville: The Last Depot.* Chapel Hill: Univ. of North Carolina Press, 1994.

———. *Mr. Lincoln Goes to War.* Boston: Houghton Mifflin, 2006.

Matheson, D. S. *History of First Presbyterian Church, Cheraw, S.C.* N.p., n.d.

McDonough, James Lee, and James Pickett Jones. *War So Terrible: Sherman and Atlanta.* New York: W. W. Norton, 1987.

McElfresh, Earl B. *Maps and Mapmakers of the Civil War.* New York: Harry N. Abrams, 1999.

McKay, Charles W. "'Three Years or during the War,' with the Crescent and Star." In *The National Tribune Scrap Book,* 121–60. N.p., n.d.

McMaster, Fitz Hugh. *History of Fairfield County, South Carolina: From "Before the White Man Came" to 1942.* Columbia, S.C.: State Commercial Printing Co., 1946.

McMaster, Richard H. *The Feasterville Incident: Hampton and Sherman.* Washington, D.C.: Published by the author, 1955.

———. "Sherman's Army in Fairfield." In Fitz Hugh McMaster, *History of Fairfield County, South Carolina: From "Before the White Man Came" to 1942.* Columbia, S.C.: State Commercial Printing Co., 1946.

McMurry, Richard M. *Atlanta 1864: Last Chance for the Confederacy.* Lincoln: Univ. of Nebraska Press, 2000.

McNeill, William J. "A Survey of Confederate Soldier Morale during Sherman's Campaign through Georgia and the Carolinas." *Georgia Historical Quarterly* 55, no. 1 (Spring 1971): 1–25.

McPherson, Tara. *Reconstructing Dixie: Race, Gender, and Nostalgia in the Imagined South.* Durham, N.C.: Duke Univ. Press, 2003.

Medley, Mary L. *History of Anson County, North Carolina, 1750–1976.* Wadesboro, N.C.: Anson County Historical Society, 1976.

Melton, Brian C. *Sherman's Forgotten General: Henry W. Slocum.* Columbia: Univ. of Missouri Press, 2007.

———. "'The Town That Sherman Wouldn't Burn': Sherman's March and

Madison, Georgia, in History, Memory, and Legend." *Georgia Historical Quarterly* 86, no. 2 (Summer 2002): 201–30.

Merrill, Adeline Godfrey Pringle, ed. *Life in Cheraw: The Civil War, Harriet Powe Godfrey, and the Town, 1901–1930.* Vol. 2 of *All in One Southern Family.* Charleston, S.C.: N.p., 1996.

Merrill, James M. *William Tecumseh Sherman.* Chicago: Rand McNally, 1971.

Miers, Earl Schenck. *The General Who Marched to Hell: Sherman and the Southern Campaign.* New York: Dorset Press, 1951.

Miles, Jim. *To the Sea: A History and Tour Guide of the War in the West, Sherman's March across Georgia and through the Carolinas, 1864–1865.* Nashville: Cumberland House, 2002.

Mills, Gary B. *Southern Loyalists in the Civil War: The Southern Claims Commission.* Baltimore: Clearfield, 2004.

Mitchell, Ella. *History of Washington County.* Atlanta: Cherokee Publishing Co., 1973.

Mitchell, Margaret. *Gone with the Wind.* New York: Macmillan, 1937.

Mitchell, Stephens. "Atlanta: The Industrial Heart of the Confederacy." *Atlanta Historical Bulletin* 3 (May 1930): 20–27.

Morgan County Heritage Book Committee. *Morgan County, Georgia Heritage, 1807–1997.* Waynesville, N.C.: Walsworth Publishing Co., 1997.

Muir, John. *A Thousand-Mile Walk to the Gulf.* Edited by William Frederic Bade. Boston: Houghton Mifflin, 1916.

Murray, Elizabeth Reid. *Wake: Capital County of North Carolina.* Raleigh: Capital County Publishing Co., 1983.

Naipaul, V. S. *A Turn in the South.* New York: Alfred A. Knopf, 1989.

Neely, Mark E., Jr., and Harold Holzer. *The Union Image: Popular Prints of the Civil War North.* Chapel Hill: Univ. of North Carolina Press, 2000.

Neff, John R. *Honoring the Civil War Dead: Commemoration and the Problem of Reconciliation.* Lawrence: Univ. Press of Kansas, 2005.

Nelson, Larry E. "Sherman at Cheraw." *South Carolina Historical Magazine* 100, no. 4 (October 1999): 328–54.

———. *Sherman's March through the Upper Pee Dee Region of South Carolina.* Florence, S.C.: Pee Dee Heritage Center, 2001.

New York [State]. Adjutant General. *Annual Report of the Adjutant General of the State of New York for the Year 1904.* Serial number 39. Albany: Brandow Printing Co., 1905.

New York [State]. New York State Monuments Commission. *In Memoriam Henry Warner Slocum, 1826–1894.* Albany: J. B. Lyon Co., 1904.

Nichols, George Ward. *The Story of the Great March.* New York: Harper and Brothers, 1865.

Northrop, Henry Davenport. *Life and Deeds of General Sherman.* Boston: B. B. Russell, 1891.

Oates, John A. *The Story of Fayetteville and the Upper Cape Fear.* Raleigh, N.C.: Contemporary Lithographers, 1981.

Obear, Katharine Theus. *Through the Years in Old Winnsboro.* Spartanburg, S.C.: Reprint Co., 1980.

Ott, Victoria E. *Confederate Daughters: Coming of Age during the Civil War.* Carbondale: Southern Illinois Univ. Press, 2008.

Paskoff, Paul F. "Measures of War: A Quantitative Examination of the Civil War's Destructiveness in the Confederacy." *Civil War History* 44 (March 2008): 35–62.

Pepper, George W. *Personal Recollections of Sherman's Campaigns in Georgia and the Carolinas.* Zanesville, Ohio: Hugh Dunne, 1866.

Perkerson, Medora Field. *White Columns in Georgia.* New York: Rinehart, 1952.

"Persons Sent from Atlanta by Gen. Sherman." *Atlanta Historical Bulletin* 6 (February 1932): 21–32.

Powell, Lillian Lewis, Dorothy Collins Odom, and Albert M. Hillhouse. *Grave Markers in Burke County, Georgia.* Waynesboro, Ga.: Chalker Publishing Co., 1974.

Presidents, Soldiers, Statesmen. New York: H. H. Hardesty, 1899.

Pringle, Elizabeth W. Allston. *Chronicles of Chicora Wood.* New York: Charles Scribner's Sons, 1921.

Pula, James S. *The Sigel Regiment: A History of the 26th Wisconsin Volunteer Infantry, 1862–1865.* Campbell, Calif.: Savas Publishing, 1998.

Quaife, Milo M., ed. *From the Cannon's Mouth: The Civil War Letters of General Alpheus S. Williams.* Detroit: Wayne State Univ. Press and the Detroit Historical Society, 1959.

Reardon, Carol. "William T. Sherman in Postwar Georgia's Collective Memory, 1864–1914." In *Wars within a War,* ed. Joan Waugh and Gary W. Gallagher, 223–48. Chapel Hill: Univ. of North Carolina Press, 2009.

Reston, James, Jr. *Sherman's March and Vietnam.* New York: Macmillan, 1984.

Robertson, William J. *The Changing South.* New York: Boni and Liveright, 1927.

Rogers, Alice Rhodes. *The Thomas Rhodes Family of South Carolina.* Florence, S.C.: Pattillo Printing, 1996.

Royster, Charles. *The Destructive War: William Tecumseh Sherman, Stonewall Jackson, and the Americans.* New York: Alfred A. Knopf, 1991.

Sams, Anita B. *Wayfarers in Walton: A History of Walton County Georgia, 1818–1967.* Monroe, Ga.: General Charitable Foundation of Monroe, Georgia, 1967.

Scaife, William R. *The March to the Sea.* Atlanta: Published by the author, 1989.

Schivelbusch, Wolfgang. *The Culture of Defeat: On National Trauma, Mourning, and Recovery.* New York: Metropolitan Books, 2003.

Sherman, William T. *Memoirs of General William T. Sherman, by Himself.* 2 vols. 1875. Reprint, Bloomington: Indiana State Univ. Press, 1957.

Silber, Nina. *The Romance of Reunion: Northerners and the South, 1865–1900.* Chapel Hill: Univ. of North Carolina Press, 1993.

Simpson, Brooks D., and Jean V. Berlin, eds. *Sherman's Civil War: Selected Correspondence of William T. Sherman, 1860–1865.* Chapel Hill: Univ. of North Carolina Press, 1999.

Slocum, Charles Elihu. *The Life and Services of Major General Henry Warner Slocum.* Toledo, Ohio: Slocum Publishing Co., 1913.

Smith, Derek. *Civil War Savannah.* Savannah: Frederic C. Beil, 1997.

Smith, Elizabeth F., ed. *The Reminiscences of James Ormond.* Crawfordsville, Fla.: Magnolia Monthly Press, 1966.

South Carolina Division, United Daughters of the Confederacy. *Recollections and Reminiscences, 1861–1865 through World War I.* 12 vols. N.p., 1990–2002.

Stout, Harry S. *Upon the Altar of the Nation: A Moral History of the Civil War.* New York: Viking, 2006.

Thomas, Edward J. *Memoirs of a Southerner, 1840–1923.* Savannah: Published by the author, 1923.

Thomas, Rev. J. A. W. *A History of Marlboro County, with Traditions and Sketches of Numerous Families.* 1897. Reprint, Baltimore: Regional Publishing Co., 1978.

Thompson, David B. "Confederates at the Keyboard: Southern Piano Music during the Civil War." In *Bugle Resounding: Music and Musicians of the Civil War Era,* edited by Bruce C. Kelley and Mark A. Snell. Columbia: Univ. of Missouri Press, 2004.

Thorndike, Rachel Sherman. *The Sherman Letters: Correspondence between General and Senator Sherman from 1837 to 1891.* New York: Charles Scribner's Sons, 1894.

Tinkcom, Harry Marlin. *John White Geary: Soldier-Statesman, 1819–1873.* Philadelphia: Univ. of Pennsylvania Press, 1940.

Town of Chesterfield, 1670–1970. N.p., n.d.

Trowbridge, John T. *The Desolate South, 1865–1866: A Picture of the Battlefields and of the Devastated Confederacy.* Edited by Gordon Carroll. New York: Duell, Sloan and Pearce, 1956.

Trudeau, Noah Andre. *Southern Storm: Sherman's March to the Sea.* New York: Harper, 2008.

Turner, Joseph Addison. *Autobiography of "The Countryman."* Edited by Thomas H. English. Atlanta: Emory Univ. Library, 1943.

Turner, Norman V. *The History of Camp Jack.* Springfield, Ga.: Published by the author, 2002.

Ulrich, Laurel Thatcher. *Well Behaved Women Seldom Make History.* New York: Alfred A. Knopf, 2007.

Underwood, Adin B. *The Three Years' Service of the Thirty-third Mass. Infantry Regiment, 1862–1865.* 1881. Reprint, Huntington, W. Va.: Blue Acorn Press, 1993.

U.S. War Department. *The War of the Rebellion: The Official Records of the Union and Confederate Armies.* 128 vols. Washington: Government Printing Office, 1880–1901.

Vetter, Charles Edmund. *Sherman: Merchant of Terror, Advocate of Peace.* Gretna, La.: Pelican Publishing Co., 1992.

Wagner, C. Peter. "Healing the Land: The Power to Heal the Past." *Prayer Track News* 5, no. 2 (April–June 1996): 1, 7.

Walker, John Ellis. *Genealogy of the Walker Family.* N.p., n.d.

Walters, Katherine Bowman. *Oconee River: Tales to Tell.* Spartanburg, S.C.: Reprint Co., 1995.

Warren, David B. "The Jordan Family of Georgia and Their Belter parlor furniture." *Magazine Antiques,* December 1998, 826–33.

Watson, Thomas E. *Prose Miscellanies.* Thomson, Ga.: Tom Watson Book Co., 1927.

Waugh, Joan, and Gary W. Gallagher, eds., *Wars within a War.* Chapel Hill: Univ. of North Carolina Press, 2009.

Weintraub, Stanley. *General Sherman's Christmas: Savannah, 1864.* New York: Smithsonian Books, 2009.

Wheeler, Richard. *Sherman's March.* New York: Thomas Y. Crowell, 1978.

Wheeler, W. Reginald. *Pine Knots and Bark Peelers: The Story of Five Generations of American Lumbermen.* New York: Ganis and Harris, 1960.

Whites, LeeAnn, and Alecia P. Long, eds. *Occupied Women: Gender, Military Occupation, and the American Civil War.* Baton Rouge: Louisiana State Univ. Press, 2009.

Wiley, Bell Irvin. *The Life of Billy Yank: The Common Soldier of the Union.* Baton Rouge: Louisiana State Univ. Press, 1993.

Wilson, Adelaide. *Historic and Picturesque Savannah.* Boston: Boston Photogravure Co., 1889.

Wilson, Edmund. *Patriotic Gore: Studies in the Literature of the American Civil War.* New York: Farrar, Straus and Giroux, 1977.

Wilson, Harold S. *Confederate Industry: Manufacturers and Quartermasters in the Civil War.* Jackson: Univ. Press of Mississippi, 2002.

Wood, Karen G. *The Power of Water: Four Early Mill Sites on Georgia's Oconee River.* N.p., n.d.

Yeary, Mamie. *Reminiscences of the Boys in Gray, 1861–1865.* Dallas, Tex.: Smith and Lamar, 1912.

Zettler, B. M. *War Stories and School-Day Incidents for the Children.* Springfield, Ga.: Page's Printing Co., 1984.

Zinn, John G. *The Mutinous Regiment: The Thirty-third New Jersey in the Civil War.* Jefferson, N.C.: McFarland and Co., 2005.

Index

Gordon, Eleanor Kinzie, 97, 107

Gordon, Sarah, 104

Grand Review, Washington, 177, 189

Grant, Ulysses S.: and Sherman, 6, 24, 36, 99, 107, 108; mentioned, 156, 172, 174, 176

Grantham's Store, N.C., 162

Granville, Daddy, 148

Graves, George Eugene "Gene": at Atlanta, 26; on foraging, 43; at siege of Savannah, 89, 90; at Savannah, 108; in Carolinas campaign, 152; at war's end, 174

Gray, Norman H., 36

Great Pee Dee River, S.C., 129, 140, 143, 144, 145, 148, 150

Green, Anna Maria, 62, 70

Green, John C., 88

Greene County, N.C., 164, 166, 192

Greenville and Columbia Railroad, 127

Grimsley, Mark, 10–11, 136

Griswold, Milon J., 20, 21, 33, 37

Groat, Esley, 165

Grover, Cuvier, 108, 112

Gum Creek, Ga., 45, 70, 71, 219n3

Guntharpe, Violet, 137–38, 181

Gwinnett County, Ga., 42

Hagood, James O., 120

Hagood, William H., 120, 230n32

Haight, William P., 87

Hall, B. C., 184

Halleck, Henry W., 107

Hampton, Wade, 123, 125, 128

Hanging Rock Creek, S.C., 138

Hanging Rock Post Office, S.C., 138

Hanna, Mattie, 63

Hardee, William J., 86, 89, 90, 91, 92, 223n27

Harns, Theodore C., 71, 77

Harper, William D., 26, 50, 76, 78

Harper's Weekly, 92, 140, 142

Harris, Abe, 133

Harris family, Savannah, 104–5

Harris, Joel Chandler, 18, 58, 59

Harris, Rebecca Ann, 62–63, 64–65

Hart, B. H. Liddell, 6, 186

Hart, John R., 170

Hartzell, Mrs. J. S., 148, 149

Healing Springs Baptist Church, S.C., 121

Hebron, Ga., 71–72

Helmey farm, Ga., 85

Henken, Elissa R., 11–12, 17, 120, 183, 193, 194

Henry, Jim, 133

Herrington, Edward G., 88

High, Emma, 49

Hightower Trail, Ga., 45, 47, 214n25

Hill, Joshua, 35

Hinman, Truman, 189

Hitchcock, Henry, 71, 99–100

Hollingsworth, Dixon, 12

Hollowell, J. M., 163

Hood, John Bell, 28, 30, 32, 36, 97

Hooker, Joseph, 23

Horse Creek, Ga., 80

Horsepen Road, Ga., 191

Horwitz, Tony, 13

Houck, Jeremiah, 165

Howard, Harriet, 70, 71

Howard, Jane Wallace, 100, 103, 105

Howard, Oliver Otis, 37

Hoyle, Imogene, 71–72

Hugaboom, Norman H., 164, 165

Hunt, Leonard L., 51

Hutchinson Island, Ga., 86, 87, 88, 89, 90, 91, 92

Independent Presbyterian Church, Savannah, 99

Inglis, Laura Prince, 145, 147

J., Mrs. L. F., 17, 72, 207n42

Jackson Branch of Whippy Swamp, S.C., 118

Jackson, Camilla, 42

Jackson, Snovey, 65

Jackson, Thomas J. "Stonewall," 6

Jarott, Mrs. C. E., 148

Jasper County, S.C., 191, 229n13

Jeffcoat property, S.C., 122

Jeffcoat's Bridge, S.C., 121

Jefferson County, Ga., 12, 74, 76, 77

Jennings, John Henry, 119, 180

Jersey, Ga. *See* Centerville, Ga.

Johnson, Andrew, 177

Johnson, Herschel V., 74

Johnston, Byron A., 22

Johnston, Joseph E., 6, 162, 174, 175, 176

Jones, David S., 112, 122, 169, 176–77

Jones, Katherine M., 9, 16, 17, 220n25

Jones, Neppie, 34, 35

Nast, Thomas, 186
National Geographic Society, 5–6
Neuse River, N.C., 162, 163, 164, 166
New Hope Church, Ga.: battle of, 21
New Jersey regiments: 33rd Infantry, 23
New York Herald, 36, 37, 61, 115, 185
New York regiments: 12th Cavalry, 165; 112th Infantry, 162; 119th Infantry, 23; 134th Infantry, 23, 88, 90; 154th Infantry (*see* 154th New York Volunteer Infantry)
New York, N.Y., 169, 183
Newberry Court House, S.C., 169
Newton County, Ga., 42, 213n6
Newton, Kitty, 55
Newton, William Henry, 55
Nichols, George W., 100, 101–2, 140
Nichols, Wellman P., 88
Northrup, Edwin D., 8
Norton, William W.: at Atlanta, 22, 25, 26, 36, 37, 38; at siege of Savannah, 90; at Savannah, 99, 107; in Carolinas campaign, 169; at war's end, 174; mentioned, 66

Obear, Katharine Theus, 130, 232n19
Oconee River, Ga., 50, 51, 62, 70
Ogeechee River, Ga., 74, 75, 86, 88–89, 191
"On the March to the Sea" (Darley), 186
154th New York Volunteer Infantry: John Langhans and, 1; histories of, 4, 5, 7, 8; depletion of, 7, 20, 26; at Atlanta, 19–39; background of, 20, 21, 28, 162; replenished by recruits, 21–22, 24, 25, 26; officer corps of, 22; deaths in, 26, 84, 113, 155, 164, 168, 173; and 1864 election, 26–27; foraging by, 28; at Andersonville, 30–31; and expulsion of Atlanta's inhabitants, 33; speculates about future in Atlanta, 35; anticipates move, 35, 36; abortive move of, 37; on March to the Sea, 41–86; railroad destruction by, 50, 73, 74, 75, 128–29, 150, 133; soldiers captured, 51, 79, 87, 138, 159, 165, 167, 168; and African Americans, 53, 97–98; and pillaging, 67; at siege of Savannah, 86–91; visited by Sherman, 87; soldiers wounded, 88, 91; occupation of Savannah, 92–111; in Carolinas campaign, 111–71; burns Chesterfield courthouse, 141–42, 194; at war's end, 171–77; distance marched, 176; in postwar years, 186, 188–89; Atlanta campsites of, 190
O'Neill, James Jasper, 167, 168–69
Orangeburg District, S.C., 121
Orme, Richard M., 66
Ormond, Elizabeth, 31, 34, 39
Ormond, James, 31, 34, 39
Oyer, Clark E. "Salty," 32, 87

Paces Ferry, Ga., 19
Palmer, John, 181
Pardee, Ario, Jr., 128, 133, 173
Park, Andrew G., 166, 167–68, 169
Park, James B., Sr., 51, 52
Park's Mill, Ga., 51, 58, 192, 215n40
Peachtree Creek, Ga.: battle of, 19, 21
Peck, Delos, 87
Pee Dee River, S.C. *See* Great Pee Dee River, S.C.
Pennsylvania regiments: 73rd Infantry, 23, 88, 90, 174; 109th Infantry, 23, 98, 163; Independent Battery E, 87–88, 91
Perkerson, Medora Field, 12
Perrysburg, N.Y., 169
Pettit, Joshua R., 38, 52–53, 88
Philadelphia Church, Ga., 59
Pigman, William A., 102–3, 106
pillaging. *See* looting
Pine Knob, Ga.: battle of, 21
plundering: *See* looting
Porter, Emma, 122
Potter County, Pa., 173
Pristell, Henry, 117
Pritchard, Josephine, 150
Puppy Creek, N.C., 155
Putnam County, Ga., 51, 54, 58, 93, 180, 192
Putnam, Joseph, 77, 189

Quillin, Martha Amanda, 42, 180

railroads, destruction of: in Georgia, 28, 29, 38, 48, 50, 73, 74, 75, 86, 96; in South Carolina, 120, 127, 128–29; in North Carolina, 150; officially reported, 172; mentioned, 33, 67, 125, 130, 162, 177, 182

Raleigh, N.C., 14, 158, 169, 174, 175, 176, 182, 188, insane asylum at, 175, 240n14
Ralling, Dr., 138–39
Ravencroft's Steam Mill, S.C., 126
Ray, Malinda B., 156
Ray, Mary Rawson, 32, 33
Reconstruction, 4, 15, 195
Red Bank Creek, S.C., 123
Reed, Almon Deforest, 109, 165
Reid, Mrs. J. R., 137
Reisser, Charlotte, 112–13
Reisser, Christopher F., 112–13
Resaca, Ga.: battle of, 21
Reston, James, Jr., 13
Revolutionary War, 86, 136, 138, 141, 146, 151, 179–80
Rhodes, George, 116
Richards, Samuel P., 34, 35
Richmond County, N.C., 150, 154, 159, 236n21
Richmond, Va., 20, 57, 148, 174, 156, 174, 176
Right Wing. *See* Sherman's army, Right Wing
Robertson, William J., 184
Robertville, S.C., 114, 115, 150, 229n13, 229n14
Robinson, Charlie, 133
Rock Bridge Post Office, Ga., 42, 43
Rockfish Creek, N.C., 155
Rockingham, N.C., 150
Rocky Face Ridge, Ga.: battle of, 21
Rocky Mount Post Office, S.C., 136, 137, 181, 233n12
Rogers, Aunt Ferebe, 54
Rooty Creek, Ga., 59, 60
Rough and Ready, Ga., 33–34
Rutledge Station, Ga., 48

Saffold, Thomas P., 51
St. David's Episcopal Church, Cheraw, 145–46, 147, 191
Saint-Gaudens, Augustus, 183
St. Stephen's Church, Milledgeville, 65
Salisbury, N.C., 169
Salkehatchie River, S.C., 118, 191
Saluda River, S.C., 125, 126
Salzburgers, 85
Sampson County, N.C., 160
Sand Hills Game Land, N.C., 191

Sandersville, Ga., 17, 72–73, 170
Sandy Grove plantation, Ga., 74
Sarver, Floris Dunkelman, 1, 3
Savannah Daily Herald, 97
Savannah, Ga.: John Langhans in, 2, 191; author's visits to, 5, 191, 193; regiment approaches, 82, 83, 84, 85, 86; siege of, 86–91; capture of, 91–92; occupation of, 92–111; Pest Hospital, 99; departure from, 111; fire in, 112, 228n6; sick sent to, 114; Sherman's postwar visit, 182; mentioned, 3, 8, 36, 37, 56, 90, 113, 155, 164, 169, 176, 185, 187, 188
Savannah Republican, 97, 98, 100, 105
Savannah River, 86, 89, 111, 113, 114, 150, 156, 191
Schofield, John M., 162, 163
Scotland County, N.C., 191
Scott, Louisa Bothwell, 76
Scott, Milton D., 26
Scott, Mrs. H. W., 146
Screven County, Ga., 12, 80, 81–82, 182, 192
Scutt, Addison L., 20
2nd Brigade, 2nd Division, 20th Corps: headquarters of, 20, 24, 25, 31, 176; composition of, 23; reviews of, 25, 113; on March to the Sea, 41, 42, 47, 74, 75–76, 80, 85, 86; at siege of Savannah, 86, 90, 91–92, 191; at Savannah, 92, 97, 98, 99; in South Carolina, 118, 119, 120, 123, 128, 133, 136, 138, 139; in North Carolina, 150, 154, 155, 158, 160, 161, 166, 172; at war's end, 173; mentioned, 22
2nd Division, 20th Corps (Geary's division): on March to the Sea, 3, 42, 45, 48, 50, 51, 52, 57, 58, 61, 70, 71, 76, 79, 80, 81, 84, 180; White Star badge of, 20, 25, 32, 99, 108, 112, 160, 174; reviews of, 25, 97, 173; hospital of, 26, 36, 84, 88, 114, 143, 158; Atlanta cemetery of, 26; Joel Chandler Harris on, 59; pioneers of, 60, 84, 111, 113, 114, 116–17, 121, 123; at siege of Savannah, 86, 89; at Savannah, 92, 93, 94, 95, 96, 99–100, 101, 103, 105, 107, 108, 111–12; in South Carolina, 115, 117, 118, 119, 121, 122, 123, 125, 126, 128, 130, 140, 141, 143, 144; in North Carolina, 154, 155,

158, 159, 160; miles marched by, 171; mentioned, 23, 104, 192

Sexual relations. *See* African Americans; Sherman's army; Southern civilians

Seymour, Horatio, 27

Screven County, Ga., 12, 79, 80, 81, 82, 182, 192

Shannon, Edgar: at Atlanta, 20, 24 32, 33; as quartermaster, 22; at Savannah, 96, 98, 101, 109; in Carolinas campaign, 162, 163, 166, 169, 172, 187

Sheffield, Ga., 45

Sherman Didn't Burn Our Recipes, 184

Sherman, Ebenezer C., 77

Sherman, Robert S., 6

Sherman, William Tecumseh: family stories of, 1; memoirs of, 2, 6, 185; biographies of, 2, 6; quoted, 2, 29, 32, 36, 37, 38, 75, 81, 90, 99, 100, 104, 107–8, 115, 143, 145, 158, 171, 173, 175, 185, 188, 232–33n9; collected correspondence of, 7; southern opinions of, 10, 16, 60, 62, 107, 135, 179, 180, 183–85, 195; northern opinions of, 10, 185; as army commander, 20, 23, 27; soldiers' opinions of, 20, 24, 28, 37–38, 108, 113, 114, 143, 156, 174, 188; on recruits, 21; accepts Joseph Hooker's resignation, 23; background of, 23–24; orders of, 24, 37, 38, 81; reviews troops, 25, 97, 158, 175; expels Atlanta's inhabitants, 32, 35; plans March to the Sea, 35–36; pride in army, 38, 90, 108, 158, 171, 175; and destruction of Atlanta, 38; staff officers of, 42, 55, 71, 99–100, 101; on March to the Sea, 71, 72, 77, 185, 188; and carrier pigeons, 84; at siege of Savannah, 86, 87, 89, 90, 91, 92, 223n27; at Savannah, 95, 99, 100, 101, 102 107–8; and African Americans, 104; in South Carolina, 113, 115, 120, 129, 136, 140–41, 143, 145; commits vandalism, 135, 232–33n9; in North Carolina, 155, 158, 159, 161, 175; and Joseph Mower, 173; and failed peace negotiations, 175; accepts Joseph Johnston's surrender, 176; in postwar years, 182–83, 185, 186; Saint-Gaudens monument, 183;

compares Georgia and Carolinas marches, 185–86. *See also* legends: involving Sherman

Sherman's army: family stories of, 1; and African Americans, 1, 17, 53, 54, 117; as Old Testament host, 2, 3; in *Gone with the Wind,* 3–4, 7; characterized by E. L. Doctorow, 7; Joseph Glatthaar on, 7, 189; incommunicado, 8; southern accounts and opinions of, 9, 16, 59, 65, 147, 149, 152, 179, 180, 182, 184, 195; recruits in, 21–22; at Atlanta, 31, 33; and 1864 election, 27; perceived as foreigners, 34, 73, 134, 179–80; journalists with, 36–37, 115; Right Wing, 37, 90, 129, 140, 151; Left Wing, 37, 47, 57, 67, 77, 89, 111, 125, 129, 140, 151, 152, 161, 173; cavalry, 37, 80, 123, 137, 144, 151, 160; as foragers, 37, 42, 43, 44; Sherman on, 38, 90, 108, 158, 171, 175; as railroad destroyers, 50; sexual relations of, 55–56, 147; at Milledgeville, 62–63; metamorphosis of, 71; at siege of Savannah, 86; at Savannah, 92; congressional resolution and, 95; seeks vengeance in South Carolina, 108, 115, 117, 150; and pianos, 118; cursed by civilian, 127; as superplunderers, 135, 146; pets kept by, 137; at Goldsboro, 162, 163; Charles Abell on, 172, 175; Levi Bryant on, 174; and Army of the Potomac, 176; in Grand Review, 177; northern opinions of, 185–86; in Herman Melville's poem, 186. *See also* bummers; legends

Sherman's March in Myth and Memory (Caudill and Ashdown), 10

Sherman's marches. *See* March to the Sea; Carolinas campaign

Simms, James, 103

Sisters Ferry, Ga., 114, 166, 191

Six Mile Creek, S.C., 125

Sloan, Thomas S., 87, 88, 91

Slocum, Henry W.: as corps commander, 23; reviews troops, 25; as Left Wing commander, 37, 151, 173; in Denhamville legend, 57; assigns guards, 62, 76; issues orders, 67, 126, 128, 152; at siege of Savannah, 89, 91, 92